Electoral Politics in Africa since 1990

Democratic transitions in the early 1990s led to a significant change in sub-Saharan African politics. Between 1990 and 2015, several hundred competitive legislative and presidential elections were held in all but a handful of the region's countries. This book is the first comprehensive comparative analysis of the key issues, actors, and trends in these elections. In the book, we ask: What motivates African citizens to vote? What issues do candidates campaign on? How has the turn to regular elections affected the push for greater democracy? Has regular electoral competition made a difference in the welfare of citizens? We argue that regular elections have both caused significant changes in African politics and been influenced by a rapidly changing continent – even if few of the political systems that now convene elections can be considered democratic and many features of older African politics persist.

Jaimie Bleck is Ford Family Associate Professor of Political Science at the University of Notre Dame.

Nicolas van de Walle is Maxwell M. Upson Professor of Government at Cornell University.

Electoral Politics in Africa since 1990

Continuity in Change

JAIMIE BLECK
University of Notre Dame

NICOLAS VAN DE WALLE
Cornell University

CAMBRIDGE
UNIVERSITY PRESS

CAMBRIDGE
UNIVERSITY PRESS

University Printing House, Cambridge CB2 8BS, United Kingdom

One Liberty Plaza, 20th Floor, New York, NY 10006, USA

477 Williamstown Road, Port Melbourne, VIC 3207, Australia

314–321, 3rd Floor, Plot 3, Splendor Forum, Jasola District Centre,
New Delhi – 110025, India

79 Anson Road, #06-04/06, Singapore 079906

Cambridge University Press is part of the University of Cambridge.

It furthers the University's mission by disseminating knowledge in the pursuit of
education, learning, and research at the highest international levels of excellence.

www.cambridge.org
Information on this title: www.cambridge.org/9781107162082
DOI: 10.1017/9781316676936

First published 2019

Printed in the United States of America by Sheridan Books, Inc.

A catalogue record for this publication is available from the British Library.

Library of Congress Cataloging-in-Publication Data
NAMES: Bleck, Jaimie, 1980- author. | Van de Walle, Nicolas, 1957- author.
TITLE: Electoral Politics in Africa since 1990: Continuity in Change / Jaimie Bleck, Nicolas
van de Walle.
DESCRIPTION: New York: Cambridge University Press, 2018. | Includes bibliographical
references and index.
IDENTIFIERS: LCCN 2018012825| ISBN 9781107162082 (hardback: alk. paper) |
ISBN 9781316612477 (pbk.: alk. paper)
SUBJECTS: LCSH: Elections—Africa, Sub-Saharan. | Africa, Sub-Saharan—Politics and
government—1960-
CLASSIFICATION: LCC DT30.5 .B583 2018 | DDC 324.967—dc23
LC record available at https://lccn.loc.gov/2018012825

ISBN 978-1-107-16208-2 Hardback
ISBN 978-1-316-61247-7 Paperback

Contents

Figures

Tables

Acknowledgments

In researching and writing this book, we have benefited from the generosity and insights of many colleagues. It is impossible to thank all of the people by name who have made this a better book as a result of some form of communication with us, a quick convention chat, a longer but less focused discussion over drinks, or an email correspondence. Many African citizens in different countries put up with our questions during various forms of field work. Their comments and insights deeply enriched our understanding of electoral politics on the continent. We can also claim the privilege of being based in wonderfully collegial departments at Notre Dame and Cornell, respectively, that have provided much appreciated intellectual, material, and moral support over the years. Much of the materials in this book were first explored in undergraduate seminars we both taught on electoral politics in Africa, in spring of 2013 and 2014 (at Cornell and Notre Dame) and fall of 2016 (at Notre Dame). We thank those students, as the class discussions generated ideas and arguments in this book.

We apologize in advance to all of these people whom we have not named individually. Still, we want to acknowledge as many of our debts as we can. Many colleagues have read and commented on different parts of the manuscript over its much too long development. For their help and encouragement, we thank Val Bunce, Sidiki Guindo, Marja Hinfelaar, Emizet Kisangani, Stephan Klingebiel, Karrie Koesel, Noam Lupu, Andreas Mehler, Anne Meng, Kristin Michelitch, Muna Ndulo, Anne Pitcher, Lise Rakner, Ken Roberts, Tyson Roberts, Steven Rosenzweig, Keith Weghorst, Suzanne Wengle, and Martha Wilfahrt. The Kellogg Institute for International Studies funded a manuscript conference at Notre Dame in late 2016 that proved to be immensely useful. This was not least because of the consistently insightful and sometimes much too nice comments from Leo Arriola, Michael Bratton, Paul Friesen, Mamoudou Gazibo, Lauren Honig, Emily Maiden, Andrea Peña-Vasquez, and Rachel Riedl, who all slogged through our very first full draft. Finally, for their close reading of the second draft and their generous comments, we are particularly grateful to Chipo Dendere, Alex Dyzenhaus, Sebastian Elischer, Adrienne LeBas, Natalie Letsa, Lindsey Pruett, Jonathan Van Eerd, and Michael Wahman.

Different parts of the manuscript were presented and garnered extremely useful feedback during presentations at Cornell, the University of Bergen, GIGA, Kansas State University, Michigan State University, Princeton, the University of Virginia, and Oxford University and at the annual meetings of the American Political Science Association and the African Studies Association.

Over the last couple of years, we have been assisted by a number of very talented undergraduate research assistants, without whom this book would not have been possible. For all their help, we thank Liana Cramer, Bright Gyamfi, Dierdre Kennedy, Thomas Mologne, Jacqueline O'Brien, Zachary Spahr, Elizabeth Steiner, Natalie Vellutini, Nicole Waddick, and Grace Watkins at Notre Dame and Enrico Bonatti, Bruno De Larragoiti, Erin Ellis, Akhilesh Issur, Sophie Lin, Temi Sanusi, and Jady Wei at Cornell.

We acknowledge permission from *Comparative Political Studies* to reuse material published in "Valence issues in African elections: Navigating uncertainty and the weight of the past," *Comparative Political Studies* 46:11 (2013): 1394–1421, in an updated and expanded version, here in Chapter 6 and from the journal *Democratization* for material that was originally developed in our essay "Parties and issues in Francophone West Africa: Towards a theory of non-mobilization," *Democratization*, 18:5 (2011): 1125–1145.

At Cambridge University Press, we thank Lew Bateman, who encouraged us at the beginning of the project, and Sara Doskow and her diligent and very patient team for bringing the book safely to harbor.

Finally, this book could not have been written without the help of our families, particularly our respective spouses, Idrissa Sidibe and Michèle van de Walle, life partners who provide us with respite, grounding, and sustenance for everything we do.

The book is dedicated to three early teachers and role models: Caroline Angell Bleck, Edouard Poullet, and Ruth M. Slominski.

The Puzzle of Electoral Continuity

I.I INTRODUCTION

The general elections that were convened in Zambia on August 11, 2016, were the eighth multiparty presidential elections and the sixth legislative elections convened since democratization in the early 1990s restored multiparty politics in that country. Between independence and 1991, Zambia had convened only one competitive presidential election and just two legislative elections that involved more than a single party. President Edgar Lungu of the Patriotic Front (PF) party was reelected narrowly over Hakainde Hichilema of the United Party for National Development (UPND).[1] The campaign rhetoric of the two parties was sharply different. Hichilema lamented the decline of democratic norms under PF rule and criticized Lungu's management of the economy, brandishing his own record as a successful businessman to argue that he would do much better. By contrast, President Lungu highlighted the administration's record in infrastructure development and contrasted his own humble background and religious faith with his opponent's arrogance, wealth, and "godlessness" (Fraser, 2017, p. 466).

The results suggested an evenly divided country, with the eastern and northern regions voting overwhelmingly for the incumbent and the southern and western regions strongly supporting Hichilema. International observers publicly declared the election to have been free and fair, although they did lament the climate of violence in which the campaign

---

[1] The present account is based largely on various newspaper accounts; see also *African Arguments* (2017), Beardsworth (2017), and Fraser (2017).

proceeded, including several significant clashes between supporters of the two parties. Observers also criticized the government for having suspended *The Post*, the main opposition newspaper, in the run-up to the election. In addition, the government jailed key leaders of the UPND, accusing them of trying to create a private militia, presumably to contest the electoral results – charges that the opposition categorically denied.

Hichilema contested the electoral results vigorously, accusing the national electoral commission of having conspired with the government to alter the results. His unwillingness to accept the results led the PF to accuse him of treasonous behavior, and he was jailed from April to August 2017 in a clear attempt to intimidate him. Pressured notably by the Commonwealth of Nations and the Zambian Conference of Catholic Bishops, President Lungu did not follow through on the indictment and eventually released Hichilema unconditionally.

International reporting on the Zambian election expressed concern about the evolution of the country's democracy. The BBC's accounts of the election characteristically lamented a decline of democracy in Zambia and argued the country was at a "crossroads,"[2] while *The Guardian* lamented the decline of popular support for democracy in Zambia.[3]

When observers such as Freedom House bemoaned the global decline of democracy in 2016, the Zambian elections were invariably offered as an example (Puddington and Roylance, 2017). Yet by Freedom House's own rankings, Zambia's record as a highly flawed electoral democracy has been fairly consistent over the past two decades. It is a "partly free" regime, in Freedom House's terms, with a long record of highly imperfect elections. Since the transition to multiparty rule, incumbents in Zambia have consistently resorted to illiberal strategies to win elections, with pressure on the independent press and attempts to intimidate the opposition.

Not all elections in the region in 2016 were as problematic. Ghana's general elections in December 2016 resulted in the victory of opposition leader Nana Akuffo-Addo and his New Patriotic Party over incumbent President John Mahama and the National Democratic Congress Party.[4]

---

[2] "Hakainde Hichilema's Treason Trial Puts Zambia at Crossroads," Thursday, August 11, 2016, accessed at www.bbc.co.uk/news/world-africa-40020950.

[3] "Zambia Goes to Polls to Elect Next President after Hard-Fought Campaign," accessed at www.theguardian.com/world/2016/aug/10/zambia-goes-to-polls-to-elect-next-president-after-hard-fought-campaign

[4] This account is derived from several sources, including "Ghana: A Turning Point Vote for the Black Star," (2016); Sarah Brierley and George Ofosu, "9 Things You Should Know about Ghana's Election," in *The Washington Post*, December 7, 2016, accessed at

Despite worries about violence and fraud, given the highly partisan electoral campaign conducted by the two main parties, the election proved to be trouble free, and Mahama conceded defeat soon after the National Electoral Commission announced the results. One reason for the lack of contestation was the elaborate effort by the Coalition of Domestic Election Observers, an alliance of thirty-four civic associations, to deploy a network of 12,000 election observers and then produce an immediate estimate of the results on the night of the elections. Thanks to smartphone and Internet technology, this estimate proved to be virtually the same as the official results reported by the commission and helped to legitimize it. Mahama's government had engaged in a spending splurge in the months before the elections in hopes of improving a worsening economic situation, but attitudinal surveys suggested that Ghanaians were disgruntled about the economy's slowdown and dissatisfied with the direction the country was taking. The Ghanaian general elections of 2016 were the seventh presidential and legislative elections since the return of multiparty politics in 1992.

The December 2016 Gambian elections also witnessed the defeat of an incumbent, but it occurred after a vitriolic campaign in which the government engaged in extensive intimidation of the opposition.[5] Unlike his Ghanaian counterpart, President Yahya Jammeh refused to accept the result, vowing to remain in power, a stance that was soon buttressed by the support of the army. Jammeh had been in power since a military coup in 1994, and his rule was characterized by regular elections combined with little respect for civil and political rights. Eventually, neighboring states were able to negotiate a diplomatic exit for Jammeh from the presidency so that the challenger, Adama Barrow, could take office. However, without the intervention of the Economic Community of West African States, Jammeh would likely still be in power.

In sum, 2016 provided the full panoply of African elections, from the admirably democratic to the evidently fraudulent. In all, there were some fourteen direct multiparty national elections on the continent that year.

---

www.washingtonpost.com/news/monkey-cage/wp/2016/12/07/nine-things-you-should-know-about-ghanas-election/?utm_term=.891f3ce3005c; and Sean Lyngaas and Dionne Searceydec, "Ghana Presidential Vote Hinges on Economic Perceptions," in *The New York Times,* December 6, 2016, accessed at www.nytimes.com/2016/12/06/world/africa/ghana-election-john-mahama.html?_r=0.

[5] See "Jammeh Tilts the Playing Field"(2016); "The Gambia's President Jammeh Concedes Defeat in Election," in *The Guardian,* December 2, 2016, accessed at www.theguardian.com/world/2016/dec/02/the-gambia-president-jammeh-concede-defeat-in-election.

Such a busy electoral calendar was no longer exceptional in an area where elections had once been rare events. Indeed, several hundred multiparty elections have been held in forty-six of the forty-nine countries of sub-Saharan Africa[6] since a wave of democratization swept across the region in the early 1990s. How typical were the very different 2016 elections in Ghana, Gambia, or Zambia? How have African elections changed in the past twenty-five years? How have parties and party systems evolved? Have elections helped to strengthen democracy in Africa, or have they contributed to political instability? What do Africans think of these elections? What do political campaigns actually look like?

In this book, we analyze a quarter-century of multiparty electoral politics in the region. Every year since the early 1990s, a dozen or so African countries have organized multiparty elections. Many of these elections have included illiberal practices, from voter intimidation to vote buying and violence. But, as is less often remarked upon, much has been normal about these elections. For example, political parties canvas and put up posters to make voters aware of predictable electoral pledges. Candidates engage in standard political rhetoric at mass rallies and undertake campaign stops around the country. Many candidates use social media to communicate with citizens. Voters reward officeholders who have delivered good economic performance, and they pay attention to the professional backgrounds and personal qualities of candidates in addition to their policy promises. Opposition parties win legislative seats and subnational offices, and more rarely, the presidency, albeit. Citizen participation in these elections has also been routinized, with varying but mostly unremarkable turnout rates in comparative terms. Moreover, these participation rates have remained fairly stable for more than two decades.

In summary, multiparty elections have been institutionalized during this quarter-century. However, we do not observe broader democratic consolidation in most of these countries. Instead, the democratization of the early 1990s remains incomplete in much of the region. Our referring to *multiparty* elections rather than *democratic* elections is intentional because, as we shall argue, many if not most of these elections either were not free and fair or were not organized in a democratic context. Despite much apparent change since 1990, many of the same men and rather fewer women remain in positions of power in the region. On the whole,

---

[6] Throughout the text, we refer to "Africa" and "sub-Saharan Africa" interchangeably, to refer to the forty-nine countries south of the Sahara.

with a few notable exceptions, the same political class that dominated national politics before transitions continues to do so.

Some elections have been free and fair and have been held in political systems with recognized civic and political rights. More elections have been manipulated by incumbent regimes and their presidents, who can leverage the advantage embedded in disproportionate executive power or, in some instances, act in a manner that is totally at odds with the procedures and spirit of democracy. Even when elections are relatively free and fair, most African political systems continue to be characterized by abuses of power and a less-than-stellar respect for the political rights of citizens. As in the postindependence era, power has remained skewed toward the executive, and we observe limited growth and institutionalization of other branches of government in most countries.

The extent to which regular multiparty elections have coincided with undemocratic practices is suggested by the examples with which we began this introduction. Despite different electoral histories in Gambia and Zambia, both the Jammeh and Lungu regimes were resorting to well-established political practices to circumvent the will of the people as expressed through the ballot. These practices suggest that not much had changed in Africa. Yet the Gambian and Ghanaian cases show that elections of varying quality can nonetheless generate opportunities for political challengers to gain executive power.

Why has the move to routine and regular multiparty elections not promoted more political change in Africa? Why did it not generate democratic consolidation? These are the puzzles we seek to unravel in this book. Many observers may not agree with the argument we make about the role of elections in ensuring political continuity. As a result, our first task, to be undertaken in the next chapter, will be to demonstrate the high degree of electoral continuity. In the rest of the book, we will use a broad survey of electoral politics in the region to explain that continuity. Both optimist and, increasingly, pessimist observations about the region disagree with our argument of continuity. This is partly because news accounts of political trends in Africa usually overinterpret the results of an individual election in a single country and extrapolate from it a striking trend for the entire continent. For instance, in August 2016, *The Economist* published a gloomy assessment of electoral democracy in Africa. "African democracy has stalled – or even gone into reverse," *The Economist* argued, pointing to the August 2016 elections in Zambia, which it viewed as marred by fraud and intimidation by incumbent President Lungu (*The Economist*, 2016). This article contrasted starkly with two more optimistic assessments of African democracy published in that magazine in the previous decade (see *The Economist*, 2002, 2010). Each of these three articles was based on one or two national elections in a region of some forty-nine countries. The fact that the news magazine could not decide whether democracy in Africa had not progressed or had actually regressed made *The Economist*'s editorial line comparatively sanguine about Africa. Elsewhere in the press and in the foreign affairs literature, a more pessimistic view has often prevailed in which a "rollback" of the wave of democratization is either described or predicted.

Gloomy academic assessments are even more common, and they are long-running, having started as the wave of democratization was still taking place in Africa and continuing since. Most scholars viewed the democratic reforms as too superficial, too ephemeral, and/or too unsustainable to be truly meaningful (Chabal, 1998; Joseph, 1998; Chabal and Daloz, 1999). Others, such as Ake (1991) and Monga (1997), argued that electoral democracy would not much affect the lives of ordinary Africans. Much contemporary academic commentary has argued that the level of democracy in sub-Saharan Africa has been regressing since the high point of the Third Wave of democratization (Diamond, 2015; for a discussion, see Bratton, 2013). Not only Africa but also the rest of the world has been affected by the Third Wave, from Eastern Europe to Latin America (see Gandhi and Lust-Okar, 2009; Fukuyama, 2015).

In contradicting these arguments, we employ various types of quantitative and qualitative data to show that the striking characteristic of the region that needs to be explained is how little negative or positive regime change has actually taken place since the conclusion of the democratic transitions of the mid-1990s. Once countries started holding regular multiparty elections, they have largely continued to do so. Military coups that used to lead to lengthy periods of nonelectoral politics now get overturned quickly as the result of both local and international pressures. Regular elections have become the default option of politics. In this book, we will often lament the inconsistency and thinness of democratic procedures across the continent. But let us be clear from the start: The turn to multiparty competition across the region in the early 1990s constituted a political and institutional revolution that should not be underestimated.

Equally striking is the paradoxical continuity that can be observed since the end of the transitions of the 1990s. Governments are more responsive, but the weight of corruption and clientelism on growth remains heavy. The authoritarian tendencies of the executive have not changed as much as might have been expected. The composition of the political class remains very similar to what it has been since 1990. Although high levels of volatility continue to characterize party politics, we observe patterns of elite circulation or *transhumance*,[7] in which the same individual politicians and networks of politicians reappear in new parties. Indeed, in a continent of youths, the political class seems to continue to be getting older.

This stasis in political life despite the introduction of multiparty elections is all the more puzzling in light of the dramatic social and economic changes that Africa has experienced during the past quarter-century at least in part, as we show in Chapter 8, because of the beneficial impact of regular multiparty elections. Two decades of steady and rising economic growth have transformed most African countries. Regular growth has swelled the ranks of the African middle class. Governments have seen their fiscal resources increase, and they have invested in new infrastructure and services and have hired more civil servants, who – in sharp contrast to the 1970s and 1980s – are more likely to get paid a living wage on a regular basis. Concurrent with the introduction of regular electoral competition have been urbanization, a rising middle class, a growing youth bulge, and the unprecedented growth of traditional and social media, as well as telephone expansion on the continent. Remarkably, urbanization continues at breakneck speed – above 3 percent annually – so towns all over the continent are expanding, and more than half of all Africans live in urban centers. The greater density of cities has created new media markets, bringing about an explosion in old and new media outlets. The increased purchasing power of Africans has also come to the attention of foreign investors, who have dramatically increased their investments in the region. In 2015, foreign direct investment levels reached a historic high in Africa, with US $61 billion yearly,[8] up from just above US $1 billion a year in the late 1980s. We argue that positive economic growth rates provide fodder for incumbents to boast about their economic management, but the rise in the middle class also suggests an increase in the numbers of more informed, independent, and empowered voters.

The radical changes in the media landscape in the past quarter-century are particularly noteworthy. In 1990, the big media innovation in Africa was the emergence of satellite news channels such as CNN, which were

[7] This French term, which designates the practice of moving livestock from one grazing area to another, is commonly used in French West Africa to refer to the tendency of individual politicians to migrate from party to party.

[8] See "Foreign Direct Investment in Africa Surges," in *The Financial Times,* May 19, 2015, accessed at www.ft.com/content/79ee41b6-fd84-11e4-b824-00144feabdco.

undermining government monopolies over information in new ways. During the wave of democratization that was then hitting the region, debates focused on whether the recently invented fax machine provided an advantage to prodemocracy groups, which could use faxes to better coordinate their action. By 2000, the explosion of cellphones all over the continent made this debate seem quaint, but even then, the Internet was in its early infancy in Africa. Today, the role of social media has dramatically expanded and influences all aspects of electoral campaigns and, presumably, how basic political news travels within African political systems. While political learning is happening at the elite level as well and incumbents are learning how to track, manipulate, and block access to these technologies, what seems incontrovertible is the increasing expansion of the availability of political information.

As we demonstrate in Chapter 7, over the past two decades, African citizens have gained unprecedented access to various media from newspapers to television and the Internet. These individuals are also increasingly likely to be members of a self-help association. While there is still tremendous variation across countries, we observe increases in citizens' political knowledge about municipal and legislative officials over time. Finally, we see gains in political interest in the 1990s and early 2000s, followed by a stabilization of interest that appears to have remained steady.

A usually unexamined presumption in much work on democratization in Africa is that progress or regression in democracy is happening as fast as in the socioeconomic arena. In fact, we will argue that there is a striking and paradoxical disjuncture between the great changes in African society and the relative stagnation in its politics, even as we recognize the change brought on by the introduction of hundreds of competitive elections over the past two decades. In this book, we will both document this disjuncture and investigate its implications for electoral politics.

1.2 EXPLAINING POLITICAL CONTINUITY: PRESIDENTIALISM AND THE LIABILITY OF NEWNESS

Given the regularization of multiparty elections coupled with changes in the media landscape and demographic trends that include higher growth rates, urbanization, and unprecedented access to schooling, why do we observe relative political stasis? We argue that two key factors promote continuity: presidentialism and the "liability of newness."

1.2.1 Presidentialism

The primary lens through which to understand political continuity is the persistence of presidentialism, by which we mean that most of the political systems in Africa remain characterized by dominant and often unaccountable executive power. Following the turn away from electoral politics after independence, African strongmen typically adopted presidential institutions, through which they personalized power to a considerable extent and weakened legislatures and judiciaries in order to escape accountability. Dominant and even abusive executive power came to characterize most African states. To be sure, the reach of these "presidents for life" was often constrained by low levels of capacity in the states they oversaw, but in political terms, the strongmen towered over the polity.

As we will discuss in Chapters 2 and 3, the transitions of the early 1990s included debates about constitutional issues and some significant changes, notably in electoral rules, but not a single country in the region decided to abandon presidentialism for parliamentary government. Not only do presidential constitutions continue to dominate the national institutional landscape, with considerable formal power vested in the presidency, but also informal institutions continue to tend to favor the executive branch of government. The executive branch continues to dwarf other branches of government in financial and political resources. Legislatures have been slow to seize the powers they have been formally granted, while the judiciary's low levels of professionalism and resources have typically subordinated them to the executive branch of government even when the country's constitution grants judicial independence.

Although the degree of presidentialism varies somewhat across the countries of the region, the variation is not related to other indicators of the level of democracy. We will also examine the handful of parliamentary regimes in the region, which are often the most stable and pluralistic democratic systems in the region – Botswana, Mauritius, and South Africa, for instance – but which also have exhibited a tendency toward executive branch dominance.

One of the striking trends in sub-Saharan Africa over the past quarter-century is the very low rate of executive alternation as the members of the old guard of nationalist politicians pass from the scene and the political class becomes younger. As we will argue, the rate of alternation may be increasing, but so far, in most African countries, incumbents seem to get reelected regardless of their performance in power.

This electoral success results from the uneven playing field that confronts would-be political challengers, who find that sitting presidents enjoy all sorts of advantages, from control of national institutions to access to state resources. Presidentialism exacerbates incumbency advantage in numerous ways, making it challenging for new actors to penetrate elite political circles. First, the president holds a substantial valence advantage in having more experience in office, controlling central levels of clientelistic redistribution, and maintaining relationships with donors and other important international stakeholders. This political dominance of the executive makes it difficult for voters to imagine a different leader governing with comparable resources and competence. As we show in Chapter 6, the preponderance of valence discourse in political debate during electoral campaigns favors the incumbent, particularly in relation to the central concern of economic development and public goods provision.

Second, in some systems, incumbents have consistently manipulated electoral processes to their advantage. This can happen through subtle control of the press, the use of state institutions for partisan purposes (Levitsky and Way, 2010), or more blatant forms of voter suppression and ballot rigging.

Third, many African economies remain state-centric, with relatively little dynamism in the private sector and a state that too often seeks to mitigate its low levels of capacity through a surfeit of regulatory ambitions – dynamics that may have their origin in the colonial state (Herbst, 2014). Thus dominant state executives can utilize state resources and rents, including foreign aid and mineral wealth, to their own advantage. Incumbents' control over state resources, including contracts and bidding processes, makes it difficult for moneyed challengers to emerge without ties to the president or party in power (Arriola, 2013). Some dominant parties have managed to exert a stranglehold on private sector development so that all new development goes through the party (Pitcher, 2017).

Finally, a key manifestation of incumbency advantage lies in the nature of party systems in the region, which also limit the prospects for political change. Relatively weak parties are buttressed when they benefit from incumbency and control of the executive. Though these parties often appear to be strong, they have quickly atrophied and in many cases completely disappeared if and when they have lost the benefits of state resources. While in power, however, they dominate the political scene, and regimes use incumbency advantage to weaken and fragment opposition parties. As a result, the turn to multiparty politics has only unevenly and very slowly enhanced party system institutionalization. Instead, we continue to observe incumbent parties that dominate the legislature – thanks to the patronage of the presidency – and are surrounded by a highly fragmented opposition in what remain lowly institutionalized party systems. Thus the democratic era demonstrates a good deal of continuity with the predemocratic era even as it reinvents politics in other ways (see Chapter 4).

1.2.2 The Liability of Newness

The second process that conditions this paradoxical combination of change and continuity lies in the fact that Africa's experience with multiparty elections is still relatively recent, and its newness shapes observed political behaviors. This is what Stinchcombe (1965) called "the liability of newness," albeit in a different context. Experience levels varied across the region. In Nigeria, the Second Republic (1979–1983) provided a kind of dress rehearsal for the multiparty politics of the Fourth Republic since 1999, while subnational politics at the state level served to train and promote a diverse and younger set of politicians who had national ambitions. Civilian single-party regimes with competitive primaries in the 1970s and 1980s, such as Kenya, found it easier to evolve to multiparty politics than did regimes without any tradition of postindependence political competition before democratization.

As we have argued elsewhere (Bleck and van de Walle, 2013), few African electoral systems could rely on previous significant experience with multiparty elections after the transitions of the early 1990s. In contrast, in Latin America, long-standing party traditions go back to previous experiments with multiparty electoral competition, albeit in systems with restricted franchises (Levitsky et al., 2016). In Argentina, for instance, the end of the military dictatorship resulted in the 1983 elections that were won by Raúl Alfonsín and his Radical Civic Union Party, which had competed in elections in Argentina since its founding in 1891. Presidents have been elected in Argentina since 1854. Perhaps better for comparison with Africa would be the former Soviet Union and Eastern Europe, in which many of the same electoral dynamics can be discerned as the ones we will document in this book. There as well, the general absence of previous national democratic experiments can be partly to blame for the disappointing record of democratization, albeit with some important exceptions in central Europe. Apart from Czechoslovakia, the entire region had enjoyed only eight years of multiparty competition before 1990.[9]

---

[9] We thank Val Bunce for bringing this fact to our attention.

Limited political experience and the absence of these structural building blocks shape both the process and the outcomes of competitive elections. Political actors stick to what they know and are wary of taking risks. For their part, new political parties with little history and few organic links to the citizens of the country struggle to develop electoral strategies or to find their natural constituencies. We argue that these fledgling electoral democracies have little or no past history of competitive elections and therefore few experienced political parties, while the structural requisites of democracy are largely absent.

Given their inexperience, political actors fall back on repertoires of strategic action from the two previous periods of political competition: the immediate postindependence era and the early 1990s when these political systems were renewed with multiparty competition. From the reemergence of the same old party system dynamics to the attempts by some of the winners of the founding election to subvert democratic principles and maintain their power or to the continuing persistence of hyper-presidential politics, the current era echoes and links back to the 1960s as well as the more recent democratization experiences of the early 1990s.

In Chapters 5 and 6, we demonstrate how incumbents benefit from the fact that opposition parties have little previous experience in power. This provides incumbents and their parties a valence advantage on most policy issues. It is challenging for most voters to assess an opposition candidate's ability to outperform the incumbent, since there is little previous evidence upon which to evaluate the challenger. The incumbent can capitalize on the great uncertainty surrounding opposition candidates.

1.2.3 Other Factors

Of course, other factors also explain the slow pace of political change in Africa. Generational change is always a delayed reaction. Many African adults were socialized in the old days, while those who have grown up in the new environment need time to emerge and take the reins. In addition, the change in urban areas is counterbalanced by the relative stagnation of the countryside, which tends to be more conservative. Africa is urbanizing rapidly, but people living in rural areas, who are far more likely to vote for the incumbent, continue to weight election results (Wahman and Boone 2018).

Changes at the international level have affected the pace of political change in the region since the mid-1990s. Africa's wave of democratization was carried out in the context of a dramatic marginalization of

Africa in the international system. International commodity prices had collapsed, and this, combined with disastrous economic policies, resulted in very weak economies in the region. As a result, African governments were bankrupt and increasingly dependent on the goodwill of their international creditors, which came to view political change as a prerequisite for economic renewal and therefore supported regime change in the region.

In sharp contrast, major changes in the international system have helped to sustain the political status quo in Africa. The commodity boom since the mid-1990s has helped to lessen African governments' dependence on foreign assistance. The promotion of the "war on terror" in the United States after September 11, 2001, and the greater prioritization of Africa on Western states' security agenda strengthened the hands of African incumbents because of the new emphasis on political stability. A number of African governments, such as those of Chad, Kenya, Uganda, and Ethiopia, bartered their assistance in the war on terror for greater Western complacency about their governance issues – a deal that the Western countries were happy to make. This tendency was then reinforced by the increasing role of China in Africa, providing an alternative to Western finance and thus weakening the leverage of the West in the region. Thus the international environment increased the leverage of incumbents across the region.

Finally, during the past two decades, multiparty elections in Africa have coincided with generally positive economic results, and perhaps this has enhanced stability (see Chapter 8). Since the late 1990s, economic growth and poverty alleviation have occurred after a long period of devastating economic crisis (Radelet, 2010). Before the slowdown in the global economy in 2013, Africa's economic prospects seemed to be on an upward trajectory, with Gross Domestic Product (GDP) increasing from 1.5 percent annually in the 1980s to 2.5 percent in the 1990s and to more than 5 percent the following decade, making sub-Saharan Africa the fastest-growing region of the world in the 2000s. Poverty levels also decreased during this period for the first time in the postindependence period. The World Bank (2016) reports that the share of Africans who are poor fell from 56 percent in 1990 to 43 percent in 2012. To what extent is this coincidental? To what extent has multiparty competition caused the improved economic performance? Could the causal arrow go largely in the other direction, with democratization having been sustained by good economic results? Or are these political and economic trends both caused by some other set of factors? There are theoretical and empirical reasons to believe each of these causal explanations. Perhaps regular electoral competition has enhanced governmental accountability and thus responsiveness, as a large proportion literature has argued (Baum and Lake, 2003; Stasavage, 2005; Masaki and van de Walle, 2014). Because of the possibility of being sanctioned by the voters, government officials now have greater incentives to improve – or at least to be viewed as improving – the lives of their fellow citizens. On the other hand, perhaps democratization has been legitimated, and thus sustained, by the better economic results. The political crises of the late 1980s and early 1990s that deposed authoritarian leaders in a number of countries were brought on, at least in part, by years of economic crisis. In contrast, these leaders' more democratic successors have been sustained in power by the better economic results, buoyed largely by high commodity prices until 2013, which are largely unrelated to the regular convening of multiparty elections (Przeworski et al., 1996).

1.3 AFRICAN ELECTIONS IN COMPARATIVE PERSPECTIVE

The focus of this book is on elections, not democracy, though we are keenly interested in the relationship between the two. The subject of our study is the more than 500 national-level elections that have been convened in Africa since 1990. We examine when elections are convened and which types of candidates and political parties win. We analyze the variation in incumbency advantage and focus at length on the actual campaigns: what candidates discuss and debate and how they work to gain the support of voters.

A burgeoning scholarly literature is emerging that analyzes specific African elections, notably the nature of political campaigns, voting behavior by citizens, patterns in electoral results, the role of political parties, the party systems that are emerging, and the implications for the progress of democracy in the region. Nonetheless, surprisingly little scholarship has focused explicitly on these elections and their comparative implications.[10] Many studies examine single elections in single countries or discuss elections in the context of a broader discussion of, for instance, democratization in the region. There are also more targeted research results focusing on specific features of elections, from vote buying to electoral turnout to the role of violence and international observers of elections. A number of

---

[10] Important exceptions include Lindberg (2006) and Bratton (2013).

excellent collections of essays have been published, but they contain too many unexamined contradictions between individual chapters to constitute an integrated analysis. Thus no single study provides an analytical and comparative treatment of electoral politics in Africa. The objective of this book is to provide such a study in order to summarize and analyze this literature, fill several important gaps, and generalize about the extent of our knowledge about electoral politics in Africa.

We also bring to our book the ambition to demystify and normalize African elections with the tools and analytical categories of comparative politics. Too much work on African politics has treated elections in the region as being shaped by purely African dynamics and has largely ignored the empirical electoral theories that have been used in studying other regions of the world. Too often, the literature has demonstrated a predilection for the darker or more exotic dimensions of African elections, from a focus on ethnic politics to the continuing role of traditional authorities, vote buying, clientelism, and electoral violence. Our objective is not to deny at least some African specificity – and in the pages that follow, we will critically discuss many of these phenomena – but rather to show that electoral politics in the region is not exotic or unique to Africa. Basic concepts that have been developed to study elections in well-established democracies – such as retrospective voting, political business cycles, issue framing and ownership, valence competition, and voter cueing – can be used to understand voting and party behavior in Africa. Electoral laws and other formal institutions structure African elections in much the same manner as elsewhere, as the comparative literature on institutions predict. Indeed, we will show that these theories from comparative politics help us to understand key patterns and variations in the elections we study.

It is at best reductionist to view African elections as little more than ethnic censuses in which voters respond mechanically to ethnic cues and vote for their coethnics, typically in the context of pervasive clientelism and violence. In fact, ethnic identity is never the only factor shaping the party system or shaping voter decisions, and in a number of countries, it is mostly irrelevant. Far from seeing a landscape empty of policy debates as we survey African elections, we are struck by the substantive nature of the electoral rhetoric, even if the discourse does not attain the level of a graduate seminar at a policy school – a standard that is very rarely attained in any contemporary democracy. Candidates use traditional campaign tours as well as social media to reach out to the electorate with messages that they hope with resonate.

Politicians in most African countries are certainly willing to campaign for the support of specific ethnoregional constituencies with coded language, or "dog whistles," in much in the way that American or European politicians do. However, African politicians pursue voters through other strategies as well and understand that they must address voters' welfare concerns and not just focus on ascriptive appeals. While violence and blatant appeals to clientelism are certainly part of the African electoral landscape, they are not the only – or often even the most important – characteristics of these elections, as their dominance in the Africanist literature might lead one to believe.

1.4 ELECTIONS AS POLITICAL MOMENTS

In very young and still unsettled electoral systems, each election provides a moment of temporary political fluidity – what could be called a "turning point," a "crisis," or an "unsettled time" (Capoccia and Keleman, 2007, p. 341). The term "political opportunity structure," found in the contentious politics literature, perhaps captures the same idea, albeit in a more sociological manner. Karl (1986, p. 85, fn 5) identified a similar dynamic in electoral periods for Latin America in the 1980s, although she calls these brief periods "political moments":

Even when organized by authoritarians, elections can shape and redefine political moments in several ways. They can narrow the options available to actors on the extremes of the political spectrum, provoke changes in the strategies of all political actors that encourage accommodation, and define new rules of the game that encourage regime liberalization – even if they were not originally intended to do so.

Regardless of terminology, we argue that elections present Africa's political systems with relatively brief periods in which political change is more likely to occur and to put the country on a new and different political path with somewhat changed institutions. Across the continent, there is variation in the probability that elections will act as political moments leading to significant changes in government leadership and policy. On average, countries with oil rents, strong militaries backing the incumbent regime, or former revolutionary parties should be better able to weather political change. However, as the cases of Nigeria and Gambia demonstrate, even in political systems characterized by an oil economy or an authoritarian grip on power, dramatic political change can occur in the wake of elections. In this book, we seek not to predict when an alternation is likely to take place but rather to stress that elections introduce the possibility of such change.

The relationship between elections and democratization has been the subject of much scholarly debate. Seminal work by Lindberg (2006, 2009) and Schedler (2002) first developed the influential argument that regular elections helped to promote democratization both through a process of political learning by the citizenry and political elites and because it helped to institutionalize the norms, practices, and procedures of competition and participation (see also Flores and Nooruddin, 2016; Edgell et al., 2017; Teorell and Wahman, 2017). This "democratization by elections" thesis holds either that each election advances democracy in a process of small incremental steps or that a history of elections will, over time, pave the way for an eventual consolidated democratic order (see Teorell and Hadenius, 2009).

At the other extreme, Collier (2011) and Mansfield and Snyder (2002) are among prominent scholars who have argued that democratic elections are fraught with danger for low-income countries and could be linked statistically with a rise in civil conflict, ethnic violence, and, more generally, political decline. These scholars argued that elections, far from promoting democracy, could bring about a backlash against democracy by increasing instability. We will discuss both of these arguments at length in later chapters. Here, we suggest only that our own position is somewhere between the optimism of the "democratization by elections" hypothesis and the pessimistic view that elections destabilize low-income countries. We find ourselves closer to the view of Carothers (2002): that most of these polities are actually relatively stable, in the process of neither democratizing nor regressing to their authoritarian past. The fluidity of the transition era is over; in Africa, as elsewhere, elections put in play both change agents and dogged defendants of the status quo. The relationship between democracy and elections is shaped by factors that vary across time and country from socioeconomic variables to state capacity and the international environment.

While Schedler is probably correct to argue that the long-term prospects for democracy are improved by the global legitimacy of procedural democracy, in the past twenty-five years that legitimacy has served more to ensure the regular convening of multiparty elections than to generate much discernible democratic deepening, though the latter may well be happening in a minority of countries. The other dominant argument in the literature – about the dangers of elections in low-income Africa – similarly offers the insight that electoral periods represent moments of vulnerability for even the least democratic regimes because elections spark mass popular participation and awareness about politics. Nonetheless, as we will show in the Chapters 2–4, the striking pattern is for elections to shore up the status quo, in both the more- and in less-democratic polities. Elections have destabilized a minority of countries, but in most, they have served as relatively predictable and peaceful instruments for the maintenance of power of existing regimes.

Our argument is thus somewhat different from the "democratization by elections" hypothesis. First, our argument is about brief political openings that can lead to institutional innovation, in contrast to Lindberg's argument, which is primarily about the behavioral effects of elections and the political learning that takes place as a result of elections. Perhaps more important, we do not believe that the change that results from an electoral political moment is necessarily positive. We eschew the teleological logic of much of the consolidation literature. Electoral moments can also lead to the rollback of previous democratic gains or the consolidation of obstacles to further opening up. The point is that elections are key moments in the life of a relatively young democracy because the choices that are open to political actors expand briefly, with lasting consequences for the political system.

Some examples will help to clarify what we have in mind. Every African country has had to decide whether or not to enforce term limits for the president (see Chapter 3). That decision, invariably made in the context of an upcoming election, forces the political system and its actors to reassess national political institutions and whether to deepen or undermine democracy. The decision is not completely context free, of course, and is constrained by economic and social legacies; but it has typically been a contingent one, in which individual actors, civil society, and political parties have weighed in heavily.

In this respect, the contrast between Benin and Togo is illustrative. President Mathieu Kerekou's decision not to force a change to the constitution to allow him to run for a third term as president of Benin in 2000 helped to put that country on a path in which Kerekou's decision considerably weakened the ability of subsequent presidents to force their way to a third term, as two-term president Yayi Boni discovered in 2016. In neighboring Togo, the constitution was similarly altered during the transition to electoral democracy in the early 1990s to include presidential term limits. Longtime strongman President Gnassingbé Eyadema managed to survive this transition and was elected in both 1993 and 1998 in the country's first multicandidate presidential elections since 1961.

This was a loose interpretation of the two-term limit rule, since Eyadema had been in power since 1967. Still, in the run-up to the 2005 elections, he forced a constitutional change that ended presidential terms limits, despite opposition. In sharp contrast to Benin's political system, that of Togo has remained much more authoritarian, and current President Faure Gnassingbé Eyadema, the son of Gnassingbé Eyadema, was able to gain a third term in 2015.

The contrasting politics around the third term are not easily explained by the structural differences between two countries with very similar histories and socioeconomic legacies. Instead, the struggles over the third term should be understood as highly contingent political struggles with long-term institutional consequences for democracy in the two countries. As we will show in Chapter 3, a large proportion of the states in the region have been confronted with the term-limit debate, typically in the run-up to an election. How the debate has turned out has shaped these countries political systems in lasting ways. Even where elites have managed to manipulate term limits, as in Togo and Burundi, these decisions have been met with tremendous popular protest and dissent.

Similarly, open-seat elections, in which no incumbent is running, provide African electoral systems a political moment in which contingent politics can push the country in different directions (Cheeseman, 2010). In some cases, the status quo has in effect won the day. In Gabon, Togo, and the Democratic Republic of Congo, the death of the long-time dictator resulted in little liberalization, as each defunct president's cronies quickly installed his son in the presidency to maintain their own power. However, in examining a broader number of cases, observers note that executives' attempts to hand power to their kin have had varied success (Brossier and Dorronsoro, 2016). In other electoral autocracies, the exit of the old autocrat has resulted in significant democratization, with a member of the opposition being elected and executive power becoming significantly more accountable. Open-seat elections have resulted in victories for the opposition and further democratization in Guinea (2008), Ghana (2000), Kenya (2002), São Tomé and Príncipe (2011), and Sierra Leone (2007). In these cases, elections created a moment of political fluidity, and the mobilization of both domestic and international opinion made a military intervention or some kind of extralegal power grab less likely. Once the moment was over, structural forces reasserted themselves but with slightly more open political institutions in place.

To be sure, there have been significant setbacks in some countries, and some cases of democratic progress have also been recorded, but we will argue that patterns of political competition and participation have rarely changed in a sustained manner. Whatever political change is happening is occurring very slowly, in sharp contrast to the dynamism and fluidity of African society. Over the course of the past quarter-century, one can observe a process of institutionalization of electoral politics in the region but relatively little democratic deepening. That is, the striking and unprecedented convening of multiparty competitive elections has become routine and mostly accepted by both political elites and mass publics in the region, but the quality of these elections and the democratic institutions that structure them have not changed dramatically in most countries.

This combination of political stasis and rapid societal change may eventually pose risks for these political systems as citizens become ever more frustrated with the unchanging menu of political choices. But the disjuncture between political society and civil society that has marked the period under study has so far been more a curious feature of electoral politics than a source of conflict or sudden change.

1.4.1 Elections as Moments of Heightened Citizenship

The regularization of elections has generated cyclical focal points for African citizens to talk about, and sometimes to engage in, politics. Like their peers on other continents, African citizens' focus on governance, their levels of political knowledge (Andersen, Tilley, and Heath, 2005), and their partisan attachments (Michelitch and Utych, 2018) are heightened during election cycles. In sub-Saharan Africa, where legal pluralism and parallel forms of governance continue to play an important role in "lived governance," the election cycle might have a particularly crucial impact on refocusing citizens' attention toward formal institutions of governance. Election cycles make parties and electoral actors more salient, especially in countries where they are relatively weak. For instance, Michelitch and Utych (2018) show that fluctuations in partisan identification are stronger in poorer countries and in countries where parties are weaker.

The institutionalization of multiparty politics has generated new information and experiences that citizens and politicians can use to orient their understanding of governance. Election cycles, regardless of electoral quality, generate increased public debate and candidate visibility. Over time, we believe, both politicians and voters will gain experience and greater confidence about the environment in which they operate. We suggest that citizens are learning incrementally about the role of elections and are changing their expectations about the accountability of elected officials. In this book, we highlight candidates' attempts to connect with the population and to discuss key issues that concern them. Across most of the continent, citizens continue to care about some key political issues from election to election: access to basic services and economic development, various freedoms associated with democracy and government corruption, issues related to security and sovereignty, definitions of citizenship, and the distribution of natural resources.

In Chapters 5 and 6, we link candidates' electoral rhetoric to issues that citizens care about, and we show that this rhetoric varies among countries and elections cycles, although it proves to be remarkably predictable. We demonstrate the recourse to valence arguments about policy, which we argue is a strategic response to high levels of political uncertainty. We can observe this in social media data, from the substantial number of hits on parties' and candidates' Twitter feeds and Facebook accounts and from the emergence of campaign advertisements posted to websites such as YouTube, as we discuss in Chapter 5. These socioeconomic changes both shape the electoral environment and affect the relationship between citizens and government, distinct from elections.

These moments of heightened citizenship around elections, it should be clear, do not necessarily only promote better citizenship or political pluralism. They can also promote exclusionary and demagogic politics, as when ethnic identity and conflict are exacerbated during electoral periods. Thus, for instance, in West Africa, the debates about indigeneity and citizenship that destabilized Côte d'Ivoire were clearly intensified by politicians seeking an electoral advantage (Keller, 2014).

Chapter 7 shows that citizens' exposure to diverse forms of media such as television and the Internet is increasing over time. Initial evidence from Afrobarometer tentatively suggests that increased access to media is associated with greater levels of political knowledge about municipal and legislative officials as well as increasing membership in self-help associations. African citizens who are more knowledgeable about, and actively engaged in, civil society will ultimately be more empowered voters. Further, African citizens appear to maintain steady interest and participation in politics, and there appears to be no clear patterns in protest behavior. These trends may disabuse critics of the idea that elected governments' inability to meet mass demands for development, public service provision, and job creation will generate skepticism that ultimately drives citizens out of participation in electoral channels into exclusive repertoires of contentious politics.

We caution that this process of learning will not happen equally quickly in all countries or even within countries. The diffusion of political ideas, parties' campaign efforts, and citizens' participation are shaped by electoral environments. While we emphasize trends in campaigning and electoral discourse, we also stress that there is no one "African voter." There is high variation in rates and modes of participation across countries. Longitudinal continuity in political participation rates in each country since founding elections is relatively striking, suggesting specific country-level dynamics around mobilization. In Chapter 7, we show that participation rates are not correlated with levels of democracy. Although political participation is evolving rapidly, voting behavior continues to exhibit a degree of deference to incumbents, particularly in rural areas, where local political brokers can still be relied upon to turn out the vote for sitting presidents. African citizens make decisions about when and how to participate on the basis of the unique incentives offered by the political system in these citizens' specific geographic location and during the particular election cycle.

The turn to regular competitive elections in combination with social changes such as urbanization and growing literacy has, at the same time, introduced a historically unprecedented explosion in political participation in the region at both national and local levels. Even when the playing field is far from level, with incumbents benefiting from various types of advantages, party competition has emerged in regular election campaigns and in legislative debates. An increasingly aggressive press, in traditional media but increasingly on social media as well, comments on politics and informs the public. And the public has responded, both in voting turnout and, even more, in their growing interaction with politicians, government officials, and local intermediaries. They join an increasing number of nongovernmental organizations and civic associations.

1.5 RETHINKING DEMOCRATIC CONSOLIDATION

The evidence we present in this book that holding regular multiparty elections does not necessarily promote the stability of democracy – or its deepening – forces a reconsideration of different theories about democratic consolidation. Theoretical discussions of democratic consolidation have undergone a number of different, somewhat contradictory permutations. It has often been said that theories of democratic consolidation are teleological, in that the term denotes both a process and an outcome. The process of democratic consolidation results in a consolidated democracy, or, as Linz and Stepan (1996, p. 14) put it, "democracy cannot be thought of as consolidated until a democratic transition has been brought to completion." This is problematic in the sense that it leads to a conflation of two distinct dynamics of consolidation. On the one hand, consolidation is viewed as the final stage of a circumscribed transition process, taking place within a couple years at the most. Procedural definitions of democracy have been based on minimal requirements: Either regimes were democratic or they were not, depending on the presence of a small number of political institutions, including the regular convening of competitive elections with a widespread popular franchise. Early democratic data sets thus defined democracy as a 0–1 variable, allowing no middle ground or ambiguous status somewhere between full democracy and full autocracy.

Consolidation was thus seen as a relatively short-term process, after which a country would no longer regress to nondemocracy. Huntington's (1991, p. 267) definition of consolidation as having taken place when two electoral executive turnovers have been registered in elections subsequent to the transition election has been much cited, not least because it is easily operationalized. In addition, it reflects the view that the regime coming out of the transition would be a new, distinct, and democratic one. The alternative to consolidation was a return to the old order via a military coup – the clear and obvious threat looming over most of the early democratizers of the Third Wave, such as Portugal, Greece, or Brazil, which had democratized from military regimes.

In retrospect, Huntington's definition of consolidation presumed wrongly that competitive elections were a sufficient condition for liberal democracy as well as a necessary one. The emergence of electoral autocracies in recent years has confirmed the dangers of what Karl (1986) called the electoral fallacy about Central America in the 1980s. In Africa today, it is clear that relatively competitive elections with executive turnovers can occur in countries that lack democratic levels of civil and political rights.

On the other hand, perhaps as a result of the emergence of nondemocratic electoral regimes, most contemporary discussions of consolidation have defined it as democratic deepening by which the thin and incomplete democratic institutions created by the transition are perfected and strengthened progressively and over time. This understanding of consolidation is more vague and perhaps less operational, but it seems to fit better the reality in low-income, low-capacity democracies. As the Third Wave of democratization moved to countries with weaker structural requisites associated with democracy, such as high levels of national income and literacy, observers were more likely to predict that the initial transition was only a first stage, resulting in a "democracy with adjectives" (Collier and Levitsky, 1997). The process of consolidation was thought to be a much longer-term process through which these adjectives would be progressively shed and thus was largely delinked from the initial transition.

Initially, Carothers's (2002) trenchant critique that too many observers seemed to assume that all recent democratizers were still in transition and moving inexorably toward a deepening of democracy may well have been true, but a reading of the academic literature on consolidation makes it clear that few academic observers are still under the spell of "the transition paradigm"; instead, the danger of "democratic erosion" (Schedler, 1998) or "democratic backsliding" (Bermeo, 2016) is the primary lens through which these countries' progress is assessed. With some exceptions (for instance, Posner and Young, 2007; Levitsky and Way, 2015), most contemporary observers lament the decline of democratic practices and values in the African region (for instance, Diamond, 2015; Gyimah-Boadi, 2015).

Our own view challenges both of these understandings of consolidation. For one thing, as we shall discuss at greater length in Chapters 2 and 3, only between a third and a half of the polities in the region ever undertook what could be meaningfully described as a democratic transition in the early 1990s. In the others countries, incumbents agreed to regular elections and some cosmetic political liberalization to placate domestic and international demands but did so in a way that did not threaten their own rule. In these countries, simply put, it is not clear what is being consolidated. Not only are some elections still so restricted that they cannot be associated with political liberalization, but even in cases of the introduction of regular free and fair multiparty elections, the evolution to liberal democracy is neither assured nor perhaps even likely. As we will show, political elites have been savvy in adapting their strategies to focus on power maintenance despite these substantial formal, institutional changes. We will argue that the past quarter-century suggests that regular elections are necessary but insufficient conditions for democratic consolidation.

More generally, the African experience of the past quarter-century suggests that approaches to democratic consolidation do not emphasize political continuity enough; despite the regular incorporation of multiparty elections, we emphasize regime continuity. Very few regimes have significantly deepened their democratic practice since the onset of regular elections. But we also insist that political and civil rights have not substantially eroded, even in most of the political systems that have undergone repeated political crises. The political backsliding that legitimately attracts much hand-wringing has been limited to a small number of countries, at least during the period on which this book is primarily focused: 1995–2015.

Further, once countries begin to hold elections, elections become demanded by the population. What are the implications of this stability, notably for the process of democratic consolidation? Has stability strengthened democratic institutions and attitudes? Or does the lack of progress point to the fragility of these institutions and the thinness of the support for democracy among the citizenry? It is easy to be pessimistic about African democracy, but what strikes us is the resilience of these fledgling institutions and the unabated demand for civic and political rights coming from African citizens.

While some of these trends and continuity stretch back to an earlier time, before the transitions to democracy, this book is not arguing that elections have not affected governance in African states. As we show, compared to the pretransition period of the late 1980s, the majority of African states are performing dramatically better in terms of political liberties and civil rights. Many states continued to move in the direction of polyarchy (a term that means "government by many") until the early 2000s. While the second decade of the twenty-first century has been associated with greater stagnation and in some instances backsliding, it is undeniable that most African citizens have greater political rights and greater accountability from government now than they did before transitions to democracy.

The apparent current stasis in the quality of political institutions is all the more paradoxical given that the region is otherwise undergoing rapid social and economic change, which we view as generally supportive of democracy. Theories of democratic consolidation rarely include a sophisticated sociology of these countries, and we know of no work that makes the same contrast that we advance between political stasis and sociological change. However, this contrast seems to us essential to understanding contemporary Africa and the long-term prospects for democracy.

1.6 ORGANIZATION OF THE BOOK

The chapters that follow this introduction analyze a quarter-century of electoral politics in sub-Saharan Africa, from 1990 to 2015. The dates were chosen at least in part for the unscientific reason that they encompass a complete quarter-century. Nonetheless, 1990 is a logical place to start, since the wave of democratization that ushered in the current era of regular multiparty elections can be said to have started in that year. We refer to some elections that took place in 2016, the year in which we were writing this book, not least because a number of the most recent elections provide great fodder for our analysis, but 2015 is the last year for which we had complete data as we started writing the book.

The book's materials are based on several types of data. First, the book uses the descriptive data set covering all national level multiparty elections, which allows for statistical generalizations about the region. Second, much of the book focuses on eight multiparty systems across the region (Benin, Ghana, Kenya, Mozambique, Nigeria, Senegal, Uganda, and Zambia). These countries were chosen to represent different regions, different colonial legacies, and different levels of democratic consolidation. In this book, we develop finer-grained data for these countries to illustrate broad trends and test some initial hypotheses. Our analysis of the issues that dominate African elections, for instance, is based on a data set of issues discussed in local newspapers during electoral cycles in these countries (Chapter 6).

Third, we have taken case studies of specific countries and elections from a wide variety of sources, based on our reading of the literature and key elections we are aware of. Too much of the scholarly literature and too many empirical conclusions about the region are based on a handful of Anglophone African countries (Briggs, 2017), and we have consciously sought to base our arguments and generalization on as broad a set of cases as possible.

We start by assessing emerging patterns in electoral results: the number of elections, reelection rates, the emerging party systems, and the strength of opposition parties and candidates, all in the context of contemporary theorizing about democratic consolidation. We ask both what impact electoral competition has on the quality of democracy in the region and whether observed patterns can be linked to the quality of democracy. We assess the progress on democratic consolidation over time and its relationship with the holding of elections. Political alternation, with the defeat of the incumbent, has happened in some countries but not in others; this turnover is not always linked to quality of democracy. We explore the role and evolution of parties in the region. The degree to which party systems are structured by ethnolinguistic factors varies as well. The book then examines candidates and campaigns before exploring a set of key issues in greater depth. It analyzes the manner in which candidates and parties conduct electoral campaigns, the issues they use to mobilize voters, and the role of ethnicity and clientelism in shaping electoral outcomes. Chapter 7 is devoted to the micro-level behavior of Africa voters, their motivations for participating, and their attitudes about democracy. Some dynamics appear to be widely shared in the region, but there is also interesting variation across our cases, which we seek to explain. We discuss distinct patterns of mobilization in rural and urban areas, but we also show the high level of variation in voter turnout across countries. We conclude with a chapter that explores the implications of the routinization of elections on the daily lives of African citizens.

Our analysis throughout this book is structured on the broad theme of political outcomes in the region being shaped by the paradoxical interaction of change and continuity.

The book proceeds as follows. Chapter 2 examines the key trends in the evolution of electoral competition in the region. It links the democratic era back to electoral trends in Africa in the decades before the transitions. Examining the transitions, we show that few countries fully democratized in the early 1900s. We then introduce data on presidential and legislative electoral results between 1990 and 2015 in the forty-six countries of the region that conducted multiparty elections during that period. We examine the evolution in terms of margin of victory, reelection rates, strength of the opposition, participation rates, and party systems, and we argue that the stability of these regimes over time is striking and needs to be explained.

Chapter 3 expands on Chapter 2 by problematizing the quality of democracy in the region and the complex relationship between democracy and multiparty elections. We document the wide range of electoral practices that often protect incumbents in both more- and less-democratic states. The predominance of presidentialism emerges as a hallmark of these regimes, in both more- and less-democratic states – one reason why the region continues to show very little electoral alternation. We identify as many as half of the countries in the region as nondemocratic, despite the convening of regular multiparty elections, and we examine elections in these states to show how elections have become instruments for power maintenance rather than for the expression of meaningful political participation and competition.

In Chapter 4, we examine the parties and party systems that compete in African elections. The chapter starts with a brief history of parties at independence to show the continuity of certain dynamics. We find evidence that the modal party system in the region comprises seemingly dominant parties in power surrounded by relatively ephemeral small parties in poorly institutionalized party systems. Although there are some significant exceptions that must be understood, this general pattern was quickly established in the transitional elections of the early and mid-1990s, and it has remained stable even when the party in power has changed. This seems to hold regardless of the quality of democracy in the country. In Chapter 4, we examine these patterns more carefully and characterize different theories of party development and party system institutionalization in the region. We show that access to funding has shaped the organization and leadership of parties in the region, and we argue that this is the main reason why parties in power with access to state resources have a substantial political advantage over opposition parties, though the latter can access significant public resources at the subnational level in the bigger countries of the region.

In Chapters 5 and 6, we explore the actual electoral campaigns in Africa from 1990 to 2015. In Chapter 5, we discuss the common attributes of presidential candidates and their typical electoral campaigns. We argue that it is important to understand the strategic nature and substantive issues that function underneath different rituals and the sometimes seemingly exotic practices that candidates undertake in the course of the elections. We highlight some key practices of electoral campaigns, including candidate tours, candidate endorsements, brokerage, political advertising, gifts, and violence at election time.

In Chapter 6, we focus on the electoral issues that dominate these elections. One cliché about African elections has it that they are comparatively empty of real debate over national issues but instead focus mostly on ethnically based appeals, lubricated by clientelism and vote buying. In this chapter, we show that this argument is untenable and that a number of issues can regularly be discerned in African elections even though they are often valence issues and not easily captured framework of specific political positions easily placed in a policy space of issue ownership reveals logical and predictable patterns in electoral discourse. The chapter also shows that the newness of these electoral systems and the inexperience of most African parties help to explain the political rhetoric the parties employ during elections, as they are still just learning how to mobilize voters and how to identify stable constituencies. Parties can use their structural position as opposition or incumbents to "own" specific issues, such as democracy and development. In this chapter, we also highlight six thematic areas that dominate electoral discourse in Africa: economic development, democracy, sovereignty, domestic security, citizenship, and the distribution of natural resources.

In Chapter 7, we turn our attention to the voters themselves. We examine the evolving attitudes and behavior of African voters by focusing on the different forms of political expression (from voting to contentious politics) as well as the role of ethnicity, partisanship, religion, and other forms of group identity in explaining the choice to participate and the nature of that participation. We analyze the various factors that influence voters' decisions, including party strength and system competitiveness, incumbent performance, the role of traditional authorities and other brokers, socioeconomic variables, and associational membership. We also assess the nature of citizen support for democracy and its evolution over time.

In Chapter 8, we ask whether or not these elections matter. In addition to concluding the book, this chapter answers the "so what" question. Do elections make a difference in the lives of Africans? We marshal evidence on behalf of the argument that democratization has had a minor but significant effect in economic and political terms and that this impact is likely to increase over time. Political liberalization has increased the accountability of state officials, albeit modestly in most countries, and the need to win competitive elections has resulted in governments that are more likely to provide services to the population. The politics that is emerging in the new Africa includes more attention to citizens and the emergence of distributive politics. It also gives more power to the business community, which is ideally suited to fund political parties to advance its own policy agenda. New social coalitions are emerging across the region as a result, with potentially profound effects for deepening of democracy in the future.

We conclude with a discussion of our expectation that continuity will diminish over time as the two factors of resilience diminish: executive dominance and the liability of newness. As ruling executives leave office and successor candidates must face open-seat elections, there will be reduced incumbency advantage and heightened opportunities for alternation during electoral cycles. As opposition parties are elected to office, they will be able to leverage those experiences to their advantage.

2

The Evolution of Electoral Competition, 1990–2015

2.1 INTRODUCTION

Democratic transitions in the early 1990s brought about a major shift in African politics. Between 1990 and 2015, 184 multicandidate presidential elections and 207 multiparty legislative elections were held in some forty-six countries.[1] Only Eritrea, Somalia, and Swaziland did not convene a single competitive national election during that time. In comparison, only nine competitive multiparty elections had been convened in the period 1985–1989.[2] This striking difference illustrates the breadth of the wave of democratization that swept through Africa in the 1990s (Wiseman, 1995; Bratton and van de Walle, 1997; Clark and Gardinier, 1997; Daloz and Quantin, 1997). Before 1990, competitive elections involving multiple political parties were rare events in Africa; after that year, they became routine. As we shall see, the record of democratization in the region remains uneven and imperfect, but there is no denying the dramatic change in political practices and popular participation, notably through elections, that has occurred since the early 1990s.[3]

---

[1] We define a multiparty legislative election as one in which at least one opposition party candidate gets elected. We do not count "independents"; we rank presidential elections as multiparty when the winner does not get 100 percent of the vote. The latter may seem a forgiving coding rule, but in fact the highest total recorded is 97.85 percent of the vote going to the winner in the 1996 elections in Equatorial Guinea, and only eighteen of the 183 elections registered totals above 90 percent.

[2] Multiparty elections were held during this period in Botswana, Mauritius, and, more problematically, Zimbabwe, Gambia, and Senegal.

[3] Among a large literature that examines the extent and sustainability of democracy in the region, see Gazibo (2005), Lindberg (2006), Saine et al. (2011), Crawford and Lynch (2012), Bratton (2013), and Cheeseman (2015).

In this chapter, we summarize the results of these elections and the broad patterns they suggest about electoral competition in Africa for the last quarter-century. In the next chapter, we relate these elections to the evolving quality of democracy in the region. Here, the intention is to catalogue some of the essential patterns and trends. The first section provides a brief history of elections in Africa since independence and summarizes the basic parameters of electoral competition since 1990. We compare and contrast the handful of elections of the independence period with those of the contemporary era to understand why multiparty elections have been sustained for over two decades. We show that regular multiparty elections have become routinized in Africa for the first time since independence. The overwhelming majority of countries in the region now conduct national presidential and legislative elections on a regular basis. In the next section, we show that the convening of elections does not constitute a process of democratic consolidation, however, since only a small number of states have democratized substantially during this period. We argue, instead, that elections constitute political moments with greater uncertainty and heightened attention to politics that can, in some cases, lead to greater democracy. Regular elections are perhaps a necessary condition for democratic consolidation, but they are not a sufficient condition, since some of the region's least democratic countries also regularly convene multiparty elections.

Then we summarize several broad empirical trends that emerge from the data. First is the key role of the transitional election in the early 1990s. We show that success in the first multiparty presidential election often proved to be the key to political dominance in the 1990s. We also show that this path dependence has attenuated over time. Second, we show that electoral competition has been dominated by the incumbent president and his party. Presidentialism has been described as one of the characteristic features of Africa's imperfect democratization, and we describe its electoral dimension. Finally, we show the very limited amount of electoral alternation that has occurred in the last quarter-century, as incumbents almost always win reelection. We conclude by arguing that we are observing a process of institutionalization of African electoral competition. The process is slow and halting, but patterns and processes are hardening and becoming more routine. Is this a process of democratic consolidation? While our analysis suggests little evidence for a regional process of democratic erosion, we argue that the quality of democracy has not improved substantially enough in most countries to speak of a continent-wide process of democratic consolidation.

2.2 A BRIEF HISTORY OF ELECTORAL COMPETITION IN AFRICA

Students of democratization have contrasted the power of structural constraints on change during times of normal politics in stable regimes with the fluidity of politics in periods of regime breakdown (O'Donnell and Schmitter, 1986, p. 3; Bratton and van de Walle, 1997, pp. 19–60). Structural factors, such as the basic structure of the economy and society, weigh more during the former, while individual agency and political contingency matter more to outcomes when institutions are in flux and the political status quo is shaken. This contrast helps to explain the slow pace of political change in Africa since the end of the transitions in the early 1990s. As political stability has returned, deepening of democratization has proved to be constrained by such persistent structural factors as the weakness of the middle class, high rates of poverty and of illiteracy in the bureaucratic languages of the state, and low levels of state capacity.

A brief detour through the region's history of elections is enlightening, as Africa's current political systems can be understood to have been shaped by two past *critical junctures*, or what Capoccia and Kelemen (2007, p. 341) refer to as a "brief phase(s) of institutional flux." During a critical juncture, structural factors weigh less heavily on politics, and the possibility of significant institutional change for the polity is heightened. Capoccia and Kelemen appear to view critical junctures as relatively rare exogenous shocks to the regime of political institution. The independence period and then the regime crises and democratization wave of the late 1980s and early 1990s represent two significant critical junctures in which rapid change took place and a new institutional equilibria were established. In the late 1950s and early 1960s, impending decolonization created the conditions for a period of intense institutional and political experimenting. New parties emerged, political elites engaged in debates about the political institutions to adopt after independence, and mobilized citizens participated in large numbers and pursued various forms of contentious politics. Most countries in the region suffered from structural conditions that were not propitious for the emergence of democratic governance, and multiparty electoral competition proved ephemeral as personal dictatorships took control. Still, the experiments of the independence period continued to exert significant influences on African politics, and some of the variation in political outcomes that we observe today can be directly related to dynamics and patterns from that period, as we will argue throughout this book.

Similarly, the collapse of African economies during the 1980s and the resulting political crisis resulted directly in the wave of democratization of the early 1990s, which constituted a second critical juncture in the region. With echoes from the earlier era of multiparty rule, the region went through a dramatic transformation involving a wholesale transition to multiparty rule. This time, the antecedent conditions were somewhat more favorable for participatory politics to sustain themselves. Multiparty elections did become routine. At the same time, many of the structural and institutional conditions that had existed after independence continue to undermine democratic consolidation.

2.2.1 The Independence Era

Sub-Saharan Africa enjoyed a brief period of multiparty competitive politics in the first years following independence. Important lessons can be learned by comparing that period to the contemporary era. The European colonial powers belatedly introduced democratic constitutions in their African colonies in the waning days of their rule in the region (Collier, 1982; Cooper, 2002, pp. 38–53, 76–84). The first national participatory electoral exercises sometimes took place within just a couple of years after complete independence, even if the recourse to local and municipal elections had come somewhat earlier, typically with a very limited franchise that excluded most African citizens. In most countries, these regimes did not last much longer than one or two electoral terms, as ruling governments soon consolidated their hold on power by curtailing civil and political rights or, almost as often, were ousted by military coups (Collier, 1982).

With the exception of the few citizens who managed to achieve assimilated status in French- and Portuguese-speaking countries, most Africans were entirely banned from electoral engagement during the colonial era (Hyden, 2011, p. 104). Most Africans had never voted in local elections, let alone national ones. Protests were usually harshly repressed, and political associations were at best tolerated when limited to very circumscribed elite circles. The short run-up to independence in the 1950s offered the first possibilities for mass political participation in most countries in the region (Collier, 1982, pp. 29–61). In contrast to the typically very gradual processes of enfranchisement in the West, the vast majority of African states extended universal suffrage to all citizens, including women, and very quickly – in a matter of years if not months preceding independence.[4]

The years around formal independence constituted an era of unprecedented formal political participation.[5] As soon as the colonial authorities tentatively opened up what had been very closed political systems, parties and various associations and unions mushroomed all over the continent (on unions in this era, see Cooper, 1996), as did nationalist-leaning newspapers catering to an African audience. Particularly in the cities, citizens joined economic and political protests in much greater numbers than had been the case before World War II. Thanks to the electoral reforms that were advanced in most colonies, Africans who had never voted were suddenly being asked to go to the polls for constitutional referenda, local elections, presidential elections, and legislative elections. In a story that could be repeated for most countries in the region, Bienen (1974, p. 89) describes the voting explosion for citizens in Mombasa, Kenya:

No African had voted in (Mombasa) municipal elections before 1960, and fewer than 1,000 were registered in the 1957 and 1958 legislative elections. By 1961, about 25,000 Africans were registered in Mombasa's district and 75,000 by 1963. Moreover, within a space of four months in 1963, Mombasa Africans could vote for the Lower House seats in the National Assembly and for the Senate, ... and for a municipal council.

It is important to contrast these dramatic increases in political participation in the late colonial era with much greater continuity in certain other political and socioeconomic dynamics. A large literature argues that the new governments drew on traditions and a political culture forged during the colonial era and that few efforts were made to adapt or incorporate indigenous political traditions or resources (Young, 1993, p. 301; Young, 2004; Willis and al-Batthani, 2010). Some scholars trace the heritage of a powerful presidency from the legacy of colonial governors and state-centric model of governance (Crowder, 1987; Young,

---

4 With the exception of the white minority settler states in Southern Africa and for women in Northern Nigeria.

5 Of course, there were many existing modes of informal participation in African societies that continue to takes place outside of the state bureaucracy regardless of the regime type. For instance, Logan (2009, p. 105) argues that a focus on formal participation through electoral channels neglects traditional systems of accountability: "For example, community-wide gatherings common to many African societies, known variously as *pitso* (Lesotho), *kgotla* (Botswana), *shir* (Somalia), *baraza* (Kenya) and by many other names, have long offered an opportunity for a wide array of community members to voice their opinions on community affairs and participate in consensus-based decision-making."

1993, p. 301). Newly independent governments also soon adopted some repressive tactics that colonial states had used to control dissenters, such as preventive detention (Crowder, 1987, p. 13).

To be sure, the commodities boom of the 1950s provided new and significant resources for state-building projects, though these resources would dissipate slowly throughout the 1960s. In addition, decolonization opened up economic opportunities for Africans that had previously been monopolized by white and Asian populations, especially in Eastern and Central Africa. Still, colonial capital and business interests, combined with a predominance of Asian and Middle Eastern networks in retail trade, were initially little affected by independence. Many new governments retained European advisors to state ministries and firms (Crowder, 1987). Kwame Nkrumah's caution to his followers, "Seek ye first the political kingdom and all things shall be added unto you," is often cited to argue that the emergent African political class viewed political power as the initial step in a process of class formation (Sklar, 1979). However, it also reflected, at least in part, the extent to which their new political power did not yet have an economic counterpart.

Despite the unprecedented opportunities for mass political participation brought about by the end of colonialism, moreover, new political systems retained the elitist character of pre-independence governance. At a most basic level, nearly all countries adopted the former colonizers' language as the bureaucratic language of government and for mass schooling (Laitin, 1992; Albaugh, 2009), though that language was rarely spoken fluently by more than a small minority of the population.[6]

The men of the fledgling political class were drawn from an exceedingly small pool of Western-educated elites. Literacy rates at the time of independence were quite low. Roughly a third of school-age children were enrolled in schools, although British colonies enjoyed higher levels of literacy, owing largely to the much greater role of Protestant missions in basic education (Brown, 2000, pp. 29–34; Frankema, 2012). College graduates were even fewer, typically well under a hundred in most colonies and notoriously only six in the Belgian Congo (van de Walle, 2001, p. 129). In many countries, the colonial state had made minimal investments in schooling or other social service infrastructure. The few Africans who had managed to achieve secondary and university degrees found tremendous opportunities for social mobility through jobs in politics or

---

[6] An exception is Tanzania, which ran a Swahilization campaign to build national unity and suppress ethnic divides (Laitin 1992).

government service in the context of state expansion and Africanization in the years following independence (Sklar, 1979; Young, 2004, p. 28; Ba, 2009), in stark contrast with the limited opportunities for the much larger number of educated youth today. Milton Margai, Sierra Leone's first president, was the first medical school graduate in his country, and Mauritania's first president, Moktar Ould Daddah, was that country's first trained lawyer.

The fledgling political elite in most countries emerged largely from the civil services, which began to be quickly indigenized to prepare for independence. Bakary (1993, pp. 80–81) notes that in the 1962 parliamentary elections in Senegal, 50 percent of the elected candidates had come from the civil service. By 1980, this total had increased to 89 percent. In Cameroon and Côte d'Ivoire in the mid-1980s, the same dynamic prevailed, with 69 and 56 percent, respectively, of parliamentarians coming from the civil service. Within the civil service, public school teachers were particularly well represented, as teaching was the first public sector profession open to Africans. First post-independence presidents Hamani Diori in Niger, Kenneth Kaunde in Zambia, Hubert Maga in Benin, Julius Nyerere in Tanzania, and Leopold Senghor in Senegal all started their careers as colonial-era public school teachers before moving into politics.

In Francophone Africa in particular, the post-independence civil service initially retained many colonial-era privileges, such as paid vacations to Paris. Independence-era administrators made cosmopolitan comparisons of their own status to that of the former French bureaucrats rather than that of their less fortunate countrymen, whose taxes would now be used to support the lifestyles of the civil service (Morgenthau, 1971, p. 7). An early critic, René Dumont (1966, p. 79), estimated that a parliamentarian in French West Africa earned 36 times more than the average peasant. Dumont added acidly, "[T]hese countries have not yet understood their poverty." He perhaps understood what the nationalist fervor around independence obscured: that these emergent party elites were hardly representative of their countries' population, with which they did not have many natural links.

This narrow political elite would form the core of the post-independence ruling class. Most of the dominant political actors in the multiparty period have come from this same pool of leaders (see Chapter 5). Despite the introduction of regular elections and tremendous socioeconomic change, the continuity of the political class is a striking characteristic of the region.

Are there lessons for the current era to be had from the failure of these fledgling attempts to sustain multiparty electoral politics in post-independence Africa? Why was this earlier foray into multiparty electoral politics so brief, and why has the current era been able to sustain it for a quarter-century? One clear difference between the two eras seems to be the lower level of legitimacy for political competition and mass participation that prevailed in the 1960s, notably as expressed by political parties. A fear of the social and ethnoregional divisions that were believed to have been spurred by the first experiences of electoral competition feature prominently in accounts from this period (see Zolberg, 1966). Moreover, the nationalist ideologies that dominated the anticolonial struggle put a real premium on party unity, which was reinforced by the Leninist doctrine of the vanguard party, which also served to delegitimize opposition.

The single party fit well the needs of ambitious dominant party leaders, who wanted to centralize power and eliminate rivals. For that purpose, mobilizing voters was useful and resulted in surprisingly high rates of turnout right around independence. Soon, however, the incentives changed, and the mobilization ambitions of emergent single parties were allowed to atrophy. Power and capacity building were transferred to the executive branch and the central administration, which was viewed as more crucial for economic development and where resources were in any event concentrated.

As Kasfir (1974) and Collier (1982, pp. 118–150) argued, established regimes preferred to contain and constrain popular participation and mass competition through a variety of mechanisms. Kasfir's (1974, p. 12) description of "the growing desuetude of participatory structures" in the late 1960s and early 1970s is authoritative:

Elections have been manipulated, legislatures have declined in importance, and important voluntary associations – trade unions and cooperative – have lost autonomy. Government parties have tended to become empty shells and local government has been virtually taken over by the center.

The influence of these measures on electoral participation was significant. Bienen (1978, pp. 90–91) notes that participation rates were well above 80 percent in the first Kenyan national elections but had declined to a third of that by the late 1960s. Even with such low levels of participation, Kenya retained more political competition than most African states, at least until the Moi presidency in the 1980s.

The short life of the participation explosion in the early 1960s diverges from the one that marked the transitions of the early 1990s in that the latter has been largely sustained to the present, marked by today's much stronger civil society and the failure of incumbents to completely stifle opposition. Whether or not state elites are more committed to democracy today is questionable, but the demand for democracy among the populations of African countries, which has been the subject of attitudinal surveys, is unmistakable and has been sustained for the last two decades (see Chapter 7).

One reason for sustained participation in the contemporary period may be the socioeconomic changes the African continent has undergone. It was overwhelmingly rural, illiterate, and disconnected from the politics of the countries' capitals in the mid-twentieth century. Today, Africa is considerably more urban, literate, and connected to regional and global networks. Ghana, one of Africa's wealthiest countries in the late 1950s, provides a good example: In 1960, Accra's population was an estimated 338,000; today, it is well over two million. Overall, the share of the urban population in Ghana has grown from 23 percent of the total population to 54 percent today. At independence, only a quarter of the population was literate; today, four out of five Ghanaians are literate. At independence, only a handful of Ghanaians lived outside of the country. Today, there are estimated to be 235,000 Ghanaians in the United States alone, who send back some $30 million USD to Ghana each year (Migration Policy Institute, 2015). These linkages, as well as increased access to social media and global news, contribute to a more cosmopolitan view of the world and greater demands on elected leaders. In sum, the socioeconomic context in which elections now take place is entirely different from that of the early postindependence years.

Moreover, the international contexts during the two democratic eras differ profoundly. There was little international support for electoral democratic politics in the early 1960s compared to the contemporary international context, which is much more supportive of pluralist politics. On the one hand, the dominant modernization theories of the 1960s suggested that economic development was a prerequisite for political development, and military governments were viewed as more capable promoters of economic growth. On the other hand, the West sought strong regimes that would serve as regional allies in their Cold War struggles. By comparison, the international support for electoral politics, while imperfect, is much stronger today.

2.2.2 The End of the First Democratic Experiments and the Authoritarian Era

The region's first multiparty era was brief, and the quickness and breadth of the descent into authoritarian rule were rather breathtaking. Between 1956 and 1966, thirty-two countries in the region attained their independence – eighteen in 1960 alone. By the early 1970s, Freedom House would rank only two of the thirty-two independent countries in the region as "free" (Gambia and Mauritius) and an additional nine as "partly free."[7] In broad strokes, the end of multipartyism followed one of two remarkably predictable scripts. In the countries that followed the first script, the winners of the first election soon consolidated their hold on power and sought to make sure they would not soon relinquish it. They accomplished this through constitutional amendments that circumscribed political competition, typically by outlawing opposition parties and weakening the legislature. In countries that followed the second script, the army overthrew civilian rule, often pointing to some failure of the latter to justify its intervention (Decalo, 1976; Bienen, 1978). By 1970, militaries had successfully undertaken or attempted forty-two coups, nineteen of which had toppled civilian governments in fifteen different countries (McGowan, 2003).

To distinguish between the path that resulted in military rule and the one that did not, Collier (1978) emphasizes that when the victorious party that emerged from the first election was genuinely popular and could integrate other political parties peacefully, the likelihood of a military coup was considerably lower. Countries such as Kenya, Zambia, and Senegal would then develop single-party systems with relatively regular electoral competition, albeit within the single party. By contrast, when the party that emerged from the initial competition was less popular or ethnoregional divisions were more bitter and repression and coercion were necessary to bring about unity, then military intervention was considerably more likely.

The 1960s were also marked by a thorough centralization of power via constitutional reforms. Great Britain left behind parliamentary constitutions inspired by its own political system when it granted independence to thirteen colonies in the late 1950s and early 1960s. Within a decade of independence, ten of the thirteen had become authoritarian presidential

---

[7] The partly free countries were Botswana, Burkina Faso, Cameroon, Kenya, Madagascar, Nigeria, Sierra Leone, Swaziland, and Zambia.

regimes or military dictatorships; only Botswana, Gambia, and Mauritius retained some semblance of the Westminster system. In francophone Africa, the constitutions that were quickly fashioned at independence closely followed the French constitution for the Fifth Republic, sometimes word for word (Le Vine, 1997, p. 184). The choice of presidential government seemed natural, but Levine points out that within three years of independence, nine out of ten francophone countries in West Africa had reformed their constitutions to reinforce executive power well beyond the French model (Le Vine, 1997, p. 187 and passim). Upper Volta had undertaken a referendum in 1959 about the desired form of government, and 80 percent of the voters supported parliamentary rule, which was adopted. However, it was made meaningless by the rapid emasculation of the legislature and the centralization of power around the president of the council (Englebert, 1996, pp. 32–36).

This quick descent into authoritarian government proved lasting. By the mid-1980s, twenty-four countries in the region were led by military governments, and of the remaining twenty-four countries, only two – Mauritius and Botswana – had enjoyed uninterrupted multiparty electoral democracy. In addition, Gambia and Senegal could claim to have reasonably pluralistic elections, although these fell well short of unrestricted multiparty competition. Otherwise, the region's regimes were authoritarian. Occasionally, the military would tire of rule and hand power back to civilians, leading to elections, but these democratic interludes were typically brief. This was the case notably for Nigeria in 1979, when General Obasanjo orchestrated the end of military rule and the transition to the democratic Second Republic. Widespread corruption, economic crisis, and the contested elections of August 1983 resulted in a military coup in December of that year, returning power to the military (Falola and Ihonvbere, 1985), which would keep it until 1999.

Some civilian regimes did convene regular single-party elections. Presidential single-party elections were not competitive and were typically won by the president for life by majorities above 90 percent (Hayward, 1987). By contrast, in cases such as Kenya or Côte d'Ivoire, the competition within the governing party was genuine and fierce in the legislative elections and resulted in the ouster of significant percentage of incumbents. Collier (1982, p. 129) reports that in the Malawian legislative elections of 1978, a 55 percent turnout resulted in the defeat of 66 percent of nominated incumbents. Indeed, presidents in these countries instrumentalized legislative elections to maintain the popular legitimacy of the regime and to discipline the backbenchers of the single party. Both Jomo

Kenyatta in Kenya and Félix Houphouët-Boigny of Côte d'Ivoire used this strategy. It allowed them to better gauge the popularity of the regime and its barons, enable the population to let off steam and express discontent, and rein in overly ambitious or unpopular members of the single party through electoral competition (Barkan and Okumu, 1978; Hermet et al., 1978; Fauré, 1993).

In many countries, the introduction of elections at the subnational level continued to generate real competition and citizen mobilization. For instance, in the 1988–1989 Ghanaian Local Assembly elections, 12, 842 candidates ran for 7,260 seats, and only 532 of them ran unopposed (Crook, 1997, p. 213, citing Ayee, 1990, and Ninsin, 1991). These elections were local and nonpartisan but demonstrated active participation even under single-party rule. As we shall see, a good deal of continuity can be discerned, since over the last quarter-century, legislative and local elections have continued to be more competitive and have generated more popular participation.

2.2.3 The Return of Multiparty Electoral Politics

By the mid-1980s, political patterns in the region appeared set, and most observers believed that a wide variety of structural and social factors favored the persistence of authoritarian rule and the absence of electoral competition. Samuel Huntington (1984, p. 216) expressed the conventional wisdom when he argued that

[m]ost African countries are, by reason of their poverty or the violence of their politics, unlikely to move in a democratic fashion. Those African ... countries that have adhered to the cyclical patterns of alternative democratic and authoritarian systems in the past are not likely to change this basic patterns, as the example of Nigeria underlines, unless more fundamental changes occur in their economic and social infrastructure.

With the advantage of hindsight, the regime transitions of the early 1990s are not surprising. Chazan (1982) had noted the rise in various forms of informal participation and contentious politics in the late 1970s, which contrasted with the quiescence of formal modes of citizen engagement with the state. The devastating economic crisis that hit the region in the 1980s resulted in a progressive increase in social protests, suggesting growing restiveness (Wiseman, 1986; Nyong'o, 1987). Although Huntington was probably correct to point to such structural factors as high levels of poverty as being inimical to democratization, other factors favored its emergence. An increasingly urban and literate population, the growth of civil society, and the change in international attitudes about authoritarian rule, notably with the emergence of the human rights discourse, all contributed to a general loss of legitimacy of Africa's poorly performing authoritarian states.

In any event, the wave of democratization that emerged in the 1990s took most observers, as well as most incumbent regimes, by surprise. The African chapter of the Third Wave of democratization is usually held to have begun with the Namibian Constituent Assembly elections of November 1989, which ended white minority rule and coincided with the Fall of the Berlin Wall several thousand miles away. For our purposes, however, the emblematic event of the renaissance of electoral politics in the region is probably the March 1991 elections in Benin, which ended the presidency of Mathieu Kérékou, who had been in power since leading a military coup in 1972 (Heilbrunn, 1993; Seely, 2005). These founding elections were convened after a long period of political unrest, amid economic crisis and the bankruptcy of the central states. Benin was the first country in the region in which a postcolonial autocrat was forced out of office by popular protests and then free and fair elections were held.

Within the next few years, a wave of democratization swept through the region as economic protests against the disastrous economic crisis then prevailing in most countries morphed into the expression of more directly political grievances (Bratton and van de Walle, 1997, pp. 98–107). The combination of mass popular protests, donor pressures, and the growing fragmentation of an increasingly skittish political elite pressured most of the regimes in the region to undertake some degree of political liberalization and to convene multiparty elections.

This turn to multiparty electoral politics proved to be broad and sustained. When Zambia convened elections in January 2015 to determine who would serve out the term of President Michael Sata, who had died in October of the previous year, it marked the seventh presidential election since the country's democratic transition in 1991. Edgar Lungu won the election with 48 percent of the vote over ten other candidates. Lungu was the fifth president elected in the democratic era, after President Kenneth Kaunde had ruled the country from independence in 1964 until 1991.

Because two of its presidents died while in office and Zambia has no constitutional mechanism for a nonelectoral presidential succession in such circumstances, the country's election totals may be somewhat inflated. Yet Table 2.1 shows well how broad and consistent the turn to multiparty elections has been. It shows that three quarters of the countries in the region have had at least four legislative multiparty elections since 1990, and three quarters of the presidential systems in the region have had their fourth such election.

The countries in the region are overwhelmingly presidential in constitutional terms. Only six (Angola since 2010, Botswana, Ethiopia, Lesotho, Mauritius, and South Africa) do not have a direct election of the president but have their executives selected by the legislature. The other states in the region are all presidential or semi-presidential regimes.[8]

Table 2.1 also shows the evolution of electoral competition over time. A couple of features stand out. First is the sheer number of elections taking place in the region and the breadth of the turn to regular electoral competition. Almost half the countries in the region have gone through four or five complete electoral cycles. In any given year, some eight to twelve national elections and many more subnational elections are held on the continent. Second, popular participation in these elections has been substantial and consistent over time, as we will discuss at length in Chapter 7. Third is the stability in the different statistics across time and elections. The number of parties competing in these legislative elections has declined slightly over time, although the effective number of parties has declined more sharply, suggesting the greater dominance of the biggest parties. On the other hand, since the second elections, there has been relatively little evolution in the percentage of either votes or seats going to the winning party. The turnout numbers are also very stable, particularly the turnout as a percentage of the voting age population. Such aggregate electoral statistics do not lend themselves to easy interpretation, but the stability they demonstrate does undermine any thesis positing some kind of major continuous change, whether it be in popular participation, the nature of the party system, or the degree of competitiveness of these elections. We turn to each of these issues in the next three sections.

---

[8] Elgie and Moestrup (2007, p. 9) identify nineteen countries in Africa as semi-presidential, including eleven of seventeen former French colonies in the region, a number that suggests the strong legacy of France's Fifth Republic. Elgie and Moestrup adopt the narrow definition of semi-presidentialism as regimes "where the popularly elected fixed-term president exists alongside of a prime minister and cabinet who are responsible to the legislature" (p. 6). They concede that this definition says little about presidential prerogatives and the constraints on presidential power.

TABLE 2.1. *The evolution of electoral competition in Africa, 1990–2015*

	First elections	Second elections	Third elections	Fourth elections	Fifth elections	Sixth elections	Seventh elections	Total or average
# of Presidential Elections	41	40	37	33	24	10	3	185
# if of Legislative Elections	46	43	44	39	34	13	1	219
Number of Parties winning seats	6.3	6.8	6.7	6.0	7.2	6.3	8.0	6.55
Effective Number of Parties	3.1	2.3	2.8	2.2	2.6	2	3.4	2.5
% of Votes to Winning Party	56.2	57.1	52.1	56.9	49.7	48.2	33.7	53.4
% of Seats to Winning Party	62.4	67.2	64.9	63.9	60.1	62.2	44.7	63.4
% Voter Turnout	64	68.2	64.2	61.1	62.0	65.6	63.3	64.2
% VAP Turnout	54.1	55.9	55.5	54.6	52.1	68.6	45.6	56.8

Notes:
Source: authors' data base on African elections
Sums and averages do not include the 7th election cycle.
VAP: voting age population.

2.3 THE ACHIEVEMENTS AND LIMITS OF
THE WAVE OF DEMOCRATIZATION

In the excitement of the initial transitions, it seemed possible that the wave of democratization would completely sweep away authoritarian rule throughout the region. Benin quickly established a stable electoral democratic system, with widespread political and civil rights. Other states appeared to follow suit, with popular protests leading to democratic founding elections and the exit of the authoritarian ruler in Cape Verde (February 1991), Sao Tome and Principe (March 1991), Zambia (October 1991), Mali (April 1992), Republic of Congo (August 1992), and Madagascar (November 1992), to cite the first half dozen such countries. Elsewhere, the changing environment led authoritarian regimes to voluntarily adopt political pluralism. In Kenya (December 1992), Ghana (November 1992), Senegal (February 1993), and Mozambique (August 1994), the first multiparty elections in a generation were part of top-down policies of political liberalization, anticipating popular protests and diplomatic pressures rather than responding to them. While leading to significant political liberalization in the short run and probably setting the stage for further democratization down the road, top-down political liberalization seemed to serve as a palliative for real democratization and allowed incumbents to remain in power.

In all, nine of the leaders who were in power at the beginning of 1990 left political power as a result of losing founding elections during the democratization wave (Hastings Banda in Malawi, Pierre Buyoya in Burundi, F. W. de Klerk in South Africa, Kenneth Kaunde in Zambia, Mathieu Kérékou in Benin, André-Dieudonné Kolingba in the Central African Republic, Aristides Pereira in Cape Verde, Didier Ratsiraka in Madagascar, and Dennis Sassou Nguesso in Congo). Another seven or so countries went through real regime change, even though the incumbent did not actually compete and lose in the transition election. In Namibia, for instance, the South African–backed white minority regime left power voluntarily, ushering in the democratically elected regime of Sam Nujoma. In São Tomé, Manuel Pinto da Costa also chose to retire rather than competing in multiparty elections he was likely to lose. In Mali, the regime of Moussa Traore was deposed in a military coup, by prodemocracy officers, who withdrew from power after democratic elections.

The limits of the wave of democratization would soon become clearer, however. In Republic of the Congo, the authoritarian president Dennis

Sassou Nguesso seemed to accept the verdict of the presidential elections of August 1992, when he was soundly defeated by opposition leader Pascal Lissouba, following the same kind of political process that had marked the transition in Benin: popular protests leading to a national conference and the legalization of opposition parties (Quantin, 1997; Clark, 2008). Sassou Nguesso would nonetheless assiduously seek to undermine the new regime and would fight his way back to power in October 1997, following a vicious civil war that involved private militias and the support of the Angolan army. His return to power effectively ended the country's experiment with multiparty elections, though Lissouba's presidency had already been marked by various abuses of power.

Elsewhere, dictators learned to undertake limited political liberalization without its threatening their hold on power. In Cameroon, for instance, popular protests led President Paul Biya to lift the ban on opposition political parties in December 1990. He survived the elections of October 1992, thanks largely to extensive fraud and divisions within the opposition, and then weathered the subsequent "Villes Mortes" popular protests and general strike by using heavy-handed repression (Krieger, 1994; Ngayap, 1999). Eventually, law and order were restored and foreign aid was renewed, which helped to restabilize the regime. Biya would eventually overturn the presidential term limits to which he had agreed in the early 1990s. He convened presidential elections in 1997, 2004, and 2011, winning each comfortably, assisted by various forms of fraud and intimidation (Albaugh, 2011).

In 1998, Baker (1998) surveyed the region and noted that twenty of the thirty-nine authoritarian leaders who had been in power in 1990 were still in power. This led him to argue that the wave of democratization had been limited in scope and breadth.[9] Table 2.2 updates and adapts Baker's data. It shows that at the end of 2015, just seven leaders (Isaias Afwerki of Eritrea, Omar al-Bashir of Sudan, Paul Biya of Cameroon, Idriss Deby of Chad, Yoweri Museveni of Uganda, Dennis Sassou Nguesso of Republic of the Congo, and Francisco Macías Nguema of Equatorial Guinea) were left over from the pre-1990 cohort. Not long before this book went to press, two sitting presidents handed over power (Dos Santos in Angola and Mugabe in Zimbabwe), but seven of the executives from the list were

---

[9] Note that Baker excludes Senegal, Gambia, Botswana, Mauritius, Namibia, Comoros Islands, Angola, and Zimbabwe from his totals. His premise is that these countries were already engaged in electoral competition in 1990, albeit of a fairly restrictive kind. Of the leaders of these countries, only Robert Mugabe of Zimbabwe remained in power in 2015.

TABLE 2.2. *Sub-Saharan African countries that did not undergo
presidential turnover, 1989–1995*

Country	Current status of president in 1989
Angola	Dos Santos steps down; new MPLA candidate wins 2017 elections
Burkina Faso	Compaore president 1987–2014
Burundi	Buyoya lost election in 1993, regained power through coup
Cameroon	Biya still President
Chad	Déby still president
Comoros	Djohar removed by coup in 1995
Côte d'Ivoire	Houphouët-Boigny died in office in 1993; Bédié ousted in coup in 1999
Democratic Republic of the Congo	Mobutu lost power to rebel army in 1997
Djibouti	Gouled retired in 1999, ceded power to nephew
Equatorial Guinea	Macías Nguema still President
Eritrea	Afwerki still President
Ethiopia	Mengistu ousted in 1991; Meles president until death in 2012
Gabon	Bongo president until death in 2009; replaced by son
Gambia	Jawara ousted military coup; Jammeh defeated in 2016 elections
Ghana	Rawlings president until term limits in 2000
Guinea	Conté president until death in 2008
Kenya	Moi president until term limits in 2002
Liberia	Taylor defeated by rebel army in 2003
Mauritania	Taya ousted by military coup in 2005
Nigeria	Babangida ousted by military coup in 1993
Rwanda	Habyaramina killed in 1994; Kagame still in power
Sierra Leone	Momoh ousted by coup in 1992; Strasser ousted by coup in 1996
Somalia	Barre ousted in 1991; Farmajo elected president in 2017
Sudan	Al-Bashir still president

(continued)

TABLE 2.2 *(continued)*

Country	Current status of president in 1989
Swaziland	**Mswati still king**
Tanzania	Mwinyi president until term limits in 1995
Togo	*Eyadema president until death in 2005; replaced by son*
Uganda	**Museveni still president**
Zimbabwe	Mugabe resigned in November 2017

Sources: Compiled by authors from various sources
Countries in bold have same executive since 1989 through the end of 2015.
Military rulers in 1989 denoted by italics.

still in power. Six of the nine were military leaders, confirming the key role of the military in power maintenance that Baker had noted. Just as revealingly, all of them except Afwerki have convened and survived at least one multiparty election since 1990, and all of them have adopted at least some political liberalization, but all of them also unmistakably have continued to dominate nondemocratic regimes.

The important point is that not all African countries underwent a real democratic transition in the early 1990s. Instead, perhaps only sixteen states can be claimed to have really changed regimes at that time, mostly through popular protests that toppled an incumbent regime (Bratton and van de Walle, 1997, pp. 120–22).

The attentive reader will have noticed the absence of Dennis Sassou Nguesso in Table 2.2. Although he lost a democratic election in 1992 to Pascal Lissouba, Sassou Nguesso returned to power after a civil war in 1997 (Quantin, 1997; Clark, 2008). Three other leaders also returned to power after the wave of transitions had subsided. In Burundi, after losing a competitive election in 1993, Pierre Buyoya returned to power via a military coup in 1996. Mathieu Kérékou returned to power more honorably in Benin by winning relatively free and fair elections in 1996 and then being reelected in 2001. In Madagascar, Didier Ratsiraka finally avenged his loss in the 1992 presidential elections by defeating incumbent Albert Zafy in 1996. Of these four men, only Sassou Nguesso remained in power in 2015. He has not repeated his mistake of tolerating fair-enough elections that might imperil his hold on power, and unlike Kérékou, he has disregarded term limits. Burundi and Madagascar have teetered on the edge of civil violence for much of this period, while Benin,

alone of these countries, has maintained a stable and reasonably democratic electoral system.

In sum, although it is important to emphasize the significance of political liberalization in the region, many of Africa's authoritarian regimes
managed to survive this wave of democratization and the attendant turn
to multiparty elections. Many African strongmen found that they could
control and survive political liberalization and the emergence of electoral
pluralism. This control is all the more remarkable in that levels of popular
participation have remained high. The days of the 99 percent electoral victories are over, and opposition parties are present in significant numbers
in most of the legislatures, even if erstwhile presidents for life have put in
place systems of political regulation that allow them to confront elections
with equanimity. These include a combination of different strategies from
what Schedler (2002) called the "menu of manipulation," which allows
regimes to perfect the many instruments available to survive multiparty
elections. We will analyze these different strategies in Chapter 3.

2.3.1 Institutionalization of Elections without Consolidation

By the late 1990s, of sub-Saharan Africa's forty-nine countries, only
Eritrea and Swaziland still had not legalized opposition parties. Figure 2.1
shows the dramatic increase in the number of multiparty elections since
1990 across the continent. From fewer than a handful of annual elections
in the 1970s and 1980s, the region now witnesses close to ten elections a
year. The figure also shows that the growing trend in multiparty elections

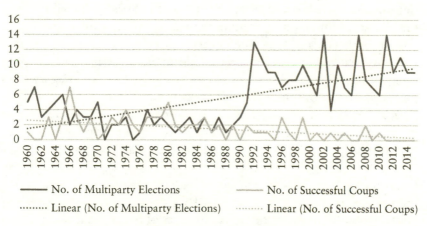

FIGURE 2.1. *Multiparty elections and successful coups by year, 1960–2015*

has coincided with an equally dramatic decline in the number of extra-constitutional alternations in power, suggesting that the turn to competitive elections has also sustained an increasingly institutionalized mode of power transfers (Posner and Young, 2007). Again contradicting the discourse of sustained democratic decline, the number of military coups and the ability of the military to remain in power after an intervention have declined over time (Lindberg and Clark, 2008). While military coups were still able to remove some twenty-five heads of state from power from fifteen countries between 1995 and 2015, domestic pressures and the threat of the withdrawal of foreign aid have increasingly convinced the military to give up power soon after their intervention in such countries as Niger, Guinea Bissau, Guinea, and Mali.

In today's Africa, civilian rule and the regular convening of multiparty elections does not necessarily indicate that a country is democratic in any meaningful sense of the word. Table 2.3 tabulates all of the presidential and legislative elections convened in the region between 1990 and 2015 in which multiple candidates or multiple parties were allowed to compete. At the same time, it divides the countries into Freedom House's typology of free, partly free, and not free regimes. For instance, the table identifies Benin as one of only nine free countries by the judgment of Freedom House, in 2015; between 1990 and the end of 2015, Benin convened six legislative elections and five presidential elections. While the precise boundaries between the three categories are fairly arbitrary, the classification can give us a sense of the relationship between freer countries, such as Benin, and less free regimes, such as Burundi, and their electoral practices.

Table 2.3 suggests that the number and regularity of pluralistic elections do not indicate much about the level of political and civil rights in the country. With only a small number of exceptions, multiparty elections appear to happen almost as often in partly free countries as in free ones. It is true that the average number of elections in the not free category is significantly lower than that the free category, but the category does include a number of countries that have convened elections very regularly over a period of a quarter-century. If the tabulation of the number of presidential elections held in a country is used as a proxy for civil rights and liberties, it is easy for observers to believe that, say, Togo is as democratic as Zambia. The mean number of legislative elections held correlates roughly with Freedom House ratings, ranging from 5.7 (free) to 4.8 (partly free) to 3.0 (not free) or 3.5 (if we omit countries that have not held elections). The difference in the number of presidential races is even closer. Free and partly free countries average nearly the same number of

TABLE 2.3. *Political regimes in Africa, 2015 (legislative elections/ presidential elections since 1990)*

Free	Partly free	Not free
Benin 7/5	Burkina Faso 6/5	Angola 3/3
Botswana 5/0	Comoros 6/5	Burundi 4/4
Cabo Verde 5/5	Cote d'Ivoire 4/5	Cameroon 5/4
Ghana 6/6	Guinea 3/5	CAR 5/5
Mauritius 6/0	Guinea-Bissau 5/6	Chad 3/4
Namibia 6/5	Kenya 5/5	Congo, Rep. 5/4
S. Tome, Principe 7/5	Lesotho 6/0	D.R. Congo 3/2
Senegal 5/4	Liberia 4/3	Djibouti 1/3
South Africa 5/0	Madagascar 5/5	Eq. Guinea 5/3
	Malawi 5/5	Eritrea 0/0
	Mali 5/5	Ethiopia 6/0
	Mozambique 5/5	Gabon 5/4
	Niger 7/5	Gambia 5/5
	Nigeria 6/6	Mauritania 5/6
	Seychelles 5/6	Rwanda 3/2
	Sierra Leone 4/4	Somalia 0/0
	Tanzania 5/5	South Sudan 1/1
	Togo 5/6	Sudan 2/3
	Zambia 5/7	Swaziland 0/0
	Zimbabwe 6/5	Uganda 4/5
Average: 5.7/5	5.1/4.9	3.25/3.0
		3.8/3.6*

Sources: Freedom House and authors' data base on African elections.
*averages if Eritrea, Somalia and Swaziland excluded.
Parliamentary regimes omitted in calculating executive averages.

presidential races (5 and 4.9, respectively), while not free countries still average 3 presidential elections since 1990.

However, the regular convening of elections by itself does not tell us much about the quality of the democracy in a country. What about the electoral results themselves? Table 2.4 compares the degree of competitiveness of elections in both more and less democratic countries since 1990, according to Freedom House. Here, the quality of democracy is discernible in

TABLE 2.4. *Degree of electoral competition, democracies and non democracies (1990–2015)[1]*

Freedom House score	Sub-Saharan African countries	
	Countries ≤ 4.0	Countries > 4.0
Average Freedom House score	5.8	11.0
Average % seats of winning party	58.4	69.1
Average % votes for president	55.4	64.1

[1]We caution that the Freedom House rating, in part reflects, the dependent variable (degree of political competition from opposition), which may exaggerate the divergence between the two categories.

the data. Margins of victory both in the presidential election and in the size of the legislative majority of the president's party correlate intuitively with the level of democracy in the political system. Presidents in less democratic countries are able to manage electoral competition more easily than their peers in the region's more democratic countries, as we argue below. Still, the numbers suggest a fairly comfortable margin of victory for the president and a very comfortable majority in the legislature, even in the more democratic countries. In the United States, for instance, during this same time period (1988–2012), across seven presidential elections, the average vote total for the winner has been just 49.7 percent. In legislative elections, the Democrats averaged 50.1 percent of the seats in the Senate and 50.1 percent in the House of Representatives across the terms of two Republican presidents and two Democratic presidents. The president's party did not control the Senate for five of the fourteen congresses and did not control the House for six of the congresses. In sum, at least relative to the United States, the executive in even the most democratic African countries seems to be in considerable control of the executive and legislative branches of government.

2.4 THE PATH DEPENDENCE OF THE EARLY 1990S TRANSITIONS

Many observers are disappointed by the democratic performance in the African region, but this feeling is probably conditioned by the lack of progress observed in recent years. The stagnation is interpreted, wrongly, as regression when it is also due to inflated assessments of democratic governance that accompanied the initial transitions to democracy.

It is more productive to ask more narrowly about the extent of political change in the region since the transitions of the early 1990s. Five countries already enjoyed multiparty electoral democracy in 1990: Botswana, Gambia, Mauritius, Senegal, and Zimbabwe. Of these, Gambia and Zimbabwe have become considerably less democratic during the last quarter-century, while Senegal has become more democratic and Botswana and Mauritius have remained relatively stable electoral democracies. What about the other states? Were the democratic gains of the early 1990s sustained? The evidence suggests that the events of the early 1990s continue to exert a degree of path dependence on electoral politics and democracy in the region, albeit to a progressively declining level.

The countries that underwent real regime transitions in the early 1990s continue to be more politically liberal than those that did not. There are, of course, exceptions. Regimes in Kenya and Ghana survived the democratization wave but nonetheless did engage in significant political reform over time. On the other side of the ledger, the Central African Republic and the Republic of the Congo, which had defeated incumbent presidents in competitive elections in the early 1990s, have not sustained their democratic progress since then. In particular, we want to investigate why the turn to regular multiparty elections has proved to be so much more lasting than it was during the first electoral era, around independence. This appears to be the case in the more democratic countries to emerge in the early 1990s and, perhaps more interestingly, in the less democratic regimes as well.

Overall, nonetheless, the difference remains significant, as shown in Figure 2.2, which compares the evolving Freedom House scores since the mid-1980s for countries that changed executives in the early 1990s and those that did not. The figure tracks the Freedom House scores for three categories of countries we have been discussing: the long-standing pluralist countries, or the handful of countries that enjoyed multiparty elections before 1989; the transition countries, which are the authoritarian countries that changed presidents in the early 1990s as a result of either a founding election or a prodemocracy coup; and the nontransition countries, that is, the authoritarian countries whose leaders managed to survive the transition era.

Figure 2.2 reveals that the transitioning countries were, on average, countries whose relatively high levels of civil and political rights had

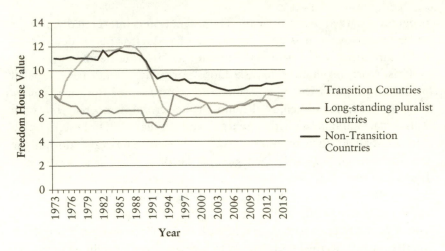

FIGURE 2.2. *Regime trajectories in Africa, 1973–2015*
Source: Freedom House data. See the text for an explanation of the categories. Note that lower values indicate countries that are more democratic on the Freedom House scale.

sharply deteriorated in the late 1970s. The trend that is of interest to us, however, is the sharp divergence of the Freedom House scores in the 1990s, in which the impact of the transitions is quite clear. Still, Figure 2.2 suggests that the impact of the events of the early 1990s is becoming attenuated over time. Facing relatively similar external environments as well as similarly minded domestic public opinion, African states are slowly converging toward political systems that have some basic similarities. The challenge in the rest of this book will be to account as much for the similarities across the forty-nine states in the region as for the differences.

Another general stylized fact that emerges from Figure 2.2 concerns how few African states have significantly changed their level of political and civil rights since the end of the transition period in the mid-1990s. The overall average combined civil and political rights scores for the forty-eight countries in sub-Saharan Africa was 9.1 in 1996, a logical beginning point for our analysis, since the region's wave of democratization could be said to have ended by then. The overall average was 8.9 in 2015 for the now forty-nine countries being graded by Freedom House. In between, the average went high as 9.2 in 1997 (indicating a decline in civil and political liberties) and as low as 8.2 in 2005 (the peak average of democratic progress on the continent). Given the vagaries of cross-national comparison for single-point annual measures of complex political phenomena, these differences strike us as nonsignificant.

If we examine single countries, twenty-eight of the forty-nine countries have received combined scores from Freedom House that varied as much as three points between 1996 and 2012. They are listed in Figure 2.3. In twelve of these countries, the net trend over the period suggests improved democratic governance; in ten of them, the trend suggests a decline; and in the remaining, six exhibit no discernible overall trend from the beginning of the period to the end. Ten of the twenty-eight countries had their scores vary by five or more points, including three (Burundi, Liberia, and Sierra Leone) that confronted major civil conflict during the period. These numbers suggest a good deal of volatility in the democratic situation in these countries rather than a clear medium- or long-term trend. State weakness, including bureaucratic weakness and the inability to control territory, continues to constrain institutional consolidation in many countries (Bleck and Logvinenko 2018), a topic to which we will return in Chapter 8. Mali, the country with the largest range of Freedom House scores in Figure 2.3, epitomizes the limits to democracy posed by state weakness. Mali's score was 4–6 from 1996 to 2011 and then increased to 12 for 2012 because of military coup and political instability that year. In 2012, as Mali approached its fifth scheduled elections, the government's inability to control a Northern insurgency ultimately led to a coup d'état. However, once elections were reinstated a little over a year later, an opposition leader took over control of the government. In the span of two years, Mali went from a democratic darling to a junta-controlled regime and back to democratically elected government. As the book goes to press, going into Mali's 2018 presidential elections, which will be their 6th multi-party race, observers cannot predict who will win, but the vast majority of the country remains outside of the government's control. In countries like Mali, state weakness, legitimate political competition, and insurgency can all coincide in limited time frames.

2.5 ALTERNATION IN POWER

We now examine the record on electoral alternation during this period, which confirms many of the trends already highlighted. In fact, incumbent African presidents rarely lose elections. For the first decade after the initial transitions, only in Benin and Madagascar did an incumbent president and his party lose power through an election. Overall, the winning party and president from the first election almost invariably won a more comfortable majority in the second election. This pattern has been

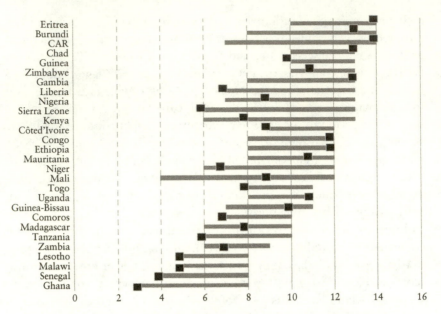

FIGURE 2.3. *African country Freedom House scores with substantial variation, 1996–2015*

Notes: Values taken from Freedom House, various years. Political and civil rights scores added together. The figure scores the highest and lowest Freedom House scores between 1996 and 2015; the black squares indicate the score at the end of 2015.

somewhat attenuated in more recent years; still, a striking pattern of African elections has been the relatively small number of alternations of executives, at least in comparison to other regions of the world. Between 1990 and 2015, we count twenty-one cases (in thirteen countries) in which a presidential incumbent was defeated. In another sixteen cases (in eleven countries), an "open" election, in which the sitting president was not running for reelection, was won by a party different from the previous president's party (see Table 3.1). In other words, between 1990 and 2015, broadly defined alternation can be said to have occurred in thirty-seven cases out of 184 presidential elections involving nineteen countries (see the Tables 3.1 and 3.2). Since nine of the twenty-one cases occurred in the founding election in the first half of the 1990s, the rate of alternation since the end of the transitions is actually lower. Twenty-nine countries in the region have not witnessed either type of electoral alternation. Interestingly, once a country has undergone an alternation, it seems likelier to undergo another one. Eight of the countries on our list have undergone two alternations, and another four have undergone three or more alternations. In comparison, Arriola (2013, p. 6) demonstrates that between 1985 and 2005, 45 percent of all presidential elections held around the world resulted in turnover. Arriola (2013, p. 7) also shows that African incumbents' average margin of victory, 40 percent, is much higher than that in other regions.

Electoral alternation has not always proceeded smoothly and has sometimes resulted in trauma for the country. For instance, in Côte d'Ivoire (2010), Guinea (2009), and Madagascar (2001), a combination of a long standoff and international intervention was needed to remove a defeated incumbent from office. In Côte d'Ivoire, President Laurent Gbagbo would not admit his defeat in the elections of 2010, and a civil war and foreign intervention took place before former Prime Minister Alassane Ouattara was allowed to begin his term in 2011. In Guinea, within six hours of the announcement of the death of President Lansana Conté, a military coup was staged under the leadership of Captain Moussa Camara, and the military retained the pride of place it had enjoyed under Conté. However, under considerable international pressure, the military was never able to consolidate power, and elections were eventually conducted in June and July 2010. They were won by longtime opposition leader Alpha Condé. Some observers argue that the first elections won by Condé were more free and fair than any previous elections in Guinea (Roberts, 2015) and arguably freer than his second victory in 2015. Freedom House ratings indicate that Guinea has made incremental improvements in terms of political and civil rights since Condé's election to office. Still, his rule has been marred by many of the same abuses of power that were seen under Conté. In Madagascar, similarly, businessman Marc Ravalomana's electoral victory in 2001 was contested by incumbent Didier Rastiraka during a seven-month standoff.

In all four cases, significant international pressures were necessary to convince the loser of the election to step down. Still, we consider these cases to be examples of successful alternation. In other cases, incumbent presidents were probably able to employ fraud, intimidation, and the benign neglect of the international community to deny effective electoral defeat. For example, many observers claim that Paul Biya's victory in the Cameroonian 1992 elections was largely fraudulent or that Robert Mugabe received considerably less than the 56 percent of the vote he claimed in 2002 in Zimbabwe.

Another type of alternation has come not through elections but as a result of the passing away or retirement of the president. Often older men, presidents have died in office. In some cases, the system was sufficiently institutionalized for the succession to proceed smoothly. In Zambia, twice (in 2008 and 2015) the incumbent passed away, and the vice president became interim president for three months before elections were convened. The passing away of the president poses special risks for the less institutionalized electoral autocracies, since the institutional mechanism to designate the successor either is not easily applied or is ignored by the regime's core elite. However, in none of Africa's less democratic systems has major regime change followed the death of the president. The death of longtime dictators seemed to provide a window of opportunity for political change, but in each case, continuity was the striking outcome. In DRC (2001), Gabon (2009), and Togo (2005), the transition was dynastic: The sons of the deceased president took over, with remarkably little change in the nature of the regime. The case of Togo is representative. When President Gnassingbé Eyadema died in February 2005, the constitution stipulated that the President of the National Assembly be installed as interim president and that presidential elections be held within sixty days. Instead, the army took control, prevented the President of the National Assembly from returning to the country from an overseas trip, and forced the Assembly to name the deceased president's son, Faure Gnassingbé, as his successor.

This example from Togo highlights the reality that the military holds ultimate veto power over the executive in many African countries. Military interventions constitute a third mode of executive alternation. They have removed the president eighteen times in some thirteen countries of the region since 1990, including multiple times in Guinea Bissau (1999, 2003, and 2012), Mali (1991 and 2012), Mauritania (2005 and 2009), and Niger (1996, 1999, and 2010) (see Elischer, 2016). With the exceptions of prodemocracy coups in Mali (1991) and Niger (1999), military interventions have not generally resulted in significant changes in the degree of political freedom. The personnel in the presidential palace changes, but the ground rules stay the same.

The default assumption in imperfectly democratic countries has to be that the likelihood of executive turnover is positively correlated with the quality of democracy, since presidents in less democratic regimes might be thought to benefit from an array of formal and informal mechanisms to win reelection in less than free and fair elections (Huntington, 1991). Yet the relationship in Africa appears less straightforward,[10] even

---

[10] See Bogaards's (2007) critique of elections outcomes as a measure of democracy.

if the multiparty era of the last two decades, and the concomitant introduction of term limits in a number of countries, has sharply reduced the number of leaders who have been in power for over a decade. Since Kenneth Kaunde was defeated in the founding election of Zambia's democracy in 1991 after twenty-seven years in office, the country has had five different elected presidents, for instance. Since Houphouët-Boigny's death in office in 1993 after thirty-three years in office, Côte D'Ivoire has had three different elected leaders. However, Côte d'Ivoire has hardly been a stable democracy during this period.

In Chapter 3, we document the various kinds of illiberal tools that autocrats use to remain in power despite multiparty elections. Still, the most democratic countries are not necessarily the ones that have experienced executive turnover. The cases of presidential Ghana and parliamentary Mauritius, with a combined five executive alternations during the course of the last two decades, suggest that democratic consolidation and party strength can foster relatively stable patterns of turnover. However, the relationship between the quality of democracy and open-seat turnover varies tremendously. In contradistinction to Ghana and Mauritius, one could cite long-standing democratic Botswana, where a quite stable trajectory of single-party domination has not resulted in authoritarianism, even if some observers view its democracy as declining in recent years (Good, 2009). In Mali, Madagascar, and Niger, electoral turnover and extrajudicial power grabs have happened in close proximity, suggesting that party weakness and the absence of democratic consolidation might be as likely to generate turnover in open-seat elections (on Madagascar, see Marcus and Ratsimbaharison, 2005). For instance, Ibrahim Boubacar Keita, the winner of Mali's 2013 presidential polls, was previously the leader of one of Mali's two opposition parties; his party, Rassemblement Pour le Mali (RPM), had previously held only eleven seats in the 147-member National Assembly. In contrast, none of the candidates running from the former president's forty-two-party ruling coalition, including the party of the interim president, were successful in the wake of the April 2012 coup.

2.6 CONCLUSION

Since 1990, multiparty elections have become routine in sub-Saharan Africa. For the first time since independence, multiparty elections are being conducted regularly in most countries in the region, and opposition parties and candidates have won seats and, occasionally, the big prize of the presidency.

In this chapter, we discussed at some length the period of political pluralism surrounding the independence era, not least because a comparison with the current era shows a kind of echo effect in which many of the same political dynamics that occurred in the independence era have arisen anew. Political stability was more likely when a dominant political coalition emerged rapidly from the turn to multiparty electoral politics, while in both periods, the failure of elections to identify a stable majoritarian political coalition led to a much higher risk of political instability.

Similarly, a comparison of the two electoral eras shows a stabilization in political participation in contrast with the sharp decline in the postindependence period. The current dynamics of political participation will be discussed in Chapter 7. Here, we simply state that the bases of political participation seem much more sound today than they did in the early 1960s. Citizens are more urban and educated, and they benefit from much denser networks and more accessible media. In addition, it is harder today and less legitimate for state leaders to criticize participation. When President Obote justified his constitutional reforms to limit constraints on his power during the debate over Uganda's 1967 constitution, his central argument was that the country was not ready for democracy, as he claimed that "there was no point in pretending that Uganda was at a stage where Parliamentary democracy could obtain" (see Kasfir, 1974, p. 10). At the time, few domestic or international observers contested him, so much was he expressing a common view among political elites in Africa and the West. It was perhaps inevitable that the new constitution significantly increased his powers and helped to precipitate Uganda toward authoritarian rule. When the aging autocrats made the same kinds of claims in the 1990s, they were much more likely to be derided as out of touch and reactionary. The region and the international climate had changed irreversibly.

In this chapter, we also examined the common view that the democratization wave of the early 1990s has crested and receded. The democratic quality of elections and of the regimes that conduct them will be a theme throughout this book. In this chapter, we have limited ourselves to the argument that there is little evidence to suggest either a decline in electoral practices or much progress. Since the wave struck, multiparty elections have become routinized in most countries and have continued to be convened with remarkable consistency. At the same time, many if not most African countries remain authoritarian, despite their adoption of regular elections. However, owing to the fluidity in the political moments, we do observe in some instances that elections can result in executive turnover.

In the rest of this book, we analyze these elections in greater detail, from the political parties that dominate them and the rhetoric and campaigning strategies they adopt to the attitudes and behaviors of the voters that candidates are trying to convince to support them. In Chapter 3, we examine in greater depth the relationship between multiparty elections and the progress of democracy, and we survey the many ways in which elections have either failed as instruments of democracy or, more rarely, have helped strengthen it. To accomplish this, we examine the role that electoral politics have played in maintaining regimes in place and protecting the political tradition in Africa or presidential dominance.

3

The Impact of Elections on Democracy

There can only be one male crocodile in the marigot.

President Félix Houphouët-Boigny, Côte d'Ivoire

3.1 INTRODUCTION

General elections were convened in Uganda in February 2016.[1] Incumbent President Yoweri Museveni was easily reelected, with just under 61 percent of the vote, compared to 35.6 percent for Kizza Besigye, candidate for the Forum for Democratic Change and Museveni's main challenger. In all, seven candidates ran against Museveni. In some respects, this was a routine election. Uganda has been running competitive multiparty elections every five years since 1996; indeed, his 2016 victory was the fourth time in a row that Museveni had defeated Besigye. The mandate for the incumbent appeared to be a national one, with Besigye winning only a few isolated constituencies, mostly in Northern Uganda. During the campaign, Museveni had vaunted his achievements as president since the mid-1980s. His posters included such slogans as "Steady Progress Focused on Job Creation and Wealth Creation" and "The Only Tested Leader." Besigye's main slogan was "For the Change We Deserve." Two presidential debates were televised nationally, though Museveni participated only in the second debate, which focused primarily on the state of the national economy and foreign policy.

[1] The following account is based on newspaper accounts, including Abrahamsen and Bareebe (2016), Africa Confidential (2016a, 2016b), Kavuma (2016), and Kron (2016).

The election revealed in different ways how far Uganda remains from being a fully democratic country. President Museveni's reelection was largely a foregone conclusion, given how he benefited from a severely uneven playing field. Although he did not orchestrate a sharp increase in public funding in the months before the election to extend his electoral support, as he had in the 2011 elections, Museveni's access to the media and use of public sector resources for his campaign gave him a huge advantage over his opponents. In addition, state institutions harassed opposition campaigns systematically to undermine them. Besigye was manhandled at events by police and arrested several times. Authorization for opposition rallies either was not provided or was retracted at the last minute, providing an excuse for police violence at the rallies, which was not uncommon and resulted in an estimated twenty deaths during the course of the campaign. Finally, various external observers and local journalists pointed to numerous election-day anomalies, which indicated that widespread fraud had taken place.

The influential news magazine on African politics, *Africa Confidential* (2016c), responded to the Ugandan election among others to lament the decline in the quality of African elections, in part because, it argued, incumbents were learning how to manipulate electoral processes better. It may be true that leaders like Museveni have learned over time how better to steal elections, but the argument that the quality of elections has declined in Uganda or in Africa more generally since the early 1990s is much harder to support. Every election since the return of multiparty rule in Uganda has been marred by much the same kinds of flaws that were observed in 2016.

Observers who argue that African democracy has been in decline in recent years tend to exaggerate the progress that had been achieved earlier. In fact, as we showed in Chapter 2, the wave of democratization covered only perhaps a quarter of the countries in the region. The other countries in the region either never had a transition and the same regime is in place as in 1990 or had an authoritarian breakdown but not a transition to democracy in the early to mid-1990s. When there is a bad election, as in Uganda, observers assume too often that the country democratized more in the early 1990s than was actually the case.

In Chapter 2, we showed that regular elections have become the political norm across the region but that the region's democratization has not advanced much since the transitions of the early 1990s. The modal African political system remains authoritarian, and there has been little alternation in power. In this chapter, we begin the process of explaining this paradoxical stability by examining the relationship between democracy and elections. In the next section, we examine the literature that has proposed theories explaining the impact of multiparty elections on political change. Sharp disagreements can be found on this key issue. Some scholars have argued for a "democratization by elections" thesis, which presumes that the conduct of even imperfect elections has a prodemocratic effect such that, over time, the quality of elections should improve. Other scholars have argued that elections are dangerous for the stability of low-income, low-capacity political systems, such as those in Africa. Finally, the recent literature on authoritarianism argues that elections are used by authoritarian regimes to maintain power. We argue for a nuanced understanding of the relationship between elections and democracy in Africa since 1990. Elections should be understood as political moments that can, but do not necessarily, push democracy forward. In time, the optimists may be right, but over the past two decades, the region seems in a relatively stable equilibrium, balanced by both minor progress and minor setbacks.

In Chapter 2, we showed how rare alternation has been; in this chapter, we explain why. In Section 3.3 we discuss the formal political institutions that account for a good deal of the variation in alternation, electoral rules, and term limits, and we explore the politics around the latter. In Section 3.4, we discuss the power of incumbency advantage under presidentialism that helps to account for the low rates of alternation. The section is focused on factors that are not specifically related to the nature of the political regime but can exist in even the most democratic systems. In Section 3.5, we focus on the most illiberal and often illegal practices to which incumbents in more authoritarian systems have resorted in order to remain in power. We conclude the chapter in Section 3.6 with a discussion of the prospects for change.

3.2 ELECTIONS AND POLITICAL CHANGE

Much recent scholarship has debated whether or not elections promote democratization and democratic consolidation. Bratton and van de Walle (1997) found that the variation in the number of elections conducted in the authoritarian regimes of Africa before 1990 helped to explain the likelihood of democratization in the early 1990s. Even fraudulent and single-party elections in the 1970s and 1980s were positively correlated with a successful transition.

More recently, some observers have argued that elections in themselves can improve the quality of democracy both by changing citizen's values and sense of personal efficacy (Schedler, 2002; Lindberg, 2006) and through learning processes that involve not only the voters themselves, but also institutional actors such as political parties, the media, electoral commissions, the judiciary, and external observers. Other scholars have argued that the legitimacy gap between winners and losers declines over time, and it becomes harder for losers to complain about electoral results (Moehler & Lindberg, 2009).

This "democratization by elections" hypothesis has received highly qualified support in the empirical literature (Lindberg, 2009; Bratton, 2013; Flores & Nooruddin, 2016; Teorell & Wahman, 2017). In Africa, regular elections since 1990 have not brought improvements in democratic quality, at least according to broad comparative data sets of regime type, such as those of Freedom House or POLITY. The lack of progress has dampened the optimism that greeted African transitions in the 1990s, and Tom Carothers's (2002) influential suggestion that Third Wave democracies in low-income countries are not likely to consolidate but will instead remain trapped at relatively low levels of democratic quality and governance has been a more optimistic view than that held by most in the public policy and scholarly community. As Lindberg (2009) has conceded more recently, it may be that regular elections are a possible path for democratization but not the only path and, indeed, not a common path.

Lindberg's early optimism was never widely shared. The more common conventional wisdom of the impact of multiparty elections in the region has made pointed reference to the electoral fallacy, first defined by Terry Lynn Karl (1995): Without improved levels of economic development or democratic consolidation, elections are largely meaningless and are unlikely to weaken the power of the oligarchic elites that govern most African countries. According to this argument, regular elections may in fact undermine democratic progress. A large academic and public policy literature advances some version of the electoral fallacy argument. Modernization theorists (Huntington & Nelson, 1976) have posited that mass political participation at low levels of economic development would lead to populist dead ends and both economic and political instability rather than successful democracy. Using a different theoretical framework, Chabal and Daloz (1999, p. 39) are similarly categorical that "multi-party elections do not ... change the fundamental rules of the game" of African politics, which they depict as patrimonial competition over public resources. These ideas have been given a new lease in recent public policy work. Collier (2011), North et al. (2013), and Khan (2014) all argue that multiparty elections in low-income countries not only are unlikely to promote real democracy, but actually promote instability and conflict.

A more subtle critique of electoralism can be found in cultural critiques of Western concepts of procedural democracy, which are alleged to fail to translate to African cultural conceptions. Thus for Schaffer (2000), Senegalese peasants do not necessarily see a link between a procedure of democracy, such as elections, and the Western ideals of participation and competition that make up the definition of liberal democracy. These kinds of cultural arguments about how African societies conceive of democracy in different and often illiberal ways are a recurring theme in much literature on contemporary Africa (see, for example, Ake, 1996; Schatzberg, 2001; Ellis & Ter Haar, 2004; Kelsall, 2008), although they get little support from attitudinal surveys such as the Afrobarometer, which have consistently found that Africans conceive of democracy in much the same manner as do publics in the West (see, for instance, Bratton & Mattes, 2001).

Finally, scholars of electoral authoritarianism have increasingly viewed "the establishment of elections as a means by which dictators hold onto power" (Gandhi & Lust-Okar, 2009, p. 404); thus they view elections as a source of stability rather than change. This literature takes a largely functional view of elections, which, it argues, promote stability because they serve to shore up the governing party (Magaloni, 2006; Greene, 2007), facilitate the regime's management of elites (Geddes, 2005; Gandhi & Przeworski, 2007; Svolik, 2012), help regimes to fine-tune their patronage strategies (Lust-Okar, 2006; Magaloni, 2006), or provide useful information to rulers about the society they oversee and where the support for the regime is soft (Brownlee, 2007; Gandhi, 2008).

The empirical evidence for these theories is quite mixed, however. Hadenius and Teorell (2007) (see also Schedler, 2013; Howard & Roessler, 2006) argue that electoral autocracies are among the most unstable regimes in the contemporary era and are most likely to lead to more democratic regimes, not less democratic ones. As Levitsky and Way (2010) have argued, some electoral autocracies have proven to be stable but the very hybrid nature of others makes them unstable, as different logics of rule and contradictory political institutions coexist.

Claims about the links between elections and conflict can be justified, but it is important to pay attention to nuances that shed light on the links between democracy and regular elections. Elections are less likely to bring about conflict in more democratic African countries (Goldsmith, 2010) than in less democratic ones. Violence is also more likely in countries with histories of violence, and electoral competition does not necessarily increase it (Bekoe, 2012). The argument that electoral campaigns spurs violent distributional conflict also has uneven empirical support, and at least one study (Stras & Taylor, 2012) finds little evidence that violence levels increase in election years compared to nonelection years. Electoral violence, such as that in Kenya during and immediately after the 2007 elections, may be a high-profile but rare event.

Each of these divergent strands of the literature on the political impact of multiparty elections provides genuine insight and helps us to understand specific country cases. In countries such as Ghana or Senegal, the "democratization by elections" thesis does help to explain how elections have promoted an incremental process of democratization over time. In addition, the "democratization by elections" thesis may be compelling in the long run, even if in the short to medium term we observe only fitful progress, too often followed by regression. By contrast, the new theories about authoritarianism have better traction in explaining the stability of electoral autocracies such as those of Cameroon (Albaugh, 2011; Letsa, 2017) and Tanzania (Whitehead, 2009; Morse, 2011), despite the poor economic performance of these governments.

We nonetheless reject the extreme versions of these different theses about the effects of multiparty electoral competition. The variation in outcomes across Africa suggests that not all elections systematically promote democratic deepening, inevitably destabilize low-income countries, or are entirely unrelated to political pluralism and serve only the needs of incumbents. First, the impact of elections is likely to vary according to the nature of the regime. In the more pluralist electoral regimes, formal democratic processes are sufficiently institutionalized and legitimated over time that reversals are less likely, and slow incremental progress along the lines of the "democratization by elections" thesis seems a reasonable presumption. By contrast, the prospects for elections having a positive effect on democratic consolidation may be poorest in the most authoritarian states. Indeed, our survey suggests a good deal of resilience and adaptation among these latter regimes. Such long-standing autocratic rulers as Paul Biya, Denis Sassou Nguesso, Idris Deby, and Nguema Obiang have made only limited concessions to survive the turn to electoral politics. Perhaps even more impressive have been the lasting power of family dynasties such as the Eyademas in Togo, the Kabilas in Democratic Republic of the Congo, and the Bongos in Gabon and the stable dominant-party systems such as those of Frelimo in Mozambique or the Chama Cha Mapinduzi (CCM) in Tanzania, which have accommodated multiple leadership changes. All of these regimes survived the period of rapid change in the early 1990s and continue to soldier on largely unchanged a quarter-century later.

Second, it is far from clear that we can distinguish among regimes in the region carefully enough to say with confidence that country A has elections that are sufficiently pluralistic to unswervingly serve the cause of democratization, whereas Country B is so authoritarian that its elections represent no threat to the dictator and his regime. We will sometimes use the language of regime analysis, and we have referred to other scholars' regime categories, but this is more for heuristic reasons than out of a conviction that regime analysis is useful in a region with so much political volatility. Africa's most democratic countries are not safe from sudden authoritarian impulses, as Mali proved in 2012, while some quite authoritarian countries have actually suddenly opened up politically, as Ghana did after 1992 or, more recently, Burkina Faso did with the protest-driven ouster of President Blaise Compaoré in 2014 (Banégas, 2015).

We argue instead that elections present discrete windows of opportunity during which there are greater possibilities for political change, both negative and positive. Elections present opportunities for the defenders of democratic consolidation but also for its enemies to topple incumbents, promote accountability, and enhance standards of public freedoms. However, elections also can lead to resistance by incumbents through various forms of fraud and violence, which can beget more violence and enhance the cynicism and defeatism of citizens. How political systems handle these countervailing opportunities largely determines whether or not they democratize over time.

We side with scholars who emphasize the uncertainty of elections in the countries of the region. We agree with Schedler's (2013) argument that elections are fraught with much too much uncertainty for authoritarian regimes to willingly instrumentalize them for their own ends, as the literature on electoral authoritarianism too often suggests. Elections are appealing to dictators, in Schedler's (2013, p. 174) phrase, "not as a source of tranquility, but a strategy of risk management." In other words, elections are always risky, even for the most hegemonic authoritarian regimes. The risks are exacerbated in Africa by the limited capacity of the state and of most political actors. Even the most autocratic regimes can exercise comparatively little control over their environments. Their fiscal base is circumscribed and highly volatile, dependent as it typically is on commodity exports with wildly fluctuating prices. The ability of the state to project power throughout the territory is limited, and many governments in the region have been vulnerable to rebellions coming out of their hinterlands that they can neither predict nor eliminate. Few autocrats can rely on a strong political party or an engaged core base of supporters. As a result, they are rarely able to mobilize citizens. In sum, low state capacity only exacerbates the uncertainty that Schedler (2013) identifies as a key characteristic of these autocratic electoral systems.

Similarly, we find much to agree with in Bunce and Wolchik's (2011) masterful analysis of democratization in postcommunist Eastern Europe showing that defeating dictators required special international circumstances, creative civil society action, and remarkable opposition campaigns. The possibilities for democratization are uncertain in these countries, they argue, but when these exceptional contingent factors were present, elections did promote democratic change. The key role played by political parties also needs to be highlighted, and we will devote Chapter 4 to analyzing them in greater depth. As Bunce and Wolchik (2011) and Brownlee (2007) argue, authoritarian stasis is helped by well-institutionalized dominant parties, but the prospects for regime change are also aided by dynamic and broad opposition party coalitions.

In sum, the political effects of elections are likely to vary across countries, which are on their own specific trajectories and vulnerable to different contingent dynamics. The impact of any specific election varies, depending on political history, the role of political parties, the international environment, and the unexpected emergence of contentious politics, not least because of the performance of specific political leaders. These institutional and purely contingent factors have to be taken into account, in addition to such structural endowments as the level of economic development and resource endowments and the degree of ethnic heterogeneity.

3.3 FORMAL INSTITUTIONS AND ALTERNATION

How, then, do elections affect political change positively? The evidence suggests that alternation in power is the political factor most associated with political liberalization and democratic deepening, so we start there. Afrobarometer data show that electoral alternation increases voters' confidence that democracy will be durable and increases public confidence in societal commitment to democratic rules, thus bolstering democracy and its chance to endure (Cho & Logan, 2013). Alternation can also lessen the perceived legitimacy gap between winners and losers (Moehler & Lindberg, 2009), and proximity to turnover is positively correlated with optimism toward democracy (Bratton, 2004). If leaders are less able to manipulate the rules, they may be less likely to convince voters that they are the central and crucial node of governing stability. In their study of Ghana, Weghorst and Lindberg (2011) argue that vote buying might lose its utility as voters gain greater experience and information. Similarly, as opposition candidates and parties gain experience in office, they could build their reputations around particular policies and lessen fears that turnover equals instability. Similar to Lindberg's (2006) arguments about elections as contributing to democratic consolidation, it seems that turnover breeds more turnover. Of all twenty-one countries that have experience with turnover, thirteen have experienced multiple turnovers.

3.3.1 Presidential Term Limits

Supporters of democracy have targeted presidential term limits as an effective formal mechanism for alternation. As we argued in Chapter 2, one of the key issues addressed in the episodes of constitutional reform following democratization was the promulgation of presidential term limits. As difficult as it continues to be to defeat a sitting African president, the number of open-seat elections that have led to effective alternation suggests that enforcing constitutional term limits can be a key mechanism to change the presidential personnel and, as a result, attenuate presidential power and enhance the prospects for democracy.

All but eight states in sub-Saharan Africa adopted term limits in the 1990s as part of the process of democratization or political liberalization (Baker, 2002; Kiwuwa, 2013; McKie, 2013). Perhaps surprisingly, a number of countries that had clearly not undertaken a democratic transition nonetheless passed constitutional reforms that included term limits. However, subsequent rounds of constitutional reforms eliminated term limits in twelve countries, and presidents in eleven other countries were able to amend the constitution so that it did not apply to them, only to their successors.

Repeated attitudinal surveys have suggested that presidential term limits are supported by the great majority of African voters (Dulani, 2015). Nonetheless, a number of states subsequently revoked them, and today, the constitutional provision of term limits seems completely safe in no more than eleven countries in the region. Term limits have been officially revoked in twelve countries, are the subject of open contestation in three or four countries at any given time, and have yet to be fully tested in as many as half the states in the region. Among the latter, one might locate Burkina Faso. In 2014, long-serving President Compaoré attempted to introduce a law abolishing the two-term limit imposed by the constitution, which would have forced him to resign after twenty-seven years in power (Bonnecase, 2015). The resulting political protests, including the setting on fire of the building housing the legislature, led the army to intervene. The army was politically close to Compaoré, and the intervention was initially intended to counter the attempts of the parliament to exclude the members who had opposed term limits from running for office (*The Economist*, 2015). However, it would eventually lead to Compaoré's decision to resign on October 31, 2014. The upshot of this complicated history is a good deal of uncertainty about the current status of term limits in Burkina Faso and a clear public demonstration of mass support for limits on executive power. A number of other countries are in a similar boat, where the status of the law is ambiguous and the current politics around term limits are closely related to attitudes toward the incumbent president and his regime rather than an abstract principle about presidential power.

Still, the status of constitutional term limits probably varies in fairly predictable ways. Clearly, term limits are linked to the degree of institutionalization in a political system, in which the personalization of power that traditionally characterized the region has abated and impersonal norms have come to dominate. It makes sense, then, that term limits appear more likely to be implemented in more democratic countries. This intuition is supported by Reyntjens (2016), who offers empirical evidence that states with effective term limits are more democratic than countries in which either there are no term limits or existing provisions have not been enforced. But this is not the end of the story. Mozambique and Tanzania have scrupulously followed the two-term limit provision, despite otherwise mediocre records on political and civil rights and public corruption. In these two countries, at least, the strength of the constitutional provision of term limits seems related to the existence of strong, well-institutionalized dominant parties that are able to impose limits on their leaders (McKie, 2016). To this day, the ability to enforce or reimpose term limits constitutes a key issue in many countries and a central dimension of the struggle for democratic consolidation, often in the context of elections. But what is striking to observers is not only the relative success of presidents so far to turn back or limit one of the key achievements of the transitions, but also the examples of massive popular mobilization against such moves.

3.3.2 Electoral Rules

The reform of electoral rules constitutes another terrain in which the ambitions to limit executive power in the early 1990s were largely not achieved. The continued impact of colonial legacy on the choice of legislative electoral systems is clear from Table 3.1: Ex-British colonies have had an overwhelming preference for a simple plurality system, while Portuguese colonies all have resorted to the party-list proportional representation (PR) system using the d'Hondt method, and the predilection for a two-round majority system on a par with the French Fifth Republic is clear in the ex-French colonies (Hartmann, 2007, pp. 151–4).

As Hartmann (2007) and others have argued, in the countries where there has been change, notably from the colonial model, the level of participatory politics largely explains the direction of the constitutional changes. In the more democratic polities, change has tended occur in a consensual direction, while the more autocratic countries have tended to increase the majoritarian nature of the electoral system. So in Cameroon, a series of constitutional revisions have been engineered by the regime to protect the status quo. Cameroon resisted the opposition's demands for constitutional changes in the early 1990s. Though President Biya conceded the legalization of opposition parties before the 1992 elections, he moved to a simple plurality system that would favor him vis-à-vis a divided opposition. When the government did refashion the constitution in 1996, it extended the presidential term to seven years and established the office of the vice president. Another constitutional modification in 2008 eliminated presidential term limits and made it harder to prosecute the executive for acts committed while in office (see Albaugh, 2011; Opalo, 2012).

In African presidential systems, an interesting difference can be noted in the different systems applied to legislative and presidential electoral rules. Needless to say, PR systems cannot be adopted for the presidency; this partly but not entirely explains the much greater variation found for legislatures, as shown in Table 3.1. On the other hand, for presidential elections, the francophone and lusophone countries overwhelmingly adopted the two-round majority system for the presidency (only authoritarian Cameroon and Gabon have adopted a simple plurality system). Among the anglophone countries, only Sierra Leone and Sudan do not have simple plurality systems for their legislatures (both adopted different systems in the last decade), and presidential elections are evenly divided between the simple plurality system they adopted at independence and

TABLE 3.1. *African legislative electoral systems, 2014*

List PR (14)	Simple plurality (18)	Two-round system (6)	Parallel (5)	Other (3)	No current electoral system (3)
Angola	Botswana	C.A.R.	Democratic Republic of the Congo	Djibouti	Eritrea
Benin	Cameroon	Comoros	Guinea	Lesotho	Somalia
Burkina Faso	Chad	Gabon	Senegal	Mauritius	South Sudan
Burundi	Côte d'Ivoire	Mali	Seychelles		
Cape Verde	Ethiopia	Mauritania	Sudan		
Equatorial Guinea	Gambia	Republic of the Congo			
Guinea-Bissau	Ghana				
Mozambique	Kenya				
Namibia	Liberia				
Niger	Madagascar				
Rwanda	Malawi				
São Tomé	Nigeria				
South Africa	Sierra Leone				
Togo	Swaziland				
	Tanzania				
	Uganda				
	Zambia				
	Zimbabwe				

Source: IDEA web site: www.idea.int/esd/world.cfm

two-round majority systems. In the end, it is tempting but difficult to link electoral engineering to regime characteristics. It may well be true, as Opalo (2012) has argued, that the ability of presidents to weaken the legislature has shaped the democratic trajectories of countries in the region, as there is a clear correlation between the institutional strength of the legislature and the horizontal accountability of the executive. But the legislative electoral rules do not appear to have been systematically manipulated instrumentally by the executive.

Examining the results of two-round systems confirms some trends that we have already discussed. Incumbency advantages are rather striking in these elections. Only 48 of the 119 presidential elections conducted in two-round systems between 1990 and 2015 actually required a second round; the winner won over half the votes in the first round in well over half of these elections. Moreover, regime instability can be associated with systems in which no clear winner typically emerged in the first round, and this appears to be the case regardless of the level of democracy in the country at the time of the election. So in the Comoros, Guinea-Bissau, Madagascar, and Niger, second rounds were required in nineteen of twenty-one presidential elections, and all four countries were marked by repeated military interventions and civil strife, often directly related to political controversies around election results. On the other hand, in Mozambique and Namibia, two relatively stable systems, a second round has never been necessary, as the winner has gained a full majority of the vote in all ten presidential elections held in the two countries.

A consensus holds that simple first-past-the-post majority rules favor the incumbent, while a two-round majority system favors coalition building in the opposition and thus is more threatening to the president. Two-round majority presidential voting systems do indeed account for a disproportionate share of the electoral defeats of sitting incumbents. A fragmented opposition is penalized relative to the incumbent in a simple plurality system. There is evidence that in some countries, incumbents have encouraged frivolous candidacies to divide the opposition. On the other hand, in a two-round system, a divided opposition is not penalized in the first round, as long as it can keep the incumbent under the necessary 50 percent (van de Walle, 2006). In the time between rounds, members of opposition parties can agree to support the opposition candidate who has the most chance to unseat the incumbent. Thus, for instance, in the Senegalese elections of 2000, President Abdou Diouf won a comfortable plurality in the first round, with 41 percent of the vote, well ahead of Abdoulaye Wade, who garnered 31 percent, and Moustapha Niassé, who won 16 percent. Between the two rounds, following negotiations between them, Niassé threw his support to Wade, who named Niassé Prime Minister when he defeated Diouf in the runoff three weeks later.

The key property of the two-round system is that it provides a window of opportunity for the opposition to strike a coalitional bargain between rounds. Therefore it is probably no accident that twenty-eight of the thirty-seven cases of presidential alternation that occurred between 1990 and 2015 came in two-round majority systems (see Table 3.2). The finding is even more striking if one takes into account that two of the five plurality cases occurred during founding elections in the early 1990s.

TABLE 3.2. *Loss of incumbents in presidential elections, 1990–2015*

Country	Election year	Open seat	Winner	Voting system
Benin	1991	N	Nicéphore Soglo	TRS
Cape Verde	1991	N	António Mascarenhas Monteiro	TRS
Zambia	1991	N	Frederick Chiluba	FPTP
Burundi	1993	N	Melchior Ndadaye	TRS
Central African Republic	1993	N	Ange-Félix Patassé	TRS
Madagascar	1993	N	Albert Zafy	TRS
Niger	1993	Y	Mahamane Ousmane	TRS
Malawi	1994	N	Bakili Muluzi	FPTP
South Africa	1994	N	Nelson Mandela	
Mauritius	1995	N	Navin Ramgoolam of the Labour Party (PTr)	
Sierra Leone	1996	Y	Ahmad Tejan Kabbah	TRS
Benin	1996	N	Mathieu Kérékou	TRS
Madagascar	1996	N	Didier Ratsiraka	TRS
Guinea-Bissau	1999	N	Kumba Yala	TRS
Cote d'Ivoire	2000	Y	Laurent Gbagbo	TRS
Ghana	2000	Y	John Kufuor	TRS
Mauritius	2000	N	Paul Berenger/ Sir Anerood Jugnauth	
Senegal	2000	N	Abdoulaye Wade	TRS
	2001	N	Marc Ravalomanana	TRS
	2001	Y	Pedro Pires	TRS

(continued)

TABLE 3.2 *(continued)*

Country	Election year	Open seat	Winner	Voting system
Kenya	2002	Y	Mwai Kibaki	FPTP
Mali	2002	Y	Amadou Toumani Touré	TRS
Guinea-Bissau	2005	N	Nino Veira	TRS
Liberia	2005	Y	Ellen Sirleaf Johnson	TRS
Mauritius	2005	N	Navin Ramgoolam	
Benin	2006	Y	Yayi Boni	TRS
Sierra Leone	2007	Y	Ernst Bai Koroma	TRS
Ghana	2008	Y	John Atta Mills	TRS
Guinea	2010	Y	Alpha Condé	TRS
Cote d'Ivoire	2010	N	Alassane Ouattara	TRS
São Tomé and Principe	2011	N	Manuel Pinto da Costa	TRS
Cape Verde	2011	Y	Jorge Carlos Fonseca	TRS
Zambia	2011	N	Michael Sata	FPTP
Niger	2011	Y	Mahamadou Issoufou	TRS
Senegal	2012	N	Macky Sall	TRS
Mali	2013	Y	Ibrahim Boubacar Keita	TRS
Kenya	2013	Y	Uhuru Kenyatta	FPTP

Both Cameroon and Gabon changed their systems in the 1990s when the incumbent seemed in real risk of losing power.

The party system can also have an effect on incumbency advantage, although here the prediction is harder to make, as can be seen in the debate between Mozaffar et al. (2003) and Brambor et al. (2007). The nature of the party system conditions electoral competition in a variety of informal ways. We might anticipate that party strength, of both the incumbent and challenger parties, could affect incumbency advantage. Such factors as the nature of the party system and its degree of institutionalization and the weakness of the opposition have been argued to constitute a factor in the power of incumbents, since it undermines accountability (Rakner & van de Walle, 2009; Crawford & Lynch, 2011).

Relatedly, strong opposition parties and political coalitions might limit the incumbent's power and his ability to resort to the panoply of informal mechanisms to hold onto electoral power. As Barkan (2008) argues, the institutional strength of the legislature can obstruct executive dominance. The nature of the legislature's constitutional powers and its ability to enforce horizontal accountability on the president, on practical matters such as the budget and on broader constitutional issues that, for instance, limit the president's power to decree, arguably could affect reelection rates.

3.4 THE POWER OF INCUMBENCY

A key obstacle to political change that also explains the low rates of political alternation is the dominance of the executive branch of government and of individual presidents in most African countries. Presidential dominance has long been argued to be the defining characteristic of African politics, both before the third wave of democratization and since. Theories of the personal nature of political power in Africa (Jackson & Rosberg, 1982, 1991; Bratton & van de Walle, 1997; Bayart, 2009) dominated the analysis of politics in the region before 1990; since then, the continuation of presidential dominance has been much remarked upon (van de Walle, 2003; Prempeh, 2007), even as observers recognize the increasing salience of formal institutions in Africa politics (Posner & Young, 2007).

Democratization in the early 1990s brought about the legalization of opposition parties and the formal acceptance of civic and political rights, usually through meaningful constitutional reforms. With the exceptions of Botswana, Mauritius, and Tanzania, every country in the region has either promulgated a new constitution or substantially revised an old one since 1990 (Hartmann, 2007). A number of countries have engaged in repeated tinkering with constitutional arrangements. Malawi, for instance, has undertaken over a dozen constitutional reforms since it formulated a new democratic constitution in 1994.

These constitutional reforms have meaningfully helped to institutionalize African politics, although important variation exists across the region in the degree to which incumbents are constrained by formal institutions. As Posner and Young (2007, p. 128) remind us, the primary causes of executive departures from office have shifted from violent over-throw or assassinations in the 1990s to institutionally regulated exits such as voluntary resignations or elections. Political participation and competition, the two main dimensions of political regimes identified by Dahl (1971), have undoubtedly been enhanced substantially by politi-cal liberalization, with regular multiparty elections, greater political and press freedoms, and fewer constraints on popular participation in politics at an all-time high.

Still, executive dominance persists in most of these countries, well tethered by the formal institutions in the region. Revealingly, no sub-Saharan African countries abandoned presidential rule after democrati-zation unlike Tunisia in 2011–14 and, earlier, several countries in Eastern Europe, where democratization resulted in the move to parliamentary government. In sub-Saharan Africa, despite a tradition of parliamentary rule and the presence of two extremely successful stable parliamentary democracies, Mauritius and Botswana, transitions to multiparty elections has not resulted in moving away from presidential government.

In any event, the link between electoral practice and democracy seems to be at its starkest in the choice of head of state, because the excesses of presidential power are so often at the root of the democratic fail-ures of countries in the region. Unfortunately, multiparty elections have attenuated the presidentialism in African politics mostly on the margins, even in the more democratic countries. Although there was considerable tinkering with electoral rules, the predictability and lack of fundamental change in these rules in the last quarter-century are striking.

In sum, presidential dominance and the low rates of executive alterna-tion probably have to do both with some features shared by all African countries and with some features that are more pronounced in less-democratic countries. We focus first on the factors that are not easily related to the quality of democracy before turning, in Section 3.5, to the specific features of less democratic countries in the region.

3.4.1 Control of the Legislature

A primary feature of presidential political dominance has been the ability of African presidents to exert close control over the main national legis-lative body and the resulting relative weakness of the latter. In eighty-eight legislative elections in thirty-two countries between 1990 and 2015 (43 percent of the total number of elections in that time period), the president's party has won more than two-thirds of the seats available,. In seventy-one additional elections, the president's party enjoyed a comfortable majority with between 50 percent and 67 percent seats. At the other extreme, the president's party won fewer than 50 percent of the seats in only forty-seven elections (23 percent) in twenty countries. Even then, the president's party did not actually control the legislature; in most cases, the president's party held a plurality of seats and exerted control through alliances with other parties and independents. For example, in countries such as Madagascar (in the elections of 1998) or Malawi (in the elections of 2004), independents won over a fifth of the seats (Rakner & van de Walle, 2009). Many of these independents join the presidential majority soon after the election, either officially or, if that is not allowed in the legislature, unofficially so that they can benefit from presidential spoils. Much the same is true of small parties. The life of the opposition party legislator is a hard one, even in countries with relatively large legislator salaries, as the opposition cannot access the resources of the state that are dominated by the incumbent's party.

The cases of real "cohabitation," in which the legislature is de facto controlled by the opposition, occurred during the last quarter century only in a very small number of cases, characterized by instability. Thus, in Niger, Mahamane Ousmane's victory in the 1993 presidential election initially gained him a comfortable coalition majority in the legislature (Decoudras & Gazibo, 1997; Moestrup, 1999). But the breakdown of the coalition forced Ousmane into a minority position by late 1995. Early elections did not produce a new presidential majority, and cohabitation resulted, with a paralysis of government and the rise of partisan rhetoric. This became a pretext for the military coup of January 1996 (Baudais & Chauzal, 2011). A similar story can be told for Guinea-Bissau, where unstable political alliances and the absence of a stable presidential majority resulted in multiple interventions by the military as well as repeated episodes of political violence, including the 2009 assassination of the country's first democratically elected president, João Bernardo Vieira, the day after the murder of one of his chief rivals (Opalo 2015, p. 242).

Presidential dominance over the legislature has been compounded by the high rates of electoral alternation in the latter. In other words, the counterpart of relatively low rates of presidential turnovers has been very high legislative turnover. Opalo's (2015) study of the Kenyan legislature estimates that only 67 percent of incumbents have even chosen to run for reelection, and 51 percent of those are reelected. Adamolekun and Laleye (2009, pp. 119–20) note that in Benin, 65 percent of the parliamentarians in office in 1999 were serving their first term and that only four had served in every multiparty legislature since 1991. In Uganda in 2001, only 43 percent of the parliamentarians had been reelected (Kasfir & Twebaze, 2009, p. 83). In Ghana, reelection rates have averaged around 44 percent (Lindberg & Zhou, 2009, p. 165), while in Nigeria's Third Assembly (2007–11), only 20 percent of members were reelected (Lewis, 2009, pp. 198–9). Such low reelection rates probably have multiple causes. Running for office is expensive, at least in part because of growing competition as well as the need to redistribute to constituents during campaigning (Lindberg, 2010). Opalo (2017, p. 15) notes that the average constituency had only four candidates in the old single-party days but the average has been seven candidates since the transition to multiparty politics after 1991. As we shall argue in Chapter 4, one dimension of this record is the weakness and low levels of institutionalization of political parties, which provide relatively little support to candidates and are usually incapable of disciplining them.

Reelection rates are also probably influenced by the quality of incumbents, and Opalo (2014) argues that weak legislatures can be expected to produce weak legislators. When the legislature lacks institutional capacity and power, individual parliamentarians are less likely to be able to provide their constituents with access to various services or favors, having to rely instead on currying favor with the executive branch. The presence of inexperienced parliamentarians who are unlikely to remain in office results in a weak legislature, lacking in the ability to counter executive power. By contrast, when political parties are stronger and there is more stability in the legislature, one would expect the president to be held to a higher standard of accountability.

3.4.2 State Resources

In many political systems around the world, incumbents have a comparative advantage based on the fact that they already occupy office and, as a result, have access to specific resources that challengers do not. This includes money to travel to constituencies, franking privileges, staff and other support to help communicate with constituents, and fundraising advantages (King, 1991; Levitt & Wolfram, 1997, p. 45). As we will argue below, this advantage is multiplied in presidential systems in sub-Saharan Africa.

Scholars have long argued that access to discretionary resources reinforces political stability, whether the resources come from natural resource rents or from a growing economy. Discretionary control of state resources provides opportunities for patronage and clientelism, to which virtually all elected governments resort in some manner. Even in the most established Western democracies, state spending always follows a least some degree of political logic, particularly during electoral periods, during which public spending almost invariably increases (Nordhaus, 1975). Not only are transfer and subsidy programs, civil service hiring, and infrastructure spending likely to follow the electoral cycle, there is a large literature suggesting that they are targeted toward specific voters (Kitschelt & Wilkinson, 2007; Hicken, 2011; Stokes et al, 2013).

Levitsky and Way (2010) discuss three ways in which incumbents in hybrid or semiauthoritarian regimes can leverage an uneven playing field to their advantage without blatant harassment or obstruction of the opposition: control of the media, use of government resources for the incumbent campaign, and the stacking of institutions in a partisan manner. Unlike the cases of blatant electoral manipulation, these "subtle" forms of manipulation can leave opportunities for opposition victory but skew the playing field toward the incumbent.

In sub-Saharan Africa, control of media can range from innocuous acts such as monopolizing airtime to more overt acts of censorship. In most African countries, most media are still state owned (Moehler & Singh, 2011), giving incumbents additional leverage over this form of advantage. In close races, incumbents have demonstrated a willingness to harass or close opposition newspapers. For instance, in 2016, the Zambian government shut down a leading newspaper – the *Zambian Post* – in the run-up to the elections. While the Internet offers citizens some autonomy and opportunities to access independent media, there is also political learning among elites. In some countries, where there are limited Internet providers, government may encourage network disruptions at politically salient moments. For instance, as social media are becoming more important, regimes are increasingly using Facebook and Twitter outages to disrupt political activity. In Mali, the government of President Ibrahim Keïta faced tremendous popular protest in 2016 after it attempted to arrest and silence Ras Bath, a very popular radio talk show host. In the days that followed, Internet users in Bamako could not access sites such as Facebook without going through a virtual private network (VPN). The Malian government denied any involvement in the Internet outage. The Ethiopian government has been more forthright in its control of access to the Internet. In June 2017, it shut down the Internet to prevent high school students from leaking copies of their exams online. Previously, the government had blocked Internet connectivity during protests in 2015–16 but later relaxed the ban to exclusively target social media sites used for political organizing, such as Facebook and Twitter.[2] Governments are increasingly requesting data about citizens' Internet usage.[3]

In African elections, candidates have unequal access to funding resources, and the incumbent party can monopolize existing resources. Since political parties have few requirements to report,[4] party financing is plagued by a lack of transparency. Dendere (2015) documents incumbents' access to networks of financing from other incumbent regimes, such as Equatorial Guinea and Libya (in the Khaddafi era), to which opposition parties have no access. Eighty-five percent of African countries provide some kind of public financing for parties and/or elections, and about a third provide regular access to this funding, but access to these resources is often controlled and manipulated by the incumbent (Dendere, 2015, p. 5). The Zimbabwe African National Union–Patriotic Front (ZANU-PF) generated public financing rules for its own benefit and denied public funding to eligible opposition parties on technicalities (Dendere, 2015, pp. 12–15). Paget (2017) argues that the costs of campaigning are increasing; he demonstrates this by noting the increasing use of helicopters during campaigns in Tanzania. In such environments, candidates need to spend time courting political financiers. Traditionally, incumbents are seen as the more credible candidates, since they are already in power and financial backers know that executive alternation is limited.

Access to resources is important for campaigns because African elections are expensive, and incumbent parties typically considerably outspend the opposition (see Chapter 5). For instance, Weghorst (2015, p. 246) found that dominant-party candidates in Tanzania routinely spent an average of 16–25 million shillings (approximately US \$7,000–11,000) more on their campaigns, than opposition candidates did but also found that winning opposition candidates spent more than losing opposition candidates did. Molomo (2000) explains that the ruling Botswana Democratic Party has amassed a campaign finance advantage through funding sources from abroad. Opposition parties have been critical of "clandestine foreign funding"; for instance, Molomo (2000, p. 78) cites a

---

[2] www.reuters.com/article/us-ethopia-internet/ethiopia-cuts-off-internet-after-high-school-exam-leaks-idUSKBN18S535
[3] See CIPESA report on government requests: https://cipesa.org/?wpfb_dl=248
[4] Dendere (2015) explains that the 2014 elections in Malawi involved requirements for parties to report on their finances.

P2.4 million donation (over US $200,000) from an undisclosed international source in the 1999 election campaign.

In Africa, political clientelism has long been defined as the use of state resources for political ends (Bratton & van de Walle, 1997; Bayart, 2009) in a process that protects incumbents and promotes political stability. These dynamics have largely continued since the wave of democratization. van de Walle (2001, pp. 103–5) argues that the numbers of government cabinets and other state offices had regularly increased after independence to provide authoritarian presidents with patronage possibilities. Arriola (2009) confirms that these practices continue in the democratic era, and he links this practice to political stability, finding, for instance, that increased cabinet size decreases the probability of a coup. The preponderance of power in the executive branch means that there are fewer checks and balances by the legislature or judicial branch on potential abuses of power or misappropriation of state funding for personal purposes.

Why should we think that this control of the state purse matters more in Africa than in other competitive electoral systems? The weakness of nonstate actors, whether in civil society or in the private sector, is the primary reason. The share of formal employment that depends on state funding is more substantial in economies in which low-paying informal sector jobs dominate. Sklar's (1979) observation several decades ago that class stratification in the region was a process largely determined by access to state resources remains true to this day, particularly in the poorer states in the region and the dozen or so oil-exporting states.

In some countries in Africa that have a strong private sector, structural changes in economies have attenuated the process described by Sklar (1979) and others. Arriola (2013) has stressed that the distribution of access to private capital can serve as the glue needed to form and maintain successful challenging coalitions in electoral politics. He argues that the process of economic liberalization that began in the 1990s now provides opposition candidates with potentially more access to private capital and, consequently, the fodder needed to build cross-ethnic alliances. Arriola (2013, pp. 256–68) notes fourteen instances in which coalitions resulted in turnover and seventeen instances in which coalitions were unsuccessful in overcoming the incumbent or the incumbent party. In the same chart (Arriola, 2013), we observe twelve instances of turnover that were not generated by coalitions. This variation suggests that the formation of an opposition coalition is neither necessary nor sufficient for executive turnover. However, it might play a role in specific cases.

3.4.3 Executive Rents: Commodity Production and Foreign Aid

Particular types of resource endowments that are common in Africa have been shown to protect incumbents. For instance, Omgba (2009) shows that oil wealth increases duration of executive leadership, and Ross (2001, p. 432) demonstrates its impact on the dominance of party elite. Omgba (2009) argues that oil resources afford incumbents patronage to coopt to potential challengers but simultaneously attracts support for the status quo from the international community. As the most extreme examples, he highlights French intervention in Gabon and Chad to squelch challenger movements. We observe no cases of turnover in either incumbent or open-seat polls in oil-producing countries between 1990 and 2015, with the partial exception of the Republic of the Congo in 1992, suggesting that oil rents insulate not only presidents, but also their parties and ruling coalitions, from political challengers. The role of the international community in the region's electoral politics in the current era is a complicated one that is well beyond the scope of this chapter, but it seems clear that substantial natural resource revenue has made incumbents less vulnerable to the inconsistent and uneven political conditionality that the international community tends to impose (see, for example, Brown, 2011).

Because foreign aid is directed primarily at governments and typically provides resources directly to the central state, it probably operates somewhat like commodity rents (Morrison, 2014; Resnick & van de Walle, 2013). On the one hand, foreign aid represents discretionary resources for the incumbent. Even if these were not instrumentalized in a political fashion and their use followed an entirely developmental logic, they would still benefit the incumbent by providing economic growth and alleviation of poverty. Incumbents can claim credit for this economic progress under their leadership. Similarly, the sudden withdrawal of donor support can serve to destabilize regimes, in much the same way that unexpected declines in commodity prices can put incumbents in temporary difficulty. Pressures from donors and the threat of a long-term boycott have also helped to convince military leaders to give up power they had gained in a coup, although this effect has seemed to be limited to the weakest and most aid-dependent countries in the region (such as Mali and Burkina Faso).

Generally, however, foreign aid clearly serves as a political resource for incumbent governments. Much evidence is accruing that aid resources are often used not in a developmental fashion but rather in a politically partisan manner by the government. Briggs (2014) finds compelling

evidence that Kenyan presidents directed foreign aid projects disproportionately to their political supporters between 1989 and 1995. In a separate study, Briggs (2012) similarly detects a distinct political logic to the
spatial allocation of aid in Ghana, a finding that Masaki (2016) replicates
for Zambia. Government distribution of donor-funded fertilizer has been
found to follow a political logic in both Zambia and Malawi. In Zambia,
Mason et al. (2016) found that the government provides fertilizer subsidies to districts that provide electoral support to the president's party
rather than being given to poor regions and that fertilizer distribution
peaks in electoral years. In their study of agricultural input subsidies,
Horowitz and Dionne (2016) found no evidence of political targeting,
but they did find significant evidence that the subsidies benefited the
incumbent party at elections time.

Finally, control of the policy agenda helps incumbents, often with
the unwitting complicity of international donors. With economic conditions worsening in recent years because of declining export receipts, debt
negotiations with international donors became more or less inevitable in
2015 and 2016. In a number of countries, including Gabon, Ghana, and
Zambia, regimes deferred policy reform and belt tightening until after
presidential elections. In Zambia, for instance, the Popular Front government oversaw an increase in debt from 22 percent of GDP to more
than 50 percent, and the government ran a budget deficit of 10 percent
of GDP in the year before the August 2016 elections. But the government
waited until after the election to change the Minister of Finance and concede that negotiations with the International Monetary Fund (IMF) were
urgent (Hill, 2016). This ability to control the timing of macro policy
constitutes a big advantage for the incumbent, not least when international institutions such as the IMF remain willing to provide adjustment
finance to the government despite its evident policy negligence.

3.4.4 Economic Performance

In the comparative context, studies have long demonstrated that retrospective voters typically reward incumbents for good economic performance (see, for example, Hibbs et al., 1982; Lewis-Beck and Rice, 1982).
In Chapter 7, we will present the growing body of empirical evidence
that voters use performance-based evaluations of candidates (Posner &
Simon, 2002; Bratton et al., 2012; Weghorst & Lindberg, 2013; Ellis,
2014). Good economic performance seems particularly important in low-
income countries, and the very survival of democracy in these countries

may depend on it; over a decade ago, Cheibub et al. (1996) showed that that low-income democracies needed economic growth to survive.

As it happens, the current democratic era in Africa has largely coincided with a period of sustained rapid economic growth across most countries in the region. Following negative per capita GDP growth in the late 1970s and 1980s, economic growth began to outstrip population growth in the mid-1990s. By the 2000s, the economy of the continent as a whole was growing over 5 percent annually. The decline in commodity prices since 2010 have dampened these growth rates in some countries, and several oil producers in the region are facing fiscal adjustments, but the IMF forecasts of April 2016 remained relatively upbeat about the region's growth potential (IMF, 2016). As Radelet (2010) and others (see, for example, Masaki & van de Walle, 2014) have noted, the past two decades have been both the region's most democratic era and its fastest-growing era since independence. Presidents may be getting some of the political credit for the rising standard of living in many countries.

Thus the economic climate has almost certainly favored incumbents. Like citizens in other parts of the world, Africans may have credited their leaders for their rising standards of living and, as a result, have voted for them to remain in power. Perhaps the recent slowing down of the world economy, the decline in commodity prices since 2013, and the resulting fiscal problems in a number of countries of the region will increase electoral pressures on incumbents. The defeat of presidential incumbents in Ghana, for instance, since the decline of commodity prices in 2013 and a resulting slowdown in growth rates suggests that incumbency advantage may have relied on good economic performance and may decline in the coming years.

Economic growth is coupled with access that incumbents have to international donors and state funding for service provision. This is particularly important for candidates, given that constituents often judge incumbents' performance on the basis of their ability to bring constituency services back home (Barkan, 2008). Even voters who are critical of an incumbent's performance may recognize that this candidate has preferred access to donor networks and existing development programs.

3.4.5 Political Culture

It is tempting to adopt a cultural explanation for incumbency advantage. Certainly, authoritarian rulers once linked presidentialism to African culture, as when President Félix Houphouët-Boigny of Côte d'Ivoire cited the traditional proverb that "there can only be one male crocodile in the marigot [river tributary]." Some scholars (Chabal & Daloz, 1999; Schatzberg, 2001) have used cultural arguments, notably about the patriarchal nature of African society to suggest that the region has a tendency toward authoritarian rule of a personal nature. Some scholars have posited that citizens' deference to presidents is rooted in African culture, providing a cultural advantage to incumbents. Schatzberg (2001) has famously written about the perception of the African president as the "father of the nation." He argues that African cultural norms place the head of state as the head of a moral matrix. As such, the leader is rarely criticized by his people, or "children" (Schatzberg, 2001, p. 25), and is seldom held to the same standards as other institutions. Similarly, Chabal (2009, p. 40) argues that because of African cultural norms, an incumbent's advanced age serves as a buffer to younger, less legitimate challengers (see also Chabal & Daloz, 1999).

It is difficult to distinguish the impact of such cultural traditions from the other factors that we survey in this section. Survey data suggest a tradition of deference to the president in many African countries. Little and Logan's (2008) compilation of the fourth round of the Afrobarometer demonstrates that citizens in fourteen of eighteen countries rank their trust in the institution of the presidency higher than their trust in any other formal institution. These rankings do not appear to be correlated with experience of turnover. Two countries that have experienced two turnovers – Côte d'Ivoire and Senegal – do not rank the president as the most trustworthy, but other countries that have experienced multiple turnovers, such as Benin, Ghana, and Madagascar, do.

The same Afrobarometer polls suggest a consistently lower level of trust in political parties, particularly of the opposition. In some cases, the opposition is deeply unpopular. Ascribing this pattern of a systematic trust gap between the president and the opposition could help to explain incumbency advantages. But is this a cultural trait? Perhaps low trust in the opposition results from the incumbents' control of the media, which results in more favorable treatment of the president, for instance. Perhaps citizens find convincing the rhetoric of presidents according to which the president "stands above the fray" of the party system while castigating party politicians for their partisanship. Perhaps, within the context of repressive regimes such as those of Uganda, Rwanda, Eritrea, and Ethiopia, citizens may literally fear the incumbent and the executive's discretionary ability to physically harm citizens.

The point is that a range of attitudes may be observationally equivalent to a cultural trait of deference. When a survey respondent says that he or she supports the incumbent because "God gave him the power to rule," this citizen could be signaling a multitude of reasons for supporting the president. As we will argue in Chapter 6, incumbents in most regimes around the world can point to their past experience in office to bolster their credentials as "issue owners." Since opposition parties have limited experience in office, incumbent candidates and parties have a strong comparative valence advantage. This advantage is heightened in sub-Saharan Africa by the inexperience of both elite actors and citizens with electoral politics and by the prominence of the executive. Voters recognize the sitting executive as a central node in a network of clientelist redistribution but also as a key mediator to links with the international community. The strength of the executive branch reinforces the role of the president as a focal point for the entire political system. It becomes difficult to imagine the political equilibrium that would be established if a new president took office, particularly in personalist systems in which the party has little power to discipline or influence the executive. This generates speculation in the context of great uncertainty. Would the new president be able to navigate domestic politics and strike acceptable bargains to build coalitions and get things done? Would he be able to negotiate with donors, foreign investors, and neighboring countries?

3.5 ILLIBERAL MECHANISMS OF POLITICAL STABILITY

Next, we focus on practices that are either illegal or in direct contravention of the spirit of democracy and that, as a result, are more likely to be prevalent in the least democratic electoral regimes. The formal and informal mechanisms to which African presidents resort in order to maintain power vary widely. As Schedler (2002, 2013) has noted, the "menu of manipulation" is extensive. We make no effort to be comprehensive. Instead, we focus on how African autocrats use elections and political repression to maintain themselves in power. We then address the implications of both kinds of strategies.

3.5.1 Electoral Manipulation

The frequency of elections alone cannot be related to the level of democracy. In Africa between 1995 and 2015, sitting presidents were electorally defeated in only a single country that Freedom House defines as "partly free" or "not free": Madagascar in 1996, when the predemocratic-era strongman Didier Ratsiraka came back to power. One could argue that several other autocrats actually received fewer votes than their challenger, despite the official results. A short list of suspicious results include those of the Cameroonian elections of 1992, the Zimbabwean elections of 2008, the Togolese elections of 2005, the Kenyan elections of 2007, and the Nigerian elections of 2011. However, that only confirms the advantage incumbents bring to these elections, since challengers cannot choose to steal elections.

One clear difference between democracies and electoral autocracies lies in the control that the executive branch exercises over elections. In the more democratic countries in the region, the president has little discretion over the electoral calendar. In electoral autocracies, the president and his ruling party enjoy at least some discretion, as we observe that elections are more likely to be delayed, rescheduled, or cancelled and are somewhat less regular. Interestingly, the difference is much more pronounced for legislative elections: The less democratic the country, the fewer the number of legislative elections. At first, this discrepancy seems surprising. Legislatures in these regimes are weak and typically dominated by the president's party, which generally enjoys a comfortable majority. Indeed, there are no examples of authoritarian countries in which the president's party does not have a substantial majority in the legislature, ensuring that the regime maintains control of the legislature. But the discrepancy makes sense if one sees presidential and legislative elections as serving different political functions: Presidential elections provide the president with needed domestic and international legitimacy, while legislative elections do not, per se. True, they may play an important function in even the least democratic states; presidents use them to shore up their own political coalitions with a mixture of carrot and stick. The president can promote key backbenchers with patronage and support and punish insufficiently loyal legislators by withdrawing the same (Gandhi & Lust-Okar, 2009). Legislative elections help to strengthen the government party and build its support throughout the territory. Still, because legislative elections do not directly threaten the president, the stakes are likely to be lower.

Autocracies typically lack an independent electoral commission, and this helps them to manipulate the electoral process. Though even francophone countries no longer have the Ministry of the Interior organize elections – a legacy inherited from France – but now typically have an electoral commission, these are usually carefully managed by the regime

(Thiriot, 2004). As Gazibo's (2006) survey of electoral commissions in West Africa notes, the formal institutional setup does not correlate with the effective degree of independence of the commission from the government. Only in the most democratic countries in the region, such as Ghana and Benin, is the commission endowed with enough capacity and independence to serve as an effective check on executive abuses (on Ghana, see Gyimah-Boadi, 2009; Debrah, 2011); on Benin, see Gazibo, 2006).

Unfortunately, Cameroon exemplifies a much more common pattern. There, the formal independence of the electoral commission betrays its near total subservience to the regime. The commission was long chaired by Enoch Kwayeb, a baron of the Rassemblement Démocratique du Peuple Camerounais (RDPC), the party in power (Pigeaud, 2011, p. 81). When the donors pressured Biya to create a more independent commission in preparation for the 2006 elections, he established a new commission (Elections Cameroon, known as ELECAM) and proceeded to name twelve members of the RDPC's central committee to its advisory board before almost entirely disempowering the body in 2011 (Pigeaud, 2011, p. 82). In Tanzania, the CCM, which is the dominant party selects the members of the electoral commission (Hoffman & Robinson, 2009). In Gabon, the controversy over the reelection of Ali Bongo in the summer of 2016 revealed to an almost comical extent the Bongo family's control of the administrative machinery overseeing the elections. The Interior Ministry is in charge of organizing elections. The minister in 2016, Pacôme Moubelet-Boubeya, was a close family friend of the Bongos and political loyalist. So was the head of the Electoral Commission, René Aboghe Ella. The Governor of Haut-Ogooué Province – the Bongo stronghold, where results indicated that 95.5 percent of the 99.99 percent of the voters who had turned out on election day to vote for Bongo – was another close political ally of the presidential family. Finally, the opposition's legal challenge of the official results was heard by the Constitutional Court, whose long-standing president, Marie Madeleine Mborantsuo, had had two children with Omar Bongo ("Bongo's Incredible Win," 2016).

The misleading rhetoric of the incumbent regime may provide another means of confusing voters and thus manipulating elections. The president refers to the electoral commission as independent, despite all the evidence that he closely controls its actions. This does not fool everyone, but at least some voters come to believe that an "independent" electoral commission cannot be fair, and this undermines support for a genuinely independent electoral commission. Indeed, the systematic adoption by a regime of the language and rhetoric of democracy to describe practices that are not democratic is no doubt designed with the narrow purposes of propaganda: to defend and justify the actions of the regime. However, they also corrupt the meaning of democracy in the minds of the public, and this serves a larger purpose for the regime.

Unfortunately, we can offer only partial evidence to support these hypotheses. Indeed, the survey evidence is far from conclusive.[5] The Afrobarometer data suggest that African citizens are fairly realistic about the imperfections of their country's democracy. At the same time, and relatively puzzlingly, their understanding of the quality of the democratic institutions does not have much effect on their level of trust in these institutions. The countries surveyed by the Afrobarometer tend to be more democratic than many of the electoral autocracies discussed in this chapter, a finding that mitigates the odd result that trust in political institutions appears to be inversely related to their quality.

In sum, control of the electoral commission and electoral logistics helps electoral autocracies to rig elections with a mixture of ingenious strategies that are pursued well before the election, from malapportionment to partisan approaches to voter registration to election-day intimidation, fraud, and vote buying.

In the 1970 elections in the Democratic Republic of the Congo (then called Zaire), ballot stuffing on behalf of President Mobutu Sese Seko was a little too enthusiastic, and over 30,000 votes more were cast for him than the total number of registered voters. In Nigeria, ballot rigging is an old tradition, practiced with impunity by successive governments going back to the first republic (Herskovits, 2007; Rawlence & Albin-Lackey, 2007). Today, such old-fashioned election-day ballot stuffing is rare. It is more likely to occur in a decentralized fashion, perhaps with the blessing of the regime elite but not necessarily its organizational assistance. Still, presidents have been elected with more than 90 percent of the vote in thirteen countries since 1991, totals that do not necessarily imply significant ballot stuffing but do suggest its likelihood. Willis and al-Bhattani (2010, p. 222) describe widespread, decentralized processes of ballot stuffing during the 1996 elections in Sudan, which were expressed in the appearance of a legitimate electoral exercise:

There were apparently some new departures in malpractice: not only were government vehicles used to bring voters to polling stations, but in some cases ballot boxes were reported to have been taken to public gatherings – to weddings, or

[5] We thank Natalie Letsa for particularly useful comments on these issues.

funerals – and people were given ballot papers to put in the boxes. These elections brought together, in striking fashion, two approaches to "changing the law": the straightforward cheating which had developed in the Nimeiri period and the combination of a fantasy of procedure with a reality of multiple local expedients to push up participation rates.

Incumbent president Omar Al-Bashir won comfortably with over 75 percent of the vote. Similarly, Rwandan President Paul Kagame's ability to garner 95 percent, 93 percent, and 99 percent of the vote in the last three elections, despite belonging to a minority ethnic group, clearly suggests election-day fraud. The political purpose of winning by such lopsided scores is not clear. More common, perhaps, may be ballot stuffing in competitive elections to nudge the incumbent's totals above those of his challenger. The 2007 Kenyan elections were also widely viewed as having been the occasion of some postvoting ballot stuffing to move the election in Kibaki's favor when electoral officials who favored the regime discovered that his vote totals were much lower than anticipated (Cheeseman, 2008).

Manipulation of the voter rolls well before election day is likely to be a more efficient way to steal elections. Fraudulent and politicized voter registration is one such approach. Analyzing the results of the recent 2013 elections in Zimbabwe, external observers estimated that the regime had added one million invalid voters in core ZANU-PF regions and had excluded up to a million real voters, mostly in urban areas where support for the Movement for Democratic Change (MDC) is strongest (*The Independent*, August 2, 2013).[6] Similar accounts describe elections in Nigeria, in which intimidation of voters and manipulation of access to voting polls and ballots in some regions of the country coincided with suspiciously high turnouts in others (Human Rights Watch, 2007; Bratton, 2008)

Electoral malapportionment to help the government control the legislature is another more sophisticated strategy. Albaugh (2011) describes an emblematic process of electoral manipulation in today's Cameroon. She notes, for instance, that voters from the president's South Province enjoyed a legislative seat for about 34,000 voters, whereas the voters from the North, historically opposed to Biya, could count on one seat for 71,000 voters (Albaugh, 2011, p. 121). She also notes various tricks used by the regime to promote voter registration in areas that favor the president and aggressively attenuate it in other parts of the country. In her fascinating study of district proliferation in Ghana, Resnick (2017) shows that successive incumbents have used redistricting to increase the number

[6] Post-July 31 Zimbabwe: Responses, managing outcomes"; and "Disputed Election Results: Biometric Future of Voting". both available at: www.theindependent.co.zw/elections-2013-2/.

of safe legislative constituencies for their backbenchers. It is interesting, in this respect, that the average African legislature has grown from 180 seats to 209 seats between 1990 and 2015, though this growth is only weakly correlated with regime type.

Malapportionment featured in the 1990s in Kenya; Barkan and Ng'ethe (1998, pp. 44–5) argue that malapportionment allowed the government of President Daniel arap Moi to manufacture a legislative majority that it otherwise would not have had. Although Wahman and Boone (2018) do not focus on electoral autocracies or examine recent efforts by incumbents to manipulate the process of districting, they show that there is a systematic rural bias in the legislative malapportionment of eight anglophone countries, a bias that plays to the advantage of the incumbent, since support for the president is more reliable in the countryside (see also Samuels & Snyder, 2001).

3.5.2 Vote or Turnout Buying, Gift Giving, and Violence

The burgeoning literature on vote or turnout buying (Schaffer, 2007; Bratton, 2008; Vicente & Wantchekon, 2009; Stokes et al, 2013) typically does not discuss the practice in the context of incumbency advantage.[7] This is odd because vote buying, when and where it takes place, is more often than not an asymmetric process in which the opposition cannot compete easily with the incumbent and his access to state resources. Conroy-Krutz (2017) provides evidence that Ugandan voters will "sell" their votes more cheaply to the opposition than to the incumbent candidate, suggesting that the voters understand the disparity of the resources available to each candidate. Thus, while there is no denying that both sides engage in vote buying, it is still useful to think of it as one of the tools in the incumbent's toolbox that can be used to remain in the power.

The fifth round of the Afrobarometer reported that 16 percent of the voters in some thirty-three countries reported having been offered money or goods in exchange for their vote (quoted in Mares & Young, 2016),[8] but this percentage varies quite a lot across the different countries

---

[7] We acknowledge that in many instances, vote buying is probably more accurately described as turnout buying, in that parties lack the ability to monitor vote choice (Nichter, 2008), but we will use the terms interchangeably in this section. In most instances, African parties are thought to be too weak to actually monitor voting (Vicente and Wantchekon, 2009; Vincente, 2014; but see Ferree and Long, 2016). Without the information and capacity to enforce the bargain, parties cannot determine whether voters act as promised.

[8] In comparison, 15 percent of Latin American voters report exposure to vote buying (Mares and Young, 2016).

surveyed, from a high of 41 percent in Uganda to less than 10 percent in Namibia. The countries where respondents have the highest expectations of gift giving vary in their turnout rates – from countries with habitually low turnout, such as Burkina, Liberia, Niger, and Mali, to places with much higher turnout rates, such as Uganda, and Sierra Leone (Mares & Young, 2016, p. 30). It is likely that gifts play different roles in different contexts, but more research is needed to understand the nature of vote buying across countries. For instance, does it typically target core constituencies or swing voters? In some contexts, such as the Sahel, vote buying might reflect general state weakness. Voters who have little confidence in parties' abilities to generate public goods once in office may focus on redistribution around election time as a way to extract goods from political actors. Interestingly, countries where respondents report exposure to fear, intimidation, or violence are distinct from the countries where voters expect gifts (Mares & Young, 2016).[9]

What vote buying and gift giving share is that both favor the incumbent. In theory, the business community can fund opposition campaigns and provide equivalent resources, but businesses are unlikely to think of such support as a sound investment unless the prospects for victory are good, which is only rarely the case in systems with few incumbent defeats. The advantage for incumbents is that they can use state resources for vote-buying practices. These practices can include both narrowly defined vote buying and general inducements to support the incumbent that are provided around election time. It is difficult but important to distinguish between vote buying, in which the exchange of money represents a formal contract for a vote, and gift giving, in which candidates provide some material benefit to voters but without a clear contractual arrangement. Young (1993, p. 304) describes how the dominant party strategically distributes development materials during election time. Campaigns are chock-full of stories of candidates distributing material goods to voters yet lacking either the ability or the intention to monitor the vote that then takes place.

Van Ham and Lindberg (2015) make the interesting argument that vote buying is more likely to be done by incumbents in more democratic countries, when the conduct of elections has become free and fair enough that intimidation and administrative shenanigans are no longer politically expedient, to promote victory at the polls. However, individual

---

[9] Only Uganda, Sierra Leone, and Kenya appear as top countries for gift giving and the use of violence, a finding that suggests the country-specific nature of these dynamics.

country case studies suggest that vote buying takes place in countries in which there is also resort to intimidation and gerrymandering, such as Cameroon, Gabon, and Tanzania. One suspects considerable spatial variation in these two practices within individual countries; the incumbent is probably more likely to engage in vote buying in swing and/or core constituencies and violence in opposition ones. While the two practices are weakly correlated for most of Africa, they are negatively correlated in West Africa, a finding that might reveal country-specific variables.

Most of the academic attention has been on vote buying, but electoral violence and threats of violence continue to play a more substantial role in electoral campaigns of the region's more autocratic states. Mares and Young (2016) use Afrobarometer data from thirty-three countries to show that nearly half of all voters surveyed reported experiencing fear, intimidation, or violence during elections. One should distinguish the violence and intimidation that is directed specifically at opposition parties and candidates from the kinds that are directed at voters. The former is less common and correlates negatively with the quality of the electoral system. Governments are more likely to treat voters with a heavy hand than opposition candidates, though there is plenty of evidence of attempts to intimidate and weaken political parties and their campaigns. In the least democratic electoral systems, violence directed at candidates is common; opposition candidates have been jailed and/or roughed up in recent elections in Rwanda, Uganda, Zambia, and Zimbabwe. Despite Rwanda's carefully cultivated reputation for gender equity, the government responded to Diane Shima Rwigara's announcement in 2017 that she would run against Kagame for the presidency by barring her from running and eventually putting her in prison when she persisted. Throughout the campaign, fake nude pictures of Rwigara were widely circulated on social media (Attiah, 2017).

Mares and Young (2016) posit that positive inducements (gifts, money, club goods) have different psychological effects on voters' than the threat of negative inducements (such as losses or violence). They cite Boone's (2011) work from Kenya, where parties are able to mobilize voters effectively by arguing that constituents will lose entitlements to land if they do not come out to vote. Young (2015) argues that negative inducements as well as appeals to anger and fear can be very powerful.

The effectiveness of threats or inducements in driving voter behavior may depend on the actors' credibility (Kramon, 2016), voters' beliefs about electoral secrecy (Mares, 2015), the strength of judicial institutions and/or the probability of punishment for electoral malfeasance (Hafner-Burton et al., 2014), or the actors' capacity to monitor (Mares & Young, 2016). Consistent with Rauschenbach's (2015) emphasis on parties' attempts to court their core constituents, Mares and Young (2016, p. 30) find that in countries where vote buying is most likely to be present, swing voters are less likely to be targeted with positive inducements, suggesting a targeting of partisans.

In some cases, the regime's legitimate attempts to ensure stability around the time of elections may lead to restrictions on civil liberties but may be largely supported by voters. In postconflict environments, there is often a tension around attempts to ensure security. In the 2012 elections in Sierra Leone, the electoral commission banned political speech, dress, and activity during polling and increased oversight for party registration (Bolten, 2016). While the international community criticized the restriction of political liberties, voters of Sierra Leone were largely supportive of these measures to prevent the types of violence they had seen in the 2007 race (Bolten, 2016).

Still, repressive tactics for the sake of supposed national security, a key issue of interest to voters that we will outline in Chapter 6, are often one sided. As presidents increase financing for the repressive apparatus in preparation for elections, they also increase public sector employment and developmental spending in the run up to the election. Even as opposition rallies are squashed and the independent press intimidated, government ministers tour the countryside and take credit for rural infrastructure and new clinics, schools, and roads.

Electoral violence should also be understood as a tool of incumbency, although it is rarely discussed in this manner in the literature. In the much covered 2007 Kenyan elections, both the opposition and supporters of the regime engaged in violence, and both sides were equally blamed (see, for example, Cheeseman, 2008). But this is unusual. Straus and Taylor (2013) surveyed organized electoral violence in Africa and found that much of it is instigated by incumbents before the election. Further, their data suggest that acts of violence by the opposition typically take place after the election in response to regime-led violence and as an expression of often well-founded grievances concerning the results of the election.

Straus and Taylor (2013) distinguish among three types of violence in terms of ascending importance, from "violent harassment" to "violent repression" and, the category of the most violence, "large-scale violence." African electoral autocracies are well represented in all three categories. Only Tanzania and the Comoros are reported never to have witnessed electoral violence. The other states all saw some degree of electoral violence during this period. In the Central African Republic, for instance, the authors report no violence in the 1998 elections; violent harassment in 1993, 1999, and 2005; and large-scale violence in 1992 (Straus and Taylor, 2013, p 25).

Examining the data of Straus and Taylor (2013) for the electoral autocracies provides two insights. First, distinguishing states that engaged in the higher two levels of violence from states that engaged in no violence or limited themselves to episodes of violent harassment suggests that not all African autocratic states rely on violence in the same manner. The governments in a core set of states (Burundi, the Central African Republic, Chad, Equatorial Guinea, Guinea, Madagascar, Togo, and Zimbabwe) seem to rely on systematically high levels of violence to remain in power. While organized political violence has been much less significant in Burkina Faso, the Comoros, Gambia, Guinea-Bissau, Mozambique, Nigeria, and Tanzania, the harassment of the opposition seems fairly standard in those countries.

Second, the level of electoral violence has declined over time. Several countries exhibited violence around elections in the 1990s, during the heyday of the Third Wave of democratization, but have managed to avoid violence in more recent electoral cycles. Thus the Republic of the Congo underwent a period of significant violence, as Dictator for Life President Sassou Nguesso lost power in the early 1990s in a very contentious election and used a private militia to force his way back into power during the 1997 elections. Since then, Sassou Nguesso has won several peaceful elections, with Stalinist-level majorities. Similarly, the Bongo family almost lost power in Gabon in the early 1990s in several very contentious elections in which opposition groups were harassed and their rallies repressed. Until the 2016 presidential elections, the Bongo clan's hold on power seemed safe. Widespread protests against the official results were repressed strenuously by the regime. This suggests that resorting to violence is a sign of a weak hold on power; the stronger the state apparatus and the more popular the regimes, the less likely it is to resort to violence.

Zimbabwe, by contrast, is perhaps the only country in which organized political violence has increased during this period, which rather confirms the argument that a weakening hold on power motivates violence by incumbents. Kriger (2005) has argued persuasively that the threat of violence and the willingness to use it was a hallmark of Robert Mugabe and his ZANU-PF party well before independence in 1980 but that it was only the rise of a well-organized opposition in the late 1990s that triggered these old reflexes.

We agree with Bratton (2013) and others who have argued that bad elections in electoral autocracies do not promote democratic progress, both because they keep tyrants in power and because they give democratic processes a bad name. Still, it seems useful to distinguish the impact of violence and repression from that of "softer" forms of manipulation in shaping the legitimacy of democratic procedures. Overt acts of repression and violence by the regime are likely to be unambiguously delegitimating for the incumbent. Political violence may cow the opposition, make elections unpopular, and weaken participation in the short run, but it is too opposed to the spirit and logic of democratic processes to be viewed in the same manner as the manipulation of democratic rules. Some Afrobarometer data suggest that African voters are overwhelmingly critical of electoral violence. Bratton (2008) reports that 79 percent of Nigerians say that it such violence "never justified." Thus the evidence suggests that repression is not viewed as legitimate and that it undermines the legitimacy of the regime, making the democratic alternative to authoritarian rule more attractive. This is probably why authoritarian rulers often combine carrot and stick: repression accompanied by patronage. Vote buying on election day, finally, accompanies violence. Bratton (2008) found that one in five voters in Nigeria was exposed to an instance of vote buying and one in ten faced threats of electoral violence.

In sum, these practices may help autocratic leaders to survive elections, but they do not buttress the legitimacy of electoral autocracies. The subtler subversion of democratic practices, we hypothesize, has the advantage of subtly undermining the legitimacy of democratic procedures. "When Mugabe used violence in 2008, he lost legitimacy, so he found to find other ways to win," said Pedzisai Ruhanya, from the Zimbabwe Democracy Institute, a Harare-based think tank. "What we have seen is a masterclass in electoral fraud. It is chicanery, organized theft and electoral authoritarianism."[10]

Some of these forms of manipulations are perhaps simply not well understood by voters. Voters probably do not fully grasp the powerful impact of district malapportionment, particularly in rural areas, since it may not be easy to compare the sizes of districts and the numbers of voters it takes to elect a legislator. Obstacles to voter registration may

---

[10] Quoted in Leo Cendrowicz, "Robert Mugabe's Zimbabwe Election Victory Was a 'Masterclass in Electoral Fraud'," in *The Independent*, August 2, 2013, accessed at www.independent.co.uk/news/world/africa/robert-mugabes-zimbabwe-election-victory-was-a-masterclass-in-electoral-fraud-8744348.html

be similarly frustrating to opposition voters, although these obstacles can easily be disguised as the result of incompetence and bureaucratic snafus rather than strategic actions. Voters in opposition districts may not know that the same frustrations do not exist in electoral strongholds of the regime, with which they have little contact. Election-day results are frustrating and may well arouse suspicions of fraud, but many voters are unlikely to understand the size of the advantage that fraud and manipulations provided to the incumbent. Moreover, accusations by the independent press and the opposition are usually countered by accusations from the government that the opposition also engaged in fraud, and they cancel each other out in the eyes of at least some voters. Many African voters may view dueling accusations as tiresome. Indeed, much evidence suggests that African voters treat partisan sniping with disfavor and blame the opposition as much as the government for it. Moreover, not all voters will be equally critical of the government. Letsa's (2017) deconstruction of the political geography of Cameroon shows well how attitudes and opinions about the government vary quite a bit in the country's different regions. In the government's core areas of support, voters generally buy the narrative of the government and are far more likely to view the country as democratic. It probably helps that these voters are more likely to be favored by both patronage and such nondemocratic practices as malapportionment.

3.6 CONCLUDING REMARKS: THE PROSPECTS FOR CHANGE

We have argued that the regular convening of elections in Africa for the past twenty-five years has not systematically advanced democratic consolidation. Multiparty elections do provide real risks for even the most authoritarian regimes, and the positive change that has occurred in some countries more often than not has resulted from elections or from national debates that relate to upcoming elections, such as debates over term limits.

Why, then, have elections not led to more positive political change? The primary reason we have advanced is that African politics has remained dominated by presidents who tend not to lose elections and who rely on an array of mechanisms to maintain their political dominance and survive electoral threats. Regular elections have thus been institutionalized but with little democratic deepening, at least since the end of the 1990s transitions.

Control of the executive branch has provided a key advantage to incumbents, which is enhanced by the lack of electoral experience that opposition politicians and parties bring to the table, given African political history. Incumbents have learned from their mistakes and have engaged in institutional learning. Although the opposition is also learning from repeated participation in electoral contests, the incumbents are at an advantage (Schedler, 2002). In founding elections, some presidents, such as the incumbents in Zambia and Malawi, miscalculated their popularity and lost (Lindberg, 2009). With greater presences of survey research and polling firms, such mistakes are now less likely. Relatedly, we increasingly see presidents being more proactive in using or obstructing social media as a tactic to maintain power and legitimacy.

The international situation is probably not conducive to positive political change. We note that as African economies continue to grow and new donors such as China increase aid to Africa, governments are less likely to be desperate for conditional financial support from the West. This cannot be confirmed until these states face another era of economic depression. Relatedly, Western governments have taken a turn away from the emphasis on good governance and may be less willing to try to ensure that elections are more than procedural masquerades. Resnick and van de Walle (2013) show the disproportionate amount of aid money being invested into elections and women's empowerment compared to any other topics related to accountability and governance. Investments continue to target issues related to horizontal accountability with few successes in addressing the overwhelming power of the executive.

In the next chapters, we will turn our attention to the African electorate. We will document its dynamism and growing impatience with the stasis of political society. The main force on behalf of positive change is that African voters are becoming more savvy and more appreciative of the electoral process. But first, in Chapter 4, we will turn our attention to political parties and party systems, which are perhaps the key institutional actors in determining the political impact of multiparty elections.

4

Political Parties and Electoral Competition

One of the strengths of SWAPO is its ability to appear to transform itself from a non-democratic authoritarian, top-down organization to a democratic, participatory organization while essentially remaining the same. It is this style of political chicanery that makes it very difficult for opposition against SWAPO.

– J. Diescho (1996, p. 15)

4.1 INTRODUCTION

Since at least V. O. Key (1942), scholars have agreed that political parties perform essential functions in political systems with regular competitive elections and that, by extension, they are crucial to democracy (see also Panebianco, 1988; Sartori, 2005). Political parties recruit and promote the main protagonists of electoral politics – the candidates and eventually the elected officeholders. Parties mobilize citizens, and they serve an important integration function, linking citizens with the government in fundamental ways. Even when they do not perform these functions well, they constitute the main organizational actor in both electoral competition and government. Parties compete to win elections, and when they win, they provide the main organizational principle for government and linkages to citizens. Opposition parties, for their part, play a vital role in the mechanisms of vertical and horizontal accountability that are key to democracy.

The increasingly rich literature on African political parties shows that most of them are weak and poorly institutionalized.[1] Parties in Africa are young and inexperienced. They are not well rooted in society and have only limited abilities to mobilize voters; instead, they must resort to ethnic appeals and brokerage mechanisms to ensure an adequate turnout (Koter, 2016). Party systems are poorly institutionalized, sprouting in the buildup to elections and disappearing shortly after the elections have been held (Kuenzi and Lambright, 2001; Weghorst and Bernhard, 2014). Opposition parties have generally remained too weak to counter effectively the power of incumbents (Bogaards, 2000; Rakner and Van de Walle, 2009).

Because political parties are critically important to democratic consolidation, it is important to better understand why African parties are weak, whether the turn to regular elections has helped them to get stronger over time, and whether variations in parties and party systems help to explain the electoral outcomes described in Chapters 2 and 3. Answering these questions is the main objective of this chapter. We show that, indeed, the political continuity in Africa over the last quarter-century of multiparty electoral politics, which we described in Chapters 2 and 3, and the failure of democratic deepening during this period are caused by the nature and evolution of parties and party systems and, in turn, prevent parties from getting stronger and party systems more institutionalized.

Our argument is again anchored by a historical analysis of the evolution of political parties, particularly their origins in the critical juncture during decolonization. This history is laid out in the next section. Lipset and Rokkan (1967) famously argued that the parties and party systems of Western Europe formed around a small number of social cleavages, largely in response to several key critical junctures in European history. Thus party systems were formed and then fixed around cleavages created by the political and socioeconomic changes that were occurring in Europe just as the electoral franchise was starting to broaden in the second half of the nineteenth century. Over time, these cleavages helped to spur partisan identity. Citizens were more likely to be loyal to parties that represented their positions vis-à-vis one or more of these historical cleavages.

---

[1] General accounts of parties and party systems in Africa since 1990 include Randall and Svåsand (2002), Bogaards (2004, 2013), Salih (2003), Manning (2005), Carbone (2007), Elischer (2013), Resnick (2014), and Souaré (2017). On party formation in the region, see LeBas (2011, 2014) and Van Eerd (2017). On the role of parties in policy making, see Pitcher (2012), Resnick (2014), and Riedl and Dickovick (2014).

In this chapter, we argue that the specific nature of African parties can similarly be related to the critical juncture of decolonization in the 1950s. In most cases, the years before decolonization and the very short period of electoral politics around independence failed to generate parties that had strong linkages to voters. Parties were made up largely of members of the newly created educated elite class. They did not seek to substantively integrate precolonial governance mechanisms or the rural masses. In addition, we argue, the genesis of parties during the nationalist struggle served to delegitimate opposition. The circumstances in which party competition developed directly shaped the nature of both parties and party systems. The era of democratic transitions in the early 1990s could have represented a new critical juncture in which political parties were dramatically reshaped , but we argue that it did not, as many of the dynamics of the decolonization era reemerged – albeit with more muted effects and greater intercountry variation – to ensure a good deal of continuity for parties and party systems.

We turn our attention in Section 4.3 to three broad empirical patterns that can be discerned in African parties and party systems since the return to multiparty rule in the 1990s. First, the political class that has dominated party politics is largely the same class that once dominated the single party, and the many new parties that have emerged strikingly often descend directly from the old single party. The return of electoral politics led to the creation of many new parties, though more often than not with a similar logic, not least because of a great deal of continuity in the political class. Second, we argue that surprisingly few of the old single parties have been able to survive losing power in the multiparty era, in spite of the organizational strengths they seemed to exhibit when in power. Third, we identify a modal African party system, in which one party has a legislative supermajority and dominates the political scene, with relatively few opposition parties having the strength to counter it and provide a legitimate chance of alternation. This pattern exists regardless of how democratic the country is, although there is some evidence of a strengthening opposition in the more democratic systems.

In Section 4.4, we explain the paradoxical combination of change and continuity that we observe in parties and party systems. To understand the resilience of these parties, we argue that it is more useful to look outside of the internal mechanics of the party to regime factors, such as incumbency advantage buffered by disproportionate access to clientelist resources and repression. We conclude by examining recent party trends, most notably the emergence of populist parties with a more strident programmatic agenda.

4.2 THE SOCIAL ORIGINS OF AFRICAN PARTIES

As we discussed in Chapter 2, the emergent political parties recruited their leadership and cadres largely from the small networks of educated elites that emerged after World War II and were heavily recruited into the civil service upon independence. Indeed, nationalist and anticolonial ideologies with a progressive rhetoric masked indigenous class divisions and the process of social stratification that marked the early years after independence (Sklar, 1979, p. 552). Nationalist movements had typically been led by urban elites with relatively high-status occupations and high education levels. They were soon joined by an indigenous business community that benefited from the procurements and licenses of the state. By any definition, the emergent political elite was drawn from a small minority of the population.[2]

As has been amply documented in studies of the era (see, for example, Zolberg, 1966), the politicians and parties that emerged in response to the belated political liberalization of the late colonial era operated in societies with a minuscule working class, at least in the classic sense of unionized low-income workers in Fordist manufacturing and mining industries, who made the electoral fortunes of the Labour Party in Great Britain and the Social Democratic Parties in northern Europe. Partly as a result, no strong leftist parties based on organized labor and representing class interests – or indeed any clear economic cleavages – emerged in the African political systems that gained independence in the 1960s.

One important consequence of this legacy is that African political parties were not then and are not today easily placed on a traditional left–right spectrum (Kitschelt and Kselman, 2010). Parties with names suggesting support for socialist ideas are common, of course, but their actual political rhetoric is rarely meaningfully programmatic on the left end of the ideological spectrum. Nor, finally, can one link the party systems across the region to the kind of historical cleavages that helped to define political parties in Western Europe early in its own democratic history as memorably analyzed by Lipset and Rokkan (1967) and which have proved remarkably resilient, even as new issues have come dominate and inspire the formation of new parties.

---

[2] For instance, Sklar (1979, p. 535) cites Markakis's (1974) estimate of 10,000 political elites among a population of twenty-five million in Ethiopia. Ngayap's (1983) estimates of the Cameroonian "ruling class" is even more circumscribed; he defines it as only the holders of the top state offices, which add up to just a thousand men and women.

Instead, given the priority of the anticolonial struggle and, in most countries, the absence of a significant anti-independence vote, parties had to adopt a nationalist rhetoric regarding the germane economic issues of the early postindependence years, including the Africanization of the army's officer corps, the extension of colonial administration salary scales and benefits to national civil servants, strict regulation of foreign direct investments, and state control over major economic interests. The importance of overt nationalist rhetoric has waned in most countries even if it remains a significant strand in the "sovereignty" rhetoric of all African parties, as we will suggest in Chapter 6 and below. One particularly salient contemporary manifestation is the issue of land assets, which retains visceral importance in the handful of countries, such as Zimbabwe (Ranger, 2004; Tendi, 2011) and South Africa (Gibson, 2009), that had a significant European settler population in the past.

The vast majority of new parties typically rejected capitalism, which they associated with imperialism and foreign interests, and embraced rhetoric that adopted some version of African socialism, in which nationalist and pan-African ideas combined with vague commitments to religion, communitarianism, and cultural heritage (Morgenthau, 1963; Sklar, 1988; Hyden, 2011). Even conservative politicians adopted the rhetoric of socialist economic planning, which was then much in vogue. In addition, ethnic divisions across parties made the rhetoric of nationalism attractive to parties that wanted to communicate the breadth of their support. Major nationalist parties soon found it convenient to criticize their opponents as tribalist to delegitimate the opposition. Anderson (2005) shows how the overt nationalism of the Kenya African National Union (KANU) was in part motivated by the desire to marginalize the Kenya African Democratic Union (KADU) and the electoral traction that it seemed to gain from its federalist policy orientation under the "Majimbo" label. KADU was derided as constituted of "tribalists who opposed the broader goals of nationalism" (Anderson, 2005, p. 547). Similarly, in Tanzania, in an essay designed to justify the move to a de jure single-party system, President Julius Nyerere (1967, p. 200) argued that "where there is one party, provided that it is identified with the nation as a whole, the foundations of democracy can be firmer, and the people can have more opportunity to exercise a real choice, than where you have two or more parties, each representing only a section of the community."

African party formation was also influenced by external events and ideas during this critical period. Thus, for instance, in francophone Africa, a number of parties emerged in the post-World War II era as the offshoots of networks fostered directly by the French Socialist and Communist parties, including perhaps the most influential single party in French West Africa around independence, the Rassemblement Democratique Africain (RDA). Its first leader, Félix Houphouët-Boigny, would eventually become the long-serving president for life of Côte d'Ivoire (Zolberg, 1969; Levine, 2004, pp. 74–81).

Still, the nationalism and anticolonial nature of the independence struggle as well as local ethnoregional dynamics proved to be much more determinative of the party systems that emerged than the outreach of the European left. Indeed, Houphouët-Boigny would learn valuable lessons on party organization and unity from the French Communist Party but would soon turn decidedly away from its ideological positions as he fashioned the Ivoirian offshoot of the RDA, the Parti Démocratique de la Côte d'Ivoire (PDCI), into the moderate, probusiness party with a strong nationalist orientation that would eventually govern Côte d'Ivoire for three decades following independence. Elsewhere, these early links to the European left would instill a progressive discourse in much party rhetoric that the African parties maintained long after their programmatic ambitions had ceased to be redistributive.

Even in the context of efforts to expand social services to rural populations, the elite ruling class in most countries continued the exclusionary policies of the colonial era, believing that the modern, educated citizens were better trusted with governance, and remained wary of the uneducated, illiterate masses. Willis and al-Batthani (2010, p. 198) describe the emergence of a norm of accepting the exclusion of potential voters in a bifurcated Sudanese state as well as institutional innovations that captured these ideas, such as additional representation for more educated portions of the population. As they explain, "the fear among the educated that the universal franchise might hand power to sectarian or tribal leaders who could command the votes of large numbers of uneducated followers, was to be a constant factor in the politics of independent Sudan" (Willis and al-Batthani, 2010, p. 198).

4.2.1 Party–Citizen Linkages

If the weakness of social cleavages in this critical time attenuated the partisan attachments of most voters, a number of other factors further served to weaken the linkages between parties and citizens, particularly outside of the capital city. The inexperienced fledgling political class that emerged just as colonialism was ending did not have multiple electoral cycles in which to learn its craft and gain the rhetoric or organizational capacity to connect with voters. Structural factors such as low literacy rates, poor infrastructure, low population densities, and large rural populations further complicated the efforts of parties.

Given these difficulties in party building, politicians quickly turned to traditional leaders and other local brokers in order to build up political support, particularly away from the capital and in rural areas. Party leaderships might be constituted by a relatively broad, cross ethnoregional alliances, but party building soon rested upon much narrower vertical networks of ethnic and religious communities, and political success relied largely on the ability to "integrate or coopt" key brokers (Hyden, 2011, p. 108). Modernizing elites were initially quick to reject or seek to sideline traditional authorities. In some countries, particularly those with large Muslim populations, tension between traditional elites and the "newly invented educated class" (Brenner, 2001), who derived their legitimacy from the former colonial state (Ekeh, 1975), was probably inevitable. Still, in most of the countries in the region, national parties eventually sought to accommodate, coopt, and support these brokers, generating a system of patronage-based politics and the creation of a governing coalition around what would become the single party by the end of the 1960s. Thus Sklar (1979, pp. 534–5) describes the formation of the dominant political class in Nigeria and Ethiopia as involving "the social and political coalescence of traditional rulers, administrative functionaries of both aristocratic and humble origins, and businessmen."[3]

The literature has long sought to establish intercountry variation on this dimension of party organization. Lemarchand (1972) was the first scholar to distinguish two types of linkages between national parties and these local brokers across the countries of the region. He argues that weaker parties and those facing less competition often settled for the pure brokerage model, in which these local linkages largely mitigated the party's weakness outside of the capital and a few major cities. In Nigeria, the Northern People's Congress (NPC) was a loose alliance of elites who relied on traditional authorities to mobilize northern voters but never established direct linkages to their electoral base (Sklar, 1963; Whitaker, 1970). Similarly, KANU in Kenya engaged in "little investment in party building" and worked largely as "a congeries of district and sub

---

[3] This is not to say that nationalist movements were completely inclusionary; many groups were excluded under the broad umbrella of nationalism (Aminzade, 2013).

district, personal and ethnic machines" that were poorly integrated at the national level (Bienen, 1974, p. 101).

Lemarchand (1972) distinguishes such parties from the Parti Socialiste (PS) in Senegal and the PDCI in Côte d'Ivoire, two dominant independence parties that also relied on local brokers but sought to integrate them in a political machine, fostering a more direct form of clientelism at the local level, leveraged with material benefits. Lemarchand's distinctions are not always empirically clear-cut, and the quality of integration achieved by the party needs to be further qualified. In Côte d'Ivoire, the PDCI worked to consolidate power and circumscribe the emergence of local political leadership outside of their networks, which strengthened the party's hold (see Zolberg, 1969, especially pp. 285–320) but would eventually result in the "de-participation" of rural voters (Crook, 1997, p. 137; on de-participation more generally, see Kasfir, 1976). Citizens came to accept the transactional dominance of the PDCI but also stopped paying attention to its rhetoric or to its participatory rituals (Fauré and Médard, 1982).

The degree of this demobilization varies across countries. Our main point is that in only a small minority of countries did the ruling party make substantial efforts to connect with and educate rural voters about policy choices, and even then, the party-citizen linkages were not comparatively strong. TANU in Tanzania, in particular, stands out in its ability to build a party organization that emphasized linkages to the countryside and develop a truly national party structure. To be sure, Bienen (1970b, pp. 12–13) pointed out that the central headquarters in Dar es Salaam in the mid-1960s included only twenty-five full-time professionals and complained about the party's "loose, decentralized forms of party organization" that hardly allowed it to promote national integration. Nonetheless, later observers would argue that TANU's decentralized organizational structure gave it a relatively strong presence in the countryside as well as flexibility and resilience, while its concerted efforts to build a party brand with a clear ideology did promote its mass appeal and legitimacy (Mihyo, 2003; Hyden, 2006).

Similarly, in Ghana during the 1950s and 1960s, Kwame Nkrumah's Convention People's Party was able to mobilize voters effectively through ideological appeals. It faced an active political opposition fueled by other elements of civil society and a comparatively large urban middle class. Local communities were actively involved in political competition and participation, which, according to Crook (1997, p. 203), "gave a political structuring to society" and oriented subsequent conflict "within the realm of the state." The parties and candidates who wanted to oppose the powerful CPP "tended to be mediated by personal links. But in the absence of such links, 'voters seemed to fall in with the powerful propaganda of the CPP" (Collier, 1982, p. 91, citing Zolberg, 1966, p. 20).

Some of the strongest parties did buttress their local presence to maintain order, usually after they came to power and could harness state resources. Writing about Botswana in the late 1990s, Holm et al. (1996, p. 48) observe the parties' relative strength vis-à-vis civil society. They claim that "no party including the primary opposition party of the last twenty-five years, the Botswana National Front (BNP), has made an attempt to mobilize existing social organizations to support their election campaigns. Rather, parties form their own local branches wherever they find supporters. These branches appeal to the voters directly in terms of communal feelings or problems." They describe parties usurping community organizations to directly address local problems. The Botswana government adopted a policy that banned members of the civil service, including teachers, army, and police, and *diKgosi* (traditional leaders) from contesting political office, thus stifling the emergence of new political players with backing from these communities (Molomo, 2000, p. 76). During independence, the state worked to minimize control by traditional authorities; in 1968, it stripped the *diKgosi* of their land allocation powers (Molomo, 2000, p. 76). This context provides an additional counterexample to the brokerage strategies relied upon by weaker parties.

Broadly speaking, one must not exaggerate the range of linkages that the main African parties managed to establish with their mass publics, particularly outside the major cities. With a few exceptions, the difference between the strongest and weakest parties is one of degree. The small number of competitive electoral cycles and the inexperience and youth of the political class, combined with the limited reach of the state institutions inherited from colonialism, ensured that political parties were on the whole not well rooted in society. We will return to this variation in the relationship between political parties and African societies below.

4.2.2 The Single-Party Era

Three distinct patterns in party strength emerged in the two decades following independence and before the wave of democratization in the early 1990s that are related to the evolution of African regimes in the 1960s and 1970s.

As we discussed in Chapter 2, one can distinguish between two sets of countries that gained their independence in the early 1960s, depending on the dynamics of the very first elections. The winners of the first elections all sought to protect their hold on power. When the winning nationalist party had managed to secure a broad national coalition, a stable civilian single-party regime overseen by this party emerged in most cases. This was true in Côte d'Ivoire, Zambia, Senegal, Kenya, and Tanzania. These regimes would conduct regular single-party elections with various degrees of internal competition until the demise of the single party in the early 1990s. They would be less likely to fall to military coups. Single parties in these regimes exhibited different levels of cohesion and integrative capacity, although they should be viewed as comparatively weak relative to parties in other regions (Zolberg, 1966). For the most part, these parties lacked the organizational capacity to mobilize citizens and did not gain the loyalty that stronger linkages with society might have given them, but like dominant parties in other regions, they maintained power through "mutually reinforcing ... political and economic monopolies," in Greene's (2007, p. 6) felicitous phrase.

A large scholarly literature shows how the emergent single parties resorted to elite clientelism to ensure the support of a wide variety of regional, ethnic, and traditional elites across as much of the territory as possible. This is what Bayart called the "reciprocal assimilation of elites" (Bayart, 1993, pp. 150–79 and passim) and Rothchild (1985) termed "hegemonial exchange." Unlike the situation in a multiparty democracy, in which a supermajority confers little extra legitimacy and governing coalitions typically limit themselves to a large enough coalition to maintain an effective majority, postindependence single-party leaders needed buy-in from a supermajority in order to legitimate their attempts to centralize power and curtail democratic freedoms. Thus civilian single-party regimes typically sought to include representative elites from most of the main ethnoregional groups of the country in their party structures and government cabinets, even when real power might be much more circumscribed. The rhetorical emphasis on national unity for the single party resulted in broad and vague programmatic platforms that would appeal to a majority of the citizenry and elide divisive issues, an issue to which we will return in Chapter 6.

In a second modal pattern of party dynamics in early independence countries, party fractionalism developed in the immediate postindependence period, and no single party managed to secure this broad reciprocal assimilation to emerge as politically hegemonic. In these countries, military governments were considerably more likely to emerge, following one or more coups, as we discussed in Chapter 2. This pattern can be seen in Benin, the Democratic Republic of the Congo, Niger, Nigeria, the Republic of the Congo, and Upper Volta (Burkina Faso). The resulting governments convened fewer elections and typically invested fewer resources in creating a strong national political party (Bratton and van de Walle, 1997, pp. 68–82). Some military governments never organized a political party, preferring to rule through decree and the state of emergency. No national legislative elections were convened in Nigeria from the end of the first republic in the mid-1960s to the beginning of the second republic in 1979 and then again from the end of the second republic at the end of 1983 to the beginning of the short-lived Third Republic in 1993.

Within this broad category of countries, military governments with a Marxist inspiration tended to try to create a more ambitious vanguard party with integrative ambitions. These include, for instance, Kerekou's Benin People's Revolutionary Party (PRPB), which won three single-party elections with overwhelming majorities in 1979, 1984, and 1989. In the Republic of the Congo, the military ruled through the Congo Labor Party (PCT) between 1969 and 1992 and again since 1997, with single-party plebiscitary elections in 1973, 1979, 1984, and 1989. Despite their nationalist and lofty Marxist-Leninist rhetoric, these fractionalized and ethnically unstable political systems created single parties that were most citizens viewed as a "vehicle for ethnic supremacy" (Bienen, 1983, p. 116).

Most postcoup military governments initially vented against the parties and politicians whose corruption and ineffectiveness had justified the military's intervention, but these governments eventually found it useful to seek electoral legitimation through the creation of a single party. Few of these parties proved effective in mobilizing citizens or providing regimes with added legitimacy. In Togo and Equatorial Guinea, the single party does not appear to have played an integrative function at all and was poorly implanted across the territory, achieving little beyond contributing clumsily to the cult of personality around the president (on Togo, see Toulabor, 1986).

It is tempting to argue that the single-party systems that emerged from military rule were much weaker organizationally than the civilian-dominated single parties. As we shall see below, however, the tangible evidence for greater organizational capacity and cohesion is actually quite weak. On the other hand, it seems clear that the civilian single parties benefited from greater legitimacy and popularity, at least in part because they ruled over countries in which there was a natural majority social coalition in power. The majority of military governments and the single parties that issued from them, by contrast, presided over much more divided societies, and the single party was often ethnically and regionally more narrow in its support base.

A third category of states comprises the late independence countries, including all of the Portuguese colonies and the settler states of Southern Africa. These countries experienced a long, more conflictual process of decolonization and a later independence.[4] The longer anticolonial struggle helped to season the political class, while the long periods of clandestine activities and active repression by the colonial authorities created party structures that were more resilient and organizationally capacious.

Perhaps as a result, party leaders in these states were older and more experienced than their postindependence peers and over time had been able to build on strong cosmopolitan networks outside of their home countries. Operating covertly during the long anticolonial struggle, these parties had needed to build up effective organizations to survive, while future party leaders also had the opportunity to prove their competence in the conflict period (Tripp, 2015). In Zimbabwe, Zimbabwe African National Union–Patriotic Front (ZANU-PF) leveraged its paramilitary roots in very local level community units in order to build a network of decentralized party leaders who could compete in elections at every level of governance throughout most of the country's territory (Dendere, 2015, p. 82; Dorman, 2016). Some parties' assistance from the Soviet Union pushed them in a Marxist-Leninist direction, and other parties were shaped by ideologically charged revolutionary leaders such as Amil Cabral and Eduardo Mondlane (Sklar, 1988), but in practice, it is difficult to see how these circumstances have informed the parties' ideological heritage in the multiparty period.[5]

The struggle to reach power forged political parties with more robust links to citizens at the local level. These parties did not necessarily enjoy close linkages to African society, given their inability to campaign publicly, but they did gain significant credit with African populations for

---

4 The Portuguese colonies gained their independence in 1974–1975, Zimbabwe in 1980, and Namibia in 1989. Majority rule was not achieved in South Africa until 1994.

5 Decades out, it is more difficult to detect how this heritage shapes contemporary policy making, as most countries have embraced capitalism (Sklar, 1988, pp. 19–20).

their struggle. In every case, these parties would gain overwhelming electoral victories following independence in the 1980s or, for South Africa majority rule, in 1994. The party brand was legitimized by the fight for independence; these parties became solid "issue owners" of national sovereignty, as we will discuss further in Chapter 6.

At the same time, the role of armed struggle in the decolonization process forged close relations between the military and the party, and in all these cases except that in South Africa, the stability of the postindependence era has been built as much on control of the means of coercion as on party organization and legitimacy, an issue to which we will return below.

Finally, we add to this category of partial exceptions the second-generation single parties that emerged after a protracted civil war in Ethiopia, Rwanda, and Uganda. These cases share with the Portuguese and settler colonies the fact that the party came to power through a long and bitter armed struggle against an incumbent regime. However, its subservience to the armed wing of the movement that came to power through the barrel of the gun lessened the legitimacy of the party once power was achieved, not least because of the ethnic divisions that prevailed in all three countries. The single-party regimes that emerged have proven to be unusually disciplined and coherent, but these regimes owe their durability more to impressive coercive capacity and success at promoting economic success than to the national legitimacy of their dominant parties (Themnér, 2017).

4.2.3 Implications

The process of party formation in the postindependence era has two important implications for contemporary African parties. First, and most generally, many leaders learned to employ elections as tools of power maintenance and legitimacy. Rather than opening up opportunities for broader political competition, the executive could use elections to build legitimacy and create networks of dependency for aspiring candidates who needed resources for their own constituencies. Legislative elections, which could be very competitive, were used by many presidents to weaken the political class, formally united under the banner of the single party, and, in the process, to buttress executive power. Presidents could manipulate nominations or primary results to discipline ambitious party members and remind them of presidential power. Moreover, by keeping competition restricted to a small network of elites, few actors outside of this network had an opportunity to participate in politics or to experiment with policy messages, find a programmatic constituency, or build a credible reputation as issue owners.

A second pattern set in the single-party era that has had lasting influence concerns the reliance on existing vertical networks of mobilization. Most African parties in this era did not become the primary organizations brokering societal linkages with the state. Parties typically outsourced their core functions of constituency service and mobilization that might typically have contributed to the growth of organizational capacity and local legitimacy. To be sure, brokerage strategies were attractive to party leaders in part because of the limited capacity of the fledgling parties that had emerged only years before independence. The growing budgetary crisis circumscribed the ability of these single-party states to use service delivery and public spending to build more coherent patronage machines. Traditional authorities and local big men proved to be cheaper, if less efficient linkage devices. In addition, although this varied across and even within countries (Bayart, 1993, pp. 150–79), the reliance on local elites was in harmony with the "reciprocal assimilation of elites" logic that undergirded these regimes. In any event, the reliance on local brokers ensured that parties did not gain these capacities and that their linkages to citizens remained relatively weak through the single-party era.

As we will discuss in Chapters 5 and 6, this legacy has meant that many parties are uncertain about their own constituencies and the preferences of the citizens who might vote for them. In this environment of uncertainty, parties typically champion safe valence issues and avoid discourse that might be too divisive, even when it would resonate with their electorates. Relative exceptions included the more successful mass parties, such as the Tanganyika African National Union (TANU) in Tanzania and its contemporary successor party, the Chama Cha Mapinduzi (CCM), which made comparatively greater efforts to communicate directly to its constituents, documented in the late 1960s by Bienen (1970b); these strategies have sustained the continued dominance of CCM in Tanzania. In describing the Tanzanian party's institutionalized strength, Weghorst (2015, p. 132) explains that the party controlled elite leadership positions. Nyerere's camp's power gradually eroded, and party leadership was determined by wealth and influence (Weghorst, 2015, p. 132, citing Southall (2006, p. 246). By the contemporary period, the party had become so organizationally strong that it could recruit young members through party-sponsored "youth soccer teams, church groups, and scouts programs" (Weghorst, 2015, p. 304). The party managed the election process carefully, and prospective candidates "had to demonstrate their mastery of the content of the manifesto" and "were no longer allowed to promise their constituencies with special favors" (Collier, 1982, p. 131, citing Maring, 1978, pp. 123–4).

4.3 CONTINUITY AND CHANGE IN THE MULTIPARTY ERA

Since the return of the multiparty era, three relatively clear patterns can be discerned relating to parties and party systems. These patterns generally reproduce historical patterns and can be explained in large part by the social origins of parties as discussed above. These three patterns are the significant continuity in the political class, in which most senior politicians can be linked back to the old single party; the paradoxical failure of authoritarian successor parties to win elections unless they maintained control of the presidency during these "transitions"; and the emergence of a modal party system, in which a party with a dominant legislative majority is combined with a constellation of small relatively ephemeral parties around it. We discuss each in turn in this section before explaining these patterns in Section 4.4.

4.3.1 Continuity in the Political Class

If transitions to independence generated a first critical juncture for the emergence of new political actors, the Third Wave transitions to multiparty democracy and subsequent elections represented similar types of junctures. In countries that permitted and acknowledged multiparty actors, multiparty politics created new incentives for a reemergence and reshuffling of political leaders. The uncertainty of the transitions themselves provided breathing room for politicians to redefine themselves and forge new alliances. Each subsequent electoral cycle represented an opportunity to prove one's comparative strength and renegotiate one's position within an existing party, to broker a coalition with allies, or to split off and create one's own party.

The first pattern that we want to highlight is the striking amount of continuity that can be observed in the political class at the apex of the relevant party structures has, even as the party landscape has proven to be transient and changing. The small political class that first emerged in the 1950s and 1960s from tight social networks of like-minded educated urban elites have proven remarkably resilient in the multiparty era. Writing in the late 1990s, Richard Crook and James Manor (1998, p. 137) describes the continuity of the political elite in Côte d'Ivoire:

> Côte d'Ivoire has been ruled not just by the same regime, but by the same small leadership group associated with President Houphouët-Boigny since 1952, when the French colonial administration decided to co-opt Houphouët-Boigny's party (the PDCI) as their local successors. Although the accession of Bédié represented a shift to a slightly younger generation (Bédié was born in 1934), the core of the elite, recruited over the decades through intermarriage and political and economic accumulation, has remained remarkably stable. The elite itself recruited heavily from the civil service, and it is now probably one of the most technocratic (and oldest in generational terms) in Africa.

More specifically, we can say that the single party was typically the paradoxical crucible for the "new" leaders of the democratic era in Africa. The overwhelming majority of politicians who were successful after the transitions of the early 1990s were men and women who had once belonged to the single party. Quantin's (1995) striking observation that not a single president elected in the early years of the democratic era had been an open dissident during the single-party era remains revealing of this continuity, even if his claim is no longer correct, as several more recently elected presidents were young enough to be able to claim links to opposition movements as students before 1990 (see also Chabal and Daloz, 1999). Alpha Condé, born in 1938 and president of Guinea since 2010, fits the definition of a historic dissident and is perhaps the single full exception to this generalization. Another partial exception is President Macky Sall of Senegal (born 1961), a much younger man, who had been active in a Maoist party as a student before rising in the ranks of the opposition Senegalese Democratic Party (PDS), as the country began to provide more space for the opposition in the late 1990s.

Few prominent candidates in early elections emerged from completely outside of the political class of the single-party regime (Young, 1993; Daloz et al., 1999). To be sure, some had left the government long enough before the transition to appear to the public as new men. For instance, Pascal Lissouba, the first democratically elected president in Congo, had been in political exile in Paris through most of the 1980s, but he had first been a prominent politician after independence, prime minister from 1963 to 1966, and on the Central Committee of the Parti Congolais du Travail (PCT) in the 1970s. In Mali, Alpha Oumar Konaré created a new political party, Alliance pour la Démocratie au Mali (ADEMA), in

1990 as opposition to the ruling Union Démocratique du Peuple Malien (UDPM) of Moussa Traoré was starting to spark the public protests that would eventually result in a transition to democracy. Relying on a grassroots network of educators and health professionals, ADEMA would eventually compete and win in Mali's first multiparty election in 1992. Konaré's training as a historian and his activities as a newspaper editor in the late 1980s gave him credentials as a civil society activist, yet he was also a member of the political elite in Bamako. He had held positions in the Sudanese Union/African Democratic Rally (US-RDA), the party of President Modibo Keïta in the 1960s, and had served as Minister of Youth, Sports, Arts, and Culture from 1978 to 1980 in the single-party regime that he would later help to topple (Thiriot, 1999). By the standards of the politicians who would emerge in the 1990s, Konaré could be considered something of an outsider. By contrast, Pascal Ange Patassé, the first democratically elected president in the Central African Republic, had served in every ministerial cabinet between 1966 and 1976 under President Jean-Bédel Bokassa before joining the opposition to Presidents David Dacko and André Kolingba. In Kenya, Mwai Kibaki, the first democratically elected president, had served in every KANU government from 1963 on before leaving the government of President Daniel arap Moi in 1991 to form his own political party.

Figure 4.1 confirms our intuition that the old single party remains the typical recruitment mechanism for the political class. We code all parties

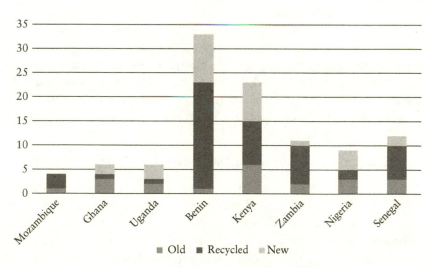

FIGURE 4.1. *Legislative parties in the multiparty era*

that have held legislative seats in our eight focus countries since transitions to multiparty elections for which we could find information about the party leadership. Parties are then sorted into one of three categories, depending on their leadership's participation in party politics before the transition to multiparty elections: pre-multiparty era party ("Old"); splinter, rebranded, or coalition party ("Recycled"); or a completely new party ("New"). "Old" parties include postindependence parties as well as single-era parties and any opposition parties during these two periods. Parties that are labeled "Recycled" are new parties with leaders who previously participated in other parties; we can trace leaders' involvement in the pre-multiparty era when they competed with other parties. "New" parties include parties with leaders who do not have clear links to parties in either era.

Figure 4.1 demonstrates that the modal party in our relatively representative eight African countries is a recycled party formed by a party leader who has left an older party, and the overwhelming majority of such parties can be traced to the incumbent party before 1990. However, we also note variations in the number of new parties in each country. Consistent with descriptions of Kenyan politics, we see a large number of splinter parties and rebranded parties, which offer new political vehicles for the same political players (Elischer, 2013). In Mozambique, all parties can trace their roots to FRELIMO or RENAMO, while in Nigeria, most parties appear to have diverse leadership from outside of the older political class. While the federal system in Nigeria may facilitate the creation of parties by outsiders, sources of this variation are important to explore in future research. Depending on parties' goals, such being elected or being incorporated into coalitions and patronage systems, and opportunities for advancement in existing parties, incentives for deserting old parties and starting new ones will differ by country. However, more generally, the figure confirms the critical historical role of the single party in the recruitment of the current political class on the continent.

4.3.2 The Failure of the Authoritarian Successor Parties

The inability of authoritarian successor parties to survive electoral defeat constitutes our second generalization about the current era. The 1990s created a new critical juncture for political parties that would undermine the logic of national unity that single parties had sought to maintain. While the extent to which opposition parties were allowed to freely compete varied widely, the widespread legalization of opposition parties created incentives for the emergence of new parties all over the region (van de Walle, 2003; Barkan, 2008; Elischer, 2013; Riedl, 2014), and a large number of new parties have indeed emerged.

The fate of the old single party in the new multiparty era reveals two primary causal factors that continue to shape African parties and party systems. First, the failure of most of these parties to forge lasting bonds with the citizenry typically condemned to oblivion the authoritarian parties that lost power during the transition. However, the era reveals the continued advantages of incumbency and control of the executive branch. Simply put, the second generalization that can be made about the current era is that the old single party either managed to remain in power or withered away in the ranks of the opposition. As we will see, only three parties that were in power in 1990 have managed to get reelected following an electoral defeat: the African Party of Independence of Cape Verde (PAICV) in Cape Verde, the National Democratic Congress (NDC) in Ghana, and the Mouvement National pour la Société du Développement (MNSD) in Niger.

Again, several distinct modal patterns can be identified among African countries regarding the party legacy left from the single-party era. We identify four patterns. First, in countries in which a transition to multiparty rule came through political protests and the defeat of old single party in the transition election, the latter was subsequently pushed to the margins of political competition or totally eliminated, as shown in Table 4.1. In other regions of the world, authoritarian successor parties have demonstrated the organizational capacity and legitimacy capital to bounce back and return to power (Loxton, 2015), but in Africa, the initial loss of power seems to have constituted a virtual death sentence (for a useful discussion on the African cases, see LeBas, 2016). The parties either have completely disappeared from current political life or have survived only on the fringes of the opposition. The case of Zambia is particularly striking. The United National Independence Party (UNIP) was widely viewed as a powerful and relatively legitimate political party from independence to the 1991 transition (Gertzel, Baylies, and Szeftel, 1984), yet it was never able to adjust to being out of power in the democratic era and quickly withered away to political insignificance (Burnell, 2001; Momba, 2003).

The single exception is, oddly enough, the MNSD in Niger, which was created only in 1989 and then was defeated in the first elections of 1993 but managed to make a comeback following a military coup, with electoral victories in 1999 and 2000, thanks at least in part to strategic alliances with other parties. However, the MNSD has not returned to power

TABLE 4.1. *The fate of the single party, following protest-driven democratization*

Country	Single party before 1990 (date of creation)	Results founding election	Latest electoral results
Benin	PRPB (1975)	Dissolved (1990)	–
Burundi	UPRONA (1958)	21% (1993)	2.5% (2015)
The Comoros	UCP (1982)	Boycotted elections (1992)	Dissolved 1996[a]
Central African Republic	RDC (1987)	NA[b] (1993)	4.6% (2011)
Democratic Republic of the Congo	MPR (1967)	Dissolved (1997)[c]	–
Lesotho	BNP (1959)	23% (1993)	4.3% (2012)
Madagascar	AREMA (1976)	Did not compete (1993)	Split into multiple factions
Malawi	MCP (1960)	34% (1994)	17% (2014)
Mali	UPDM (1976)	Dissolved (1991)	–
Namibia	DTA (1977)	29% (1989)	5% (2014)
Niger	MNSD (1989)	31% (1993)	12% (2016)
Republic of the Congo	PCT (1969)	NA[d] (1992)	NA[b] (2012)
São Tomé	MLSTP (1960)	31% (1991)	25% (2014)
South Africa	NP (1915)	20% (1994)	Disbanded, 2005
Zambia	UNIP (1959)	26% (1991)	0.2% (2016)

Percentage of popular vote in the legislature.
[a]The UCP was reformed for the 2015 elections but received just 0.5 percent of the vote.
[b]In 1993 elections, vote totals were not available, but RDC won 13 of 85 seats.
[c]Under popular pressure, President Mobutu ended the single-party regime in 1991, but no legislative election was convened until 2006.
[d]In 1992 elections, vote totals were not available but PCT won 18 of 125 seats; in the 2012 elections, PCT won 89 of 139 seats.

since another military coup in 2009. To be sure, the PCT reemerged in the Republic of the Congo, but only in the context of the electoral autocracy that Denis Sassou Nguesso imposed after the civil war that brought him back to power in 1997. The PCT had little capacity to win a relatively free and fair election, making a violent overthrow of the elected government its only viable option for a return to power (Bazenguissa-Ganga, 1996, 1999). One might also note the more honorable partial exception of the MCP in Malawi, which has remained a viable if minority legislative party, thanks to a strong ethnoregional base in central Malawi. It should be noted that of these three exceptional cases, only Malawi was categorized above as having had a stable broad-based civilian single-party regime before 1990. Indeed, one of the puzzling findings of this exercise is how little the age of the single party seems to matter for its sustainability in the multiparty era.

The three other modal regime trajectories are composed of the states in which the party in power did not initially give up power as a result of the protest-driven democratic transitions of the early 1990s. These countries are listed in Table 4.2. Here, we can distinguish three variants. First are the countries where the single party was able to negotiate the return to regular electoral competition and the legalization of opposition political parties in the early 1990s but with few enough other political concessions that it was able to remain in power. These former single parties have more often been able to remain the dominant party when they have been able to combine regular elections with an uneven playing field that allows them to retain various advantages of incumbency. In the resulting electoral autocracies, in Cameroon, Chad, Equatorial Guinea, Gabon, Tanzania, and Togo, the single party has remained dominant, albeit often with the help of the kinds of the antidemocratic practices that we discussed in Chapter 3.[6] After the mid to late 1990s, these regimes were firmly in control and almost entirely untroubled by electoral competition.

Closely related is a third group of parties in regimes that emerged from liberation struggles. The dominant parties in the Portuguese colonies and the settler states of southern Africa provide examples of pre-1990 parties that have done exceptionally well in the past quarter-century. They include the Popular Movement for the Liberation of Angola (MPLA) in Angola, FRELIMO in Mozambique, African Party for the Independence of Guinea and Cape Verde (PAIGC) in Guinea-Bissau and its offshoot PAICV in Cape Verde, ZANU-PF in Zimbabwe, South West Africa's People's Organization (SWAPO) in Namibia, and the African National Congress (ANC) in South Africa. To be clear, there are various reasons contributing to these parties' continued success. Some of them have managed to remain in power through fairly overt antidemocratic manipulation and coercion, such as ZANU-PF in Zimbabwe and the MPLA in

---

[6] Côte d'Ivoire also fits this category but more awkwardly, since it formed an electoral alliance with the RPR in the mid-1990s and reentered power as a junior partner in President Alassane Ouattarra's governing coalition following the 2011 elections.

Angola (Soares de Oliveira, 2015), But others have done well in the democratic era because of a combination of their ideological and nationalistic brands and solid party organizations. The only unambiguously successful authoritarian successor party is the PAICV in Cape Verde, which returned to power via the presidency in 2001 and regained its legislative majority in 2006, keeping it to the present.

TABLE 4.2. *The fate of the incumbent parties that survived the 1990s transitions by regime trajectory, 1990–2015*

Regime trajectories	Single party in 1990 (date of creation)	Results in first multiparty elections	Latest electoral results
1. Autocratic Survival			
Burkina Faso	CODP-MT[a] (1989)	48.5% (1992)	13.2% (2015)
Cameroon	RDPC (1960)	45.5% (1992)	78% (2013)
Chad	MPS (1990)	49.6% (1997)[b]	58.5% (2011)[b]
Côte d'Ivoire	PDCI (1946)	71.7% (1990)	28.9% (2011)
Djibouti	RPP (1979)	74.5% (1992)	61.5% (2013)[c]
Equatorial Guinea	PDGE (1987)	69.8% (1993)	99.9%(2013)[b]
Gabon	PDG (1945)	52.5%	74.2% (2011)
Gambia	PPP (1959)	69.4% (1992)	Boycotted (2012)
Guinea	– (PUP, 1993)	53.5% (1995)	0.05% (2013)
Mauritania	– (PRDR, 1992)	67.7% (1992)	0.02% (2013)[b]
Seychelles	SPPF (1964)	59.5% (1993)	49.2% (2016)
Tanzania	TANU/CCM (1954)	79.6% (1995)	55% (2015)
Togo	RPT (1969)[d]	43.2% (1994)[b]	68.1% (2013)[b]
2. Late Independence/Post-Conflict			
Angola	MPLA (1956)	53.7% (1992)	71.6% (2012)
Cape Verde	PAICV (1956)	34% (1991)	53% (2011)
Ethiopia	EPRDF (1989)	88.5% (1994)	91.2% (2010)[b]
Guinea-Bissau	PAIGC (1956)	46.4% (1994)	48% (2014)
Mozambique	FRELIMO (1962)	44.3% (1994)	55.9% (2014)
Uganda	NRM (1986)	66.8% (2006)[b]	51% (2011)
Rwanda	RPF (1979)[d]	73.8% (2003)	76.2% (2013)
Zimbabwe	ZANU-PF (1963)	63% (1980)	61.1% (2013)

(continued)

TABLE 4.2 *(continued)*

Regime trajectories	Single party in 1990 (date of creation)	Results in first multiparty elections	Latest electoral results
3. Top-Down Democratizers			
Ghana	– (NDC 1992)	77.5% (1992)	46.4% (2012)
Kenya	KANU (1944)	59.6% (1992)[b]	2.4% (2013)
Senegal	PS (1958)	82.2% (1976)	– (2012)

Notes: Countries that experienced sustained conflict such as Liberia, Sierra Leone, and Somalia are not included, given long interruptions in elections. Also excluded are Nigeria and Sudan, which did not fit any of the modal patterns discussed in the text, and Botswana and Mauritius, which did not have an authoritarian episode before 1990.
[a]The OPD-LM would add several junior partners and change its name to the Congress for Democracy and Progress (CDP) in 1996.
[b]Share of seats (voting totals were not available).
[c]The RPP incorporated four other parties in 2003 to form the UMP in 2003.
[d]In Togo, the RPT was renamed the UNIR (Union pour la Republique in 2012); in Rwanda, the RPF was initially called the Rwandese Alliance for National Unity (RANU).

Over time as well, these parties gained credibility as issue owners of the national sovereignty. For instance, SWAPO leveraged its former status as a liberation movement to gain recognition from the international community as the "sole and authentic representative" of the Namibian people, which is evident from their party slogan "SWAPO is the people and the people are SWAPO" (Melber, 2010, p. 203). As a political party, SWAPO often invokes its "struggle narrative" as the "liberator of the people" to legitimize its position as a dominant party (Melber, 2003). Melber (2013, p. 57) argues that SWAPO's alliances with civil society organizations during the struggle for liberation has made these groups less critical and more easily coopted in the multiparty period. SWAPO denounced the opposition as "agents of imperialism and remote-controlled pawns acting in the interest of regime change" (Melber, 2010, p. 205). Similarly, the ANC continues to exploit its unique role in the liberation struggle to distinguish it from all other South African parties (Ferree, 2010). The ANC has attempted to brand opposition parties as "white" to damage their credibility (Ferree 2010). Liberation parties maintain power by drawing on their legitimacy as issue owners of sovereignty, but also through coercive power born of the regime's close relationship with the bureaucratic state (Southall 2013).

In a fourth pattern, in Ghana, Senegal, and Kenya, top-down political reform was often more incremental and not completed until after 2000, but in the end, it was considerably more thorough, and it has brought about real political alternation as the old single parties have found it hard to survive the loss of power.[7] In Senegal, the formerly dominant PS did not fully recover from its defeat in the presidential elections of 2000 (Diop, 2006; Resnick, 2013b) and is not currently represented in the legislature, although it remains a minor player in Senegalese electoral politics, having notably won the municipal elections in the capital Dakar in 2009. In Kenya, a complex process of factionalism and fragmentation has turned KANU into a minor party following its defeat in the 2002 elections (Throup and Hornsby, 1998; Wanjohi, 2003; Lynch, 2011). Ghana presents us with a more curious exception: President Jerry Rawlings's NDC lost power to the New Patriotic Party (NPP) in the elections of 2000, following top-down democratization and Rawlings's retirement. Nonetheless, the NDC managed to maintain itself in opposition and returned to power in 2008 before losing power back to the NPP in 2016. Indeed, Ghana constitutes perhaps the only case in contemporary Africa of two fairly evenly balanced political parties engaged in regular alternation over multiple electoral cycles (Whitfield, 2009; Osei, 2016).

In sum, the ability of the incumbent authoritarian parties to remain relevant after the transitions to multiparty politics in the 1990s seems almost entirely related to their ability to retain control of the presidency, in more cases than not because of the tilting the electoral field in their favor that results from the discrete exercise of incumbency advantages to aggressive repression and coercion, often buttressed by the intervention of the military. The argument that interparty variation in party building and organization explains why some parties were able to survive even after they had lost the benefits of incumbency does not appear to pass the smell test, despite a very small number of sui generis exceptions, such as Ghana. In other cases, it is too early to be sure. In Tanzania or Uganda, say, incumbent parties could yet prove us wrong by losing power someday and subsequently managing to return to power.

---

[7] We did not include Nigeria in this category, but its trajectory is in many respects similar, since there has been progressive political liberalization since the 1999 elections. The People's Democratic Party was the dominant player in politics until its defeat in the 2015 elections. It still managed to retain 125 seats in the 360-seat House of Representatives and may yet return to power.

4.3.3 Dominant Party Systems

Finally, a third generalization concerns the party systems that have emerged in the region. A paradox confronts us when we look at the emerging party systems in Africa over the past quarter-century: the dizzying number of political parties that appears in each election cycle combined with a very small number of parties with a meaningful role in the legislature after the election. The number of registered parties is typically substantial, generally over 100 (Kelly, 2018). The number of parties fielding candidates in either legislative or presidential elections is much smaller, the number of parties actually present in the legislature is even smaller, and the number of parties with more than one or two legislators is smaller still.

In Senegal, some 174 parties were registered in 2010 (Kelly, 2018), yet only twenty-four parties fielded candidates in the legislative elections of July 2012. The incumbent president's new coalition party, United in Hope, won 119 of 150 seats, and the outgoing majority party, the PDS, won 12 seats. The remaining nineteen seats were shared across eleven parties, seven of which won a single seat.[8] These results were not unusual for the region, although Senegal's elections are unusually well documented. Thirteen parties competed in Zambia's 2016 legislative elections, including six new parties. Two parties shared 138 of the 156 seats, but 14 independent candidates won seats. Over 150 parties were registered in Madagascar, and 31 parties won seats in its 2013 parliamentary elections (no data were available on unsuccessful parties), although 22 of them only won 1 single seat and an additional 25 independents won seats. In Benin, where over 125 parties are registered, only 20 parties competed in the 2105 elections, and 56 of the 83 seats were won by 3 parties.

How can one explain this proliferation? In some cases, a politician wanted to run under the dominant party label but was not selected to run by the party hierarchy or lost in some competitive primary. The politician then chooses to run either as an independent or as head of his or her own party, hoping to be reintegrated eventually into the dominant party. This phenomenon drives the proliferation of splinter parties that was mentioned above. Many African political parties do not adhere to democratic and transparent intraparty candidate selection. In Tanzania, Weghorst (2015, p. 23) has documented the secrecy and politicization of

---

[8] Fourteen candidates also competed in the February 2012 presidential elections, nine of them getting aggregate less than 2 percent of the vote.

party primaries, which often thwart the public's preferred candidate from running.

In other instances, new parties or politicians profit from electoral dissatisfaction with incumbents at the legislative or municipal levels. Opalo (2015) has documented the very low reelection rates in legislative elections in countries such as Kenya or Zambia, which are often no higher than 50 percent. He argues compellingly that these low reelection rates serve to weaken parties, particularly those in the opposition, but at the same time, the low rates of reelection also serves to encourage the creation of new parties.

In other cases, a party is formed around a minority ethnic group, with just one or two candidates, whose strategy is to win the seat and then attempt to gain the presidential majority by leveraging the support of their ethnic community into a position of influence in the government and, they hope, resources for their constituents. In contrast to ruling or dominant parties, opposition parties are more likely to be ethnic or have a regional base (Cheeseman and Ford, 2007). Raising and guaranteeing resources to support coalition formation is considerably more complicated for such parties that are not in power (Arriola, 2012), and they are less likely to have access to national networks to build their party, thus increasing the allure of a deal with the incumbent.

It should be added that cross-national variation in party and party system trends in the region follow logics that are well explained by comparative theories of party systems. Bigger countries and greater ethnic or cultural heterogeneity in the electorate lead to a greater number of parties, ceteris paribus (see Elischer, 2013; see also the debate on this in Brambor et al., 2007; Mozaffar et al., 2003), even if the salience of ethnic voting varies widely across countries (Koter, 2016). Institutional effects found elsewhere also seem to apply to the region; proportional representation and multimember districts seem to increase the number of parties, as elsewhere (Brambor et al., 2007).

In any event, the effective number of parties in African legislatures is actually quite low, despite this plethora of candidates and parties. As Table 4.3 indicates, the average party system in Africa over the course of the past two decades has been roughly two to three effective parties represented in the legislature. Ghana, in which two major parties alternate in power and evenly shared all of the seats in the 2016 elections (eleven parties were competing), arguably has a "two-party system." Yet Ghana is fairly unusual, and the "effective number of parties" statistic does not seem very useful in conveying party dynamics in countries such as Senegal or Zambia.

TABLE 4.3. *Legislative parties, by election, 1990–2015*

Election	No. of countries	Winning party, % of seats	Winning party, % of votes	No. of parties winning seats	Effective no. of parties	2nd party % of seats
1	46	63.1	56.2	6.4	3.1	18.6
2	43	67.8	59.1	6.8	2.3	16.6
3	44	64.7	53.4	6.8	2.8	19.9
4	39	65.2	54.1	6.1	2.2	20.2
5	34	61.6	49.6	7.4	2.6	21.1
6	13	59.2	48.2	6.6	2.0	24.7
7	3	44.7	33.7	8.0	3.4	22.6

Table 4.3 also suggests that the modal party system in the region is characterized by a dominant party with around two-thirds of the parliamentary seats. That party is invariably the incumbent president's party. In general, opposition parties are more likely to be associated with a single ethnoregional group, whereas the government party is more likely to include broad national support even if the core leadership of that party can significantly overrepresent a narrower ethnic base (Wahman, 2017). The causal arrow in this relationship is not clear, however. Are national parties more likely to be in power and ethnic parties less likely? Or is it that once in power, parties are more likely to become national parties, while the costs to opposition parties to retain a narrow ethnic base are smaller? Whatever the causal chain, it seems clear that this relationship reinforces the advantages held by the incumbent party.

It is true that eighty-eight elections in thirty-two countries resulted in only a plurality of seats for the president's party, but even in these countries, the president typically enjoyed a comfortable working majority in the legislature, either because the president got the reliable support of independents or because he was able to leverage the support of several small parties with ministerial appointments. In a minority of cases, the party system really is fractionalized, and the president is unable to assert control of the legislature; the result is political paralysis and rule by decree. For instance, in Benin, the 1991 elections that brought Nicephore Soglo to power gave his party, the Union for the Triumph of Democratic Renewal (UTRD), only twelve of sixty-four seats in the legislature, and thirteen other parties won seats, at least in part because of the proportional representation system that the transition had put into place. Soglo laboriously sought to maintain a shifting coalition of support for his policies but with uneven success, and his term was marked by legislative paralysis. By contrast, his successors have typically run as independents and then managed to avoid Soglo's difficulties by cobbling together a legislative supermajority based on expansive patronage (on Benin elections, see Banégas, 2003; Bierschenk, 2006; Koter, 2016, pp. 82–95).

Using the president's control over state resources to establish control over opposition parties in the legislature has been much more common in these elections. In addition to Benin, winning presidential candidates have run as independents in recent elections in Mali and São Tomé. In other countries, even when the president has not been an independent, he has orchestrated a coalition between his own party and others to form a dominant bloc in the legislature. Thus in Senegal, Macky Sall left the ruling PDS of President Abdoulaye Wade in 2008 and formed his own party, the Alliance for the Republic (AR). For the 2012 elections, the AR led a coalition of parties, United in Hope, which grew as it became clear that Sall would win and ended up controlling 119 out of 150 seats in the legislature. Senegalese commentators have imaginatively called the practice of moving to the presidential party phagocytosis, in which "the incumbent ingests the opposition" (Koter, 2016, p. 97); others in French West Africa have called this the phenomenon of transhumance, in which politicians readily migrate from their party to the presidential party (Rakner and van de Walle, 2007).

The cost to the government of these arrangement can be substantial. One tentative if imperfect piece of evidence is provided by the size of ministerial cabinets, which, as Arriola (2009) shows, expanded for the first decade of democratization in the region, though we have no systematic data indicating the number of legislative candidates in these cabinets. However, anecdotal evidence shows this process at work. In two-round majority systems such as that in Senegal, deals between presidential candidates after the first round serve to buttress the winning president's legislative majority. The prospects of a Wade victory in the 2000 elections led Moustapha Niasse, who had come in third in the first round, to endorse Wade formally. He then joined the government as prime minister, and the eleven seats that his Alliance of the Forces of Progress party won in the subsequent legislative elections provided extra support to the president's party in the so-called Sopi[9] Coalition. Similar coalition building can be identified in many countries.

---

[9] "Sopi" is the Wolof word for change.

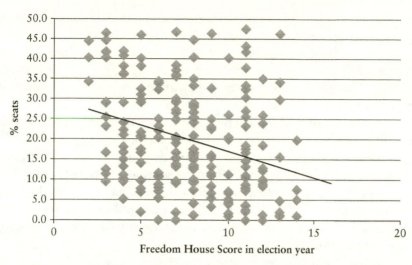

FIGURE 4.2. *Share of main opposition party seats, by Freedom House score*

In sum, Table 4.2 and plenty of other evidence suggest that most party systems in Africa can be characterized by the presence of a single disproportionately powerful party in control of the state along with a larger pool of smaller, more volatile parties (van de Walle 2003; Manning, 2005; Lindberg, 2007). These strong parties leverage their incumbent position to further build their own electoral advantage. The power of incumbency appears to be significant even in the most democratic countries in the region. On average, throughout the period, the biggest opposition party controlled fewer than a fifth of the seats, a number that has increased only marginally over time. This average disguises quite wide disparities. In a quarter of African legislatures since 1990, the formal opposition controlled under 10 percent of all seats. In twenty-two legislatures in thirteen countries, the main opposition party managed over 40 percent of the seats. The share of seats going to the second biggest party is graphed in Figure 4.2, with the country's Freedom House score on the x-axis. As might be expected, the electoral strength of the second party is linked to the quality of democracy, but interestingly, with a Pearson's coefficient of −30.3 percent, the estimated correlation is surprisingly weak.

Africanists have borrowed Sartori's (1976) definition of dominant party to describe parties that are able to win an absolute majority in at least three consecutive elections (Greene, 2007; Bogaards, 2008; Erdman and Basedau, 2013; Doorenspleet and Nijzink, 2013). Sartori did not exclude the possibility of dominant parties in fully democratic regimes. More recently, Greene (2007, p. 12) has specifically linked party dominance to electoral autocracies, explicitly defining a dominant party system as a hybrid regime in which "elections are meaningful but manifestly unfair." Though difficult to establish without ambiguity, a distinction needs to be made between parties that remain in power largely because of electoral fraud and intimidation, with incumbent regimes that will not allow electoral defeat, and parties that may be gaining an advantage from incumbency but where the rules of the game are free enough that the incumbent could conceivably lose an election. In the latter situation, dominant parties win because of their legitimacy and governmental performance rather than because of the democratic deficits of the system. Cameroon and Gabon are examples of the former, while South Africa is an example of the latter.

Another distinction must be made between the classic definition of a dominant party system, in which there is a single dominant party for multiple election cycles and decades of uninterrupted rule, and a system in which the dominant party changes over time but the incumbent's dominance stays roughly the same.[10] An example of the latter is Zambia, in which UNIP (in power until 1991), MMD (in power 1991–2011), and the PF (in power since 2011) have held power in succession, the first two with strong legislative majorities. In Senegal, the PS (in power until 2000), the PSD (in power 2000–12), and the Union for Hope (in power since 2012) have all enjoyed comfortable legislative majorities over multiple terms. Neither Senegal nor Zambia has a constituted dominant party system in the strict sense of Sartori's definition, but presidential control of the legislature has been consistently "dominant."

Most of the systems in the region with a dominant party are in fact relatively volatile and exhibit low levels of institutionalization. Many of the dynamics described in this chapter reflect low levels of party institutionalization in the region (Kuenzi and Lambright, 2005; Weghorst and Bernhard, 2014), with many parties effectively emerging and collapsing around each election cycle and few parties enjoying voter identification.[11] Even with greater multiparty competition, observers have not noted a rise

---

[10] We thank Ian Cooper for alerting us to this key distinction.

[11] Institutionalization is typically thought of as having four dimensions: regularity of electoral competition, stability of constituencies, legitimacy of actors and outcomes, and programmatic appeals. Weghorst and Bernhard (2014, pp. 1713–14) focus specifically on constituency stability, which they operationalize through legislative seat volatility.

in party institutionalization (Hyden, 2011), and some have even observed an increase in volatility (Bogaards, 2008).

High party volatility and politicians migrating from old parties to join new parties are not unique to Africa. Jacques Chirac, French politician and stalwart of the Fourth and Fifth Republics, was a member of seven different parties in his lifetime: the RPF (created 1947), CNRS (1954), UNR (1958), UDR (1968), RPR (1976), UMP (2002), and Republicans (2015). These parties often lasted only two election cycles. Still, each of the parties Chirac joined had a legitimate chance to lead a government or win the presidency.

In Africa, by contrast, party volatility appears to be partly an artifact of the high number of temporary political parties in the opposition, particularly small parties that form around as few as a single legislative candidate. Because this volatility invariably weakens the opposition and strengthens the president's hand, it seems linked to the quality of democracy in the region, and party system institutionalization can be linked to democratic consolidation (Kuenzi and Lambright, 2005; Rakner and van de Walle, 2007; but see Weghorst and Bernhard, 2014).

Weghorst and Bernhard (2014, p. 1718) offer a more optimistic perspective in their comparative analysis of party institutionalization in Africa, noting that while parties continue to enter and exit the political system at high rates (largely owing to the incentives just discussed), a recent rise in "healthy" volatility can be discerned, in which established parties are increasingly winning and losing voters to other established parties.[12] The former type of volatility (type A), associated with the entry and exit of parties, is higher than type B volatility (based on change in vote share between legitimate parties), but type A volatility peaked in the 1990s and has declined in the following two decades as type B volatility has increased (Weghorst and Bernhard, 2014, p. 1728). Their research finds that inequality in basic needs satisfaction is associated with higher levels of volatility; they theorize that this is due to conflicts over redistribution and economic voting (Weghorst and Bernhard, 2014, p. 1719).

Interestingly, type B volatility is associated with a country having a more rural population, which suggests that despite the presence of brokers and bloc voting in rural areas, even these constituencies are willing to switch their votes to support a party or candidate that offers them (and/or their brokers) a better deal (Weghorst and Bernard, 2014, pp. 1726–7).

---

[12] In contrast to research in other regions, Weghorst and Bernhard (2014, pp. 1723–4) find that higher district magnitude is associated with lower volatility and that parliamentary systems are not less volatile than presidential systems.

Dominant party systems can be relatively institutionalized and do not necessarily experience cycles of multiplication, and rebranding of opposition parties and shifting coalitions as are common in other party systems in Africa. For instance, as Figure 4.1 suggests, Mozambique's FRELIMO is dominant, but the country is characterized by a stable party system with a relatively strong opposition party, RENAMO. Similarly, in Botswana, the Botswana Democratic Party (BDP), in power since the mid-1960s, qualifies as a dominant party, but the Botswana National Front has consistently been the leading opposition party, with between a fifth and a third of the vote during the same period.

4.4 EXPLAINING PARTY AND PARTY SYSTEM EVOLUTION

How can the paradoxical patterns observed in Section 4.3 be understood? We focus on two broad-related political factors: the continuing weakness of party institutionalization, which remains a powerful legacy of the past, and the role of political clientelism with state resources that particularly buttress the nondemocratic advantages of incumbency, which both serve to weaken opposition parties.

4.4.1 Party Institutionalization in the Multiparty Era

In Section 4.3, we identified a striking lack of electoral resilience on the part of parties that had seemed so dominant when they enjoyed the benefits of incumbency. What factors help to explain the fate of the old single parties? Why have so few parties managed to survive in the opposition? An increasingly rich literature has examined this issue. First, the level of democracy before and after 1990s could be thought to have played a role. Writing shortly after the transitions, Bratton and van de Walle (1997) argued that the more competitive single-party regimes were more likely to democratize successfully than other pre-1990 regimes. This reflected the widespread view that the weakness of political parties is typically a consequence of low-quality democracy, even as the prospects for democracy are simultaneously viewed as being undermined by weak parties (Mainwaring and Scully, 1995; on the African cases, see Randall and Svåsand, 2002; Kuenzi and Lambright, 2005).

Two important recent studies of African parties have argued that significant variation exists in the strength of parties in the region and offer two distinct arguments about the reasons for this variation. In her compelling study, Riedl (2014) argues that strong authoritarian parties before 1990 with adequate organizational resources and extensive linkages to society were more likely to survive but also more likely to structure more highly institutionalized party systems. Her study contrasts the strong party cases of Ghana and Senegal with the weak party cases of Benin and Zambia. LeBas's (2013) sophisticated comparison of party formation in Zimbabwe, Kenya, and Zambia similarly emphasizes the role of party organization but argues that investments in organization for all parties are spurred by the degree of conflict and polarization they face and the role of organized labor. Corporatist authoritarian regimes were likely to create comparatively strong labor unions, which could then provide a base for the opposition when the transitions began in the midst of a tremendous economic crisis.

Making the case that regime type before 1990 can explain the ability of the authoritarian party in power to survive in the multiparty era is nonetheless not straightforward. The Ghana of Jerry Rawlings in the 1980s was a hard-edged dictatorship that tolerated little contestation; it did not rely on a cohesive party until the NDC was established in 1992, in preparation for the first national elections in over a decade. The Kenya of President Moi, by contrast, was a single-party regime for the same period, and the seemingly vibrant and competitive KANU (Throup and Hornsby, 1998) had dominated Kenyan politics since its creation before independence. Today, however, KANU seems much the weaker party. It is similarly difficult to make the case that the ability of Paul Biya in Cameroon or Gnassingbé Eyadema in Togo to maintain authoritarian power through the multiparty era results from a lower level of democracy before 1990 than existed in countries such as Mali or Benin, in which single parties were swept away. One could repeat such examples. In sum, the linkage between past regime type and parties is deeply ambiguous.

Morse (2015) distinguishes authoritarian parties with real integrative capacity from those that relied almost entirely on coercion and political repression to rule. He suggests that the former were more likely to transition to more democratic systems and political alternation. Morse's key argument is to point to the possibility that repression can palliate effectively for the absence of party organization or legitimacy. Still, it is significant that the single parties in the regimes that did survive democratization were not demonstrably stronger or more legitimate than the ones that collapsed and then disappeared. The ability of regimes to survive democratization seems only very partly related to the strength of the single party and much more related to their ability and willingness to make use of the army and the rest of the coercive apparatus to deal with the popular protests threatening the regime in the early 1990s. Perhaps this ability is related to the cohesion of the regime, but this can be almost entirely unrelated to the integrative capacity of the single party.

Commodity resources and external support from the West help to explain the variation in regime outcomes considerably better than party strength does. Smaller nations with access to offshore oil and foreign allies, such as Gabon and The Republic of the Congo, were able to distribute patronage across wide segments of society and to coopt or crush opposition development (Yates, 1996; Clark, 1997, 2002). The Republic of the Congo is the only oil exporter in the list of countries with a change of governing party due to democratization in Table 4.1; that change was quickly reversed as Sassou Nguesso reasserted himself as president through an insurgency. In the eleven countries that we code as authoritarian survivors in Table 4.2, we note five oil exporters and six presidents with military backgrounds. Tanzania and the Seychelles are the only country in the category with a civilian regime and no oil revenues during this period.

The main reason for this lack of salience of African political parties in democratic transitions is simply their generally low organizational capacity combined with their inability to command adequate societal loyalty when they come under pressure. The partial exceptions to this generalization were discussed above; they consist of ruling parties in the Portuguese colonies and settler states of southern Africa as well as postconflict states in eastern Africa.

With its stable two-party system emerging from a military government and then top-down democratization, Ghana emerges from this discussion as a signal exception, well worth a longer look. Riedl's (2014) thesis works well for Ghana, since the NDC clearly confronted democratization with solid organizational cohesion and societal support. Indeed, the evidence strongly suggests that both the NDC and the NPP have invested considerable resources in organizational capacity since the democratization of the 1990s, and both have constituted stable party machines that can survive outside of power. Osei (2016; see also Bob-Milliar, 2012) emphasizes the investments of both parties in local party organization to account for the ability of both parties to survive their stints in the opposition. The NDC is the more centralized and a more traditional political machine, with core voters having long benefited from the party's patronage; the NPP is more reliant on a decentralized leadership and electoral control of a specific region of core support.

But what explains this unusual degree of local investment? Several factors seem germane. First, most observers agree that both the NDC and the NPP have built up a strong political tradition or brand, going back to independence, that instills loyalty among voters (Nugent, 2007, pp. 260–3; Whitfield, 2009; Osei, 2012, pp. 126–8). Although it is a new party, created in 1992, the NPP can trace its roots to the oldest party in Ghana, the United Gold Coast Convention (UGCC), which was created in 1947, as well as its different offshoots: the Northern Peoples Party (created in 1954), the Progress Party (which ruled briefly (1969–72) during the Second Republic, and the Popular Front Party, the main opposition party during the Third Republic (1979–81). The NPP is associated in the public mind with wealthy Akan elites in a manner that goes back to the Busia-Danquah tradition. It is criticized as elitist in some quarters, but the NPP has skillfully branded itself as representing a pragmatic concern for the rule of law, democracy, and economic growth.

The NDC's party roots are more diffuse. It was originally designed mostly to be a vehicle for Jerry Rawlings, but over time, it has managed to appropriate an ideology of social justice and concern for the common man that harkens back to a Nkrumahist past. Other parties had long explicitly claimed the founding father's legacy (Nugent, 2007), but by combining a rhetoric espousing economic equity with populist and anti-poverty policies, the NDC has appropriated this legacy and has marginalized the true party heirs of Nkrumah.

Second, it is tempting to link both main Ghanaian parties' electoral resilience to the notion that they have been able to retain an essentially ethnoregional base, but an examination of their voters suggests a more complex reality (Lindberg and Morrison, 2005; Osei, 2012, pp. 118–30). The NPP's base could be viewed as more clearly ethnic in nature, since two-thirds of its voters self-identify as Akan, the ethnic group that makes up roughly half of the population of Ghana, but the Akan are notoriously composed of multiple subgroups with different loyalties. In fact, a fifth of NDC voters have self-identified as Akan. In general, the NDC's ethnic support is more heterogeneous, although it clearly enjoys a regional base in Northern Ghana and in the Volta region with majority support of smaller ethnic groups.

Nonetheless, most observers of Ghanaian politics suggest that ethnoregional loyalties explain only part of the resilience of the two parties, as perhaps a majority of Ghanaians are not motivated primarily by ethnoregional factors in their vote choice (Whitfield, 2009). We have already alluded to party traditions, which link parties to certain ideas and policies. In addition, Osei (2012) and Nugent (2007) have pointed to egotropic and sociotropic factors in vote choice, in which the perceptions of governmental performance have shaped voting patterns in the Fourth Republic and have favored alternation.

Finally, political competition has played a role in motivating party organization, as suggested by LeBas's (2016) recent work. The competition between the two parties clearly spurred both to invest in stronger party structure and helped both to build partisan attachment. Bob-Milliar (2012) shows well how both the NDC and the NPP publicly committed themselves to renewed party organization and stronger internal procedures after their electoral defeats in the Fourth Republic. Part of their resilience can be linked to their ability to process leadership changes in response to electoral competition. The NDC survived factional struggles and reinforced its internal procedures following the retirement of Rawlings. Similarly, John Kuofor's retirement in 2009 and the transfer of the NPP leadership to Nana Akufo-Addo was contentious but was ultimately negotiated satisfactorily.

Of course, plenty of other parties across the region have lost elections and have not invested enough in party organization to return to power. Ultimately, the Ghanaian exception remains only partly explained.

4.4.2 Political Clientelism and the Power of Executive Incumbency

Presidential dominance characterizes most of the regimes in sub-Saharan Africa. Even with the introduction of a legal opposition, incumbent parties still find myriad ways to exploit their position in power, many of which serve to weaken the other parties. A second reason that African opposition parties are weak and ephemeral relative to the incumbent is the presidentialism that prevails in the region. As the detective asks, "*A qui profite le crime?*"[13]

Presidentialism is expressed in several ways. First, presidents have clearly made active efforts to weaken the opposition. Particularly in the less democratic countries of the region, the weakness and volatility of opposition parties are manipulated and exploited by incumbent parties and the presidency, which rarely want an effective and powerful opposition. For instance, Opalo (2015) has noted that in many African constitutions parliamentary sessions are opened by the president, who controls when the parliament is working. Extremely short sessions are

---

[13] "Whom does the crime profit?"

the norm, weakening parliament's ability to exert mechanisms of horizontal accountability on the president and undermining the visibility of parliamentarians. Executives can also pass legislation that favors their own parties. For instance, Botswana's high voting age (21 years) and its choice to give migrant labor a vote provide a clear electoral benefit to the BDP (Young, 1993). Similarly, parties in Kenya and Côte d'Ivoire have enforced partisan technicalities in party registration and regulations about meetings that targeted opposition parties (Young, 1993, p. 303). Many observers have applauded the large number of African countries that have introduced gender quotas over the last two decades (Bauer and Burnet, 2013). However, scholars may have reason to be more skeptical for the basis of their adoption, given that quotas have been found to give an edge to incumbents (Goetz and Hassim, 2003; Muriaas and Wang, 2012), particularly in single-member districts (Fréchette et al., 2008).

Second, even when incumbents do not have an active policy to weaken the opposition, presidential clientelism still serves to weaken party institutionalization. This dynamic is particularly clear when the differences between rural and urban voting are compared. Scholars have long noted the tendency of African rural areas to vote for the incumbent, while urban voters are more likely to back opposition parties (Koter, 2013; Harding, 2010; Resnick, 2014). This pattern cuts across both parties and candidates. Koter (2013) notes that in Senegal, Abdoulaye Wade won the urban vote as an opposition candidate but came to rely increasingly on the rural vote once he was in office. What seems clear is that it is easier for the government to assert incumbency advantages in the countryside. Brokerage dynamics are more common there, as it is easier for brokers to monitor voting behavior in small villages, given their greater social homogeneity. Media coverage is thinner and less consistent in rural areas, so it is also probably easier to engage in various kinds of fraud there. Rural voters are more likely to be poor and illiterate (Sahn and Stifel, 2003), and paradoxically, their lower likelihood of getting government services and benefits makes them more vulnerable to the persuasion of state-funded clientelism. Indeed, Wahman and Boone (2018) find that the difference in voting patterns between urban and rural areas is conditioned by these economic factors. Richer rural areas are more likely, ceteris paribus, to vote for the opposition, while poorer urban areas are more likely to vote for the incumbent.

The phenomenon of the quixotic candidacy, in which a politician runs multiple times over a decade (often within different parties) and never manages to win, does not seem to be motivated by programmatic or ideological concerns, since one hardly ever witnesses an explicit nego-tiation over programmatic issues when the politician joins the presiden-tial majority. Instead, the contract seems to be that the president will provide the rallying politician with some kind of office or benefit in exchange for public support. Politicians who have a larger public profile and can claim a larger constituency will be able to negotiate a more important position, all the way to ministerial cabinet positions.

These strategies are typically circumscribed to a single electoral cycle, and another strategy can be elaborated for the next cycle. The absence of strong party ideology probably lessens the costs to individual candidates of switching parties or joining coalitions that benefit them as individuals. On the other hand, the access to state resources and the sharp imbalance in funding between the incumbent party and the opposition increases the cost of not seeking to join the presidential majority in some manner.

These processes evoke the kind of party coalition building that is the hallmark of most democracies, but there are two significant differences. First, in Africa, the rallying politician often abandons her party to join the presidential party, thus contributing directly to the volatility of the party system. The arrangement takes place not between two parties, as in the kind of routine coalition governments that exits in parliamentary demo-cracies, but between an individual politician and the presidential party. Second, in Africa, the process leads to greater party volatility because it is more likely to be reiterative, in that at least some of the politicians who have left their party to join the presidential majority then compete in the next election again as independent or small party candidates.

In Malawi, members of parliament officially cannot change parties without having to run for office again, but this rule has often gone unen-forced (Svåsand, 2015, p. 90). In addition, this rule does not apply to independents, an omission that further weakens party discipline. After his victory in 2004, President Peter Mutharika formed a new party, the Democratic Progressive Party (DPP), having left the United Democratic Front (UDF), under whose colors he had run for office, following disputes with the rest of the leadership. It was only after winning the 2009 elec-tions that Mutharika was able to build a stable majority, but the careful distribution of favors and appointments to cabinet of parliamentarians was a key governance mechanism of his first term and a key instrument for building up the UDF's legislative presence. During this time, the size of cabinet almost doubled, from twenty-four members in 2004 to forty-two in 2007 (see Rakner and van de Walle, 2007, pp. 214–15). In neigh-boring Zambia, much the same dynamic was present in the presidency of Fred Chiluba, who by 1994 had appointed forty-eight members of parliament to deputy minister positions (van de Walle, 2001, p. 266) in addition to adding full cabinet status and various other leadership roles in parliament itself. Perhaps over half of Chiluba's presidential majority were thus beholden to him personally.

The difference in salary and perks for a backbencher compared to a leadership position in Parliament or a ministerial position is significant, and politicians are well aware of the difficulty of surviving a long spell in the opposition. Even opposition politicians who do get elected know that it will be difficult to provide constituency services without the support of the administration, which will naturally give first priority to the majority's backbenchers. The presence of a Constituency Development Fund attenuates this reliance on the president, one reason that it is so attractive to parliamentarians, but the general point is clear: Being a member of the presidential majority provides one with much greater access to the resources of the state.

4.5 EMERGING TRENDS IN PARTY POLITICS

We find little evidence that the party systems that we have just described are changing, although in a few countries, such as Mauritius, Cape Verde, and possibly Nigeria, the patterns described above for Ghana may be evolving, and regular alternation between multiple strong parties may be in the process of emerging as different parties respond to political competition by investing in organization and closer linkages with citizens. Beardsworth's (2018) careful work on the progressive emergence of the United Party for National Development (UPND) in Zambia suggest that party is following such a script. So, possibly, is Chadema in Tanzania; the party has increased its share of the vote slowly but surely since a marginal result in 1995.

On the other hand, it is easier to see experimentation at the individual party level in many countries, and we hypothesize the emergence of several new types of organizing principles for political parties. First are parties that adopt an explicitly populist approach, as embodied by the PF of Michael Sata, the former president in Zambia, but that might also include the PDS of President Wade in Senegal or the Orange Democratic Movement (ODM) of Raila Odinga in Kenya (see Resnick, 2014). In each case, candidates eschew brokers to make direct appeals to youth voters in urban areas. The leaders of these parties understand that African demographics are changing, becoming younger and more urban, and have adapted their strategies accordingly. In most instances, when they win office, these candidates do not translate their campaign rhetoric into systematic attempts to carry out a new programmatic agenda. Many fall back instead on the patronage structures that have long characterized the political status quo. However, the emergence of many young populist opposition candidates, such as Julius Malema of the Economic Freedom Fighters in South Africa and McHenry Venaani in Namibia (Weylandt, 2015), suggests that we will continue to see new candidates embrace these types of strategies. As older systems of vote mobilization through brokerage break down, we may see the emergence of populist candidates who are able to mobilize rural voters. In dominant party systems linked to liberation struggles, younger generations of voters, who did not live through turbulent period of political conflict, do not have the same high levels of partisanship that their parents do and might be more willing to vote for an opposition candidate (Friesen, 2017). These younger candidates can leverage social media to effectively target the youth and urban voters during campaigns – the very demographic that is probably most likely to support their message.

Second is the introduction of true outsider candidates who have no previous political experience and no evident relationship to the old single party. Many of these outsiders are relatively young members of the business communities who are able to self-finance campaigns without the need for support from or deference to incumbents. Some of these candidates claim a clear reformist agenda aimed at improving domestic institutions as well as the economy. Their independence from existing networks of power enables them to adopt bolder policy platforms. Two front-runners in the Benin 2016 elections were businessman who ran as independents. The eventual winner, cotton mogul Patrice Talon, made good on campaign promises to curb executive power and quickly sought to instate policies to limit presidents to one term in office.

A subtler but related dynamic is the emergence of business-backed candidates from the political elite. In these instances, private business is strong enough to provide resources for opposition coalitions to beat the incumbent (Arriola, 2013). These candidates reflect the priorities of business communities. Uhuru Kenyatta is the son of the former president but also arguably the largest landholder in Kenya, and he is able to leverage strong support from the Kikuyu business community. In his independent bid for president of Benin in 2006, Yayi Boni relied heavily on financing from local entrepreneurs, two of whom would split from him and challenge him in the 2016 elections. Because of the pervasive incumbency advantage and the heavy costs of campaigning in Africa that we will discuss in Chapter 5, campaign financing is key for challengers who do not have access to state resources during the campaign. Arriola (2013) argues that the political economy of countries at independence shaped the feasibility of the development of an opposition over time. Specifically, private banking emerges in countries where the president's ethnic group, rather than an outsider group that could pose threats to executive power, was involved in cash crop production for export. The availability of private capital stemming from this era is associated with the availability of greater resources, independent of the state, for opposition coalition formation in the multiparty period. As the private sectors grows in some countries, entrepreneurs whose fortunes are independent of the state can play extremely important roles in financing opposition candidates and coalitions.

A third area of potential party innovation is in the relationship with organized religion. Religiosity is increasing across African countries, as a large literature makes clear (Haynes 1996; Gifford, 1998; Miles, 2007; Ranger, 2008; Riedl, 2012). The influence of organized religion on politics is increasing, from the calls for sharia law in West Africa (Miles, 2007; Kendhammer, 2016) to the growing willingness of Pentecostal churches to flex their political muscles in countries as varied as Ghana and Zambia (Riedl, 2012; Anderson, 2013; McCauley, 2012; Grossman, 2015).

Yet even when politicians have cooperated with religious leaders, overtly courted them, or sought their blessing, these networks have not so far been translated into formal political parties, defined as parties with a specific formal link to a religious organization and with an explicit ideology to advance religious belief. In contrast to both Europe and Latin America, no Christian Democracy tradition exists in sub-Saharan Africa, despite the large proportion of voters who are regular members of various Christian churches. Similarly, there appears to be no African equivalent of the Muslim Brotherhood, which has competed in elections in several Middle Eastern countries. Christian and increasingly Muslim religious influence on political parties appears to be rising across Africa (see Chapter 5), but this far from negligible influence has so far been expressed only through relations of brokerage and informal linkages rather than formal incorporation into political parties.

Will this change? While the influence of the Christian churches may be increasing faster, our bet is that there are enough precedents in Islamic parties in other regions of the world that it is only a matter of time before Islamic actors exert even greater influence on politics in West Africa.

The politics around sharia law in Northern Nigeria, well described by Kendhammer (2016), and resistance to women's equality legislation (Soares 2009; Kang 2015) suggests that such a process is already underway.

Certain national characteristics can assist in the development of the opposition. Countries with sources of funding and organization other than the state can compete with incumbent parties and their hold on the state. As we suggested above, a strong private sector can provide a counterweight to the state. In addition, LeBas (2013) is probably correct that the labor movement can provide that base. Unfortunately, few countries can claim unions as strong as those in southern Africa, on which she bases her claim. Perhaps over time, as these economies continue their structural transformations, the possibilities for larger nonstate organizations will emerge. Third, the control of subnational offices can provide opposition parties with both governance experience and access to public resources with which to build a party organization (Conroy-Krutz, 2006). One would therefore predict that stronger opposition parties will emerge in federal states such as Nigeria, South Africa, or now Kenya or in more urban countries with big primary cities.

Finally, rapid rates of urbanization and the vast expansion of access to telephone and the Internet lower the campaign costs for opposition parties and may help to improve their prospects in the future. Candidates today campaign in environments of unprecedented political information and discussion. As we will discuss in Chapter 5, in many countries, opposition parties are already making strong inroads by winning seats and mayors' races in regional capitals. Furthermore, increased access to information and communications technologies and related tools, included money transfer software and online fundraising applications, may make it easier for opposition parties to raise money from the diaspora and to distribute that money to regionally based candidates and field offices. Over time, it will be difficult for incumbent parties to hold onto the campaign monopolies that they currently enjoy in some rural areas.

5

Candidates and Electoral Campaigns

According to Moupo, a BNF activist, factors that explain Koma's personality cult are "his lack of vanity, his unshakeable devotion to the party's cause, resilience and perseverance against overwhelming odds (the formidable strength of the BDP and its vicious campaign of personal slander and political intimidation against him)."

Molomo, 2000, p. 80, citing *Mmegi* (*Gaborone*),
May 29–June 4, 1998

There are ... strategic reasons ... for Congressman A not to focus too heavily on specific issues. To do so would be unnecessary and potentially divisive ... he is a stabilizer, a maintainer. And so, when asked to speak formally, he often responds with communitarian homilies: "I believe if there was a promised land, that land is America; and if there was a chosen people, those people are Americans." "If a man isn't proud of his heritage, he won't have a heritage to be proud of. And that goes for his family, his community, his country." These utterances are not the secret of his success, but they do testify, again, to his continuing efforts to articulate a sense of community, to construct and reconstruct a web of enduring personal relationships and to present himself as totally part of that web.

Richard Fenno (1978, p. 69).

Electoral democracy offers all groups in society unparalleled opportunities for participation and competition through the extension of universal suffrage. Across the African continent, candidates compete for votes in very different political geographies with varying levels of competition, constituency support, and engagement on their behalf by a political party.

In this chapter, we discuss common campaign practices in sub-Saharan Africa. Given the dominant position of the president, discussed in Chapter 3, we focus our primary analysis on executive elections at the national level and leave important questions about legislative, gubernatorial, and municipal elections to future researchers. We show how the two factors that promote continuity – the liability of newness and the advantages of incumbency – condition campaigns in sub-Saharan Africa. First, the liability of newness factors create uncertainty in the electoral environment. Few candidates have served in the executive office since independence, so most candidates and parties have little basis on which to build their political reputations. Incumbents play off of this uncertainty by arguing that a new candidate could always perform more poorly than the incumbent does. Further, the ideological similarities of most political parties, discussed in Chapter 4, means that it is difficult for a candidate to campaign on a unique programmatic platform. With the exception of dominant parties, most presidential races in Africa remain candidate based; parties draw their reputation and brand from their executive candidate rather than the inverse. Finally, most parties, especially emerging parties, do not have a clear understanding of their voting base. Some parties can draw on regional and ethnic cues to make guesses about prospective voters, but there is still a great deal of uncertainty about voters and their preferences, particularly so-called swing voters.

This uncertainty translates into some systematic advantages for incumbent parties and candidates. Most campaign rhetoric is valence based; that is, candidates stress their own competence to address key issues and highlight personal characteristics that are valued by voters. Sitting presidents can draw on past experience in office, including development trajectories and economic growth while in office, which we will discuss more in Chapter 6. Incumbent presidents can also highlight their role as a central node among the political and business elites that is critical for building societal coalitions and getting policy implemented. Presidents demonstrate their connections to an international cosmopolitan elite, including potential donors, trading partners, and private companies that are looking to invest. Opposition challengers need to leverage aspects of their own biographies to prove competence and political capability. They may discuss their own background as business leaders or areas of technocratic expertise to gain traction on policy issues that resonate with the public. Alternatively, candidates leverage aspects of their biography that demonstrate homophily with potential voters. Typically, these are ethnic or regional cues, but they can also take the form of populist, religious, or employment-based appeals.

Campaigning is onerous. Touring the country, gaining endorsements, and securing brokerage arrangements are all expensive, time consuming and exhausting, and few candidates can rely on a fully professionalized staff. This gives the better-financed incumbents an advantage. A national campaign entails exorbitant expenses, owing to the cost of travel into remote rural areas as well as voter expectations for campaign swag in the form of rice, T-shirts, or, increasingly, the provision of club goods in the run-up to the election (Lindberg, 2010b).[1] Publicized campaign costs are imprecise and often exaggerated, but reports that Goodluck Jonathan spent between US $2 billion and $3 billion in his failed attempt to secure reelection in Nigeria in 2015 are eye-opening, regardless of their veracity.[2] In Uganda, the *Daily Monitor* newspaper reported that incumbent president Yoweri Museveni had spent US $231 million on his 2016 campaign, outspending all of his opponents combined. Runner-up Kizza Besigye had spent only US $4.5 million. The contrast provides a sense of the financial incumbency advantage that holds in African elections.[3] Polling and other forms of electoral data gathering are relatively expensive in sub-Saharan Africa in comparison to other regions, giving an advantage to incumbents who have adequate resources.[4] Further, as we discussed in Chapter 3, incumbents can leverage access to state institutions and resources as well as dominant control of the media for additional comparative advantages (Levitsky and Way, 2010). This resource discrepancy is key.

In this chapter, we start by placing African electoral campaigns in the comparative perspective. We show that many exoticized aspects of African elections are in fact present in electoral competition across the world. Then we take a look at the politicians themselves. We try to understand the ways in which they try to leverage their personal biographies to differentiate themselves from other candidates and attract potential voters. We then examine campaign strategies, including targeting supporters, brokerage, campaign tours, and campaign appeals. In Section

---

[1] The Westminster Foundation for Democracy reported that transportation costs accounted for 25–30 percent of the total campaign cost for a typical Ghanaian member of parliament in recent elections. See http://www.wfd.org/wp-content/uploads/2016/07/Ghana-Cost-of-Politics.pdf.

[2] As reported in Mwanawasa et al. (2017, p. 13).

[3] See *Daily Monitor*, July 10, 2016, available at http://www.monitor.co.ug/News/National/Museveni-expenditure-Shs773b-2016-campaign-report/688334-3287766-bwgej4z/index.html.

[4] In the United States, election polls typically cost $1–3 per respondent, but individual polling in the run-up to the 2013 Kenyan election was reported to cost $20 per head (Mwanawasa et al., 2017, p. 10).

5.4, we examine the use of different types of media, including posters, advertisements, and the emerging use of social media. In Section 5.5, we briefly examine how these dynamics play out in legislative, gubernatorial, and municipal campaigns. In Section 5.6, we summarize the content of the chapter.

5.1 AFRICAN CAMPAIGNS IN THE COMPARATIVE PERSPECTIVE

In this chapter, we explore the evolution of the profiles of political candidates as well as their campaign rhetoric and strategies. In doing so, we analyze African campaigns in a comparative perspective and demonstrate how much they have in common with Western elections in many fundamental ways.

Political rhetoric and ritual in the African context are often portrayed as unimaginative, nonprogrammatic, and largely focused on fueling clientelist relationships. In the stereotype of an African electoral campaign, a candidate travels out to rural villages to distribute gifts to favored constituencies. Emerging from a shiny four wheel drive car, he talks about his familial origins in the region and vaunts the merits and authority of the local big men. He brags about his own personal wealth, offering it as a guarantee of his political acumen and the personal generosity he will demonstrate once he is in office. National policies are not mentioned; instead, the candidate promises to deliver specific goods to that particular village. During a visit to the local chief, he promises money for the village youth soccer team, and the chief makes a vague promise to deliver the votes of all of his subjects. As the politician gets ready to leave, his aides hand out bags of rice and cold, hard cash to villagers. Pretty much the same scenario plays out in neighboring villages.

This description of rural campaigning is not completely inaccurate, but the standard interpretations of these actions in academic and journalistic accounts often seem to imply that African electoral practices are exceptional and folkloric, missing the unexceptional substantive logic that lurks behind them. First, African politics are not exceptional and should not be held to programmatic standards that are rarely met in any democracy. As the chapter opening quotation from Richard Fenno's (1978) celebrated ethnography of US politicians reveals, the campaign discourse of many US politicians shies away from direct appeals to substantive issues. We need look no further than the 2016 electoral race in the United States to see candidates engaging in similarly bizarre populist rituals, employing xenophobic rhetoric to mobilize voters, or making desperate attempts to communicate their relatability to constituencies. In every electoral system, candidates try to leverage valence characteristics, which are personal attributes or experience that are valued by the electorate. For instance, German voters are often reminded that Angela Merkel gets by on 4h of sleep a night but has breakfast every morning with her husband and loves to eat German sausages washed down with large mugs of German beer, as attested to by countless campaign reports in newspapers and on the Internet.[5]

Coded rhetoric and populist ritual are common in all democracies. In the United States, observers note the posturing by politicians to flaunt their heartfelt patriotism (in the 2008 election, candidate Barack Obama's initial reluctance to wear a flag pin on his lapel was criticized as suggesting inadequate patriotism). Heads of state of NATO countries have almost all visited their national troops based in Afghanistan in recent years, leading to the inevitable carefully posed photos of the politicians in helmets and flak jackets. Almost as important as demonstrations of patriotism, politicians' attachment to family values and the rural way of life is carefully cultivated. Visiting county fairs, eating regional specialties, and praising the quality of the local livestock are inevitable rituals for national politicians running for office in most of the oldest democracies. These practices are viewed as a way for politicians and parties to signal both their recognition of the political power and legitimacy of rural interests and their support of a policy agenda that will support these interests. In France, a visit to the annual Salon de l'Agriculture (a national agricultural fair held on the outskirts of Paris) is a well-practiced ritual that few national politicians fail to undertake. In the run-up to the 2012 French elections, the *New Yorker* noted that then-candidate Francois Hollande had spent more than 12h at the Salon, hobnobbing with the crowds and farmers presenting their wares, to dispel the notion that he was an urban technocrat with no knowledge of or appreciation for the rural world and its needs.[6]

In these cases, rhetoric and ritual do not preclude a substantive understanding of policy issues; they represent the idiom of electoral practice, the prerequisite exercises through which candidates empathize with and

---

[5] See for instance, http://www.businessinsider.com/angela-merkel-daily-routine-2017-7. Googling "Merkel eating food" led to several dozen pictures of the German chancellor consuming some form of food or beer in recent campaigns.

[6] Laura Collins, "Come to the Fair," *The New Yorker*, April 4, 2016, accessed at http://www .newyorker.com/magazine/2016/04/04/inside-the-salon-international-de-lagriculture.

communicate to voters, notably about substantive issues. The precise idiom changes from country to country, though less than is sometimes assumed, but the links between the rituals and folklore and substantive policy are no less real in Africa than in the democracies of the Organisation for Economic Co-operation and Development (OECD).

Much has been made of the clientelist character of African elections and handouts during campaigns (Chabal and Daloz, 1999; Basedau et al., 2007; Wantchekon, 2003). Scholars of African democracy lament that candidates promise gifts and kickbacks to particular constituencies rather than engaging in "programmatic policy platforms." We argue that when it comes to actual candidates and voters, the theoretical distinction between programmatic rhetoric and clientelism can be quite ambiguous. While the substantive policy relevance of such rituals can be difficult to discern when very little explicit discussion of the party's policy platform takes place, the political function and symbolism of the rituals should be recognized as it is by local voters. True, the purpose of these political rituals is often veiled by their clientelistic attributes, as they provide public venues for the distribution of patronage, but in poor, underserved constituencies, most voters care most passionately about issues related to service provision and economic development that will directly affect their own welfare. These voters are more concerned with the certainty that these goods will be delivered than with the mechanism of distribution. Low-income African voters may in the abstract value public goods, but like voters all over the world, they are more impressed by evidence that the candidate will improve voters' own lives. In an uncertain environment in which the state has historically been lackadaisical, at best, in service provision, the candidate campaign tour, in which resources are distributed and practical promises are made to local big men, is about as good a deal as most voters expect from politics.

Furthermore, campaigns often employ mixed strategies. Indeed, as Resnick (2012) has argued, many recent candidates combine different forms of linkages, including ethnic, charismatic, and programmatic strategies, all under a general clientelist umbrella. If African voters are most interested in the provision of social services, including schools and health clinics (Ichino and Nathan, 2013; Weghorst and Lindberg, 2013; Kramon, 2016), then politicians' discussions of these outcomes might be seen as programmatic even if the mode of delivery is not transparent or achieved equitably.

A similar disdain can be discerned among some scholars for the dominance of so-called ethnic politics in African electoral discourse, sometimes labeled the "politics of belonging" (Geschiere, 2009). Ethnic politics is often viewed as antithetical to programmatic politics. However, like some other scholars (see, for example, Ferree, 2006; Fridy, 2009; Conroy-Krutz, 2013), we conceptualize ethnic politics as a heuristic device that can help politicians to address constituencies and their needs. Programmatic issues are typically embedded in ethnic appeals. Just as some US candidates may pledge to stop deportations as a veiled ethnic appeal to a Latino base, so Kenyan candidates' pledge to support Luo interests could be a coded commitment to decentralization and the promotion of development in the neglected Western region of Kenya. Ethnic politics might increase candidates' programmatic appeal in areas in which the candidates can use ethnic group density to identify a large voting base and its preferences (Ichino and Nathan, 2013).

Candidates can also mobilize citizens' perceived ethnic identity by using ethnic cues (Conroy-Krutz and Kerr, 2015). Candidates can heighten divisions between ethnic insiders and outsiders by using xenophobic rhetoric, warning of redistribution to others if voters do not come out to the polls. For instance, in a comparative study of Kenya and Côte d'Ivoire, Klaus and Mitchell (2015) show how land grievances can mobilize supporters if they believe that the outcome of the election constitutes either a credible threat to their land security or an opportunity. Caricatures of African elections stress ethnic mobilization through threats and scare tactics, but it is important to note that identity appeals are present in most culturally diverse electoral political systems. As was seen in recent elections in Europe and the 2016 US presidential election, many candidates have resorted to more or less incendiary ethnic appeals. For instance, stoking fear about the redistributional threats posed by immigrants or minorities has been a staple in campaign speeches across OECD countries. In countries as varied as France, Denmark, and Poland, the recent electoral resurgence of right-wing political parties has led even mainstream politicians to respond with public declarations of their intention to limit immigration and threats to sanction immigrant groups whose public behavior did not "fit in" with the dominant national culture.

5.2 IDENTITIES OF PRESIDENTIAL CANDIDATES

Because of the central role of the executive in African governance, we explore the traits of presidential candidates and how they leverage these characteristics in the multiparty era. This includes their work backgrounds and family relationships, their structural position as challengers or incumbents, and the traits they share with their constituents.

5.2.1 Who Are the Candidates?

Like African candidates in the postindependence period and much like their counterparts in other regions of the world, most African presidents are highly educated older men. Only eight women were among the 193 most competitive candidates in elections throughout Africa between 2009 and 2016.[7] Female presidential aspirants included three sitting presidents – Ellen Sirleaf Johnson of Liberia, Ameenah Gurib-Fakim of Mauritius, and Joyce Banda of Malawi – as well as challengers in Mauritania, Mauritius, Rwanda, South Africa, Sudan, Uganda, and Zambia. Only São Tomé had more than one female candidate; Elsa Pinto and Maria das Neves both ran as independents in the 2011 race.

The average age of a presidential candidate competing in these election cycles was fifty-eight years, six months. This is actually comparable to the mean age of US presidential candidates over the last century (fifty-six years, six months).[8] The youngest candidate in Africa was Julius Malema of the Economic Freedom Party of South Africa, who ran in the 2014 elections at the age of 33. On the other end of the spectrum, Robert Mugabe and Abdoulaye Wade competed in the most recent elections cycles at the ages of 89 and 85, respectively. The high average age of presidential aspirants is perhaps especially striking in Africa given the youth bulge; the median age in Africa is 20, compared to a global average of 30, and only 5 percent of the African population is over 60.[9] This disparity may explain why older politicians have adopted more modern political idioms and postures that they believe will resonate with this growing segment of the population. However, we may see a change over time as the political class associated with the old single-party era dies out and younger candidates are forced to adopt more creative strategies to court voters.

---

[7] We coded the demographic information for each of the top five vote-getting candidates for one election cycle between 2009 and 2016. The original coding was done in fall 2015. A supplementary coding was done in fall 2016. The Excel sheet is available in the online appendix.

[8] Authors' calculation using data from http://fivethirtyeight.com/features/can-a-candidate-be-too-old-to-run-for-president.

[9] http://www.un.org/esa/population/cpd/cpd2012/Agenda%20item%204/UN%20system%20statements/ECA_Item4.pdf, p. 1.

As we discussed in Chapters 2 and 4, a common thread linking most presidential candidates is their social origins in the highly educated and cosmopolitan political elite. Most have international degrees, networks, and connections. Like postindependence politicians, most present-day African presidential candidates come from among the educated elite. It is not uncommon for a full slate of presidential competitors to have received their university degrees in Europe or the United States. Given the perceived importance of international ties and networks, it is unsurprising that parties or voters would prefer candidates with these types of profiles. For instance, Uhuru Kenyatta graduated from Amherst College, Ellen Sirleaf Johnson of Liberia earned an MPA from Harvard, Togo's Faure Gnassingbé received his BA from the Sorbonne and a Masters from George Washington University, and Ameenah Gurib of Mauritius has a PhD in chemistry from the University of Exeter. However, being too cozy with a foreign power can also be damaging. In the 2014 electoral race in Malawi, there was much debate and negative speculation about whether Peter Mutharika, a world-renowned law expert, with degrees from Yale University and a long professional affiliation with Washington University of St. Louis, had dual citizenship with the United States.

Because of these common social origins, many African politicians share experiences of political socialization. This makes it difficult for them to differentiate themselves on programmatic grounds. We observe that many candidates and sitting presidents can still trace their initial foray into politics to the single-party era before multiparty elections. In Senegal, for instance, it is hard to find a prominent presidential aspirant in the last couple of elections who did not cut his or her teeth in politics within the Parti Socialiste (PS), the dominant party in the independence era, which can be traced back to the Bloc Démocratique Sénégalais, created by Leopold Senghor in 1948. In the 2012 presidential elections, five of the top six vote-getting candidates had at one point in their careers served in the PS, even if Macky Sall, the youngest of the candidates and the eventual winner, had not. Of course, politicians try to convince voters that their past political prominence is evidence of both their competence and their ability to manage and navigate party networks, which will be useful when they are elected.

Successful businessmen have increasingly sought to convert their economic acumen and personal wealth into political office. These include cotton mogul Patrice Talon in Benin and Hery Rajaonarimampianina, an accountant and former CEO of Air Madagascar, both of whom won recent presidential races; Adama Barrow, a real estate executive, who won the Gambian presidency in December 2016; and Hakainde Hichilema, a Zambian businessman who was narrowly defeated in the 2016 presidential elections.[10] These candidates are interesting in that they come from outside the political establishment and therefore have fewer obligations to the existing political class, suggesting greater willingness to shake up policy. Indeed, Patrice Talon ran on a platform of reducing the presidential term limit to just one term in office, and it appears that he remains committed to curbing executive power.[11] As a result, these candidates often attract defectors from the existing political class within their coalitions.

In postconflict countries, some current presidential candidates originally gained notoriety and credibility in the context of a violent struggle. These include former military leaders such as Muhammadu Buhari in Nigeria and Omar el Bashir in Sudan and commanders of insurgencies who fought their way to power, such as Robert Mugabe in Zimbabwe, Paul Kagame in Rwanda, and Museveni in Uganda. These "warlord democrats," to adopt Themnér's provocative term, often have a military background but have more recently sought to rebrand themselves as civilian politicians to get elected as democratic leaders (Themnér, 2017). Relatedly, candidates who represent independence parties can point to their role as part of the liberation struggle as part of their political profile.

At the same time, conflict environments generate opportunities for politicians outside of the pre-transition political establishment. For instance, Tripp (2015) shows that women are represented in greater numbers in the legislatures and governments of postconflict countries, and argues that the disruptions of war altered gender power relations and have provided women with greater political opportunities in postconflict environments.

Dynastic politics still carry substantial weight; family connections to a past executive suggest that a candidate will have access to the same networks of his or her predecessor, generating less uncertainty for the political system. Brossier and Dorronsoro (2016) identifies twelve countries in Africa that have experienced familial transmissions of power; half were continuous, but the other half were discontinuous. Families have already "eaten" at the hands of the state, so there is less concern about greater elite redistribution. When Uhuru Kenyatta entered office in Kenya, he

---

[10] http://africa.tvcnews.tv/2016/09/02/gambia-election-businessman-barrow-challenge-president-jammeh.

[11] http://www.beninto.info/2016/08/03/le-mandat-presidentiel-unique-defi-obsessionnel-de-patrice-talon/.

carried the legacy of his father Jomo Kenyatta but was also one the country's richest citizens. Since the Kenyatta family already had access to state resources and Kenyatta's fortune was already made, a popular claim was that Uhuru Kenyatta would be less likely than the other candidates to pillage the state for additional wealth. In other instances, biological heirs are installed outside of electoral competition. This was the case for Joseph Kabila in DRC, Ali Bongo in Gabon, and Faure Gnassingbé in Togo, three men who appear to have devoted most of their adult lives to working for their fathers before inheriting their political power. But even some of Africa's most democratic regimes provide examples of familial succession. Botswana's President Ian Khama is the son of the first president. Navin Ramgoolam, the three-term premier of Mauritius, is the son of Mauritius' "father of independence," former Prime Minister Seewoosagur Ramgoolam (Kasenally, 2011, p. 162).

These attempts to place kin in political positions are not always successful. African citizens are increasingly wary of presidential attempts to usurp party procedures in order to place a biological heir in office. President Abdoulaye Wade may have had the ambition of grooming his son Karim to someday replace him. The son held a number of ministerial positions, but his eventual arrest, trial, and prison term for corruption only confirmed his lack of popularity among Senegalese voters.[12] Similarly, rumors in Burkina Faso in 2014 that President Blaise Compaoré was grooming his younger brother François to replace him was one of several issues that led to Compaoré's downfall. Also raising concerns are the rumors that President Paul Biya of Cameroon will designate his unpopular son Franck as his successor,[13] current speculation about the possibility that businesswoman Isabel dos Santos, the daughter of the current president of Angola, will become the MPLA's candidate in the upcoming Angolan elections and that Ugandan President Museveni is grooming his son, Muhoozi Kainerugaba, to replace him someday.

5.2.2 Valence Characteristics

In large part because of the ideological similarities across most African party platforms as well as their uncertainty about their own constituencies,

---

[12] See "Super Minister Wade," *Africa Confidential*, October 22, 2010; and "Senegal: Ex-President's Son Freed from Jail after Legal Pardon," *The Guardian* June 24, 2016.
[13] http://www.africareview.com/news/Cameroon-diaspora-want-Biya-son-indicted/979180-1651064-1110dgt/index.html.

most candidates engage in valence competition, in which candidates and parties attempt to convince voters that they are best placed to address the key problems and issues of the day. Rather than drawing cues from the reputation of relatively new and weak political parties, many voters form their vote choice on the basis of the characteristics and experiences of individual politicians. These valence characteristics of politicians say little about their distinct programmatic positions but are nevertheless valued by voters. As popularized by Stokes (1963, 1966), these traits can include rhetoric (Grose and Husser, 2008), character (Kartik and McAfee, 2007), credibility, and attractiveness (McGuire, 1969; Andersen and Kibler, 1978). Unsurprisingly, candidate qualities play a stronger relative role in the context of weak parties and in countries where candidates have indistinguishable similar programmatic ideologies.

In the US context, scholars discuss the valence advantage of incumbents; this advantage is enhanced in presidential systems in sub-Saharan Africa for the reasons that we discussed in Chapter 3. Incumbent presidents can draw upon their previous experience in office to prove not only their notoriety and the viability of their winning with a sufficient coalition of supporters, but also existing diplomatic relationships with donors and their web of relations in the domestic system. Challengers face greater hurdles in proving their competence and ability to win if they lack previous experience in executive office.

As with valence issues, which we will discuss in Chapter 6, these candidate traits are context specific but are typically valued by the entire voting population of a specific country.[14] For instance, in some electoral contexts, religious identity or piety is an important qualifier for the presidency. Similar to the American exigency that a president be a Christian, candidates in some countries must demonstrate their piety or deference to popular religious leaders. For instance, in Senegal, Abdoulaye Wade explained to journalists that his religious affiliation earns him some electoral support. He responded to journalists' questions about his televised visit with a Mouride leader by saying, "I have never hidden that I am a Mouride – anyone who votes for me knows they are voting for a Mouride ... Any power must have a popular base, and as it happens I benefit from this very broad popular support."[15] In Zambia, Frederick Chiluba relied heavily on backing from the growing and influential

---

[14] In some instances, valence traits can be qualities that are valued by specific sectors of the population such as a particular voting base (Stokes, 1966).

[15] http://www.reuters.com/article/us-senegal-brotherhoods-idUSTRE80M12U20120124.

Pentecostal population, going so far as to declare Zambia a Christian nation without prior approval from his own party (van Klinken, 2014).[16]

Candidates can emphasize aspects of their biographical background that might be viewed as valence characteristics. For instance, given African countries' reliance on international partners for foreign investment community it is important that candidates prove their ability to broker relationships with these communities. An incumbent, who is already in office and has managed state diplomacy, has less to prove, but challengers will want to signal that they have a cosmopolitan orientation that will enable them to work with these international communities. Challengers might stress their education abroad or past experience working for international institutions. Many presidents have previously served as members of international bodies before returning home to compete for domestic office. Alassane Ouattara, President of Côte d'Ivoire, had risen to a high rank in the International Monetary Fund. Nicéphore Soglo of Benin had worked at the World Bank, and his compatriot Thomas Yayi Boni had long worked at the Central Bank of the West African States before entering politics. These high-level professional positions abroad were specifically advertised in the candidates' self-presentation to the citizenry.

In another example of candidates' leveraging their background to gain credibility on the issue of foreign relations, in the 2016 presidential race in Gabon, challenger Jean Ping stressed his mixed Chinese-Gabonese heritage (his father was a Chinese trader, and his mother was Gabonese) to reinforce his identity as someone who was open to innovation and change but also to imply subtly that this identity could reinforce Gabonese ties with China. As described in a Newsweek article,

The half-Chinese diplomat has said that his mixed heritage would help him to lead Gabon if he is confirmed as president. "This cultural mix had a profound impact on my childhood," Ping told Quartz, saying that the experience of "looking different" made him "more open-minded." There is also speculation his links with China could benefit Gabon economically – Ping helped arrange the 2004 visit of former Chinese President Hu Jintao to Gabon. Trade between the two countries already stands at around $745 million as of 2013, with Gabon considered a significant trading partner in Africa for China, despite its tiny population of less than 2 million.[17]

---

[16] We note that candidates' religious orientation can also be portrayed in a negative light by challengers. For instance, Nigerian President Muhammadu Buhari's previous support of sharia and religious piety enabled critics to label him "radical" (Kendhammer, 2016, p. 22).

[17] John Gaffey, "Who is Jean Ping, Gabon's Presidential Challenger?" in Newsweek, accessed at Aug 30, 2016 www.newsweek.com/who-jean-ping-gabons-presidential-challenger-494551.

However, personal background can also create political liabilities and generate fodder for attacks from opponents. Observers of US politics watched members of the Tea Party movement question the origin of Barack Obama's birth certificate as well as his "Muslim-sounding" middle name to question his patriotism and loyalty to the United States and its values. In the 2016 presidential race in Benin, the dual nationality of the incumbent president's hand-picked successor, Lionel Zinsou, was called into question. Zinsou, the nephew of former president Émile Zinsou, was born in France and had spent most of his professional life working in finance in France before becoming prime minister of Benin in 2016.[18] Skeptics suggested that Zinsou's loyalties might lie with Europe rather than Benin.[19] A decade earlier, Côte d'Ivoire's President Laurent Gbagbo had unsuccessfully tried to block foreign-born Ouattara's candidacy with a similar argument.

Aside from critiques by incumbents, opposition candidates with no previous experience in office face hurdles in establishing credibility in issue areas in which they have no proven track record. One campaign strategy is to draw on their personal background and work experience to prove their competency in certain policy areas. In the 2016 presidential race in Benin, candidates Patrice Talon and Sebastien Ajavon both vaunted their business backgrounds in an appeal that resonated with constituents. Supporters of the two men celebrated the departure of a corrupt political class but also the management experience and financial acumen that these candidates could bring to the office. In Nigeria, General Buhari was able to flaunt his military credentials when discussing Boko Haram and his ability to address corruption. However, at the same time, this military background made him vulnerable to critiques by the People's Democratic Party (PDP) about his nondemocratic tendencies, since he had previously come to power after leading a coup in the 1980s.

[18] Tyson Roberts, "Here's Why Benin's Election Was a Step Forward for African Democratic Consolidation. And Why It Wasn't," *Washington Post*, March 22, 2016, accessed at https://www.washingtonpost.com/news/monkey-cage/wp/2016/03/22/heres-why-benins-election-was-a-step-forward-for-african-democratic-consolidation-and-why-it-wasnt.

[19] Zinsou had dual French and Beninian citizenship and had previously been an advisor to the French prime minister, an investment banker, and the head of a private equity firm (PAI Partners) in France. (See https://www.issafrica.org/iss-today/will-benin-get-another-international-president-in-2016).

5.2.3 Issue Ownership

In countries that are characterized by party weakness or lack unique party platforms, candidates leverage their own past experiences and professional positions as a type of valence characteristic. These experiences signal their competence, experience, or commitment to a specific issue. In much the same way that parties gain ownership over political issues on which they are perceived to be more competent, candidates can bring their biographies to own issues. Where opposition candidates have had limited experience in office, such as most countries in sub-Saharan Africa, it is often easier for an incumbent to capitalize on good policy performance than it is for an opposition leader to make a counterfactual argument that he or she would have done better. For instance, in their analysis of the 2011 elections, Conroy-Krutz and Logan (2012) find that Museveni's victory was largely due to positive assessments of the economic growth and better security under his tenure rather than to vote buying or intimidation.

As we will see in Chapter 6, candidates use their structural positions as incumbents or opposition to signal credibility on an issue. For instance, incumbents typically attempt to claim credit development projects accomplished under their tenure, even when these projects were funded entirely by foreign donors. Opposition candidates will stress their role in the trenches, fighting for the common people against pervasive corruption in the incumbent regime.

For instance, rather than appealing to a specific ethnic constituency in the run-up to the 2016 presidential race in Gambia, Adama Barrow, the challenger and eventually presidential victor, criticized Yahya Jammeh's two-decade rule and promised to "bring about change" in light of the "suffering that all Gambians irrespective of age, sex, religious, or tribal background," have experienced. Barrow continued his speech by highlighting the incumbent party's abuse of the rule of law:

The past twelve months have marked the beginning of drastic change in this country. It started in Fass Ngagga Choye when our Party leader and the UDP convoy going on a countrywide tour were stopped from continuing their tour. The standoff that followed led to the capitulation of government and granting of a permit to continue. The demonstration by our youths led by Solo Sandeng our Organizing Secretary in April this year which led to their illegal arrest and detention and subsequent death in custody of Solo, was the turning point in the history of politics in our country.[20]

[20] https://jollofnews.com/2016/09/02/gambia-in-acceptance-speech-udps-adama-barrow-vows-to-kick-jammeh-out.

Barrow's position as a young challenger from outside the political system made such critiques more credible.

5.2.4 Ethnicity and Other Appeals through Homophily

Candidates can also bring attention to identity attributes that resonate with more specifically targeted constituencies. In elections around the world, candidates draw on their biographical backgrounds to attract bloc constituencies of voters who value a candidate's homophily, or perceived degree of shared attributes (Rogers and Shoemakers, 1971). To do this, a candidate may employ a local broker who can vouch for the candidate's credibility and mobilize networks of vertical support or who can make direct appeals. Western candidates attend county fairs and tour agricultural salons to prove their links to rural communities. Similarly, African candidates are likely to emphasize familial or cultural connections to a constituency by citing family heritage, speaking the regional language, or working with local and regional elites to establish credibility through endorsements.

The most prominent manifestation of homophily in African politics is through ethnic or regional appeals. Evidence suggests that ethnic constituencies do cue on a candidate's ethnicity or regional origin to guide their vote choice among candidates with similar ideologies (Ferree, 2006; Fridy, 2009; Conroy-Krutz, 2013). Identity attributes are not limited to the candidate. New research has shown that candidates can strategically leverage the ethnicity of a non-coethnic spouse to attract supporters from that ethnic group and build a larger multiethnic coalition (Adida et al., 2016). Candidates who marry spouses from other ethnic groups, as Jerry Rawlings did, or have parents from different regions, such as Amadou Toumani Touré in Mali, will attempt to make use of these aspects of their identity to generate a greater base. Similarly, candidates of mixed ethnic background vaunt their mixed heritage to appeal to larger swaths of voters.

To be sure, ethnoregional networks and ethnic identification have been shown to help constituents to overcome information problems. They offer cognitive clues as to which candidate to vote for and offer informal insurance that a candidate of one's own ethnic group will redistribute goods and services in one's favor (Fridy, 2007; Habyarimana et al., 2007; Dunning, 2010). Candidates operating without ethnic networks have less easily identifiable constituencies of support. This problem is exacerbated by vertical patronage linkages between a diverse group of supporters and the political ambitions of a small number of individuals, often a single politician. This suggests that ethnic parties that know their constituents may be more likely to adopt clear positions, a point to which we return below.

We suspect that ethnic constituencies lessen uncertainty about where young and inexperienced political parties should court and expect votes, and politicians can make more informed decisions about position issues that are of concern to their specific constituencies. A classic example is provided by the Kenyan political system, in which party names and coalitions change each election cycle but voters remain loyal to specific ethnic elites (Elischer, 2013). In Kenya, Raila Odinga can continue to court votes with regional appeals for decentralization that resonate with Luo constituents who feel marginalized by the Kikuyu business class and the economic power of Nairobi, regardless of Odinga's shifting allegiances to different party coalitions from election to election.

There are many reasons why ethnic appeals could be effective in an electoral context characterized by uncertainty. A coethnic candidate could have a valence advantage because the common origin signals a congruence of general policy preferences, the candidate will be easier to sanction in case of a misstep (Fearon and Laitin, 1996), or the candidate could be easier to approach to communicate needs through shared relationships.

However, shared ethnicity is not the only identity characteristic employed by African candidates. In fact, relying too heavily on this one dimension of identity might constitute an electoral liability. Unless parties can bet on a majority number of votes from coethnics, they will need to ensure that identity politics associated with their party are palatable to other coalition partners. They need to be wary of creating insider–outsider divisions that would threaten future coalitions. Furthermore, even in political systems in which ethnicity is highly salient, members of smaller ethnic groups may opt out of a coethnic vote if "their" candidate is not seen as nationally viable. Precolonial political history can condition other types of political alliances across groups. For instance, Dunning and Harrison's (2010) work on voter preferences and candidate selection in Mali shows that cross-cutting networks of *sanankuya*, stemming from the Malian Empire's thirteenth-century constitution, play an important role; voters are as likely to favor a non-coethnic cousin as a coethnic, and parties are more likely to run a candidate with a large number of cousins (rather than coethnics) in specific districts. In addition, African countries had very different expressions of nationalism at independence. In some instances, such as Julius Nyerere's Tanzania, nationalism encompassed all ethnic groups and fostered a supraethnic identity, while in other countries, such as Sudan or Rwanda, nationalism favored certain ethnic groups over others. Straus (2015) argues that these experiences at independence have profound effects not only on the use of violence but also on expressions of citizenship decades later. These dynamics of political insiders and outsiders are likely to shape the prospects of coalitions and coordination among subnational groups in the multiparty context. Robinson (2016) demonstrates how strong sentiments of nationalism can mediate levels of trust among coethnics and the general population.

5.3 CAMPAIGN STRATEGY: TARGETING APPEALS

With finite resources, parties must prioritize their campaign strategies and how to target their appeals. Most parties are poorly funded and have limited information about their voter base. They have to make guesses about who constitutes their base and where they might be able to gain swing voters. Candidates' level of certainty about supportive constituencies will vary depending on the availability of heuristics such as historic regional and ethnic voting blocs.

For instance, Kenya is a country with evolving parties and coalitions but fairly consistent ethnic voting blocs (Elischer, 2013). In contrast to the stereotype, some scholarship suggests that presidential campaigning in Kenya occurs outside of the candidate or party's ethnic strongholds. Recent analysis of campaign rallies in the Kenyan 2007 election, showed that candidates actually target swing voters, defined as voters without a coethnic candidate in the race, rather than ethnic strongholds; candidates compete in the same communities rather than trying to court opposing ethnic coalitions (Horowitz, 2016, p. 330). Parties can identify high-quality local candidates in ethnic strongholds for lower-level races and can rely on these same candidates to conduct door-to-door mobilization efforts in these strongholds (Horowitz, 2012, 2016). Candidates need to employ diverse strategies to appeal to different audiences.

In presidential races, the cost of campaigning in rural areas gives an advantage to better-funded incumbents. In fact, in some countries where skeptical voters may populate urban areas, incumbent parties will rely predominantly on voters in rural areas, where the incumbents have a comparative advantage. For instance, in recent Zimbabwean elections, the Zimbabwe African National Union-Patriotic Front (ZANU-PF) has concentrated its campaign efforts in rural areas (Dendere, 2015, p. 142).

The party's strategy also involves restricting opposition movement into these rural areas and even the use of violence to maintain control of rural areas (Dendere, 2015, p. 156).

The density, accessibility, and low cost of campaigning in urban areas create opportunities for opposition candidates who do not have the same access to resources as incumbents. These are also the places where opposition members are most likely to find voters who are sympathetic to their cause. Opposition parties that are particularly cash constrained might focus their campaigning in areas where they have a strong local elite candidate (Stroh, 2010). Increasingly, opposition candidates are making successful forays into urban slums. Control over regional capitals gives opposition some initial momentum that they can leverage onto the national stage. In the 2009 elections, the Democratic Movement of Mozambique split off from Resistência Nacional Mocambiçana (RENAMO) to run a presidential candidate, Daviz Simango, a former mayor of Beira. It made direct appeals to young voters who had weaker connections to RENAMO and FRELIMO's salient political history (Nuvunga and Adalima, 2011). The nascent party went on to capture three of the four largest cities in Mozambique in the 2013 municipal races in a party system that had been dominated by two large parties for nearly twenty years (Jentzsch, 2014).[21] Emerging research suggests that opposition parties adopt similar strategies in rural zones, first targeting the rural areas with the most populous towns and cities (Boone and Wahman, 2015). Campaigning in rural areas is more expensive but is necessary for candidates who want national-level support.

Resnick (2015) describes the emergence of populist candidates who are courting votes of young, unemployed urbanites by using a special brand of populism that promises more social inclusion while denouncing the existing political class but that may also include nationalistic or xenophobic rhetoric. Cheeseman and Larmer (2015) find that ethnic appeals can be effectively mixed with populism to form "ethnopopulist" campaigns in environments with a history of urban radicalism and identity politics and urban–rural remittance streams that bridge urban and rural voters around populist candidates.

It is important to note that in some of the more authoritarian-leaning regimes and in some countries, the opposition will have limited

[21] http://africasacountry.com/2014/11/how-frelimo-rehabilitated-renamo-in-time-for-mozambiques-elections. MDM is led by two brothers; one is party president, and the other is head of the parliamentary group (Nuvunga and Adalima, 2011, p. 4).

opportunities to campaign. Incumbents can restrict opposition mobility and use state security apparatus to limit opposition campaigns. In recent contests in Zambia and Uganda, incumbents used police and security forces to threaten opposition leaders and supporters (Mwanawasa et al., 2017, p. 15).

5.3.1 Brokerage and Endorsements

One strategy that candidates use to make campaigning more efficient is to identify brokers who can help to deliver large blocs of votes. Brokers are typically nonparty actors who are well implanted in a community where they enjoy a combination of social power, prestige, and resources that allows them to reliably deliver blocs of votes to candidates by drawing on vertical networks. Democratic candidates in US races are often photographed touring a factory floor, shirt sleeves rolled up and wearing a hard hat to demonstrate solidarity with union workers. They work directly through unions that attempt to mobilize card-carrying members.

Brokerage has long been documented as a process through which credible and respected local leaders mobilize constituents to vote for a specific candidate or party (LeMarchand and Legg, 1972; Beck, 2008). Some brokers can operate at a national level, such as certain religious leaders, or regionally within ethnoregional constituencies, as may be the case for some traditional leaders or paramount chiefs. Most brokers are local big men, whose political influence is limited to the village, neighborhood, or constituency level. In the course of the campaign, candidates court brokers and seek to strike deals with them, providing some resources or the promise of club goods, such as local infrastructure, in exchange for electoral support. Baldwin (2016) argues that voters may agree to this in the rational expectation that the local chief will then be able to deliver welfare-enhancing benefits to the community.

Candidates often think of rural brokers as being able to deliver more credibly on promises of turnout than brokers in urban areas can, in part because of the vertical nature of networks from traditional or religious authorities down to their constituencies, but also as the result of a communal logic around candidate selection for legislative races (Koter, 2016, p. 134).[22] Geographically targeted brokerage, in which traditional leaders mobilize constituents from villages where they have influence, enables

---

[22] However, we note variation in the power of traditional authorities in different countries in Africa (Logan, 2009; Koter, 2013).

parties to monitor at the group level, which is less costly and requires less capacity than monitoring individual votes (Gottlieb and Larreguy, 2016). Urban brokerage, which may include horizontal brokerage within a union or across an association, can also deliver votes, but as will be described below, we increasingly see patterns of direct appeals to urban voters. Collier (1982) makes a distinction between autonomous and mobilized participation; she argues that the latter has more to do with the capacity and credibility of a vote broker than voter-level variables.

Willis and al-Batthani (2010, p. 210) describe how they used broker-age in internally displaced persons camps to efficiently capture a large number of votes; candidates emphasized the importance of using the chiefs, since they "controlled" the people. Displaced persons and other vulnerable populations might be particularly susceptible to brokerage practices and, subsequently, more obedient at the polls, which makes them attractive targets of candidates hoping to court brokers with faithful constituencies.

Local and regional leaders vary in their brokerage abilities. Candidates and parties need to determine who will be able to credibly deliver large numbers of voters to the polls (Baldwin, 2015; Gottlieb and Larreguy, 2016) and which leaders will commit to their candidates. Candidates will seek public endorsements from brokers to ensure that these brokers will not switch their support to other candidates and parties. However, such statements also provide signals of power and influence for the candidate as a trusted figure assures the audience that the candidate has the acumen to get the job done but also that the candidate can penetrate and work with existing networks. Union leaders or traditional authorities who coordinate votes among their constituencies will publicly endorsement candidates and provide a heuristic for their followers. These leaders are counted upon to negotiate the types of policies or kickbacks that benefit their constituencies with the understanding that they have the weight and credibility to mobilize their bases.

Candidates are eager to win the support of potential brokers and attempt to paint themselves as better allies than their competitors. In Senegal, candidates disseminate video and pictures of themselves seeking counsel and endorsement from religious leaders. Part of the campaign tour involves a visit to Touba, a Mouride-led, self-governed religious city within Senegal's borders.[23] In this symbolic deference, politicians acknowledge the real power of Islamic authorities. In Zambia in 2011,

[23] http://www.reuters.com/article/us-senegal-brotherhoods-idUSTRE80M12U20120124.

Michael Sata criticized President Rupiah Banda's threats to remove Senior Chieftainess Nkomeshya by framing the issue as an infringement on the power of traditional authorities.[24]

In the pure brokerage model, voters give away their vote to the broker, who will then deliver a bloc of votes to the candidate. Although the logic probably operates on a continuum, this can be distinguished from political endorsements, in which a candidate is praised and voters are encouraged to vote for that candidate but voters retains autonomy over their vote. Local traditional leaders can signal that politicians share identity, empathy for, and commitment to specific communities (Posner, 2005; Baldwin, 2015, p. 44). During the campaign, politicians will work to publicize endorsements by various traditional leaders (Baldwin, 2015, p. 121). Trusted brokers can endorse a wide range of figures, even those from outside their own communities. Recent research by Arriola et al. (2016) shows that in Kenya, candidate endorsements issued by a respected coethnic can affect voter evaluations of non-coethnics; under some circumstances, this effect is even large enough to overcome favoritism toward a coethnic candidate.

In some instances, candidates are constrained in their ability to leverage brokers and their networks. For instance, religious and traditional leaders can be reprimanded as being overtly political for endorsing specific candidates. During the 2011 campaign in Zambia, residents of Luanshya criticized a Christian leader who killed a chicken during a Patriotic Front Rally to symbolize the end of control by the Movement for Multiparty Democracy (MMD) of that district. Constituents asked that he cease committing non-Christian acts and return to the pulpit.[25] In Kenya's 2007 elections, the Catholic Church tried to rein in two of its bishops who spoke out in support of different candidates, thus violating the church's commitment to being nonpartisan. In some instances, religious leaders in Muslim majority countries flirt with endorsements of specific candidates but often abstain from backing secular politicians and "dirtying their hands" in electoral politics.

Another type of endorsement comes from former presidents or other prominent national politicians. These endorsements carry significant weight, not only because these politicians are among the few who

---

[24] Sata later attempted to remove Paramount Chief Chitimukulu in a similar fashion https://www.lusakatimes.com/2011/09/08/opinion-poll-correct-elections-held-yesterdaysata.

[25] https://www.lusakatimes.com/2011/09/01/father-frank-bwalya-condemned-beheading-live-chicken-pf-rally.

understand what it takes to do the job, but also because they are perceived to be important gatekeepers to the elite political class and the international community. By signaling their support for candidates, they are essentially saying that the candidate will be able to work within the existing political establishment. In Ghana, Jerry Rawlings has been known to dominate the stage when campaigning for National Democratic Congress (NDC) candidates; his personality may dwarf the prospective candidate, but it carries real weight with voters. Conversely, a lack of endorsement or a statement of criticism from a former president or party leader can prove damaging for a candidate. Goodluck Jonathan lost a lot of credibility as the incumbent candidate after former Nigerian President Olusegun Obasanjo called in a public letter for Jonathan to step down for mishandling security in the north and corruption and piracy plaguing the oil sector.[26]

A third type of endorsement comes from party members who attempt to signal support for different factions or from leaders of smaller parties who are looking to jump onto the bandwagon of a more successful candidate's campaign. A long-standing challenge for opposition parties has been fragmentation (Arriola, 2013) and a tendency toward political nomadism, in which opposition elected officials leave their parties and join the presidential coalition (see Chapter 4). Weak incumbent parties and coalitions can face similar challenges in the context of open-seat elections (Cheeseman, 2010). In the 2016 presidential election in Benin, the incumbent Cowry Forces for an Emerging Benin (FCBE) party became fragmented as party members accused Lionel Zinsou of having been selected in an undemocratic matter. At other times, the parties show their weakness in their inability to coordinate with or control candidates who are running under the party banner.[27] In the run-up to the 2011 Zambian elections, the MMD had difficulty disciplining affiliated candidates who were making claims that they were backed by the President Banda.[28]

Resources are key to gaining the support of future coalition members from inside or outside a candidates own party. As described by Arriola (2013), the countries that have been successful in forming opposition coalitions are the countries that have a thriving private sector independent from the state that can back opposition candidates. It becomes important

---

[26] http://www.bbc.com/news/world-africa-12192152.

[27] In less democratic contexts, incumbents might coerce or coopt elements of the opposition into making endorsements to further fragment those opposition parties.

[28] https://www.lusakatimes.com/2011/06/09/mmd-aspiring-candidate-claiming-president-bandas-support-disqualifiednyangu.

for candidates and coalition members to signal whom they plan to support because backing the winning (or best-funded candidate) could translate to significant financial gains or lucrative appointments. These types of endorsements are particularly frequent during second-round runoffs, when candidates hope to trade votes from their electoral bases for coveted positions in the future administration. Entrepreneurial third candidates can play decisive roles in breaking ties between two leading candidates, and this can generate individual payoffs in the winning administration. Minor candidates with aspirations for ministerial or cabinet positions can trade the support of their constituencies, by endorsing other candidates, for these lucrative posts. In two-round systems, these last-minute pacts often prove consequential in determining the winner.

In authoritarian-leaning regimes, candidates may attempt to buy or coopt endorsements from opposition or civil society to build their credibility, especially in the face of a boycott by other members of the opposition. In Niger's 2016 election, fifty weak parties decided to support President Mahamadou Issoufou during the second round, although the strongest parts of the opposition boycotted the second round.[29] The public endorsement by some opposition parties made the opposition boycott less powerful. There were similar dynamics in the 2016 Gabonese election after the main opposition leader's challenge of the results.

5.3.2 The Campaign Tour

A candidate tour of the countryside is a critical component of African electoral campaigns regardless of the level of democracy (Jourde, 2005). Rauschenberg's interviews with Ghanaian politicians highlight the need to actively engage with their constituents. In an interview with a member of NDC's national campaign team (Rauschenberg, 2015, p. 83), the politician explains the importance of political rallies in the context of candidate tours: "Coming to them, makes you get the vote. If you don't show them that respect [by coming to their region] ..., then you'll not get the votes. Some will decide not to vote at all."

Candidates are expected to traverse poor infrastructure and log many hours in the car so that they can meet with voters in rural constituencies. Their physical presence at the campaign site is very important, as is the journey they take to visit rural voters; many campaigns have been derailed by a candidate's choice to fly out to an area rather than drive to

---

[29] We thank Mamoudou Gazibo for bringing this argument to our attention.

visit a constituency. For its part, the ritual rural campaign tour serves to highlight the infrastructure needs of rural constituencies and allows candidates to demonstrate their humility and willingness to meet voters in their own backyard. Their visits to remote regions are highly publicized to all of their constituents; this reach also signals their ability to mobilize resources for the expensive rural vote. In the 2013 Malian elections, candidates documented their campaign movements through Facebook posts and even real-time Geographic Information Systems (GIS) tour trackers on their websites.

During the 2002 Malian presidential elections, Soumaïla Cissé faced popular criticism for making a helicopter to visit a village rather than driving on the rural roads. He eventually lost the presidential race. However, candidates now increasingly rely on planes and helicopters for gains in efficiency, particularly in richer countries, where campaigns have relied on broader and larger sources of funding. Paget (2017) documents the increasing use of helicopters in recent Tanzanian elections. He estimates that during the 2016 elections, the Chama cha Demokrasia na Maendeleo (CHADEMA) opposition party relied on six helicopters to get legislative candidates to rallies in their districts. The record for helicopter use may have been set in Kenya, where CNN reported that eighty-six different helicopters were registered for use in the 2017 elections, at a cost of US $3,000 for an hour of flight time.[30] Voters may prefer candidates who brave awful rural roads to get to their town, but Paget (2017) emphasizes the theatrical advantage of the helicopter, which noisily circles around the town a couple times to announce the candidate's visit and attract a crowd.

Candidates seek to address issues that resonate with constituencies. For instance, when visiting Bunyoro, an oil-producing region of Uganda, both Museveni and Besigye were expected to frame their appeals in terms of "management of oil proceeds, land, ethnic tensions and infrastructure."[31] Candidates can also employ important indigenous imagery that resonates with particularly constituencies. Bolten (2016, p. 1032) discusses how a candidate in Sierra Leone brought members of the *poro* (male initiation) society to demonstrate his ability to draw on the occult.

Once at a constituency site, candidates will stand onstage with respected leaders including religious figures or traditional leaders. With their

---

[30] http://www.cnn.com/2017/08/04/africa/kenya-election-helicopters/index.html.
[31] As reported in the *Ugandan Daily Monitor*: http://www.monitor.co.ug/News/National/Museveni-Besigye-camp-Bunyoro/-/688334/3044500/-/ffqssjz/-/index.html.

presence onstage, local electoral brokers provide their informal endorsement. On the rally stand, they typically pledge support to projects and services that will directly benefit that community. Outside of the context of strong, dominant parties, candidates are probably more likely to discuss their own past personal experience and actions to guarantee their competence as a candidate rather than relying on party brand. These rallies also serve as ways to generate down-ballot support for legislative and municipal offices.

Sometimes demonstrations of solidarity are more symbolic. Candidates stage soccer games as well as hip-hop concerts, a symbol of youth, to demonstrate evidence of an interest in local communities and commitment to addressing the pervasive problem of youth unemployment (see, for example, Manirakiza, 2010; Baller, 2014; for two examples of how soccer and politics intersect at the national level in the region, see Kamaté and Banégas, 2010; Deets, 2016). Populist candidates employ theatrical tactics during campaigns to gain attention and credibility around issues. Kenneth Koma, referred to as "modern Moses," campaigned wearing shabby clothes and used Setswana in his speeches to foster populist ties with certain constituencies (Resnick, 2012, p. 20, citing Motlogelwa, 2009). After Koma's death, the president of Botswana's ruling Democratic Party began to copy Koma's strategy, touring periurban areas and even riding a bicycle into some constituencies to show solidarity with the grass roots (Resnick, 2012, p. 20).

More generally, the campaign rally is designed to entertain potential voters. Paget (2017, p. 15) notes the reliance on fancy public address systems that provide loud danceable music both before and after the formal part of the rally. This may partly explain the allure of the campaign rally. Paget (2017, p. 7) estimates that – 69 percent of all Tanzanian voters attended a political rally during the 2015 campaign.

It is not uncommon for campaigns to distribute goods to people who attend a rally or to bring a larger gift intended to benefit the community. It is important to stress the difference between these campaign practices and vote buying, which is a quid pro quo exchange of material goods for turnout or a vote for a specific candidate, which is a dominant theme in the literature on African politics. In campaign distribution, candidates need to demonstrate their commitment to constituents at the rally. This often involves a distribution of goods or money or a donation of a public good to a targeted community (Lindberg, 2010, 2013). Candidates can also use this type of material distribution to stress their personal wealth and resource base. ZANU-PF distributed seed grain to rural voters in packaging that incorporated the party symbol (Dendere, 2015, p. 59). In work on Ghana, scholars have emphasized the importance of pre-electoral redistribution in validating a candidate's electoral and leadership potential (Lindberg, 2012; Paller, 2014). In other words, this kind of distribution serves as an initial test that all politicians must pass before they can be seen as viable candidates. Similarly, Kramon (2016) argues that most parties do not have the ability to monitor vote choice, so electoral handouts serve as a mechanism to provide information to voters about candidates' commitment and ability to provide resources to the poor. He draws on experimental evidence from Kenya to argue that initial handouts can make promises of future resource distribution more credible. Candidates seek to demonstrate their awareness of voters' needs but also to prove their own material viability. Electoral handouts prove that a candidate has the personal resources and backing to make a legitimate run for office. In addition to signaling the candidates' ability to win, handouts suggest that the candidates will not need to pillage the state resources, since they can rely on a sizable base of personal assets.

Anecdotal evidence suggests that the nature of relationships between voters and parties has been changing over time. In some instances, village leaders and politicians make pacts to bring development projects or public goods to specific zones. For example, in Mali, historically candidates delivered tea, sugar, or salt to rural villages in an attempt to win votes. In the run-up to the annulled 2012 presidential elections, political parties were increasingly having to offer more sophisticated types of club goods.[32] During village visits in northern Mopti in January 2012, *Alliance pour la Démocratie au Mali* (ADEMA), Mali's strongest political party, was promising cataract surgeries, while Ralley pour le Mali (RPM), the current President Keita's party, was handing out televisions and solar panel generators to villages so that they would be able to watch the Africa Cup of Nations soccer tournament.

5.4 CAMPAIGN MEDIA

One of the most celebrated achievements since democratic transitions in sub-Saharan Africa has been increases in media access and freedom. The last twenty years have been characterized by unprecedented growth of cellphone networks as well new fiber-optic cables that connect

---

[32] As was noted during data collection for Bleck and Michelitch (2015).

African capitals to high-speed Internet. In addition, transitions to democracy enabled rural radio expansion across Africa (Hyden et al., 2003; Moehler and Singh, 2011), and radio continues to be the popular communication source in Africa (Bleck and Michelitch, 2017). However, as we discussed in Chapter 3, even in environments with a relatively free press, African presidents hold an incumbency advantage when it comes to media, owing to their ability to leverage state resources during the campaign (Levitsky and Way, 2010). In more restricted environments, incumbents wield the power of the media more forcefully. After the 2016 Ugandan elections were plagued with irregularities and highly criticized by observers, the government prohibited media coverage of the opposition's Defiance Campaign and banned political demonstrations before the inauguration ceremonies (Tripp, 2017, p. 92). In another extreme example, from the 2016 election in Zimbabwe, the government arrested journalists, shut down a privately owned newspaper, and thus provided the state broadcaster with a communication monopoly for the duration of the campaign (Tripp, 2017, p. 99). However, relatively competitive electoral environments have also involved incumbents who are willing to use heavy-handed tactics to their advantage, as the case of the Zambian 2016 election demonstrates. In Sierra Leone, a journalist was arrested and detained for eleven days after making a comment that was critical of the government's Ebola relief efforts (Tripp, 2017, p. 99). In Kenya, a 2016 media bill was much more threatening than the previous law, imposing fines and jail sentences for journalists found guilty of defaming the Kenyan parliament (Tripp, 2017, p. 99). In Tanzania, the government passed a similar "media services act."[33]

Traditionally, incumbents typically have greater resources to use for an advertising advantage during campaigns. This is important as candidates seek to establish name recognition and provide voters with information about how to vote "correctly," littering urban areas with political posters (Conroy-Krutz and Moehler, 2014; Giannini et al., 2017). Similar to visual appeals in US political campaigning, advertisements for African candidates, as well as Latin American presidential candidates, tend to feature candidates' pictures, their names, and images that connect candidates to their constituencies (Giannini et al., 2017, p. 20). In fourteen African and Latin American elections, party symbols were the second most employed element of their visual appeals, followed by valence and, finally, position appeals (Giannini et al., 2017). Candidates' choices to

---

[33] We thank Keith Weghorst for this observation.

include ballots in their advertisements seem to be shaped in part by efforts to educate voters about how to use the electoral ballot, particularly in countries where there are low levels of political information or literacy (Reynolds and Steenbergen, 2006). The best-financed candidate can have more professionalized poster images and a wider variety of types of posters. Opposition candidates with more meager budgets may be restricted to one or two images. It is not uncommon to observe swaths of opposition posters that have been destroyed by "supporters" of incumbents. The preponderance of undamaged posters for incumbents and defiled posters for challengers is an additional show of incumbent dominance.[34]

Local radio, which may be affected by dominant political coalitions in the region, can play an important role in shaping citizen attitudes and mobilizing citizens out to vote (Young, 2004; Tower, 2008; Horowitz and Long, 2016). Television advertisements are used less frequently and carry less significance in many countries in sub-Saharan Africa than in the rest of the world (Wittman and Thiam, 2006). Radio and television advertisements can prove difficult for opposition candidates, as they often face censorship by state run or state-influenced media. However, some authoritarian-leaning states offer relatively equal airtime. Ahlin et al. (2015, p. 172) explain that coverage of candidates in the 2015 Togolese election on public media was impartial and that nearly every candidate was given equal access. Even so, incumbents may be at an advantage, as they can seek support from private stations and pay the higher cost of running spots on television.

Television advertisement, which are gaining ground in South Africa, help to illustrate the different campaign strategies of the different parties. In 2009, the African National Congress (ANC) ran its first national advertisement. Narrated by an older man in a local language with English subtitles, the spot focused on the historical role of the ANC in both fighting apartheid expanding service delivery.[35] In the run-up to the 2014 South African elections, both the ANC and the Democratic Alliance (DA) poured money into television advertisements.[36] The ANC advertisement ran in different national languages and focused on pictures of its policy; it invoked images of Nelson Mandela but included no images of unpopular leader Jacob Zuma. In contrast, the DA spent a lot time focusing on the personal history of Helen Zille, emphasizing her coming of age within

---

[34] We thank Michael Wahman for this observation.
[35] https://www.youtube.com/watch?v=Suu3en5u6fQ.
[36] https://www.enca.com/south-africa/anc-da-unleash-tv-ads-campaigns.

the struggle against apartheid. Zille talks about corruption and the DA's plan for job creation, and she pleads with viewers to "give us a chance to show what we can do."[37]

When opposition campaigns cannot run advertisements on television, many candidates post campaign advertisements on social media. As we will discuss below, social media levels the playing field in that it is less costly and less likely to be censored than traditional forms of media. Candidates generate Facebook profiles, circulate videotaped messages to prospective voters, live-tweet during campaign tours, and even spread "fake news" about opponents.

More broadly, social media provide access to international audiences, including expatriate voters, election observers, and the increasing number of Africans who are spending their disposable income on access to Facebook (as we will discuss below).[38] Divergent social media strategies suggest the variety of ways in which candidates can use online platforms. For instance, Zambian opposition leader Hakainde Hichilema, who lost a tight and disputed race to Patriotic Front candidate Edgar Lungu in 2015 and again in 2016, spent much of his electoral energy on courting the poor, rural parts of Zambia. A well-produced campaign video stressed his humility, family values, and love of cattle. He was shown milking cows and interviewing young schoolchildren about their dreams, drawing parallels to his background as a young student who received a government scholarship to continue his studies. When noting his commitment to access to schooling for every Zambian child, he explained, "I went to public schools on a government scholarship ... I feel indebted to the children of Zambia."[39] In the same video, Hichilema leveraged his background as an economist to critique the Patriotic Front's irresponsible borrowing and rising debt loads over the past few years.

In contrast, Edgar Lungu's Patriotic Front campaign did not create an official website but relied exclusively on a Facebook page, thus catering to the Internet habits of Lungu's young, urban base. His campaign video featured urban Zambians, many speaking in the local language, lauding Lungu, and it closed with Lungu in his office promising to continue the "good work of the PF."[40] Lungu's campaign may have prioritized

---

[37] https://www.youtube.com/watch?v=oywX1AlAE7U.
[38] We note that the sharing of media using USB flash drives and external drives means that consumers are not required to be connected to the Internet to view it. Telephones are key conduits for all types of media, even in the absence of connectivity.
[39] https://www.youtube.com/watch?v=8SGcVDBgrEU.
[40] https://www.youtube.com/watch?v=jPTjqxEidgw.

Facebook rather than a YouTube video, anticipating that that this was the medium most likely to reach constituents.

5.4.1 Social Media as a Tool to Combat Incumbency Advantage

The explosion of cellphone use and Internet access in Africa over the last fifteen years has provided opposition candidates with a cost-effective tool for engaging with younger and tech-savvy voters. Candidates and parties do not have to broker posts through journalists but instead can use Facebook, Twitter, and Instagram to engage directly with their constituencies. While governing elites may have strong control over traditional media channels, opposition candidates can leverage private radio, cellphones, and the Internet to get their message out. Cellphones also substantially reduce the costs of campaigning for new parties, since candidates can prearrange campaign tours without scouting visits and continue to broker relationships with village leaders over the phone. These efforts directly inform citizens about the nature of governance and current events. Increasingly, Africans share files in MP3 format, so campaign media can be shared directly without a need for expensive data connections. Similarly, access to information through cellphones and the Internet increases possibilities for regional diffusion and collaboration. Friends in different geographic zones can use WhatsApp group messages to share localized information and rumors.

Facebook is acknowledged to be the most prolific social media tool in the world. In 2016, 1.71 billion people were using Facebook. As of January 2016, 9 percent of Africans use social media. Nigeria was home to 15 million Facebook users, Kenya to 4.5 million, and South Africa to 12 million.[41] South Africans are among the most active Facebook users in the world, spending 3.2 h a day online compared to the global average of 2.4 h.[42] One author's recent fieldwork in Mali reveals that many young urbanites save up for cheap (approximately US $25–50) Chinese-made smartphones exclusively to have access to Facebook. The shutdown of Facebook in the wake of protests after the 2016 arrest of a popular Malian radio DJ suggest that the Malian government is aware of the potential for political mobilization that Facebook offers.[43] Therefore

---

[41] http://www.cnn.com/2016/01/13/africa/africa-social-media-consumption.

[42] http://www.cnn.com/2016/01/13/africa/africa-social-media-consumption.

[43] The DJ, Ras Bath, was later acquitted by the Bamako Court of Appeals in November 2017. http://sahelien.com/en/mali-polemicist-ras-bath-acquitted/

an exploration of Facebook provides a helpful way to explore how candidates are engaging with social media.

As well as Facebook posts, during the Kenyan elections in 2012, presidential candidates flaunted their social media prowess through ongoing Twitter commentary, Instagram photos, and online streaming of debates and addresses. These new types of technologies are less likely to be used by older voters or those in rural areas, but they appeal to many in the opposition's base: young urban voters. Social media offers cheap platforms for organizing and discussion of political information through applications such as Viber and WhatsApp. Mobile money platforms facilitate campaign logistics by allowing resources to be easily deployed to distant geographic locales. Like their peers in other countries in the world, candidates who use these forms of social media give the impression that they are tech savvy and have cosmopolitan networks across the country and even the continent. In economies that are increasingly seeking innovation, change, and opportunities for young people, mastery of online resources can be seen as a valence characteristic.

It is significant that these technologies are being adopted at rates nearly parallel to those in the United States and Western Europe. Younger candidates who are more familiar with social media platforms are using their comparative advantage to build online campaigns that rival the campaigns of their better-financed peers. Hardworking opposition candidates can provide daily logs of their visits to various constituencies, their charitable actions, or their meetings with important foreign dignitaries. Governments' attempts to shut down social media during elections or at times of political crisis demonstrate the salience of social media for opposition and civil society. In the 2016 Gambian election as well as the 2011 and 2016 Ugandan elections, there were bans on social media leading up to the elections.[44] In Mali, public protest of the 2016 arrest of a popular radio DJ and later protests against proposed constitutional amendments led to social media blackouts. In Ethiopia and Zimbabwe, the governments have passed laws that allow them to monitor citizens' Internet use (Tripp, 2017, pp. 99–100).

5.4.2 A Snapshot of Social Media Usage

Two of candidates' most powerful political platforms on social media are Twitter and Facebook. Table 5.1 captures Facebook usage among the top

---

[44] On Uganda, see Tripp (2017, p. 91).

twenty-five most active presidential candidates over the most recent election cycles as of September 19, 2016. The left-hand set of columns rank candidates by the number of friends or "likes" from their supporters. The right-hand columns show how many posts candidates had put up recently on their own Facebook wall. The number of supporters is likely to proxy for popularity, outreach efforts, and campaign resources. We acknowledge that this could be due to supporters' true appreciation of a candidate, but it could also reflect incentives around "liking" powerful candidates. The measure of recent posting is more likely to capture the efforts of candidates or campaign staff and the reliability on Facebook as a campaign tool.

This measure is biased by proximity to a recent election. For instance, in the aftermath of the Zambian election controversy, both President Lungu and challenger Hakainde Hichilema are in the top twenty-five, as are three competitors in the December 2016 Ghanaian elections. However, many of the most recent posters are posting outside of the most intense part of the electoral or campaign cycle.

Unsurprisingly, there appears to be clustering on Facebook in certain countries, such as Kenya, with three candidates listed as most active in each metric, and Ghana, where the leaders of Ghana's two main parties, the NDC and the New Patriotic Party (NPP), rank among the five candidates having the most friends or "likes" and the most active candidates. Portuguese-speaking candidates are notably absent from the top twenty-five, which might reflect a slower adoption of Facebook by the lusophone world.

Table 5.1 suggests that many opposition candidates use social media actively. They make up more than a third of the twenty-five most popular candidates (right side) and nearly half of the top twenty-five most recent posters (left side). While seventeen of the top twenty-five candidates with the most "likes" are current or former presidents, there are also quite a few secondary opposition candidates who are taking advantage of the social media platform, such as Peter Kenneth of Kenya and Cellou Diallo in Guinea. We also see opposition candidates from relatively closed regimes resorting to online media, including Kizza Besigye in Uganda and Morgan Tsvangirai in Zimbabwe. This illustrates the equalizing power of inexpensive social media, which can be leveraged by savvy opposition candidates with limited budgets. Minor opposition candidates in Zimbabwe, the Republic of the Congo, Gabon, Uganda, and Guinea had all posted on their sites within 24 h of the day our coding was completed, suggesting a good degree of activity on the site. It is notable that many

TABLE 5.1. *Presidential candidates' Facebook usage rankings**

Number of friends or "Likes" on official page				Most recent posting	
1	Uhuru Kenyatta	Kenya	2,596,026	1 *Nana Akufo-Addo*	Ghana
2	Goodluck Jonathan	Nigeria	2,106,653	1 *Yoweri Museveni*	Uganda
3	John Dramani Mahama	Ghana	1,007,041	1 *Welshman Ncube*	Zimbabwe
4	*NANA Akufo-Addo*	Ghana	949,394	4 *Mathias Dzon*	Republic of the Congo
5	Paul Kagame	Rwanda	634,625	4 *Casimir Oyé-Mba*	Gabon
6	Joyce Banda	Malawi	597,670	4 John Dramani Mahama	Ghana
7	Raila Odinga	Kenya	554,941	4 *Cellou Dalein Diallo*	Guinea
8	Alpha Condé	Guinea	550,488	4 Mahamadou Issoufou	Niger
9	*Peter Kenneth*	Kenya	419,958	4 Paul Kagame	Rwanda
10	Edgar Lungu	Zambia	407,538	4 Macky Sall	Senegal
11	Ali Bongo Ondimba	Gabon	402,763	4 Jacob Zuma	South Africa
12	Paul Biya	Cameroon	380,643	4 *Norbert Mao*	Uganda
13	*Hakainde Hichilema*	Zambia	363,480	4 Edgar C Lungu	Zambia
14	*Cellou Dalein Diallo*	Guinea	336,327	14 Paul Biya	Cameroon
15	*Helen Zille*	South Africa	281,318	14 *Paul Abine Ayah*	Cameroon
16	*Muhammadu Buhari*	Nigeria	258,016	14 *Paa Kwesi Nduom*	Ghana
17	Mahamadou Issoufou	Niger	241,651	14 Uhuru Kenyatta	Kenya
18	*Soumaïla Cissé*	Mali	240,645	14 AmeenAh Gurib-Fakim	Mauritius
19	Macky Sall	Senegal	237,234	14 *Kizza Kifeefe Besigye*	Uganda
20	Yoweri Museveni	Uganda	236,761	14 *Hakainde Hichilema*	Zambia
21	Jacob Zuma	South Africa	221,817	21 *Henry Herbert Lartey*	Ghana

TABLE 5.1 *(continued)*

22	Denis Sassou-Nguesso	Republic of the Congo	176,818	21	*Raila Odinga*	Kenya
23	*Morgan Tsvangirai*	Zimbabwe	134,242	21	*Musalia Mudavadi*	Kenya
24	*Kizza Kifeefe Besigye*	Uganda	122,139	21	*Arthur Peter Mutharika*	Malawi
25	Robert Mugabe	Zimbabwe	104,590	21	*Soumaïla Cissé*	Mali

*All indicators were ranked as of September 19, 2016. Opposition candidates are italicized.

of these electoral systems are characterized by restricted freedom of the press. Social media appear to offer a good alternative by which opposition candidates can spread their message.

Social media campaign tools might be particularly attractive to opposition candidates in that they have a low cost and cater to an urban youth population, which could be more likely to support emerging candidates such as McHenry Venaani, who at age 25 became the youngest member of Namibian Parliament in 2003. He made a presidential bid in 2014 with the Democratic Turnhalle Alliance (DTA), during which he capitalized on clever use of social media and adopted innovative strategies such as sleeping in informal settlements and riding municipal buses,[45] reminiscent of campaigns of US candidates such as Corey Booker. The opposition party leveraged Venaani's charisma while Frente de Libertação de Moçambique (SWAPO) relied on its historic message of anticolonial liberation.

Table 5.1 suggests that social media can be an effective tool, even for candidates who are campaigning against entrenched regimes. This is particularly true of young, tech-savvy candidates. Dima Shima Rwigara, a Rwandan businesswoman and activist, had her presidential campaign derailed by the incumbent regime when she was accused of submitting insufficient numbers of signatures and using names of the dead to fill her electoral petition. Although she was unable to run and later jailed, she has used social media to publicize her plight as well as the broader struggle

---

[45] As described in Weylandt (2015).

for political rights in Rwanda.[46] Her Twitter account includes a message that reads, "Account currently managed by her assistant while she is legally detained."[47] In South Africa, Julius Malema's party, the Economic Freedom Fighters, had their advertisement banned by the South African Broadcasting Corporation for potentially inciting violence. The black-and-white advertisement, focused on police brutality, featured graphic photos of the Marikana massacre, the most lethal use of force by South African police in the postapartheid era. After being posted online, the advertisement received over 500,000 hits.[48]

5.5 LEGISLATIVE, GUBERNATORIAL, AND MUNICIPAL CANDIDATES

In this chapter, we have focused mostly on presidential candidates. We end with the little we do know about the profiles of legislative, gubernatorial, and municipals candidates, a topic that is ripe for further research. Like their peers in executive races, legislative candidates continue to tend to be better educated than average citizens and more likely to come from the existing political elite and often the ranks of the civil service (Barkan, 2008). They also appear to be predominantly male, although the number of female cabinet members and legislators has increased steadily since 1980 (Tripp and Kang, 2008; Arriola and Johnson, 2014).[49]

As one might expect, younger and outsider candidates can gain initial experience at the legislative or municipal level, where barriers to entry are lower than those in presidential races. Barkan (2008) has noted the emergence of new "reformer" legislators, whom he describes as outward looking and most likely to view institutions in a global, comparative perspective, thus being quite different from establishment politicians.

For example, nearly all reformers are computer literate and use the internet, unlike most of their counterparts from the previous political generation who sustained the clientelist foundation of the one-party state. Many are also entrepreneurs in

---

[46] https://www.washingtonpost.com/news/global-opinions/wp/2017/08/02/what-happened-when-i-tried-to-run-to-become-rwandas-first-female-president/?utm_term=.2e45f547240e.

[47] https://twitter.com/shimarwigara?lang=en.

[48] http://memeburn.com/2014/04/lessons-in-the-streissand-effect-sabc-bans-eff-ad-as-das-ayisafani-gets-half-a-million-youtube-views.

[49] Gender representation at municipal level still appears to be skewed heavily toward men. In the 2009 Malian municipal elections, women made up fewer than 10 percent of all mayors nationwide (Bleck, 2015, p. 162).

the private sectors. They place greater emphasis on performance than loyalty cemented by patronage. (Barkan, 2008, p. 133)

However, prospective candidates are still constrained in that they must have wealth or a backer to be able to sustain a campaign. Legislative candidates need to visit and interact with their constituents; these visits can be expensive. In Ghana, Rauschenberg (2015) documents not only candidates' distribution of T-shirts or *pagnes* but also very specific demands from voters for personal favors such as fishing nets or money for school fees.[50]

Even in dominant party settings, candidates are expected to self-finance a large percentage of the campaign (Weghorst, 2015; Dendere, 2016). In an interview with a Tanzanian member of parliament, Weghorst (2015, p. 248) highlights the tremendous personal resource base needed to run a campaign:

In the campaign, you are responsible for about 80% of the expenses or more. In my case, the campaign cost 65 million [roughly US $40,000]. Of that, the party contributed about five million shillings. The party does pay for some expenses, like print materials. But these are shirts for the president. If you want your own information on them, you will have to pay for them yourself. I used money on the salaries for campaigners, t-shirts for my own campaign. I also made my own posters, pamphlets, paid for a speaker system for rallies and radio-advertising. These were all private expenses.

Dendere (2016) documents solidarity among youth candidates from Zimbabwe's dominant ZANU-PF, who set up a self-help fund in which they could pool money and support each other candidacies. Lindberg (2010) suggests that demands on members of Parliament (MPs) have been rising over time as constituents have learned about the "ability to harvest" at election time. He describes the experience of an MP in Ghana Lindberg (2010, p. 125):

in 1992 and 1996 local party executives were given spare parts for bicycles or in some cases used bicycles; by 2000 they all requested new bicycles; in 2004 some started to demand motorbikes; and in 2008 no one asked for bicycles – everyone wanted a motorbike and in some cases even cars. When they ask for money, party executives at constituency level demand the equivalent of US$100–500 on a regular (monthly or bi-monthly) basis. Even the young, unemployed 'boys' who help with campaigning demand mobile phones, motorbikes, jobs and start-up capital for their businesses ventures.

---

[50] As noted in Rauschenberg's (2015) study of Ghanaian campaigns.

In Chapter 6, we show that the issue of economic growth and develop-ment dominates electoral discourse because this is what voters care about. This is particularly true for legislative elections. The primary concern of voters is whether or not MPs can provide resources to their constituents in the form of development goods or generate redistribution of resources (from centralized state coffers) to these areas (Barkan, 1995). In a survey of 1,600 Ghanaians, Lindberg (2012, p. 5) found that when asked about pri-mary expectations for their MPs, nearly 70 percent of potential voters are most concerned with constituency; another 15 percent prioritize personal support. This is consistent with what Ghanaian MPs report; constituency service is their most taxing obligation as voters expect personal assis-tance and community development (Lindberg, 2010). The overwhelming emphasis on constituency service and development can be explained by the fact that citizens believe that these elected officials are responsible for bringing developmental goods and responding to citizens needs.

This means that campaign appeals in legislative races center on proving one's ability to deliver developmental goods in the form of public goods, infrastructure, or job creation. Citizens' heightened expectations are somewhat unfair to legislators, who are at best intermediaries between the state and the local communities of their constituency. They can lobby the executive branch of government for development expenditures for their district, but they do not control the resources. Access to the exec-utive branch provides an additional incumbency advantage to the party of the president, as it is presumably easier for backbenchers of the presiden-tial party to get developmental resources from the executive branch. The fact that legislative reelection rates are so low in sub-Saharan Africa may be related in part to the difficulty for legislators to respond adequately to these rising expectations from constituents.

In legislative races, endorsements from key party members or local elites play an even greater role, as voters are less likely to have evidence to evaluate candidates' character, personality, or experiences (Andersen and Kibler, 1978). In stronger party environments, candidates may draw on party strength and reputation through party endorsements. In the run-up to the 2012 elections in Ghana, Francis Egyarku Donkoh, the Central Regional Youth Organizer for the NPP, pledged to modernize and expand the Mankesim market to include a police station, a health clinic, and a fire post if his party was voted into power on 7 December.[51]

---

[51] http://www.ghanaweb.com/GhanaHomePage/politics/NPP-promises-to-modernise-Mankesim-market-255881.

In local and subnational races, candidates can champion their relationships with governing executives at the presidential or gubernatorial level to build their credibility in terms of being able to deliver development.[52] Party coordination plays an even stronger role in these races; citizens are aware the parties will need to coordinate with other political actors to secure developmental goods. Unlike presidents, who have great policy autonomy, lower-level executives and members of other branches of government will need to work with others to secure funding or to achieve policy goals. Campaigns try to convince voters that parties will be able to establish the political coalitions and cooperation to get these tasks completed. In Nigeria, Majah Umeh, a chief and former Commissioner for Information and Tourism in Anambra State, tried to convince citizens to vote for the party of the governor because it would make coordination and communications between party representatives and the governor easier, resulting in better outcomes for their community. Umeh said, "Currently, all the serving Senators from Anambra are not from our great party. They do not come to discuss issues of interest with the governor because they belong to different political parties. We want the APGA to win all the three senatorial seats for proper and effective representation."[53] He went on to cite the governor's success in building infrastructure and addressing local security challenges.

Candidates can also draw on their past experience in office, as their performance would be highly visible to constituents. In Nigeria, Dr. Orji Uzor Kalu, a former governor of Abia State, competed for a Senate seat in Abia North District by touting his past experience in office. He explained that "he brought the only development to the area and since he left office, things have fallen apart. He also rallied for all people, of all parties to vote for Jonathon. He called for greater unity amongst brothers."[54]

The critical roles that mayors and MPs play in brokering and generating development for their home regions and municipalities may be one of the reasons that we see relatively high (in the comparative context) turnout rates for these races. Citizens understand that they can punish and reward these candidates, who may have access to party resources but ultimately do not benefit from the same kind of incumbency advantage as executives do.

---

[52] This is similar to the logic of citizens voting with chiefs who can show connections to political candidates (Baldwin, 2015).
[53] http://sunnewsonline.com/new/why-apga-must-win-national-assembly-seats-umeh.
[54] http://sunnewsonline.com/new/kalu-kicks-off-senatorial-campaign-in-abia-north.

In francophone Africa, municipal races are often referred to as *élections de proximité* because they require that candidates have a personal reputation at the local level and can mobilize networks of friends, family, and colleagues (Bleck, 2015). This means that municipal candidates need to have a reasonable degree of name recognition and existing networks before running. Local elections are more personal in that many voters actually know about the candidates, their backgrounds, and their families. The limited literature on municipal candidates suggests that in stronger party systems, candidates can emerge with the backing of the party machine, but many others draw on personal reputations as past advocates for their communities and use grassroots organizing to beat dominant parties (Bierschenk, 2006; Ndletyana, 2007). These facts may help to explain the high rates of turnout that local elections appear to generate fairly consistently.

Municipal candidates can campaign on very concrete policy proposals. particularly if the political establishment is not addressing a localized concern. These races often revolve around very concrete issues such as water and electricity cuts, government sales of public land, and poor trash collection. Dynamic candidates, particularly in urban areas, can use social media as a platform to build constituency support by championing solutions to these unaddressed local issues.

Some scholars view local-level elections as good indicators of the progress of democratic consolidation in new democracies (see, for example, Lehman, 2007). But as Riedl and Dickovick (2014) argue, the relationship between national-level democracy and the degree of decentralization is deeply ambiguous. Authoritarian systems sometimes have a greater incentive to promote local-level elections than do more democratic systems, depending on the interests of political parties (see also Aalen and Tronvoll, 2009; Poteete and Ribot, 2011). In some cases, opposition parties that are unable to establish themselves at the national level view local elections as a way to get a foothold in the political system.

Willis and al-Batthani (2010, p. 209) interviewed a National Islamic Front candidate about his electoral strategy in Sudan for the 1986 elections to show that even in a context of parties with strong ideological differences, candidates relied strongly on familial and regional networks:

I went to all the centres, places you can find people, where you have access: clubs, football clubs especially, and the social clubs. Otherwise, the mosque. Every week, to visit the mosque, to say prayers and speak with them, informally. So I find a lot of blood relationship, area allegiances where I come from in the north, and ideologically people were really unsure ... It is family connections which you can bank on.

Bierschenk's (2006) analysis of the 2002 municipal elections in the Benin city of Parakou similarly notes the strategy of the eventual winner – focusing on youth associations and his notoriety as owner of the city's football team – to mobilize young voters on his behalf. At the same time, Bierschenk (2006) makes clear that local concerns and issues have to be contextualized within national party politics, in which each of the main campaigns leverages linkages to national parties and resources.

In Weghorst's (2015, p. 246) study of Tanzanian candidates, an interviewee described running for municipal office as a way to gain skills and build name recognition for a future bid in the legislative elections. Indeed, local elections are viewed as particularly attractive to opposition parties, which may be shut out of national-level political offices and view local elections as a way to gain a foothold to better compete at the national level, thanks both to the experiences gained in campaigning and to the resources that holding office provides. Opposition candidates are also attracted to big urban areas, where voters are more likely to support their reformist political agendas. Conroy-Krutz (2006) thus notes the large number of capital cities in the region with elected mayors from opposition parties.

5.6 CONCLUSION

African elections should be studied in a comparative context. Many of the concepts that are used to describe and evaluate elections in the Western world are also relevant to races in sub-Saharan Africa. Similarly, the emphasis on folkloric traditions and candidates' use of their own biography and characteristics, which we see in the study of African elections, could be used as an analytic lens to study elections in the rest of the world.

In this chapter, we have demonstrated the typical profile of candidates, which is not unlike that of candidates in the rest of the world: male, older, and well educated. We have stressed how candidates leverage their own experiences and characteristics to build credibility and own issues. We have highlighted some staple components of electoral campaigns, including campaign tours. We have also showed the ways in which politicians try to be strategic about where to target their political appeals and how they use systems of brokerage to capture rural voters. We have showed how incumbency advantage creates significant hurdles for opposition candidates' campaigns.

In this chapter, we have stressed continuity with the single-party era, including many recycled politicians with experience in the pretransition era. We have also showed how the campaign environment compounds incumbency advantage by giving sitting presidents a comparative advantage in an environment of uncertainty. Incumbents leverage their experience in office and resource base to a comparative advantage, while challengers need to provide evidence in their own biographies that they can lead capably and have enough resources to win.

However, we have also showed some changing trends, including opposition victories in urban areas and the emergence of new, younger candidates who can utilize social media to their own advantage. While their strategies cater to a younger, urban base and might not translate into voter turnout or resonate with rural voters, increasing urbanization and the fact that recent studies link social media usage to political participation (Dimitrova et al., 2014) suggest that these technologies might eventually have a real impact. Voters appears to be responding to compelling appeals from new actors, as we will discuss at greater length in Chapter 7. However, in Ghana, as chronicled by Lindberg (2010, p. 24), voters' expectations for redistribution and provision of goods by legislative candidates appear to be increasing, raising a resource requirement for interested candidates.

Finally, we have stressed that campaigns do not all take place on equal footing. The degree of incumbency advantage and the willingness of incumbents to use violence at election time – and, consequently, the window for opposition victory – depend on the level of democracy and on state strength.

6

Analyzing Issues in Presidential Campaigns

If the people trusted him, he would make this regional capital one of the most beautiful cities in the country – with infrastructure and adequate equipment. Its location makes it the heart of Senegal. The highway – Dakar – Thies – is one of the projects of future President Macky Sall. His wish is to extend it to Touba – passing through Diourbel.

> Babacar Faye, *Le Soleil*, February 22, 2012
> (reporting from Macky Sall Campaign Rally in Diourbel)

6.1 INTRODUCTION

Long-standing conventional wisdom among scholars argues that contemporary electoral politics in Africa lacks substantive issues. Most of the discourse around elections is said to focus either on the identity characteristics of the politicians and their constituents – typically through the lens of ethnicity – or on a reductive vision of elections as primarily a venue for violent threats and the distribution of money and gifts to buy votes (see, for example, Chabal and Daloz, 1999; Leonard, 2009). In part, this is argued to result from the expectations of voters and the general political culture, even in the more democratic regimes in the region. As Bierschenk (2006, p. 548) puts it without qualification about Benin, one of the region's more democratic systems, "politicians are elected not to defend policy issues, but to ensure that government resources are channelled to their region of origin."

In this chapter, we argue that such a view oversimplifies a complex reality. As in other regions, individuals in Africa often do vote expressively and on the basis of emotional appeals or identity, but this does not mean that African elections are less meaningful or that voters do not understand their electoral choices in substantive terms. We argue that African elections are often rich in policy discussions and issues appeals but that parties tend to couch their rhetoric in valence terms that everyone can agree are important rather than taking precise positions on divisive issues. It is true that elections in the region rarely elicit appeals to class cleavages, but the absence of debate involving economic ideologies should not be confused with a dearth of programmatic politics.

The first focus of this chapter is a discussion of the overwhelming use of valence issues in African election cycles. Parties employ valence discourse for the reasons we discussed in Chapters 4 and 5. The origins and evolution of the African party system have shaped parties' ability to own issues as well as the types of issues they tend to champion. This includes the shared origins of most members of the political class and the limited experience of most opposition parties that are in power. These factors limit issue ownership beyond broad categories of "incumbent" and "challenger."

The lack of experience on the part of both voters and politicians heightens the degree of uncertainty about the electoral environment. Voters have not yet developed partisan attachments to parties, while politicians are unsure about their pool of potential voters and about the specific issues that would appeal to their base, so they focus on issues that appeal to everyone. We have stressed the weak, disconnected nature of most political parties in Africa, particularly when they do not control the state apparatus and its resources. Traditionally, many parties lack human resources and organization outside of the capital or their regional stronghold. Valence issues offer safe topics, which parties know will be salient and will appeal to shifting constituencies. As weak parties face uncertainty in the political system, they embrace valence issues, which all of society agrees upon, rather than taking on divisive position issues. As a further consequence of this liability of newness, most parties and candidates have not yet established reputations as ideological issue owners. Instead, most competition revolves around trying to prove that a candidate is best placed to attack an issue that voters care most about.

In this chapter, we show that politicians actively champion many issues that resonate with citizens. We introduce six key substantive issue areas that have been reliably present in electoral campaigns in Africa since the transitions to electoral politics a quarter-century ago: constitutionalism and democracy, economic development, security, sovereignty, citizenship, and the distribution of natural resources. Many of these issues have their roots in the postindependence period and represent themes that resonate with prospective voters. As we will show, incumbents and opposition parties constitute the main explanatory distinction when examining electoral rhetoric. Consistently, we find that experience in office allows the incumbent to claim ownership over development projects and – if there is an economic upturn – growth and job creation. These are the issues that incumbent campaigns emphasize. Opposition candidates, by contrast, are more credible watchdogs of governance and civil liberties. They can plausibly attack the incumbent for attempts to usurp other branches of government or for corruption scandals. They are therefore much more likely to steer the electoral debate toward these issues.

After discussing each of these six sets of issues, we turn to an empirical examination of issues from election cycles in eight focus countries: Benin, Ghana, Kenya, Mozambique, Nigeria, Senegal, Uganda, and Zambia. We draw on local newspapers to demonstrate the types of issue areas and the ways in which issues are framed by incumbent and opposition parties in recent campaigns. We show the overwhelming use of valence issues by incumbents and opposition parties in these countries as well as the predominance of issues related to economic development and democracy. We also demonstrate that the issues and framing are embedded in the electoral context and are contingent on the salient issues and debates of the day. There is substantial variation in the types of issues the dominate discourse in each country but also across different election cycles.

6.2 UNDERSTANDING VALENCE ISSUES IN AFRICA AND BEYOND

Scholars of comparative electoral politics circumscribe a larger class of programmatic debates by focusing exclusively on position issues. Programmatic issues, that is, concerns about policy issues and government performance, are often conflated with position issues, which are conceptualized as specific positions along a policy spectrum that typically relates to specific societal cleavages. For instance, left-wing and right-wing parties adopt different policy positions with regard to the desirable level of economic redistribution. Downs (1957) argued that these positions could be compared and even meaningfully measured in a "policy space" in which left-wing party positions would be positioned to the left of right-wing party positions. This Downsian understanding of party competition has dominated academic discussion of elections around the world. Citizens' concerns about public service provision or resource distribution from the state are often portrayed in a clientelist framework.

In focusing on a clientelist depiction of party competition, scholars have discounted the substantive weight of valence issues, or issues around which there is broad societal consensus. Stokes (1963) first noted that relatively little campaign rhetoric can actually be measured in this manner. Instead, in his seminal critique of the Downsian model of party competition, he labeled as *valence issues* those more common issue areas over which there is actually broad agreement, such as law and order and national defense. In each case, disagreement focuses not on the ultimate objective of policy, about which there is consensus, but instead on how to attain desired goals and who is more likely to succeed in doing so. Most issues can be framed through either a position lens or a valence lens; it is not the content of the issues themselves as much as politicians' choice about how to frame them that determines whether the issues are examined in valence terms or along a spectrum of distinct positions. As Stokes (1963, p. 373) explained, position issues are often "lurking behind valence issues," but these positions go unarticulated in the valence discourse. However, even when it references substantive issues and debates, valence language does not clearly map onto an ideological platform. When scholars ignore the important programmatic role that valence issues and valence discourse play in African election, they trivialize issues that voters care very much about.

In sum, in addressing valence issues, partisan rhetoric focuses on proving competence with regard to the issue rather than on the rightness of a specific position on policy objectives. Valence is context specific. Valence issues are issues upon which there is agreement among constituents in a particular country context or throughout political discourse in a specific country. For instance, in the United States, candidates seek to prove their patriotism by showing deference to the American flag, but in Germany, such acts would be considered signals of extremist ideology and largely unaccepted by society. While debates about gay rights have polarized constituencies throughout much of the world, gay rights show up in political discourse in most African countries as a populist, valence issue, and nearly all politicians speak out against recognizing gay rights.

Politicians derive a valence advantage from being viewed as more competent or charismatic, having more campaign money, providing better constituency service, or coming from a party that "owns" a particular issue (Egan, 2008, p. 22). As we discussed in Chapter 5, candidates can leverage valence characteristics to convince voters that they would be more capable or competent than other candidates in addressing a key issue that all voters care about, such as tackling corruption or creating more jobs. Valence issues can give incumbents an advantage due to their past experience in office, but this advantage holds only when the incumbents are doing their jobs well. Given their experience and resources, incumbents are typically conceptualized as having a strong valence advantage. In other words, when programmatic approaches are held constant, an incumbent will typically benefit from a valence advantage (Groseclose, 2001; Stone and Simas, 2010). Furthermore, incumbent politicians might avoid staking out positions to preempt negative evaluations by voters and seek to hide in a vague policy space where they are less vulnerable. In his comparative study of seventeen democracies, Hellwig (2012) found that during economic downturns, incumbents can shield themselves from negative evaluations through retrospective voting by aligning their policy positions with those of challenger parties.

This incumbent advantage is likely multiplied in the African context, where incumbents have an even more exaggerated comparative advantage in terms of resources and experience. Sitting presidents can leverage access to state resources or subtly manipulate institutions, such as the press, to create greater visibility for the president or to portray the president in a more positive light (Levitsky and Way, 2010).

We suspect that valence discourse is prominent in most electoral campaigns across a wide variety of political systems around the world. In the sections below, we demonstrate the pervasive presence of valence issues throughout most African election cycles. We argue that the use of valence appeals is particularly pronounced in sub-Saharan Africa, owing to the historical origins of African governance and political economy and lingering uncertainty in the political system.

First, the predilection for broad general valence competition in Africa is reinforced by the newness of electoral systems, the inexperience of parties, and the resulting uncertainty facing individual politicians. Of course, as we showed in Chapter 4, there are some relatively old parties in the region, primarily the old single parties that are still in power today, such as Chama Cha Mapinduzi in Tanzania and South West African People's Organisation (SWAPO) in Namibia, or those that are now in the opposition – the United National Independence Party (UNIP) in Zambia, for instance, or the Parti Socialiste (PS) in Senegal. But even the old single parties have relatively little experience of competitive electoral campaigning.

The limited experience of opposition parties in power and the shared profiles of the political class make it difficult for them to "own" diverse issues. Parties typically earn ownership of issues over time as their performance is tested and they gain credibility as being able to manage and resolve those issues (Petrocik, 1996). Voters who prioritize those issues come to support the parties who promote and protect these interests. As we showed in Chapter 4, most African parties are no more than two decades old and have competed in only a small number of electoral campaigns. The homogenous political class – mostly urban, educated, upper-class, and quite distinct from the rest of the population – is less likely to attach specific issue identities to their parties.

Individual politicians, uncertain about future allegiances or coalitions, also face incentives to use valence discourse. Many African countries are characterized by fluid party membership and the tendency of parties to form supercoalitions, in which weaker parties jump on the bandwagon of the incumbent party, or candidates that act as political nomads and join the side of the aisle that offers the greatest short-term returns (Rakner and van de Walle, 2009). In newer democracies, many party elites compromise ideological or past coalitions to secure a slice of the government pie in what Slater and Simmons (2013; see also Slater, 2011) have evocatively called "promiscuous power-sharing." The threat of authoritarian reversal and the ability of the incumbent parties to monopolize state resources for their own benefit further incentivize getting on the bandwagon with incumbent parties. Valence issues about which there is broad consensus offer a safer strategy for politicians who may be considering switching parties or alliances in the near future. This strategy applies beyond the African context; for instance, McGraw (2008) demonstrates that the major Irish parties avoid salient programmatic issues to have the flexibility to join coalitions and court centrist voters.

Second, taking positions on controversial issues requires coordination and leadership within the party. Parties can play a role in shaping voters' imagined cleavages (De Leon et al., 2009) and articulating voters' preferences, but this practice requires coordination and decentralized information sharing. Weak parties with limited resources have more difficulty in conducting research on voters' preferences or shaping the issue agendas of constituencies. This process is further complicated when parties cannot rely on an organic constituency that has clear policy preferences. Most African parties are uncertain about the identity and preferences of their constituents. Politicians are less likely to anticipate the preferences of voters if they cannot identify their electoral base. Stokes (1963, p. 372) explains the importance of locating issues that resonate with public opinion:

Political fortunes are made and lost according to the ability of party leaders to sense what dimensions will be salient to the public as it appraises the candidates and party records ... But the skills of political leaders who must maneuver for public support in a democracy consist partly in knowing what issue dimensions are salient to the electorate or can be made salient by suitable propaganda.

Instead, politicians operating with unknown constituencies fear that by articulating a specific policy position, they risk alienating voters who disagree with that position.

A third level of uncertainty tending to reinforce the preference for valence competition concerns African policy makers' ability to uphold a policy position once elected to office. Poor African countries are uncommonly budget constrained because of their low fiscal capacity, their reliance on highly volatile flows of foreign aid, and the conditionality imposed on them by international financial institutions (Moss et al., 2008). These constraints probably undermine the credibility of specific campaign promises that are not approved by donors. Because African voters are likely to engage in "retrospective voting" (Fiorina, 1981; Posner and Simon, 2002), incumbent candidates may believe that it is best to keep their promises vague and general to avoid demonstrating their impotence relative to donors. Valence discourse is safer, as it is harder for donors to assess the macroeconomic implications of general promises and harder for citizens to measure progress toward promised outcomes. Again, this uncertainty is not specific to Africa but could affect any regime that is dependent on foreign aid or subject to stringent donor conditionality.

Finally, valence discourse is perpetuated by great uncertainty in the political system. As African parties compete to establish themselves in nascent electoral systems, they must navigate uncertainty on multiple levels. Organizationally, these mostly young parties lack resources and experience, and they are poorly informed about their potential electoral constituencies. Constantly shifting party alliances also lead to uncertainty and caution. At the systemic level, the potential of regime change and/ or shifting democratic rules in what remain unconsolidated democracies constitute another source of uncertainty. We argue that parties adopt valence discourse in response to this overwhelming uncertainty.

6.3 TYPOLOGY OF ISSUES IN AFRICA ELECTIONS

While variation in levels of party institutionalization, certainty about clear ethnic constituencies, or reform politicians' commitment to a specific issue agenda might open space for position issues that cater to loyal voters, most politicians espouse the types of issues that all voters care about. Electoral issues are driven largely by the specific electoral context, as we will see in subsequent sections. The types of issues and the ways in which they are framed can change dramatically from one election cycle to another depending on what is most salient.

Below, we survey secondary literature about recent presidential elections to emphasize six categories of issues that are very prevalent in African elections: constitutionalism and democracy, economic development, security, sovereignty, citizenship, and the distribution of natural resources. We developed this list through an inductive study of political campaigns in francophone West Africa (Bleck and van de Walle, 2011). We then tested the fit of these categories by coding newspaper accounts of political issues during a single election in seven countries (Bleck and van de Walle, 2013). We now expand the analysis to include two electoral rounds and add an eighth country, Senegal. Research assistants read local newspapers for a randomly chosen day of the week during a six-month campaign cycle and were asked to note any political issues.[1] The initial list of issues included everything from attacks on political character to party infighting as well as substantive issues discussed during campaigns. After they were flagged, these issues were coded as one of the six categories or as "other." During coding, we found that were able to fit the vast majority of political issues we encountered in these six categories.

6.3.1 Economic Development

The most prominent theme in African electoral discourse is that of economic development. Much political rhetoric addresses the population's legitimate concerns about the process of economic development and the improvement of people's welfare and income. Barkan's (2008) work on legislatures stressed how consumed many legislators are with "delivering the goods" to their home constituencies. He argues that constituency service is so demanding that it often impedes elected officials' ability

---

[1] See the description in Section 6.4. Full coding instructions are included in the online appendix.

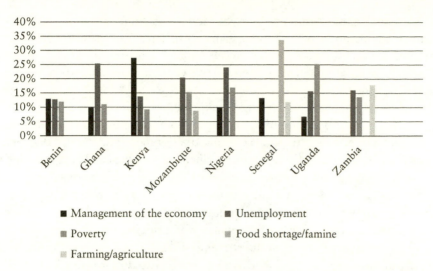

FIGURE 6.1. *Afrobarometer respondents' top three most pressing problems*
$N = 11,787.$
Source: Afrobarometer Round 4 results: Benin, Ghana, Kenya, Mozambique, Nigeria, Uganda, Senegal and Zambia. 2008. www.afrobarometer.org (Question 56, part 1).

to legislate or invest in checking incumbents' power (Barkan, 2008). Decentralized constituency funds, such as the Harambee Projects in Kenya and later constituency development funds in a wider group of countries, are designed to placate constituents and ease these pressures (Barkan, 2008; Widner, 1993).

This focus on development is consistent with citizens' preferences. Recent analysis of citizens' policy preoccupations in Afrobarometer data demonstrates that respondents are most concerned about access to jobs, health, and poverty and about infrastructure such as transport, sanitation, and education (Dome, 2015; Leo et al., 2015). These demands are consistent with the fact that access to basic public services, particularly in rural areas, is still very constrained in many African countries (Bleck and Michelitch, 2015) as well as the pressing problem of youth unemployment (Resnick, 2012). Figure 6.1 shows public opinion on the top three issues identified as most pressing issues by Afrobarometer respondents in each country.[2]

The survey asked respondents the following open-ended question about their top priorities for government intervention: "In your opinion,

---

[2] Respondents were allowed to provide three priority issues, but the figure captures only the first selection.

what are the most important issues facing this country that the government should address?" The vast majority of top three responses from all countries focused on economic development. Concerns about unemployment, poverty, and management of the economy are shared in almost every country.

A focus on development is to be expected in low-income countries, in which a large proportion of the voting population still lives in conditions of absolute poverty. In fact, economic development and service delivery have been key to political framing since independence. The aspiration for economic development was one of the major justifications for independence. Later, development was used to justify authoritarian rule, and most governments in the region sought to legitimate their hold on power by citing the development the regime was bringing about. The growth of foreign aid in recent decades means that a large proportion of the African professional class works for a donor or a donor-funded nongovernmental organization (NGO) whose primary activity is the promotion of economic development. State television in many countries often portrays a parade of new development projects and meetings with donors to secure future resources. In sum, economic development in its various forms holds a substantial place in African public life.

This theme relates to a variety of subthemes of service delivery, economic development, job creation, and infrastructure. These themes are important for national elections but disproportionately dominate discourse in municipal and legislative elections. Legislators face tremendous pressure to deliver development goods to constituencies that are hungry for access to services and economic development (Barkan, 2008). Candidates of all parties vaunt their ability to promote job creation, poverty alleviation, access to food, or education.

Incumbents will emphasize the projects, including state projects but also private sector and NGO-driven campaigns, that have been completed during their term in office or new partnerships with donors or other groups that will bring development to the region. They emphasize their role as a key broker for development and future prosperity. Incumbents attempt to claim responsibility for recent economic growth and ownership of these development projects. We observe that incumbents use nearly identical language to ask voters to "allow them to continue the work that they have started."

In virtually all democracies around the world, politicians who are out of power criticize the performance of incumbents. In Africa, this often takes the form of criticism of the slow pace of development. Opposition politicians will point to pervasive poverty or other tangible challenges to development that persist as evidence of the lack of political will or capability of incumbents.

Developmental discourse, as in any other issue area, can be couched in valence or position language. In some instances, parties distinguish themselves by promoting a specific development policy. Weghorst (2015) highlights how the Civic United Front, the Tanzanian opposition, emphasized the importance of privatization, particularly management of the clove market so that Zanzibar could become the "Hong Kong of East Africa." He suggests that this campaigning primed voters to prefer economic policies that were more free market than the platforms offered by either party (Weghorst, 2015, pp. 202–206). In the 2011 race in Zambia, the Movement for Multi-party Democracy (MMD) championed an urban-to-rural migration program to try to encourage young people to return to farming to invigorate the agriculture sector. Members of opposing parties in parliament questioned the types of support that the government would provide for this transition.[3]

6.3.2 Constitutionalism and Democracy

As we have discussed in this book so far, most multiparty systems in Africa are relatively new and generally unconsolidated. With just a few exceptions, the turn to reasonably free competitive elections took place during the 1990s after a long period of authoritarian rule following independence (Bratton and van de Walle, 1997; Lindberg, 2007). Democratic regimes have fallen to coups in a small number of countries (Niger, Mauritania, Guinea-Bissau) or have suffered a sharp decline in democratic rights (Zimbabwe, São Tomé). The threat of a reversal or a backwards slide into authoritarian or military rule remains significant throughout the region. This historical context has helped to shape a hegemony of ideas about democratic politics that continues to influence parties' agendas.

Elections continue to be viewed as important in Africa, and democracy continues to be valued by citizens over all other forms of governance (Bratton and Mattes, 2001; Mattes and Bratton, 2007). In recent cases of democratic backsliding, public opinion showed that citizens continue to champion elections as the only acceptable form of government and the solution to governance crises (Coulibaly and Bratton, 2013). Similarly,

---

[3] www.lusakatimes.com/2011/06/23/government-promote-urban-rural-migration.

we see strong citizen attachment to freedom of expression and freedom of association. Logan (2008) finds that allowing populations greater freedoms generates greater support for incumbents. Politicians leverage their relative position to champion the expression of democratic values and institutions valued by the public, including good governance, anticorruption campaigns, commitment to rule of law, freedom of press and association, and the virtues of democratic institutions.

Incumbents can also employ governance rhetoric by extolling their historical role in the democratization process. These strategies typically focus on building credibility to abide by and maintain the general democratic rules of the game. Opposition actors frame themselves as defenders of democracy and criticize incumbents for actions that can be portrayed as limiting freedoms or consolidating the incumbent's own power. Support for constitutional rule and democracy is often pronounced in public, and a standard insult against one's opponent is to doubt his or her commitment to democratic virtues, a criticism that has real weight since much of the political class was politically active before democratization. This governance rhetoric includes claims of support for the principles in the constitution, as well as stands against political corruption and executive abuses of power, which can be powerful. In the May 2014 elections, President Joyce Banda, the Malawian incumbent, was voted out of office at least in part because the opposition was able to tie her to the so-called Cashgate corruption scandal, in which members of Banda's government had been investigated for large-scale embezzlement of government funds (Dulani, 2015; Zimmerman, 2015).

Issues related to democracy and good governance can also be portrayed through a position lens. In some elections, there are more nuanced debates about democracy, including how decentralization should work, the structure of the political system, or specific elements of the constitution, such as electoral rules. As we described in Chapter 3, there has been significant debate around position issues related to the democratic rules of the game. Debates about presidential term limits have become divisive and partisan issues in Nigeria (in 2006 and 2015),[4] Senegal (in 2012 and 2016),[5] the Democratic Republic of Congo (in 2015),[6] Burkina

[4] Riedl 2015   on term limit debates in Nigeria: www.washingtonpost.com/blogs/monkey-cage/wp/2015/02/16/are-efforts-to-limit-presidential-power-in-africa-working.
[5] Kelly 2016   on newest term limit debates in Senegal: www.washingtonpost.com/news/monkey-cage/wp/2016/04/03/heres-everything-you-need-to-know-about-senegals-recent-referendum.
[6] Wilmot 2015: http://africanarguments.org/2015/10/05/how-and-why-term-limits-matter.

Faso (in 2015), the Republic of the Congo (in 2015), and Burundi (in 2015).[7] Afrobarometer data show that citizens strongly support term limits; nearly three quarters of citizens surveyed in thirty-four countries between 2011 and 2013 supported limiting presidents' tenure in office.[8] Thus we observe some races characterized by an incumbents' desire to stay in office and opposition's claims of term limit violations, generating a higher percentage of position issues.

6.3.3 Security

The issue of security involves all threats to the security of individual citizens. In a Gallup International Millennium Survey, 81 percent of all Africans surveyed expressed "a great deal of concern" about the level of crime in their own country.[9] African newspapers consistently feature news stories about urban insecurity, reflecting the rise in urban crime in recent years. Among the countries in our sample, Kenyan newspapers are particularly noteworthy for their amount of coverage of domestic security issues. Incumbent government officials announce new security initiatives or flaunt threats of instability to invoke fear in the eyes of citizens who might consider voting for the opposition. Opposition candidates, church leaders, business groups, and civic associations are in the forefront of complaints about insecurity as a result of government negligence.[10]

Fear of crime is more pronounced in certain countries and communities. Data from South Africa Round 2 of the Afrobarometer survey revealed that 35 percent of respondents listed crime as the most pressing problem that they face. Concern about crime was higher among white and Indian respondents – 67 percent and 57 percent of them, respectively, listed crime as the most pressing problem – than among blacks and coloreds (25 percent and 39 percent, respectively) (The Changing Public Agenda: South Africans' Assessments of the Country's Most Pressing Problems," Afrobarometer Briefing Paper 5, 2002).

In countries where democracy is not yet consolidated, the threat of a coup d'état, insurgency, or civil war can focus debate on security in

---

[7] Wilmot2015:http://africanarguments.org/2015/10/05/how-and-why-term-limits-matter.
[8] http://afrobarometer.org/sites/default/files/press-release/global/ab_r6_pr_term_limits_africa_day15.pdf.
[9] The poll interviewed 57,000 respondents in sixty countries worldwide in 1999. See www.gallup-international.com/ContentFiles/millennium10.asp.
[10] For instance, this news story about tourist sector association bemoaning the negative effect of crime: http://allafrica.com/stories/201104260013.html

presidential elections. For instance, ongoing peace negotiations during the run-up to the 2014 Mozambican elections meant that most candidates prioritized security issues in their discourse. Given the terrible violence and political displacement of the 2012 Kenyan elections, many candidates spent time communicating their commitment to peace to their constituencies.

One need only look to the ousting of President Goodluck Jonathan in 2015 to see that security issues, such as the Nigerian government's inability to thwart Boko Haram, hold real weight. Kendhammer (2016, p. 12) describes the issue of the kidnapped "Chibok girls" as the most important issue in the national elections. Increasingly, a transnational terrorist threat, which has manifested itself in attacks on civilians in urban centers in Kenya, Uganda, Mali, Nigeria, Côte d'Ivoire, and Burkina Faso, also poses significant challenges to domestic security apparatuses. Incumbents attempt to harness rally effects after security threats to build support for their governments (but also partisan camps), while opposition politicians point to the inability of existing political actors to manage these burgeoning threats. Significant debates have been generated about the role of international peace keepers or about foreign intervention, such as the role of France in Mali or the placement of a US drone base in Niger. These debates overlap with national discussions of sovereignty, which we discuss below.

6.3.4 Sovereignty and International Relations

The set of issues involving sovereignty and international relations seen in debates about the nature and exercise of national sovereignty include such issues as colonial interference, foreign security, border disputes, the influence of international donors, and the influence of religious and traditional actors. In other words, it can relate to both internal and external threats to the exercise of sovereignty by the national government. Some countries adopted quotas for national ownership for certain types of enterprises or assets.[11] Nationalist discourse of the 1960s emphasized economic, political, and ideological independence. The relatively recent processes of decolonialization and the lingering economic and political influence of many former colonial powers fuel the salience of the sovereignty issue in the contemporary context. This category also captures

---

[11] For example, see Sklar's (1979, p. 536) depiction of Nigerian efforts at "indigenization" of capitalist enterprise in the 1970s.

border and trade negotiations with neighboring countries as well as lobbying and diplomacy in international forums.

Earlier research on French West Africa pointed to the importance of
religious sentiment, in particular lively debates in such countries as Mali,
Senegal and Niger about the legitimate role of Islam and the relationship
between the state and Islamic leaders (Villalón, 2010; Bleck and van de
Walle, 2011; Kang, 2015). These debates are often framed in terms of
protecting domestic sovereignty from Western overreach into domestic
affairs or criticizing Middle Eastern pressures on traditional Islamic practices. Newspaper accounts of the debate over the constitution in Kenya
in 2010 suggested a similarly energetic national discussion about the
legitimacy of sharia law, a debate that has also long festered in Nigeria
(Kendhammer, 2016).

Other sovereignty issues include controversies about the conditionality of donors such as the International Monetary Fund and the undue
influence of the ex-colonial power. In French West Africa, criticism of
France has waxed and waned as a political strategy but remains fairly
common in countries such as Côte d'Ivoire, Mali, and Cameroon. The US
plan to move the headquarters of its Africa command led to heated public criticism in South Africa and Nigeria (see van de Walle, 2009). In the
2012 elections, Uhuru Kenyatta was able to leverage his own prosecution
by the International Criminal Court (ICC) to an electoral advantage by
framing it in a sovereignty lens. Western diplomats walked out during a
spring 2016 inauguration of Yoweri Museveni after the Ugandan president made comments denouncing the ICC, again clearly a winning strategy of political rhetoric aimed at domestic audience.[12] Similar rhetoric
has been used against the UN Security Council. In 2013, the European
Court of Human Rights ruled that persecuted members of the Lesbian,
Gay, Bi-Sexual, and Transgender (LGBT) community from Senegal,
Uganda, and Sierra Leone could apply for asylum. In light of international pressure, leaders such as Macky Sall and Museveni have defended
their countries' laws against homosexuality as a larger issue of national
sovereignty. Museveni has sought to limit international adoptions by
people from countries that recognize same-sex marriage. During a trip to
Senegal, Barak Obama criticized the country's criminalization of homosexuality. Macky Sall's cautious rebuttal earned him national support.

---

[12] President Bashir of Sudan (currently wanted by the ICC) was sitting in the audience (see
www.bbc.com/news/world-africa-36278479).

The Senegalese newspaper *Le Pop* ran a front-page headline extolling Sall's ability to stand up to the world's most powerful leader:

In front of the most powerful man in the world, fully armed with his mission to influence the decriminalization of homosexuality, Macky Sall was able to say, "No," the editorial continued. "And we are in a country of free men, who have built a strong state."[13]

In the current era, sovereignty can also take the role of economic nationalism. Thus rhetoric about the importance of sovereignty over the national economy and its assets is increasingly common, particularly in countries with recent oil discoveries and countries that are involved in large land deals. The Ugandan government has publicly taken a highly nationalistic attitude about the oil deposits in Lake Edward. The proposal by the Madagascar government to grant a vast land holding to a South Korean company in 2008 led to mass protests and eventually the ouster of Marc Ravalomanana's administration. In Uganda, Acholi women launched protests with displays of nudity to shame the government for seizing and selling land to a South African investor, leaving 6,000 people evicted from their homes in northern Uganda (Tripp, 2017, p. 103). In many countries, women have been vocal advocates of land reform laws in order to increase their ownership rights (Tripp, 2017, p. 105). In Ethiopia, threats of land seizure by the Chinese or by Arab monarchies are painted as attacks on domestic sovereignty.

Opposition parties might criticize government policies for putting the interests of foreign powers before the needs of their own constituents or of weakness in the face of the impositions of donor conditionality. Incumbents can champion their ability to stand up to international actors as a way to gain domestic respect. However, these tactics are mediated by the domestic context and voters' attitudes toward various donors. The diverse positions on China's role in Africa demonstrate the importance of contextual variables related to individual election cycles. For instance, in the 2011 Zambian elections, Michael Sata's populist criticism of Chinese intrusion into the Zambian economy helped him to unseat the

[13] Adam Nossiter, *New York Times*, June 28, 2013, accessed at www.nytimes.com/2013/06/29/world/africa/senegal-cheers-its-president-for-standing-up-to-obama-on-same-sex-marriage.html?_r=0.

incumbent party.[14] While other candidates were unwilling to touch on China, Sata's critiques had become a key discourse in his previous bids as president (Larmer and Fraser, 2007, p. 628). *The Economist* noted in 2015 that the Chinese focus on government to government deals has led to public criticism of Chinese investments by civil society and opposition politicians in countries as varied as Senegal, Tanzania, Nigeria, and South Africa (The Economist, 2015). However, in other instances, candidates such as Sata's successor, Edgar Lungu, have publicly adopted a pro-China view. In December 2015, Zimbabwe made headlines after choosing to adopt the yuan as its primary international currency.[15] This choice reflected President Robert Mugabe's increasingly close ties to China, which have been criticized by opposition leaders. The variety of perspectives of the role of Chinese investment and influence in Africa means that it can be debated as a position issue.

6.3.5 Citizenship

The issue of citizenship is exemplified in debates about who is a full-fledged citizen and what this implies for duties and rights of individuals and groups, including women's rights, immigrants' rights, emigrants' rights, and the rights of ethnic minorities. In the 1960s and 1970s, many countries in Africa adopted indigenization measures, which sought to push immigrants out of the country or out of key sectors of the economy. Tactics included forced emigration (as was the case for more than 80,000 Asian residents of Uganda), limitations of immigrant participation in certain labor sectors, and the confiscation or nationalization of foreign-owned businesses (Wilson, 1990; Young, 2004; Biersteker, 2014). In Northern Nigeria, where women did not earn the right to vote until a military decree in 1976, there have been vigorous debates about the drawbacks and merits of women's political participation (Kendhammer, 2016, pp. 98–99).

In recent years, a number of high-profile debates have taken place across the region about the nature of citizenship (Herbst, 1990; Manby, 2013). In Zimbabwe, Mugabe's attacks on the small minority of white farmers have been based in part on the implicit argument that these

---

[14] Sata criticized salaries paid to Zambian workers by Chinese companies, calling the salaries "slave wages" (see www.wsj.com/articles/SB10001424053111904194604576582093246107906).

[15] http://thediplomat.com/2016/01/zimbabwe-chinas-all-weather-friend-in-africa.

people should not be considered full-fledged citizens, a view that many
Zimbabweans hold (Tendi, 2010). The rise of ethnic polarization over
the course of the last quarter century and the subsequent collapse of
the Ivoirian state was caused by debates about the citizenship rights of
Ivoirians who had migrated from neighboring countries and the northern
regions of Côte d'Ivoire itself (Roubaud, 2003).

A controversial 2002 law in Mauritius gave any foreigner with over
$500,000 permanent residency status, and as a result, the number of mil-
lionaires in Mauritius grew by 20 percent in 2016.[16] This influx of rich
and influential foreign residents has spurred political movements, such as
the Patriotic Movement, that aim to address inequality and poverty in a
context of heightening foreign excess.[17]

The issue of gay rights and the criminalization of homosexuality, as
discussed above, also fall into the category of citizenship. Thirty-four
countries still have laws against homosexuality that are associated with
jail time, and three of those countries – Sudan, Northern Nigeria, and
Mauritania – have a death penalty (Tripp, 2017, p. 100). In 2016, Nigeria
passed an anti-gay law, joining many other countries on the continent
that penalize members of the LGBT community. In Botswana in 2016,
the Court of Appeals upheld a ruling that protected gay rights groups
from an increasingly anti-gay government.[18] In some instances, civil society has been able to push back against harsh legislation, but this occurs
in a minority of cases, as many political actors and institutions remain
divided about the issue, and in some instances, domestic perceptions of
gay rights campaigns as imposed by the West make this a sovereignty
issue (Tripp, 2017, p. 101).

Elites simultaneously draw on global narratives and local discourse to
frame issues in ways that resonate with domestic audiences. In Northern
Nigeria, champions of sharia played into popular anxiety about the
"prospect of a secular society" and the "victory of Western culture"
(Kendhammer, 2016, p. 91). Debates over domestic laws and women's
rights have generated lively exchanges as well as large-scale protests
throughout the Sahel (Kang, 2015).

This category of issues also concerns parallel governance structures
within the state, that is, the role of government as compared to that of

[16] https://qz.com/964440/the-number-of-millionaires-in-mauritius-is-growing-faster-than-anywhere-else-in-africa.

[17] www.lemauricien.com/article/mouvement-patriotique-lutte-contre-la-pauvrete-et-l-ine galite-economique.

[18] www.pinknews.co.uk/2016/03/16/botswana-government-lose-battle-to-ban-gay-group.

traditional and religious authority. The role of traditional chiefs – notably in relationship to the state – and the responsibilities and privileges of individual chiefs are emerging as a contentious issue in a number of countries. Relatedly, religious leaders' abilities to adjudicate disputes or to govern marriage are typically debated. Increasingly, discourse around emigrants' rights and the treatment and reintegration of deportees is prevalent in large sending countries such as Senegal.

6.3.6 Distribution of Resources

The issue of distribution of resources is seen in debates about the who, how, and why of the distribution of a country's resources, including discussions of land tenure, oil revenue, and fishing rights. This issue includes questions about economic distribution, such as subsidies and programs targeting specific constituencies. The management of national resources is at the center of contentious politics in the region. Independence found the control of natural resources largely in the hands of foreign companies. In many countries, Africans found themselves dispossessed of their ancestral lands. As a result, in the public imagination, national control over natural resources remains an important objective of government.

The unequal allocation of control over national resources in the independence era resulted in a few "well-integrated hegemonic groups" (Sklar, 1979, p. 540). In many countries, government elites and their networks had unique access to national assets, a situation that fueled subsequent inequality. Many ethnoregional appeals make reference to the need for redistribution favoring historically neglected regions to compensate for existing inequalities. Thus this category also involves quotas or redistribution targeting specific groups. This category would also address decentralization, transitions to federalism, or special status or investments for particular geographic zones. For instance, Nigerian debates about indigeneity status have been intimately tied to federalism (Kendhammer, 2016, p. 94).

In southern African countries with a history of substantial numbers of European settlers, nationalism around land issues and calling for land redistribution have proven to be winning issues at the ballot box. In Zimbabwe, the 2000 land reform generated a violent struggle that party officials likened to the liberation struggle (Dendere, 2015, p. 153; see also Alexander and McGregor, 2001). Ranger (2004) and others have documented well how the Mugabe regime promoted a "patriotic history" of the country that emphasized the key role of the Zimbabwe African

National Union-Patriotic Front (ZANU-PF) in the struggle to reclaim land from European settlers, to great political effect, notably during the 2000 electoral campaign (Alexander and McGregor, 2001).

The management of natural resources is an issue that increasingly divides Africans as well. With internal migration and growing demographic pressures, struggles over access to land and the allocation of property rights have become an increasingly contentious issue in a large number of countries (Klopp, 2000; Peters, 2004) and one that politicians are willing to instrumentalize for political purposes (Ribot, 2003; Boone, 2009).

Opposition politicians may appeal to marginalized regions or groups with promises to allocate more fairly the distribution of national income and services, or they critique the imbalance of resources controlled by the executive at the national level and the slow and inconsistent processes of decentralization and devolution. Because incumbent executives continue to control a disproportionate amount of national resources and have control over policy making, they can leverage their position to court constituencies that are hoping for a larger slice of the national pie.

6.3.7 Unclaimed Issues

Sometimes, issues that clearly resonate with citizens nonetheless remain unclaimed by political parties because these issues fall outside of the realm of imagined politics or are risky for elite actors to address. Anticipating the challenges that they will face once in office, parties are hesitant to champion issues that they feel that they won't be able to control or reluctant to shine a light on tough policies that are likely to be politically unpopular.

Many of the countries in sub-Saharan Africa are characterized by high levels of dependence on foreign aid and have incentives to avoid issues that divide foreign donors and their domestic populations, such as populist religious movements or desire for greater resources for parastatals. Some scholars have gone so far as to argue that this dependence on foreign aid and the subsequent need to adopt certain policies because of donor conditionality curtail parties' ability to promote certain types of economic policy, thus generating a "choice-less democracy" (Mkandawire, 1999). Opposition politics has constituted a game played by secular elites who were tasked with balancing populations' urgent demands for development with meager national budgets and the concerns of donors, challenging incumbents' hold on power without dividing the population, and attracting aid to help fund development projects. While candidates may be tempted to court voters by taking a populist religious position, they do not want to compromise their other relationships, or they might lack the relationship with the authentic nonstate actors who actually own that issue to make a credible statement.

While we believe that politicians still have considerable autonomy in pursuing issues unpopular with an international audience (for example, Museveni's championing of anti-gay legislation in Uganda or Kenyatta's strategy to leverage the ICC charges against him to his own electoral advantage), in some cases politicians would rather ignore the most socially contentious issues in the campaign or send them to a referendum once the candidate is in office. For instance, despite increasing programmatic debate in Kenya, politicians have refused to touch Kenya's recent privatization of the government's shares of lucrative hotels held under the Kenya Tourist Development Corporation.[19]

6.4 CAPTURING THE ISSUES IN THE DATA

To assess the presence of valence discourse in a systematic way, we examined political issues in newspaper articles in eight countries from three different regions in Africa: Benin, Ghana, Kenya, Mozambique, Nigeria, Senegal, Uganda, and Zambia. Our scope conditions required that we select countries that had experience with reasonably regular elections but exhibited some degree of variation in the quality of democracy. We were further constrained by the availability of online media, as we discuss below.[20]

We drew on more than 1,500 local newspaper articles from eight countries over sixteen presidential election cycles: Benin (in 2011 and 2016), Ghana (in 2008 and 2012), Kenya (in 2007 and 2012), Mozambique (in 2009 and 2014), Nigeria (in 2007 and 2015), Senegal (in 2012 and 2007), Uganda (in 2006 and 2016), and Zambia (in 2008 and 2011). We coded the types of thematic issues that parties raised during the campaign cycles as well as trends and variation in their engagement with valence and position issues. Given the dominance of presidentialism in these countries, we focused on presidential races, but we also coded issues in legislative and gubernatorial races that were concurrent with the presidential race.

---

[19] www.afriquesenlutte.org/afrique-de-l-est/kenya/article/kenya-privatisation-of-parastatals.

[20] Our online appendix includes data about the specific sources as well as links to the articles that we coded. Instructions for the coding appear in online Appendix 1.

Information on the newspapers, our coding rules, and links to all of the articles are available in the online appendix.

Political issues are discussed on street corners, during candidate speeches, on local radio, and increasingly in online discussions. They feature in the party manifestoes that appear during campaigns. To gain preliminary information about the pattern and nature of political issues in a wide set of countries, we decided to focus on local newspapers that were available online. Our focus on print media might bias the results, leading us to overstate the importance of issues that are marketed to literate urban populations. Of greater concern, newspaper reporting might offer more coverage of incumbent politicians and less controversial critiques of the politicians than radio would, thus restricting the types of issues that are covered in our analysis. We remain aware of this potential pitfall as we move forward. The advantage of examining online versions of print media – aside from sheer practicality – is that we can include the article links in the online appendix, thus increasing the transparency of our coding and promoting replicability.

We selected from each country newspapers that offered complete online archives that could be reviewed in their entirety by date.[21] We considered using a keyword search in newspaper archives, but preliminary tests using Nigerian print newspapers from the 2011 election cycle demonstrated that this method failed to capture most of the political issues discussed in the newspapers. Once we identified an appropriate newspaper with an online archive, we used an online randomizer to select a day of the week and skimmed the newspaper for that day every week for the six-month period leading up to the elections. We first recorded the type of thematic issue area that was being discussed. In addition, every article was coded for valence or position issues, using coding criteria listed in the online appendix. Valence issues related to posturing about credibility and capacity of actors, whereas position issues included a broader ideological justification for a particular position. It is important to distinguish between policy issues and position taking. In many cases, candidates outlined policy promises but in forms that were not debatable and therefore were not coded as position issues. For example, an incumbent member of parliament (MP) candidate in Ghana pledged to revive the shoe, meat, and tomato factories to spur youth employment; although a challenger might have argued that this was not an efficient way to create jobs, he or she could not have argued against employing

---

[21] A list of all newspaper articles and weblinks is available in the online appendix.

youth. Because of the contextual nature of valence and position issues as well as coded jargon within thematic appeals, coders were encouraged to highlight any uncertain coding in yellow. One of the authors went through the coding work by all research assistants to double-check contentious coding decisions.

To compare the frequency of different actors' valence appeals, each article was also coded for the list of actors making a claim: political parties or candidates (opposition or incumbents) and civil society actors, including NGOs, religious groups, unions, student groups, traditional authorities, private enterprise, and think tanks. Actors that were grouped into the "other" category included former politicians or government officials, distinct government institutions such as the federal bank or the education commission, donors, and other international entities. Statements from the "other" actors are not included in the discussion in this chapter.

Each statement by each actor in an article was coded as one observation. For instance, if an article reported on an opposition party and a civil society group both lobbying for a particular bill to pass, the article was coded as two observations: a position issue for the party and a position issue for the civil society group. To minimize the bias introduced by the various newspapers, we excluded any direct newspaper editorials (such as campaign endorsements by newspaper staff) and focused instead on reports of issue discussions by different actors.

We coded the thematic content of different issue statements into six broad categories, as described in the previous section: democracy, development, the distribution of resources, sovereignty, domestic security, and citizenship. We coded different thematic areas within each statement as unique observations. For example, in an article reporting on a candidate speech addressing both unemployment (coded as development) and women's rights (coded as citizenship), we pulled out and coded two separate issue statements.

We also tracked things like political endorsements, party in fighting, and candidates' celebrations of their unique skills and experience. However, we did not include these types of topics in the analysis unless they contained an explicit reference to an issue. For instance, a constituent saying that a candidate was intelligent and responsive to a constituency would not feature in our categorization. By contrast, if the article included an endorsement by a political leader saying that the candidate's extensive educational background and intelligence would help him to promote better schooling in the country, we would code this issue as development. Future research could analyze these character-based

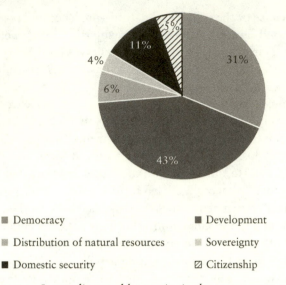

Democracy ■   Development ■

Distribution of natural resources ■   Sovereignty ▨

Domestic security ■   Citizenship ▨

FIGURE 6.2. *Issues discussed by parties in the most recent two
presidential election cycles*
N = 1,464.

appeals, but the focus of this specific chapter is on the substance behind
electoral discourse.

6.5 EVALUATING CAMPAIGN DISCOURSE: EXPLORING
THE ISSUES AS REPORTED IN LOCAL NEWSPAPERS

We start our evaluation by examining the types of issues that political
parties raise during campaign periods. Figure 6.2 depicts the issues raised
by political parties in our eight chosen countries over the most recent two
campaign cycles. The figure shows the types of thematic issues that parties discussed over these election cycles. Consistent with the fact that citizens are most invested in economic development, that issue takes up 42
percent of all parties' discourse in election cycles. Development captures
social service provision, access to jobs, and more general issues related
to the economy. The second most cited issue is development; nearly a
third of issue statements in elections relate to electoral rules, civil liberties, and candidates' extolling the importance of democracy. Issues of
domestic security are the third most discussed issue in the 2012–16 election cycles, which could be influenced by antiviolence rhetoric in Kenya

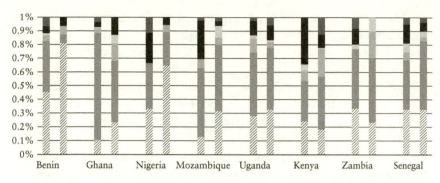

FIGURE 6.3. *Political parties' issue statements for each election cycle*
Most recent election is listed first. N = 1,464.

as well as rising tensions between Frente de Libertação de Moçambique
(FRELIMO) and Resistência Nacional Mocambiçana (RENAMO) in
Mozambique. Discussions of the distribution of resources and citizenship
make up 6 percent and 5 percent, respectively, of all coded statements.
Finally, issues of sovereignty and international relations are the least dis-
cussed in either election cycle, making up 4 percent of content.

Figure 6.2 masks important variation by country and between election
cycles. Politicians respond to current issues and salient political debates;
instead of seeing rote repetition of party platforms or issues that are
owned by a specific party, the electoral context shapes issue statements in
a dynamic way. Figure 6.3 displays the issues raised by political parties in
each electoral cycle and shows the variation both across countries and for
each electoral cycle. Development is the most frequently cited thematic
issue area in all countries except Benin, Nigeria, and Kenya.

In Benin, democracy is the most discussed issue, followed by development. This is largely due to debates in Benin about electoral rules and
registration as well as corruption scandals during the 2011 elections.
There were rumors that incumbent Yayi Boni wanted to extend term limits and increasing criticism of corruption in his government. Statements
about democracy subsided a bit in the subsequent elections when Boni
agreed to step down in 2016. Benin was well into its sixth multiparty
elections, and the discussions coded as "democracy" had to do with specific issues of the functioning of democratic institutions. For instance, an
MP raised a serious inquiry about the transparency of hiring practices in

the Ministry of Finance.[22] In 2016, eventual winner Patrice Talon entered the presidential race with a fairly controversial platform to limit a president to one term in office as well as a broader circumscription of executive powers.[23]

In Kenya, concerns about domestic security trumped all other issues in the 2012 elections. The concern about security during elections likely referenced the violence and massive population displacement around the 2007 elections. Candidates were invested in passing a message of peace and nonviolence to assure voters that this will not happen again under their watch. In Nigeria, accusations about corruption and interference with the election made democracy the most talked-about issue.

In Ghana, discussion of development dwarfs all other types of political debate. Issues such as access to jobs, infrastructure, social services, and economic growth made up 78 percent all issues discussed in the 2012 elections and 44 percent in the prior election cycle. This may be in part because Ghana has consolidated its democracy to a point at which security concerns and vote rigging are no longer in the forefront of voters' minds.

Country-level variables such as the competitiveness of elections or the threat of instability or war can affect the types of issues that candidates raise. In Uganda, where Museveni was competing to govern for his fifth electoral term and begin his fourth decade in office, there was little need for the challengers to raise detailed position issues. Instead, they could focus on the most obvious issue: Museveni was continuing to rule as a dictator despite democratic progress in neighboring countries. In the most recent election in Mozambique, citizens were very wary that the situation could devolve into civil war, and the number of party statements about the importance of peace, security, and unity increased.

Figure 6.4 shows issue statements by incumbent and opposition parties. Incumbency status endows a candidate with a valence advantage for campaigning. In African elections over the past two decades, this valence advantage has been enhanced by the ability to take credit for government- and donor-funded infrastructure projects as well as stable economic growth rates. Incumbents have the comparative advantage of

---

[22] www.actubenin.com/?Le-depute-Dakpe-Sossou-demande-des-comptes-au-gouverne ment-au-sujet-du-dernier. This MP, a former mayor of Lokossa, had been a vocal critic of government corruption (see http://beninwebtv.com/2016/06/benin-dakpe-sossou-interpelle-le-gouvernement-sur-une-irregularite-financiere-de-8-milliards.)

[23] www.jeuneafrique.com/mag/305843/politique/presidentielle-benin-ajavon-talon-milliardaires-campagne.

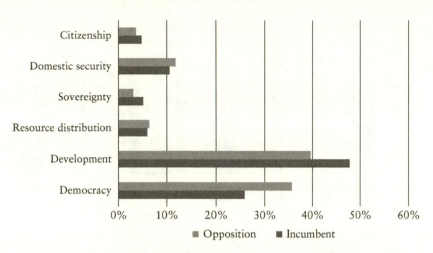

FIGURE 6.4. *Incumbent and opposition statements by thematic area*
Incumbent statements: N = 588; opposition statements: N = 859.

development issues; they "own" issues related to donor investments as well as services and infrastructure provided by the state. Since members of the incumbent party are development issue owners, we might expect them to discuss development more often than opposition candidates do. Figure 6.4 shows support for this.[24] Incumbent parties reference development in a higher percentage of their statements than do opposition parties.

As we pointed out in Chapter 2, many semiauthoritarian regimes hold elections. Twenty years after most countries have transitioned to multiparty democracy, the voting population is well aware than their president is playing by different rules than those of their more democratic neighbors. Even in more competitive systems, democracy remains fragile and unconsolidated. In many poor democracies, countries may hold regular elections and allow for freedom of association and freedom of the press while corruption remains rampant. Thus opposition candidates are best positioned to critique the incumbents' commitment to democratic ideals. Challengers have a comparative advantage on democracy issues. They should own issues related to corruption, rule of law, and civil liberties on the basis of their structural position as challengers. Figure 6.4 reveals that opposition actors raise democracy issues more frequently in their

---

[24] Because Kibaki stepped down and did not endorse a candidate, we did not code any parties as incumbent parties in Kenya.

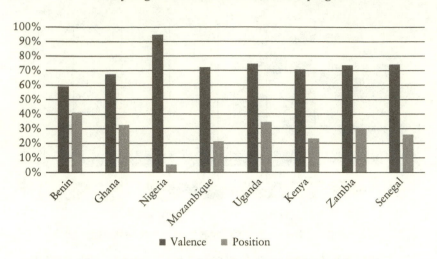

FIGURE 6.5. *Percentage of valence and position appeals used
by parties over two election cycles*
N = 1,423.

statements than incumbents do. It appears that opposition actors and
incumbents are just as likely to raise issues related to security, sovereignty,
citizenship, and resource distribution.

Figure 6.5 evaluates the use of valence and position appeals. In every
country, valence appeals are employed more frequently than position
appeals. Given the lack of issue ownership by parties, the newness of
electoral competition in Africa, the legacy of unity platforms, and uncertainty about constituencies, parties have incentives to champion valence
issues on which everyone agrees.

In Benin, Ghana, Senegal, and Zambia, which have more competitive
and less violent elections, politicians are slightly more likely to employ
position issues than is the case in the countries that have less competitive
or more violent elections: Kenya, Mozambique, Nigeria, and Uganda. It
might be that greater certainty about electoral rules and experience with
elections over time generates greater position discourse. Appeals for unity
and nonviolence can inflate the number of valence statements. Political
parties in Kenya had made position statements in nearly half their communications in the 2007 election; in contrast, there were far fewer position statements by parties (around 23 percent) in the 2012 election.
Recent experience with violence or threats to sovereignty might force
candidates to focus on issues that are at the forefront of citizens' minds.

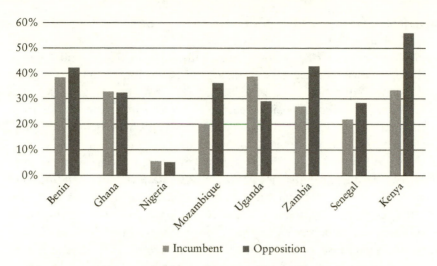

FIGURE 6.6. *Percentage of position discourse by incumbents and opposition in the most recent two election cycles*
N = 1,423.

After the electoral violence and population displacement of Kenya's 2007 elections, candidates in the 2012 race were much more cautious about using ethnic appeals and spoke during the campaign about the importance of unity and peace. Thus while the 2007 election included many position issues, such as the debate over federalism and promotion of free schooling, discourse in the 2012 elections was dwarfed by a concern over this general valence issue.[25]

Just as the electoral context shapes the thematic issues discussed by political actors, election-specific variables, including the actors who are competing for office and their records, the major issues facing the country, and the broader regional and international political and economic environment, shape choices about valence and position appeals. This means that the character of elections, in terms of the political issues that candidates discuss, the level of ethnic or unity discourse, and the use of valence or positions appeals might change from cycle to cycle.

Figure 6.6 examines position taking by incumbent and opposition parties. Although we expect these trends to be shaped by election-level

---

[25] Similarly, after the coup in Mali and a Northern occupation of more than two—thirds of the country, candidates in Mali's 2013 presidential election were all focused on reestablishing peace and democracy. Candidates departed from the typical discourse about development.

variables, we note that opposition parties are more likely to take positions than is the incumbent party. Only in Uganda did the incumbent president take more positions than challengers. In Ghana and Nigeria, the opposition and incumbent parties raised position issues with about the same frequency.

We might expect opposition parties to be more likely than actors from the majority or incumbent party to advance position issues. Although subject to the same constraints posed by uncertainty, opposition parties have less to lose and more to gain by using a flamboyant position appeal. Because they did not have access to state resources and because citizens typically trust incumbents at a higher rate (Ishiyama and Fox, 2006; Logan, 2008), incumbents have a valence advantage. In his study of European democracies, Shefter (1993) observed that opposition parties invested in issues more quickly than did parties that were in power. Other studies have found that opposition parties are more likely to take on extremist positions, while incumbents with a valence advantage hold to more moderate positions (Groseclose, 2001; Stone and Simas, 2010). In dominant party systems, challengers are willing to make niche appeals to minority constituents (Greene, 2010).

Opposition parties needed to use positions to get into power. The logic of what Riker (1986) called heuresthetics, or the creation of new cleavages and the defining of issues in a politically favorable manner, is more likely to appeal specifically to political entrepreneurs outside the majority party, since they have a much greater incentive to innovate and change the nature of political debate. Because African incumbent parties have more state resources for campaigning and already benefit from greater public confidence, we would expect them to be slower to respond to position issues that resonate with public sentiment. For their part, challengers will feel less tied down by the need to please supermajority constituencies and more willing to take risks to find and mobilize constituencies. Incumbents may view themselves as less likely to sway voters with strong ideological appeals and therefore maintain valence strategies.

Figure 6.6 seems to provide initial evidence that in most countries, opposition parties are more likely to employ position discourse than incumbents are. We see evidence of the opposition tackling salient position issues in attempts to heighten their credibility. For instance, in Benin, the opposition criticized Boni's continued collaboration with the Group Bollore on railroad construction despite a constitutional court ruling demanding that the work stop because of a dispute over the way in which Boni awarded Group Bollore the contract. The opposition was thus able

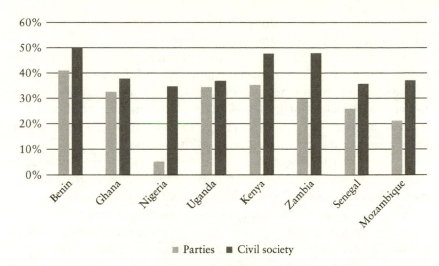

FIGURE 6.7. *Position statements by civil society and political parties in recent elections*
N = 1,851.

to capitalize on a position issue that reflected disparate views among Benin's ruling institutions and use it in their campaign against the prime minister who was running as Boni's successor.[26]

Figure 6.7 compares the percentage of position statements by civil society compared to those by political parties.[27] If uncertainty is a root cause of politicians' inability and unwillingness to take positions, then we should observe other actors, who do not face the same levels of uncertainty and who may have a narrower and more clearly identified constituency, to be more willing to take positions than political parties or candidates. We suspect that groups from civil society, such as NGO leaders, academics, religious leaders, and union leaders, will be more likely to raise position issues than will political actors, in part because of the lower levels of uncertainty and risk that those from civil society face. However, some actors from civil society, such as traditional leaders, rural

---

[26] For more on the contested railroad project, see http://cotonou24news.com/boni-yayi-lionel-zinsou-et-bollore-desavoues-par-le-niger-dans-le-dossier-boucle-ferroviaire/www.actubenin.com/?Boni-Yayi-prend-fait-et-cause-pour-le-Groupe-Bollore.

[27] Mozambique had no civil society actors reported in newspaper articles in our sample in the most recent election cycle. In one of the election cycles, there was only one statement by civil society actors in Uganda and Kenya, so those election cycles were also excluded in order not to distort the averages.

constituencies, or NGOs with political links to parties, might be as constrained as, or more constrained than, parties.

In most countries, civil society raises position issues more frequently than political parties do. However, the margin of difference is affected by the electoral environment. In authoritarian-leaning countries such as Uganda, civil society might have a weaker voice and might also be less likely to be reported on in news media. In contrast, we can observe the vocal role of civil society in Kenya in staking out positions.

Civil society actors have less internal uncertainty. Their constituencies and their missions are clearer than those of the nonideological political parties discussed above. Civil society actors can speak directly to the interest groups or the ideological or epistemic communities they represent. In some instances, civil society groups are older and more experienced than political parties, and although many electoral laws ban foreign funding of political parties, some civil society groups, especially NGOs, have a larger and more consistent funding base. Unlike politicians, they do not have to worry about coalition or allegiance building, nor do they fear retribution or punishment from a constituency if their goals are not realized. These groups can play an advocacy role without having to consider future compromises or the success of their platforms.

We do note that civil society seemed far less vocal and/or received far less newspaper coverage during the most recent election cycles, at least in the pages of newspapers in some countries. We coded very few issue statements from civil society in our sample from Uganda ($N = 2$) and Kenya ($N = 2$) and none in Mozambique in the recent elections. We wonder whether their access to the press was restricted or whether, owing to the tense environment of insecurity, these actors were self-censoring.

6.6 CONCLUSION

In this chapter, we have demonstrated the dynamic and evolving nature of African electoral debate. The framing and types of issues raised in each election vary by country but also by the specific election cycle.

We do observe some important trends. First, the dominance of development as a thematic issue in African electoral campaigning is striking, although this should perhaps not be surprising in a low-income political system. Development is followed by candidates' discussion of themes related to democracy, including good governance, rule of law, electoral rules, and corruption. Incumbents, because of their structural advantage in the electoral system, own development and employ those issues in a higher percentage of their issue statements. In contrast, opposition parties appear to own issues on democracy and draw on that language a higher percentage of the time in comparison to incumbent actors. That is not to say that opposition actors cannot promise to build wells or change trade tariffs or that incumbent actors cannot celebrate their role in democratic consolidation; the point is that opposition politicians and incumbents have comparative advantages in certain issue areas.

We observe the dominance of valence discourse in countries. As we argued earlier in this chapter, we think that this is due to the specific heritage of African party systems and to lingering uncertainty in these electoral systems. We have presented some evidence suggesting that opposition actors are more likely to take positions than incumbents and that civil society actors are more likely to use positions than are political parties.

7

The African Voter

R1: They give each of us a bit of money, but that doesn't build a hospital. To throw money around that doesn't change our situation.

R2: During the campaigns, politicians come during elections to distribute salt and sugar. We've learned from past electoral cycles and now we're requiring more.[1]

The important thing is that after this election the Nigerian new breed politicians would, hopefully, have learnt one basic lesson of party politics – that it is sustained by a proper mobilisation of the electorate through active marketing of each party's program called political campaign, not empty slogans and vile abuses. An active electorate cannot be taking for granted; it must be courted and embraced with party manifestoes and program that speak to their needs.[2]

7.1 INTRODUCTION

In this chapter, we explore continuity and change in voting behavior and more contentious forms of political participation among African citizens since 1990. Although much remains to be learned, in the nearly twenty-five years that have passed since the first transitions to democracy in the region, the evolving motivations and attitudes that African citizens bring to voting and other forms of participation have been the subject of

---

[1] Field notes from Bleck and Michelitch (2015): Focus group respondents, Village Leadership, Koulikoro Region, Mali, October 19, 2011.
[2] Rotimi Fasan, "Nigerian Politics and the 2015 Election Campaigns," *The Vanguard*, April 15, 2015, accessed at www.vanguardngr.com/2015/04/nigerian-politics-and-the-2015-election-campaigns.

considerable research, some of it seemingly contradictory. In this chapter, we review and synthesize findings in order to compare patterns of political behavior in sub-Saharan Africa with those in other regions and to formulate some generalizations.

In this chapter, we look at citizens' responses to the two broad changes that we have emphasized throughout the book: the introduction and institutionalization of multiparty elections across most countries in sub-Saharan Africa and the massive demographic changes of the last twenty-five years, which include urbanization, increased access to traditional and social media, increased rates of education, and an emerging African middle class. In the first half of the chapter, we examine how citizens have responded to the regularization of elections across regimes in sub-Saharan Africa. Have citizens seized new opportunities for electoral participation since the 1990s? We show that country-level participation rates have remained relatively constant since 1990 and have not gone through the same quick drop in electoral participation as occurred in the postindependence period, a half-century ago.

As we argued in earlier chapters, many African party systems include a dominant party in power, surrounded by a large number of smaller parties, in the context of a good deal of party volatility (see Chapters 2 and 4). African political systems cede extraordinary power to the executive branch, and executive incumbents are reelected at higher rates in Africa than anywhere else in the world (Chapter 3). Other nonelected authorities, such as regional ethnic big men, religious leaders, and traditional leaders, play important roles as brokers to the political system (Chapter 5). How do these institutional characteristics shape citizens' levels of participation, including voting, party affiliation, and campaigning? What other types of participation, including contentious action, are incentivized by formal and informal power structures in sub-Saharan Africa? As we argued in earlier chapters, there is a good deal of inter-country variation, including the political salience of ethnicity, the strength of parties, population density, and regional differences within countries.

We demonstrate that the impact of the cross-national variation in the quality of democratic governance is surprisingly muted. We find little difference in turnout whether the country is well on its way toward democratic consolidation or stuck in a relatively repressive mode of electoral authoritarianism. We hypothesize that the reason for these findings is that voters are motivated to go to the polls by different incentives and by forces that vary across different political systems. This somewhat paradoxical situation of different processes and logics leading to similar outcomes can be seen throughout the chapter.

There is, of course, no single African voter, despite the title of the chapter. Voters respond to the political context in which they live; this context varies by country, but can also vary within countries and by election cycle. Voters' valuation of the "D term" – individual-level characteristics or incentives for participation, including sense of duty, their own identity, or efficacy, that are independent of outcome (Riker and Ordershook, 1968) – is linked to the range of available candidates and parties, their platforms and promises, and their ability to deliver on these promises. It is also linked to the relative strength of formal and informal institutions, including local vote brokers, as well as negative and positive inducements linked to election day. The specific electoral context matters, as we discussed in Chapter 3; election-day participation may be incentivized by monetary handouts or dissuaded through voter suppression, depending on the distribution of electoral violence or vote-buying efforts in a particularly country or region.

In the debate about the extent to which African voters are rational or making choices entirely on the basis of ascriptive categories (Lindberg, 2013), we fall squarely on the side of rationality. In this chapter, we provide plenty of evidence of African voters making reasoned choices even if their votes are influenced by phenomena that could be, and has been, viewed through a culturalist prism, from vote buying to the influence of traditional authorities and other rural brokers. But the variables that explain participation in the traditional literature on voting behavior in mature democracies have real salience in Africa, from retrospective voting to the impact of partisanship and party identification on voting to voters' assessment of candidates' character-based valence attributes.[3]

In the second part of the chapter, we examine the ways in which sociodemographic shifts and the explosion of media and access to information and communication technology shape political participation. Do we see any discernible differences in how citizens engage with the state in an increasingly urbanized and information-saturated environment? To be sure, we observe learning. We present initial evidence of rising levels of access to television and the Internet, growing political knowledge, and increasing associational membership in most countries. As the quotes at the beginning of this chapter suggest, Africans are learning to be more

---

[3] For a discussion of these traits and their heightened salience for voters during the electoral period, see Abney et al. (2011).

demanding of their politicians, and parties are beginning to realize that they will be judged on their performance. Still, what is striking from the empirical evidence is how stable participation levels have been across time, the persistence of incumbent advantages (although these vary sharply in executive and legislative elections), and the stability in voter motivations, whatever these may be. We also show relatively stable levels of political interest and political discussion.

7.2 CONTINUITY AND CHANGING PATTERNS OF ELECTORAL TURNOUT ACROSS AFRICA

We start by exploring the cross-national and longitudinal variation in turnout since 1990. Most African voters have experienced over twenty years of regular elections. Some observers predicted that democratic participation would decline over time, as occurred in the postindependence period (Kasfir, 1974; Bienen, 1978; Collier, 1982), as the excitement of the transitions to democracy waned and voters became disgruntled with the imperfections of their democracy (Carothers, 2002). Similarly, O'Donnell and Schmitter (1986) predicted that we might see high turnout in founding elections followed by a decline as elections became routinized and elected officials failed to meet voters' expectations.

However, no dramatic variation in turnout over time is discernible in the data. Instead, indeed, electoral participation rates appear remarkably stable in the overwhelming majority of countries that convene multiparty elections.

Voter turnout in presidential and legislative elections has increased slightly in the last fifteen years compared to the period between 1990 and 1999. Since 1990, the average turnout for executive races is 61 percent, and that for legislative elections is 56 percent. Mean turnout rates for executive elections vary widely across countries – unsurprisingly, perhaps, given the range of political regimes and country characteristics. Turnout for presidential elections since 1990 has ranged from a high of 98 percent in the Seychelles in the presidential elections of 2001 to a low of 23 percent in Burkina Faso in 2010. Similarly, turnout in legislative elections rose from an average of 52 percent in 1990–9 to 56 percent in the period between 2000 and 2015. This stability contradicts the narrative of declining global electoral turnout in the last twenty-five years.[4]

---

[4] Dan Kopf, Voter turnout is dropping dramatically in the "free world" Quartz, February 1, 2017. Accessed June 3, 2018 https://qz.com/899586/global-voter-turnout-is-dropping-dramatically-across-the-world.

It is comparable to turnout rates reported for India (around 61 percent since 1967) (Diwakar, 2008) and the most recent US election (56 percent). It is a bit lower than registered voter turnout reported for a sample of Asian, Middle Eastern and Northern African, and African countries from 2004–8, as reported by Brownlee (2011).

In this book, we argue that the regularization of elections should not be conflated with the institutionalization of democracy. We perceive elections as political moments, or periods of heightened uncertainty and fluidity, which can occasionally offer the opportunity for real political change. This change is more likely to occur in countries where the state has less capacity to repress opposition.

Most observers agree that higher participation rates in sub-Saharan Africa do not always correlate well with the level of democracy[5] (see, for example, Kuenzi and Lambright, 2011), in part because the reasons for the level of turnout can vary by level of development but also because of differences in the state's capacity and motivations to control the electoral process. Owing to the variation in the types of opportunities that elections represent, turnout numbers may not be a reliable measure of citizens' efforts to communicate their political attitudes to candidates and government. The underlying mechanisms of what motivates voters to turnout under what conditions are likely to be very context dependent. In some countries, turnout might represent a "consumption act" (Fauvelle-Aymar, 2008) or a way to signal support and solidarity with more powerful actors rather than any hope of affecting the outcome of the race; in other countries, the act of voting is meant to trigger a government response to grievance or policy preferences. It could also be an expressive act linked to patriotism or hope for further democratization, or it may stem from pressure from family members or local vote brokers. Motivations might also vary depending on voters' allegiances to incumbent actors. For instance, Letsa (2015) argues that in Cameroon, nonpartisans, incumbent supporters, and opposition supporters vote "expressively" for different reasons, such as reasserting allegiance to the ruling party or to express their belief in democracy despite poor practices by the current government.[6]

---

[5] In Latin America, levels of democracy are associated with higher turnout for legislative and presidential races (Fornos et al., 2004). Similarly, Brownlee's (2011) analysis of registered voter turnout for presidential races in Africa, the Middle East and North Africa, and Asia between 2004 and 2008 reveals that countries coded as "electoral democracies" average slightly higher turnout, 68.6–66.8 percent, than nondemocracies in his sample.

[6] This is similar to Brownlee's (2011, p. 818) characterization of authoritarian regimes in the Middle East; he describes elections as moments for clientelistic transactions and elections as "performances" to display a regime's power to voters.

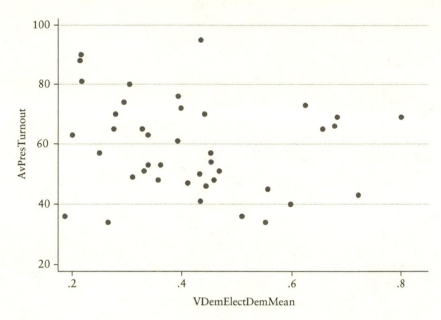

FIGURE 7.1. *Average presidential turnout (VAP) by average V-Dem score for electoral democracy*

Figures 7.1 and 7.2 take an average of countries' Varieties of Democracy (V-Dem) scores on electoral democracy[7] and average turnout since 1990 (VAP).[8] Countries are ordered from most democratic to least democratic by using their average V-Dem ratings. Figure 7.1 suggests that levels of democratization do not explain high or low levels of turnout. As expected, we do not see a clear relationship between levels of electoral democracy and turnout.

Instead, we suspect that other factors might explain the variation in turnout across countries. For instance, higher levels of democratic consolidation are linked to above-average turnout rates in Ghana (73 percent) and Cape Verde (69 percent), but some more authoritarian-leaning countries also have high average turnout rates, including Angola

---

[7] This score measures whether electoral opportunities are free and fair. It is an index of the following: the weighted average of the indices measuring freedom of association (thick) (v2x_frassoc_thick), clean elections (v2xel_frefair), freedom of expression (v2x_freexp_thick), elected officials (v2x_elecoff), and suffrage (v2x_suffr) and, on the other, the five-way multiplicative interaction between those indices (V Dem Codebook, V 7.1, p. 49, May 7, 2017).

[8] VAP rates are captured from 1990–2015, while V-Dem takes the mean of scores between 1990 and 2016.

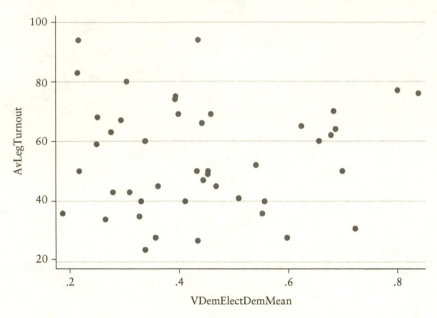

FIGURE 7.2. *Average legislative turnout (VAP) by average*
V-Dem score for electoral democracy

(88 percent) and Equatorial Guinea (81 percent). Interestingly, contrary to much of the literature on electoral autocracies, not all of the countries with the lowest electoral democracy ratings are uniformly able to boost turnout or "cook the books" to reflect as much. In contrast to Equatorial Guinea and Angola, other closed regimes are less able to get voters out to the polls, including Cameroon (51 percent turnout) and Zimbabwe (49 percent turnout). This may reflect different political dynamics in the countries of the region that do not correlate well with regime type, from party systems to cleavage structures, or it may reflect the political strategies of incumbent regimes.

Country characteristics and varying levels of state capacity may also shape turnout. Mobilizing citizens to go out to the polls may be more difficult in weak or sparsely populated states. For instance, most countries from the Sahel have had lower than average mean turnout in executive elections since 1990, despite having very different levels of democratization: Burkina (34 percent), Mali (40 percent), Niger (45 percent), Nigeria (47 percent), and Senegal (43 percent).[9] Literacy and development

---

[9] The exception is Chad with an average turnout at 70 percent since 1990.

indicators in the Sahel are among the weakest in Africa. These countries are also among the least densely populated[10] and have some of the most meager rural road networks, which would make voting more time consuming and onerous for voters. If we examine Sudan and Mozambique, two states in a different subregion but with similar characteristics, we also observe lower than average turnout at 36 percent and 50 percent, respectively.

As in other regions of the world, voter turnout appears to be generally enhanced by a close race (Kuenzi and Lambright, 2007; but see Fauvelle-Aymar, 2008, for the South African countercase). Participation is higher where the electoral outcome is uncertain, as in recent elections in Ghana, Kenya, and Nigeria. Still, the tightness of electoral competitions is not well captured by regime type, given the preponderance of dominant-party systems in the region.

In Chapter 3, we discussed that countries have very different patterns of gift giving and the use of violence, which do not clearly map onto their level of democracy. Country-level variation in the use of these tactics can affect citizens' decisions about whether to go to the polls. Existing literature suggests that election violence reduces voter turnout (Bratton, 2008; Collier and Vicente, 2014), particularly among undecided voters (Wallsworth, 2015).[11] Some electoral violence is aimed to suppress participation, but in other cases, voters abstain out of dissatisfaction with these kinds of electoral practices; increasingly, evidence shows that voters do not like violent tactics. Drawing on a survey experiment, Rosenzweig (2015) demonstrates that voters, even copartisans, do not like violent tactics at the polls. In their study of the notoriously violent 2007 election in Nigeria, Collier and Vicente (2014) show that antiviolence campaigns reduced turnout. Bratton (2008) argues that African voters also abstain when any kind of illegitimate campaigning occurs, including vote buying.

7.2.1 Legislative Elections

In other regions of the world, turnout rates for legislative elections are lower than those for executive elections. We might anticipate that turnout in legislative elections would be particularly depressed in the context

---

[10] www.indexmundi.com/g/r.aspx?v=21000.

[11] Hickman's (2009) study of electoral violence in Sri Lanka shows that violence by specific partisans reduces opposition turnout in that district. See Berkoe and Burchard (2017) for a more nuanced argument that the evidence on the impact of violence on turnout in African elections is actually weak.

of presidentialism, since power is concentrated in one branch. However, despite the political dominance of the executive branch, the gap between participation in executive elections and legislative elections for sub-Saharan Africa is small (an average of 5 percent for the continent). Some countries actually consistently demonstrate higher average turnout in legislative elections than in presidential elections, including Burkina Faso, Cape Verde, Guinea-Bissau, Kenya, Liberia, and Rwanda.

Figure 7.2 also demonstrates more variation in average turnout for legislative elections than for presidential elections. Tremendous variation across elections cycles is also striking. For instance, Equatorial Guinea boasted a 75 percent turnout for the legislative race in 2004 but only a 25 percent participation for the legislative election in 1999. Again, the data suggest country-specific and election-cycle-specific factors that might boost or suppress turnout.

Studies of voter turnout in other regions of the world have found that concurrent elections increase legislative turnout (Garand and Sharpe, 2000; Jacobson, 2000; Fornos et al., 2004; Geys, 2006), so we investigate whether jointly held legislative and presidential races yield a higher turnout in Africa. Interestingly, concurrent elections do not appear to increase turnout at the legislative level. We categorized countries as those that held all concurrent elections, those that did not hold concurrent elections, and those that held concurrent elections during some election cycles but not others. The mean turnout in these three sets of countries is relatively the same: 54.4 percent, 54.9 percent, and 55.1 percent, respectively. Note that only five countries have held concurrent elections for every election cycle during this period.

7.2.2 Local Elections

Another interesting finding is that African citizens seem to turn out for local races in relatively high numbers, at least compared to other regions of the world. While Figure 7.3 also shows the tremendous variation in turnout across countries, these patterns diverge from those in elections in the United States and Europe, where turnout for presidential, legislative, and gubernatorial elections is consistently higher than that for local elections (Morlan, 1984; Hajnal and Lewis, 2003).[12] Furthermore,

---

[12] Figure 7.3 reflects available turnout data from local-level elections, including municipal, regional, village council, and gubernatorial races. We treat these data as a rough estimate, as some of the data are reported as VAP and other data are reported as turnout

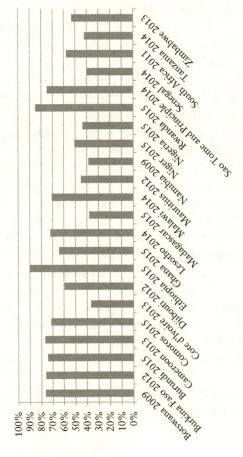

FIGURE 7.3. *Turnout in the most recent local elections*

municipal elections in some countries, such as Burkina Faso, Cameroon, the Comoros and Mali, have attracted higher turnout than recent presidential or legislative races have.[13]

Turnout may be high for legislative and municipal elections because these politicians are most visibly responsible for bringing goods and services back to their constituents. African voters are very concerned about constituency, service, and these elections determine the central players in that game. It may also be that higher levels of visibility of outputs at the local level help voters to better monitor and sanction municipal officials, thus being enabled to engage in informed retrospective voting (Pande, 2011).

High levels of participation in these elections also be the result of voters' estimation that they are more likely to be able to affect the outcome. Greater uncertainty prevails in legislative and municipal elections because incumbent candidates do not enjoy the same degree of incumbency advantage as the president, as we have discussed in Chapter 3. Consequently, voters can sanction an official who is underperforming and might be more motivated to vote in legislative elections to change constellations of power at the regional and local levels. We know that Africans actively exercise their political voice to generate more responsive local governance. African voters contact politicians at higher rates than do their peers in other countries. Mueller (2018) used Afrobarometer data to demonstrate that 33 percent of Africans had contacted a politician in the past year,[14] compared to 22 percent of citizens in the United States and fewer than 10 percent of British, French, or Swedish voters. Using original survey data from Niamey in Niger, Mueller (2018) found that most contact is for programmatic concerns, such as fixing community infrastructure, rather than for clientelistic concerns such as personal favors or gifts.

Finally, higher turnout for municipal races could be fueled by mobilization for different types of elections. For instance, municipal elections in

---

among registered voters. In some instances, these races are concurrent with legislative or presidential races or with referenda. We note that certain countries, including Angola, the Central African Republic, Guinea-Bissau, Liberia, the Republic of the Congo, the Seychelles, Somalia, South Sudan, and Sudan, hold no popular elections for local office.

[13] Other countries follow a more traditional trend of pronounced executive turnout and weaker participation rates in municipal elections. For instance, in South Africa, national-level participation dwarfs that of municipal elections; in 2014, 73 percent of registered voters cast a presidential ballot, compared to only 58 percent of registered voters participating in the 2011 municipal elections.

[14] Mueller (2015) notes that religious leaders were contacted at even higher rates.

some countries are referred to as "elections of proximity," in which people mobilize for friends of friends, coworkers, and neighbors whom they can situate within their local network rather than on the basis of specific partisan loyalties (Bleck, 2015; Cruz et al., 2015). This contrasts with elite-centered legislative and executive races, in which the likelihood that voters actually know the candidates is considerably lower. Furthermore, brokerage mechanisms between traditional authorities and legislative or municipal candidates would also take on a more personal character. Rather than negotiating with a party official, leaders could repeatedly negotiate with the candidates themselves, which might generate higher incentives and motivation to mobilize turnout through their vertical networks.

7.3 WHO VOTES?: FACTORS INFLUENCING TURNOUT AND VOTE CHOICE

In Section 7.2, we emphasized that voters might come to the polls for multiple reasons: to choose the candidate they want in office, because they were encouraged to do so by a broker, to assert a specific partisan identity at the polls, or to demonstrate allegiance to an incumbent. Therefore, it is very difficult to capture and compare voter motivations across countries. In this section, we discuss Africa-specific factors that tend to be emphasized when we discuss political behavior on the continent, including ethnic politics and brokerage but also traditional explanatory variables that influence turnout, such as partisanship and the competitiveness of the race.

7.3.1 Dispelling the Ethnic Politics Myth

The dominant narrative of party identification in Africa highlights the importance of ethnic and regional bases as the core determinants of partisan identification and vote choice. An older literature essentialized African parties and viewed elections as "ethnic censuses" (Horowitz, 1985). In addition to voters being able to express their identity when going to the polls by voting for a coethnic (Horowitz, 1985), shared ethnicity can serve as a heuristic for shared policy preferences (Ferree, 2010). Elections can heighten ethnic identity (Eifert et al., 2010), which in turn may stimulate attachment to ethnic parties. It is also possible, as Bates (1974, p. 472) posits, that ethnic groups can coordinate to sanction underperforming elites by voting them out of office; he provides evidence of groups voting cabinet members out of office due to their "failure to serve local interests." Other groups of people do not have the same access to information, organizational networks, or abilities to police behavior (Fearon and Laitin, 1996). Using an experiment in Uganda, Carlson (2015) shows that coethnic candidates are preferred only when they perform well and that voters prefer coethnics because they do not believe that non-coethnics will provide future goods. Indeed, ethnic concerns cannot always easily be analytically separated from other voting motivations, such as the economic performance of the incumbent or other economic motivations. A vote for a coethnic incumbent from whom the voter believes he or she has benefited can be viewed equally as an economic vote or as an ethnic vote.

Even the broadest understanding of ethnic voting is not a useful frame through which to view much of the region's voting behavior. The ethnicization of parties and party systems actually varies substantially across the region (Dowd and Driessen, 2008; Basedau et al., 2011; Elischer, 2013; Koter, 2016). Other group identification, such as levels of nationalism, can mediate preferential trust of coethnics (Robinson, 2016). Ishiyama and Fox (2006) found no correlation between heightened ethnic identification and heightened partisanship. Increasing evidence suggests that ethnic appeals are only one of many tactics for mobilization and only one of many predictors of voter behavior (Bratton and Kimenyi, 2008; Elischer, 2013), and the degree to which such tactics are used and their effectiveness vary substantially across both time and place (Posner, 2004). While it is true that many parties operate through ethnic heuristics, when and how ethnic heuristics are employed may depend on the proportion of different ethnic groups and the possibilities for multiple winning coalitions (Mozaffar and Scarritt, 2005; Posner, 2005; Ferree, 2010; Arriola, 2013) and the types of alternate candidate choices that are available to voters (Kasara, 2007). Bratton et al. (2012) demonstrate that most Africans engage in both ethnic and economic voting as part of very pragmatic strategies.

Ethnic homogeneity of districts could signal greater certainty of club goods being given to prospective voters in these districts if they vote for a coethnic (Ichino and Nathan, 2013a; Boone and Wahman, 2015), which might mean more united and consistent voting blocs. Ejdemyr et al. (2017) found evidence that members of parliament in Malawi provide more local public goods to districts where ethnic groups are geographically segregated and target that investment to coethnics.[15]

---

[15] Kasara (2007) argues that incumbents are better able to control competitors in their homeland region, thus exploiting the populations that support them.

While ethnic parties can be great tools for mobilization, ethnic reputations can also be stifling and may limit party growth. Ferree (2013) shows how the Democratic Alliance (DA) party in South Africa tried to shed its apartheid image as a "white party" but the African National Congress (ANC) went to great lengths to ensure that the DA was still branded a white party of the apartheid era. Indeed, quite a few incumbents, including Thomas Boni Yayi of Benin, Amadou Toumani Touré of Mali, and Yoweri Museveni of Uganda, have run as independents on a unity platform and make allusions to their mixed ethnic heritage to brand their campaign as explicitly nonethnic.

7.3.2 Incumbency Advantage, Competitiveness, and Retrospective Voting

Bratton et al. (2012) demonstrate that voters associate themselves with incumbent parties because candidates of those parties are more likely to win and therefore will be in a better position to access resources and avoid punishment after elections. This phenomenon is most exaggerated in dominant-party systems, in which opposition is weak and has a low chance of winning. A shift from a multiparty system to a dominant-party system is associated with a 31 percent higher likelihood of voting for the ruling party (Bratton et al., 2012). In these settings, vote choice is constrained by patronage systems linked to the dominant party. At an individual level, women and rural voters are more likely to vote for the ruling party (Bratton et al., 2012). Vicente and Wantchekon (2009) argue that during campaigns, incumbents' promises about what they will do if they win are more credible than those of the opposition, mostly because of the incumbents' control of the executive branch and of state resources. In their analysis of the Malawian presidential elections, Ferree and Horowitz (2010) showed how voters shifted from ethnoregional voting patterns to broad support for Peter Mutharika in the 2009 presidential election because of support for government performance and perception of inclusivity by the ruling party.

Additionally, growth rates over the last ten years have generated relatively favorable economic environments for incumbents. Logan (2009) finds that positive evaluations of economic performance and strong performance in the provision of social services increase trust in both the ruling and opposition parties but that increases in trust associated with economic growth have disproportionately large effects on the ruling party. Conversely, when perceptions of corruption are high, the ruling party receives more of the blame.

A large gap remains between trust in the ruling party and in the opposition; the gap is largest in countries that have not yet experienced peaceful electoral turnover of ruling parties (Bratton and Logan, 2015). Only four countries have a majority of citizens who think the opposition has a viable plan to govern: Ghana, Madagascar, Malawi, and Namibia (Bratton and Logan, 2015). Logan (2009) found that African voters tend to side with presidential incumbents to preserve the status quo; furthermore, voters who are more deferential to the power of the president also express more trust in the ruling party and less trust in the opposition, exacerbating the trust gap between ruling and opposition parties. The fact that Africans are likely to attribute local public goods to the president underscores the perceived dominance of the executive branch (Harding, 2015). Logan (2009) offers some evidence that poor respondents are more likely to trust opposition parties than are other respondents. Cross-country analyses of Afrobarometer data demonstrate that respondents in the middle class are most likely to support the opposition and to hold prodemocratic views (Cheeseman, 2015b).

Incumbents have also benefited from strong economic growth rates since transitions to multiparty elections, but these macro-economic trends do not always translate into money in everyone's pocket. An Afrobarometer survey conducted in 2005 showed that, consistent with growth rates in the first years of the twenty-first century, more Afrobarometer respondents were optimistic about future economic performance (56 percent) than were pessimistic (25 percent) (Bratton et al., 2012). Respondents were more likely to report variation in whether their personal economic conditions were worsening (35 percent) or improving (34 percent). Interestingly, two-thirds of respondents thought that the government was managing the economy badly, which Bratton et al. (2012) attributed to austerity measures aimed at reducing government spending. Like other voters, African voters are likely to evaluate the economy on the basis visible indicators of how it affects them or their families.

Incumbents are hardly immune to being held accountable for poor performance. Traditional retrospective voting models appear to have explanatory power in Africa as well. African voters, as in other regions, calculate economic considerations on the basis of the health of the general economy rather than their own personal well-being (Bratton et al., 2012). Favorable evaluations of the government's policy performance increase the likelihood of voting for the ruling party by 37 percent (Bratton et al., 2012). Relatedly, citizens who are non-coethnics of the incumbent and report discrimination by the governing regime are far less likely to state that they plan to vote for the ruling party (Bratton et al., 2012). Weghorst and Bernhard (2014) found that incumbents who manage development issues poorly are voted out. Similarly, economic conditions and the provision of public goods have been shown to play an important role in Ghana's recent elections (see Weghorst and Lindberg, 2011, 2013). Ellis (2014) found that voters reward and punish performance and that retrospective voting is a strong predictor of incumbent support but far from the only factor influencing vote choice. Bratton et al. (2011) show that voters' assessments of an incumbent's economic performance has double the effect on partisan identification as identity does. In 2014, Malawian President Joyce Banda was voted out of office in the wake of a corruption scandal known as Cashgate (Dulani and Dionne, 2014), and evidence suggests that this negatively affected voters' assessment of the sitting president (Zimmerman, 2015). Incumbents have been voted out of office in Nigeria and extrajudicially removed in Mali after failing to manage national security issues. Although it is too early to tell, the slowdown of African economies since 2013 may well lead to a loss of electoral support for incumbents. The defeat of incumbents in Nigeria in 2015 and Ghana in 2016 and the problematic reelection of incumbents in Gabon and Zambia in 2016 can all be viewed as evidence of incumbents being held to account for the recent downturn in economic performance.

Dominant parties are not immune to voter criticism. South West African People's Organisation (SWAPO), Namibia's dominant party, had to battle criticism that it had lost touch with ordinary people based on a series of events leading up to the campaign, including a woman being shot by police during a protest, a party leader shouting "Clap, you peasants" at a political rally, and accusations of land grabbing (Tjihenuna et al., 2014; Weylandt, 2015, citing Muraranganda, 2014). Although these critiques ultimately had little impact on electoral outcomes – SWAPO won the vast majority of seats as well as the presidential election – they signal a creeping possibility of displacement by credible challengers over time.

While incumbency advantage clearly exists at the executive level, data suggest that it does not hold for other levels of elections. In Chapter 3, we discussed low rates of legislative reelection.[16] Recent work on Zambia shows a tangible incumbency disadvantage in local government elections

---

[16] Incumbency disadvantages among legislators are common in some other regions of the world. Uppal (2009) argues that the incumbency disadvantage for state legislators is due to competitiveness and voters' perceptions of inadequate levels of public goods provision.

and no incumbency advantage at the parliamentary level for elections between 1991 and 2011 (Macdonald, 2014). Evidence from that study suggests that disadvantages are associated with zones where there are higher levels of voter information (local radio) but poorer economic conditions. In other words, informed voters who are not benefiting from government infrastructure are punishing the incumbent at the local level. In zones where there was limited access to radio ownership or high levels of electricity provision, the incumbent was advantaged (Macdonald, 2014).[17] This behavior is consistent with findings from other regions that show incumbency disadvantage to be stronger in places where citizens are dissatisfied with public goods provision, incumbent responsiveness, or an economic downturn (Trease, 2005; Uppal, 2009).

7.3.3 Partisanship

Political parties in Africa remain relatively weak in comparison to parties in other parts of the world.[18] As Cheeseman (2010) demonstrates, incumbency advantage benefits only the actual executive – not successors from his party – in open-seat elections, suggesting that party loyalties remain personalized and thin. Partisan attachment is also comparatively weak, even for incumbent parties but particularly for opposition parties (see Chapter 4). At the same time, research has shown that partisan sentiments, once developed, are very real for citizens in some countries. Sixty-three percent of all Africans reported feeling close to a political party in 2008–9 (Michelitch 2015). In a sample of eleven countries, Kuenzi and Lambright (2011) found that identification with a political party is one of the best predictors of participation, a finding that echoes a long-standing empirical finding in participation research in mature democracies. In a more recent analysis using Round 6 Afrobarometer data, Harding and Michelitch (2017) show the same results.

Emerging evidence suggests that partisanship effects identity and political evaluations. In a study of price discrimination in Ghana, Michelitch (2015) shows that non-coethnic partisans are more likely to receive price discounts on taxi fares, while riders who were neither coethnics nor copartisans face higher levels of price discrimination. In Uganda,

---

[17] Macdonald (2014) found that competitiveness had no effect on incumbency advantage in Zambian municipal races.
[18] For instance, see, Democratic Accountability and Linkages Project (DALP): http://sites .duke.edu/democracylinkage.

Carlson (2015) finds that supporters of Museveni overstate what they have received from government and are more likely to blame private actors for bad outcomes, while opposition reporters underestimate what they have received and are more likely to blame the government. Also in Uganda, Conroy-Krutz et al. (2016) show that partisan cues influence voters decision making at the ballot box. They found that partisan cues on a mock ballot increased the selection of majority-party candidates over independents, votes for copartisans, and straight-ticket ballots.

Parties play a key role in mobilizing political participation in most of the world, so it makes sense to hypothesize that the variation in turnout is related to the nature of parties and party systems. The strength of partisanship and the strength of political parties vary dramatically across countries. In an analysis of Rounds 1–6 of Afrobarometer data, Harding and Michelitch (2017) find that institutionalization of a party system and the presence of a liberation party are associated with higher rates of partisanship. Partisanship does not appear to be increasing over time. Weghorst and Bernhard (2014) note increasing volatility over time, which might reflect increasing competitiveness within the political system and/or increasing willingness of voters to change their vote to align with the party or candidate they best think reflects their interests. However, consistent with global trends, a cyclical pattern is discernible in which citizens become "more partisan" during election time (Michelitch and Utych, 2014).

Where parties are strong and perceived as having access to resources or are linked to the party of the executive, a party label can signal that a candidate will perform well in office (Conroy-Krutz et al., 2016). Some parties, such as Frente de Libertação de Moçambique (FRELIMO) in Mozambique and the ANC in South Africa,[19] can draw upon their revolutionary origins to rally partisans, but many other parties remain far too dependent on individual personalities. Harding (2012) argues that noisy informational environments, caused by party volatility and ethnic heterogeneity, make it difficult for voters to know which parties best represent their interests. However, in these noisier systems, more highly educated voters are better able to interpret information cues and more likely to have party attachment (Harding, 2012).

Devra Moehler and Jeffrey Conroy-Krutz's work suggests that nascent partisan identity in Africa may be more malleable than the entrenched

---

[19] As "born-frees" make-up an increasingly large percentage of the population, some of these parties may need to rebrand or modify their strategies.

partisan identities found in the United States. They show that when exposed to cross-cutting messages from alternative partisan perspectives, less sophisticated voters are persuaded by these new messages instead of formulating a counterargument as many US partisans do. When exposed to perspectives from the other party, less sophisticated voters have decreased preference for their party, a lower extremity of attitudes toward the opposition party, greater willingness to vote for the other side, and greater likelihood of selecting a "national" rather than a partisan key chain (Conroy-Krutz and Moehler, 2015). Relatedly, exposure to both partisan and nonpartisan media increases political interest, and cross-cutting media messages increase ambivalence and reduce participation (Moehler and Conroy-Krutz, 2015). In their study of mock ballots in Uganda, Conroy-Krutz et al. (2016) found that the presence of partisan cues increases the selection of major candidates over independents and votes for copartisans. This work, much like research on swing voters we describe below, suggests that African voters are ready to incorporate new information when exposed to pluralistic messages.

7.3.4 Who Are the Swing Voters?

Voting tendencies vary within countries. In systems in which ethnicity is salient in politics, Horowitz (2016) conceptualizes swing voters as voters without coethnics running for president. Using data from the 2013 Kenyan elections, Horowitz (2017) found that these voters are two and a half times more likely to change their vote choice over the course of the campaign. However, Weghorst and Lindberg (2013) demonstrate an even broader group of swing voters in Ghana. These citizens base their voting decision on assessments of public goods provision rather than party loyalty. The strength of partisan attachments also mediates parties' strategies to court swing voters. Drawing on evidence from Ghana, Rauschenbach (2017) argues that parties are more likely to target swing voters when the parties are certain of core voter support. Conversely, in environments where core voters have weak partisan attachments, parties will pursue these voters' support in electoral campaigns.

The greater tendency for urban voters to support the opposition while their rural brethren are more likely to support the incumbent is conventional wisdom in the Africanist literature (Koter, 2013; Harding, 2010; Resnick, 2014). But while opposition parties find it more difficult to capture the vote in the president's home region or in sparsely populated and poorer rural zones, (Wahman and Boone, 2018) found that voters in urban areas and in the richer rural areas appear to be more willing to abandon the incumbent and vote for an opposition party. Those voters are in a better position to use performance-related criteria when costs for opposition campaigning are lower, so these zones are more accessible. According to this logic, less educated, more economically marginalized voters are already less autonomous, but when they live in rural zones that opposition candidates are less likely to visit, the voters have more difficulty getting access to pluralistic political information. They are most likely to follow the candidates that are proposed by the traditional brokers in their region – in many cases, the incumbent candidate. Wahman and Boone (2018) refer to these groups as "captive constituencies." They find that presidential incumbents from areas with lower than average population density, such as Festus Mogae and Seretse Khama in Botswana, Daniel arap Moi in Kenya, and Jerry Rawlings and John Mahama in Ghana, enjoy particularly high levels of support (Wahman and Boone, 2018). In keeping with this logic, zones with low population density are often dominated by the historically strongest party, such as Alliance pour la Démocratie au Mali (ADEMA) in Northern Mali and the Cameroon People's Democratic Movement (RPDC) in southern Cameroon.

7.3.5 Socioeconomic Status Variables

Modernization theory might predict that educated urban voters with greater resources vote at higher rates. However, traditional socioeconomic indicators that were posited by modernization theorists to increase participation do a poor job of predicting patterns of turnout in Africa.[20] Little evidence links wealth or class with higher voting rates (Kuenzi and Lambright, 2007, 2011). Ishiyama and Fox (2006) find that relationships between wealth and partisan identification vary by country. People who benefit from remittances are most likely to engage in difficult or contentious participation (Dionne et al., 2014) but are less likely to vote (Ebeke and Yogo, 2013).

One reason that socioeconomic status variables do not have much predictive power is that parties are more likely to target poorer voters with vote-buying tactics (Bratton, 2008; Mares and Young, 2016),[21] as

---

[20] These individual-level variables also do a poor job of explaining turnout in Latin America (Fornos et al., 2004).

[21] Mares and Young (2016) show that in two countries – Benin and Mali – the poor are actually significantly less likely to be targeted by vote-buying offers.

parties believe that such short-term material incentives are most likely to bolster the participation of the most marginalized voters. Furthermore, using cross-national evidence from countries around the world, Kasara and Suryanarayan (2014) show that rich voters turn out at higher rates only when the state's bureaucratic capacity is large enough to ensure redistribution through taxation. It may be that wealthier Africans do not feel the need to defend policies that protect them at the polls, since the poor cannot credibly threaten to change policy.

Unlike the strong positive correlation that has been found between education and voting in the United States (Converse, 1972; Rosenstone and Hansen, 1993; Verba et al., 1995), existing evidence demonstrates that the most educated African citizens are not the most likely to vote (Isaksson, 2010; Isaksson et al., 2014; Mattes and Mughogho, 2009; MacLean, 2011b; Bleck, 2015). However, citizens with some education are more likely to vote than are citizens with no education at all.[22] In that sense, the large push to increase access to schooling since the early 1990s may result in more active political consumers. In Nigeria, Larreguy and Marshall (2017) found that primary and secondary school education increases voting rates; they argue that introduction of universal primary education has increased turnout by 3 percent points in Nigeria.[23]

However, as we stress throughout this chapter, citizens' decision to vote may also be shaped by the regime context. Education also creates healthy skepticism, and exposure to information about the process creates more distrusting democrats (Moehler, 2006). Recent work has shown that higher education levels are associated with a broader political disengagement in authoritarian-leaning regimes. Higher education in Zimbabwe was associated with decreases in voting as well as in contacting a politician or attending a community meeting (Croke et al., 2015).

Lower turnout among the most educated may be due in part to the fact that most educated citizens are less likely to be targeted for electoral mobilization (Isaksson et al., 2014) including vote buying (Kramon, 2010).[24] However, it may also reflect their general skepticism about politics. More educated citizens and those with access to more information are more

---

[22] In Mali, voters with primary school education report voting at higher rates than those without any education, while university-educated voters are not significantly more likely to vote than their noneducated peers (Bleck, 2015).

[23] This is consistent with results from India, where higher rates of literacy are associated with higher turnout (Diwakar, 2008).

[24] Some authors have found that vote buying boosts voter turnout (Collier and Vicente, 2014), but Bratton (2008) reports the opposite for Nigeria.

likely to be critical of government policy (Mattes and Mughogho, 2009). Civic education has been found to raise expectations about politicians' performance (Gottlieb, 2015) and to increase knowledge (Bratton et al., 1999) and sharing of information with others (Finkel and Smith, 2011).

In contrast, education is associated with increases in participation, including campaigning, contacting an official, and willingness to run for office (Wantchekon et al., 2013; Larreguy and Marshall, 2014; Bleck, 2015), as well as community-level involvement such as attending a community meeting, contacting a government official, or joining an association (Mattes and Mughogho, 2009; MacLean, 2011b; Isaksson et al., 2014). Even Islamic and non-formal education has been shown to stimulate knowledge and local-level participation (Kuenzi, 2006; Bleck, 2015). Higher levels of formal education are correlated with political knowledge, willingness to offer a political opinion, and greater interest in politics (Mattes and Mughogho, 2009) and with greater willingness to criticize the government and support the opposition (Croke et al., 2015).

Rural turnout rates and partisanship typically exceed or rival participation in cities (Ishiyama and Fox, 2006; Isaksson et al., 2014; Harding and Michelitch, 2017). This may be in part because the process of moving to an urban area does not necessarily bring the access to jobs, education, media development, and social services that modernization theorists envisaged (Lerner, 1958; Lipset, 1959). Approximately two-thirds of Africans live in rural areas, and those who move to urban areas face difficult living conditions and distance from the kinship networks and welfare of the village; 65 percent of urban Africans reside in slums, and 61 percent work in the informal sector.[25] Harding (2010) found rural voters to be more supportive of incumbents and more satisfied with democracy but that this effect lessens with greater rates of urbanization; he argues that this is ultimately because elections generate more prorural policy. It seems likely that rural participation matters because real policy outcomes are at stake.

Rural turnout is also bolstered by the ubiquitous presence of vote brokers that can work through vertical patronage networks, as we discussed in Chapter 5 (Koter, 2013). In this context, voting is not an individual act but a collective endeavor in which brokers mobilize constituents out to the polls (Collier, 1972). While their votes count in the

---

[25] These figures are taken from the African Development Bank Group (see www .afdb.org/en/blogs/afdb-championing-inclusive-growth-across-africa/post/ urbanization-in-africa-10143).

same way, the motivations of voters who participate in collective voting and those who make autonomous choices at the ballot box may be very different.[26] We discuss brokerage in greater depth below. There are similar findings in India, another electoral environment characterized by brokerage where urban areas are associated with lower turnout (Diwakar, 2008).

7.3.6 Programmatic Issues

What is the role of substantive policy issues in shaping participation? In Chapter 5, we argued that politicians focus rhetoric on such key valence issues as development. It turns out that these are also the issues about which voters care the most. As shown in Chapter 6, the widespread need for infrastructure and basic services as well as youth unemployment makes many African citizens prioritize economic development. Therefore, many candidates focus their discourse on these and other key issue-areas most citizens care about." Voters are often faced with choosing among parties that have indistinguishable ideology and a reticence to tackle salient, divisive political issues. In this context, political actors focus instead on showing their competency and strategies to address the issues upon which everyone agrees (Ferree, 2010; Conroy-Krutz and Lewis, 2011).

Demands for development goods are mostly consistent across gender. Gottlieb et al. (2015) found that women are more likely to prioritize poverty alleviation independent of other factors and that men's and women's preferences are most likely to diverge in places where the participation gaps are the greatest. Existing literature shows that women who are most constrained by the traditional division of labor are more likely to prioritize access to clean water, a concern that is typically within women's purview (Chattopadhyay and Duflo, 2004; Olken, 2010). Evidence indicates that women are more supportive of the status quo; for instance, they tend to be less trusting of opposition parties (Logan, 2009).

As we described in Chapter 6, incumbents have a valence advantage on economic development issues, a key voting criterion for many voters. Incumbents can leverage state resources, connections with foreign

---

[26] In the comparative context, Dalton (2007, 2008) discusses the distinction between "engaged" citizenship and "duty-based citizenship related to partisan mobilization."

diplomats and donors, and fear of the unknown to their own advantage. For instance, by leveraging its control of development funding, a newly formed incumbent party in Malawi was able to promote an inclusive food security program to court voters from beyond a narrow ethnoregional base and ultimately win the 2009 parliamentary elections (Brazys et al., 2015). Relatedly, Grossman (2015, p. 344) argues that valence advantages can include "morality" politics, in which incumbents take a stand against the international community to "signal credible commitment," a tactic that is unavailable to opposition parties. He gives the example of President Museveni of Uganda signing anti-gay legislation despite international pressure against the bill.

Rauschenbach's (2015) work in Ghana highlights incumbents' ability to leverage credibility to provide development goods to capture swing voters. She found that the opposition candidate focused primarily on ethnic partisans, while the incumbent mobilized both potential supporters and indifferent voters. The text of campaign speeches reveals the incumbent candidate's attempt to own a diplomatic contract with the Chinese government for his own campaign:

In this area there are many communities waiting for electricity. I want to assure you, we have signed the Memorandum of Understanding with the Chinese government and some poles have been delivered. I want to assure you as president of this country that in no time your electricity is coming and the next time I come to Pusiga all your communities will be shining as bright as the stars (Rauschenbach, 2015, pp. 66–67).

Similarly, Ahlin et al. (2015) describe how, in the 2015 Togolese elections, President Faure Gnassingbé was able to leverage his incumbency to highlight developmental efforts that had been conducted under his watch, including building a third pier for the port of Lomé.

Programmatic commitment to economic development might not be completely independent of vote-buying and gift-giving strategies. As we described in Chapter 6, many candidates distribute resources to prove their credibility as candidates and to assure voters that the candidate will provide public goods one elected. In a relevant experiment in the Philippines, which the authors characterize as an environment in which vote-buying "is the currency of electoral mobilization," information about major spending program and the proposed allocations of mayoral candidates raised voters' expectations of incumbents, particularly in their strongholds, which triggered greater vote-buying efforts by incumbents (Cruz et al., 2015).

7.3.7 Marginalized Citizens: Women and Youth Participation

As in most other regions of the world, there is a large gender gap in formal political participation except for voting, for which the gap is much smaller or nonexistent (Logan and Bratton, 2006; MacLean, 2011b; Isaksson et al., 2014). This may be due to collective mobilization and voter brokerage, which we will discuss at greater length in Section 7.4. This gap also persists for political knowledge and opinion formation (Logan and Bratton, 2006). Cross-national analysis of Afrobarometer data demonstrates that those underlying factors that typically mitigate the gender disparity in the comparative context, such as resource endowments or employment, do little to decrease the gender gap in Africa (Isaksson et al., 2013). The gap tends to be highest for interelectoral participation, such as getting together with other people to raise an issue or contacting a government official (Isaksson et al., 2013).

Several factors appear to decrease the participation gap. For instance, the gender gap is lower for women living in matrilineal societies, where they are assured of inheritance rights (Gottlieb and Robinson, 2016). In a study of rural Malian women, women with greater mobility and household decision-making power were more likely to be politically knowledgeable, to have justified opinions, and to support pro-woman policy reform in the Family Code (Bleck and Michelitch, 2018). Barnes and Burchard (2013) find that as more women are elected to the legislature, the predicted probability of female constituents' political engagement increases, including their reported interest in politics and whether they talk about politics, contact a party leader, contact a member of the legislature, or participate in a demonstration. These trends hold across countries and in the same country over time. However, in contrast, mandated quotas for female councilors have been shown to depress women's political engagement if citizens feel that these affirmative action policies have been forced upon them (Clayton, 2015).

As in the comparative context, African youth are less likely to vote or to express partisanship (Isaksson, 2010; Resnick and Casales, 2014). In Cameroon, Letsa (2015) argues that poorer, younger voters in urban areas are less likely to identify with a party. However, unlike youth in the rest of the world, African youth are not more likely than older citizens to protest (Resnick and Casales, 2014). Nonetheless, the general trend of youth disengagement hides some significant variation. In some countries, students continue to play an important role as mobilizers and conduits between parties and their home constituencies. Bolten's (2016) depiction of youth participation in the 2012 Sierra Leonean elections emphasizes students' willingness to save and sacrifice to participate in the electoral process. One interviewee explained how he skipped breakfast for a few weeks to save money for bus fare in order to vote back home. In another anecdote, Bolten (2016) describes how the university had difficulty recruiting youth to work as surveyors during the election, even with a lucrative salary of $60 a day, because they were so eager to vote in their own districts. In less democratic contexts or countries with histories of political violence, youth can also be deployed to harass voters and stuff ballots for political patrons (Bolten, 2016). Young people who discuss politics more often or are members of voluntary associations are more likely to participate around election time (Resnick and Casales, 2014).

It is clear that youth feel marginalized from the elite levels of African politics. While most parties have youth wings, many are run by older men waiting for their turn to enter the "regular" party leadership. Similarly, young candidates are rare even at the municipal and legislative levels. There is some evidence that youth have greater opportunities within opposition parties in the context of dominant-party systems, particularly in response to secretive and politicized party primaries (Dendere, 2015; Weghorst, 2015). Still, many leaders of youth movements within parties are well into middle age.

This is compounded by the problem of youth unemployment and the limited job opportunities for recruitment into the bureaucracy, as many older technocrats hesitate to leave their posts. A university diploma that might have guaranteed entry into the civil service or party leadership generations ago no longer offers such opportunities for young Africans. As we emphasized in Chapter 5, African elections are still expensive enterprises, and candidacy requires significant financial resources or backing. There are more youth opportunities in countries with stronger private sectors and business-friendly regulations that encourage small and medium enterprise development, but it is much harder for younger people to amass economic power that they can trade for political clout.

Some recent trends point to the emergence of a nonpartisan youth agenda in countries such as Uganda, where youth from all parties work together on legislation related to unemployment, including the Youth Jobs Bill in 2010,[27] and where youth protesters have been very active in

---

[27] www.actionaid.org/sites/files/actionaid/at_crossroads_youth_rngagement_in_policy_in_uganda.pdf.

trying to block Museveni's efforts to eliminate the age cap of seventy-five years for presidents.[28] Given the growing youth bulge in sub-Saharan Africa, we may see more candidates who try to cater to the youth population with a popular vote. While many older candidates attempt to play the role of "youth candidate," we documented in Chapter 5 the emergence of some legitimate youth candidates for office. Over time, young social media–savvy candidates might be able to build a following, accrue campaign contributions from peers abroad, and gain enough credibility to run for office, particularly for municipal and legislative offices.[29]

As ruling elites from the pre-democratic era die off and dominant parties that have drawn credibility from a revolutionary struggle face young voters who do not remember the parties' legacy, we may see some dramatic reshuffling of party politics in Africa (Friesen, 2017).

7.4 BROKERAGE

In many rural areas, mobilization to vote constitutes collective action rather than an individual autonomous choice. As we discussed in Chapter 6, brokerage and endorsements by traditional and religious leaders can play a key role in organizing the rural vote in many communities. Thus, to understand electoral participation in these areas, it becomes important to focus on the relationship between parties and regional and local brokers.

Typically, local and regional elites mobilize constituencies in exchange for access to goods and services provided by candidates in the run-up to the election or afterwards, once the candidates are in office, through subsequent patronage and/or public goods extension to their areas (Baldwin, 2015). There are multiple theories as to why citizens vote with the chief. The chief might activate norms that urge constituents to vote out of deference, or the chief might use his knowledge and power within the village to monitor voting behavior to reward correct voting and withhold resources from individuals who do not vote the village line (Baldwin, 2015). Baldwin (2015) has argued that chiefs are "development brokers" and that citizens vote along with the chief when they think the result will be a greater probability of development goods coming to their village. Voters evaluate the relationship between the chief and the parties

---

[28] www.africanews.com/2017/09/21/ugandan-police-bans-demo-as-parliament-debates-presidential-age-limit.

[29] We thank Brian Mukhaya for this insight.

to determine whether they are close enough to facilitate coordination and collaboration to bring developmental goods to the area. Work by Auerbach and Thachil (2016) from urban India suggests, similarly, that citizens choose brokers on the basis of their perceived connectedness to state bureaucracy and their ability to access resources there.

The stereotypical broker mobilizes coethnics to the polls, but brokers take on many forms and work through various networks that draw on different types of influence. Glennerster et al. (2013) found no evidence that Sierra Leonean chiefs from ethnically homogenous communities are better able to maintain order than are chiefs who rule over ethnically heterogeneous communities. Politicians and parties work through "local leaders who command moral authority, control resources, and can control electoral behavior of their dependents" (Koter, 2013, p. 189). In Koter's (2013) analysis of nonethnic brokers in Senegal, these intermediaries attempt to locate the best deal possible from different parties, regardless of ethnicity, which generates a more competitive electoral terrain. This is not unique. Rural voters have demonstrated a willingness to switch parties in different electoral cycles (Weghorst and Bernhard, 2014), suggesting that voting blocs organized by these flexible brokers might actually force parties to be more accountable to them. This environment generates greater pressure on parties to deliver to local constituencies and thus might ultimately force greater accountability to individual brokers. In many countries with weak parties, voters' interactions with parties are temporal, in contrast to more long-standing and permanent relationships with traditional or religious authorities (Englebert, 2000; Bleck, 2013). This creates an environment in which brokers enjoy greater credibility than party agents have.

In addition to local level elites, religious actors play an important role in electoral and contentious mobilization. For instance, scholars have shown the power of the Mouride brotherhood in dictating political support for different parties in Senegal (Villalón, 1995; Beck, 2008; Camara, 2014) but have also shown the role of religious authorities in mobilizing protests to constrain government policy, such as family code reform, in the broader Sahel (Wing, 2012). Religious movements can also play a strong role in providing political information and shaping voter preferences. Mattes and Shenga (2007) found that Mozambican citizens who seek out religious leaders the most frequently for help in solving problems are also more likely to demand democracy and to form preferences about what that democracy should look like, acting as "critical democrats."

In the near future, a culturally conservative vote may emerge in some African countries. Michelitch and Weghorst (2013) suggest that country-level religious interpretation plays a powerful role in forming citizens' views about the role of religion and politics; within-country gaps between Christians and Muslims on women's roles are smaller than between-country gaps. In a survey experiment in Tanzania, Michelitch and Weghorst (2013) found that pro-woman leadership endorsements from imams improved acceptance of female political leadership among Muslims and found a similar effect for ministers' messages on Christians.

The influence of religion is not limited to Islam. In the context of economic crisis and a weak state, emerging Pentecostal networks are displacing ethnic big men in urban areas in a number of countries (Maxwell, 1998; Marshall, 2009; McCauley, 2012). Although these networks are often concentrated in areas outside of electoral politics, such as Islamist groups in the Sahel, they derive their resources independently from the state and thus are well positioned to challenge government. For instance, Grossman (2015) shows the power of these networks in pushing anti-homosexual legislation in Uganda and more broadly in Africa. He found that two factors lead to the increased saliency of Lesbian, Gay, Bi-Sexual, and Transgender (LGBT) issues: the growth of the Pentecostal Evangelical, Renewalist, or Spirit-filled Churches coupled with greater political competition born out of democratization (Grossman, 2015). Unlike the Catholic Church, which has enjoyed a comfortable historical relationship with many African states, Protestant and Muslim networks derive their patronage and resources from outside of state channels, which gives them autonomy and leverage to critique the political establishment. These groups can create substantive opportunities for their constituencies to challenge government policy through the use of contentious politics and shaping political discourse through the dissemination of information and ideas in local media. In countries with weak parties, such as countries in the Sahel, these grassroots outreach activities dwarf any efforts made by parties (Idrissa, 2008).

The presence of regional brokers, as well as the accessibility and responsiveness of elected officials, might determine whether or not communities' collective capacity scales up or maps onto partisan action. Naturally, some traditional and religious leaders will have more sway than others (Boone, 2003; Beck, 2008; Baldwin, 2015). Gottlieb and Larreguy (2016) argue that incumbent parties seek brokers with high "coordinating capacity" by looking for communities that have shown themselves able to mobilize constituents to vote in previous elections.

7.5 SOCIOECONOMIC CHANGES AND
POLITICAL FORECASTING IN AFRICA

In this book, we stress many types of continuity, despite the large-scale sociodemographic changes among African populations, including sharp increases in urbanization, heightened educational enrollment, a growing middle class, the youth bulge, and the rapid expansion of traditional and social media. For instance, the proportion of urban populations in Africa climbed from 15 percent in 1960 to 40 percent in 2010 and is expected to reach 60 percent by 2050 (Freire et al., 2015, citing UN Habitat, 2011). In this section, we forecast how these changes might affect political participation over time. Urbanization has coincided with a dramatic increase in the adoption of cellphone and Internet technology as well as the proliferation of private radio stations and, increasingly, television stations. In 2002, only one in ten adults in Ghana, Kenya, Tanzania, and Uganda, owned cellphones; today, South Africans and Nigerians are as likely to own cellphones as Americans are.[30] The number of mobile subscriptions tripled between 2010 and 2015 to 300 million and is expected to grow by another 250 million by 2020.[31] The growth in ownership and use of cellphones has enabled increasing technological innovation, notably online banking, which has leapfrogged traditional banking and made some African countries, such as Kenya, genuine global standard setters. In recent years, there have been more efforts to increase access to 4G networks to accommodate a growing smartphone market, enabled by the increasing availability of low-cost devices.

Urbanization and greater communication infrastructure make information flows and political coordination easier. Social media might also be able to encourage participation by citizens who are less likely to use traditional channels of participation (Grossman et al., 2014). For instance, Grossman et al. (2017) showed increased participation in text-reporting systems when politicians added personalized prompts to generate greater perceived internal and external efficacy among users.

Governments are also responding to these dramatic changes, particularly in attempts to control new information flows and related forms of political organizing. However, it is unlikely that regimes will be able to move away from multiparty elections because citizens are attached to

---

[30] www.pewglobal.org/2015/04/15/cell-phones-in-africa-communication-lifeline.
[31] GMSA Mobile Africa 2016 (see www.gsmaintelligence.com/research/?file=3bc21ea 879a5b217b64d62fa24c55bdf&download).

this form of governance; we will discuss this topic further in Chapter 8. Therefore incumbent politicians will need to continue to compete with opposition candidates in an environment of greater information flows and an increasingly connected citizenry. In the following subsections, we explore how an increasingly educated, urbanized, informed, and connected population is likely to engage with regularized multiparty elections over time.

7.5.1 Civil Society

African citizens join together with others to take political action or to solve problems for themselves. Strong civil society can serve as an important counterweight to predatory or unresponsive government action. In the African context, a strong civil society is often merely a coping mechanism for a weak state presence (Ake, 2000; Bleck and Michelitch, 2015). We note the continued strength of associational life as well as the as the resilient role of nonelected traditional and religious authorities (Englebert, 2000; Logan, 2013). In the multiparty era, young citizens who are eager to engage in a political system that typically leaves them sidelined can exercise political expression through associational membership and contentious politics.

The evolution of the elite civil society organizations that ushered transitions to (and back to) democracy exhibit significant variation. In some places, activists have leveraged new technologies to shed light on regime transgressions, redefine political debates, and generate substantial institutional reform. For instance, in Kenya, lawyers and human rights activists made substantial gains in institutional reform in the wake of Kenya's 2007 electoral violence. In other countries, elite civil society continues to be too embedded in government networks to issue credible challenges to those in power. To understand the potential role of elite civil society in constraining or contributing to the state, it is crucial that we first understand the organization of civil society vis-à-vis government (Bratton, 1989).

While strong associational life has characterized the African landscape since the colonial period, civil society in Africa is growing far beyond its professionalized, elite base "as a response to urbanization and commercialization" (Bratton, 1989, p. 411). This includes labor unions, farmers' movements, professional groups, religious movements, and ethnic welfare associations. As Figure 7.4 shows, Afrobarometer data suggest that membership in these associations is continuing to grow over time.

This may be due to increased urbanization as well as the availability of media and new technologies for communication. In the current period, grassroots civil society groups can capitalize on available technologies for organizational and mobilization purposes.

In recent campaign cycles, civil society have played vital roles in distributing information, sensitizing voters, and monitoring the polls on election day. In addition to international and regional teams of observers, a large role is increasingly being played by domestic observer teams. In the 2016 Ghanaian elections, Coalition of Domestic Election Observers (CODEO), a coalition of domestic observers, deployed 8,000 observers and used innovative techniques such as parallel vote tallies and geographic information systems (GIS) mapping of election violence or irregularities. Their statement in support gave Ghanaian voters greater confidence in the electoral results.[32] Civil society actors have also played an important role in focusing political energy on term limits. Tripp (2017) provides examples of church coalitions, women's organizations, and legal watchdogs stopping executives' third-term attempts to remove term limits in Malawi and Zambia.

While historically ignored by political parties, blocs of religious constituencies are emerging on the political stage to rally around what might be termed "cultural-religious populism." The Family Code protests across the Sahel shows the power of Islamic actors as harbingers of a type of cultural populism that political parties have been unwilling or unable to court (Bleck and van de Walle, 2011). For instance, a 2013 Afrobarometer poll from Niger shows that 67 percent of respondents agreed with the adoption of sharia law in the Nigerien constitution; most of this support was coming from rural zones (Alou and Adamou, 2015). While Islamic actors in West Africa have been reluctant to engage explicitly in the electoral sphere (Bleck and Patel, 2018), an emerging constituency seems likely to respond to religious appeals.

Youth protest movements use WhatsApp and Facebook to diffuse political information and organize protests. By leveraging video and audio recording capability on these platforms, organizers can reach illiterate or semiliterate youth. Citizens in areas with poor connectivity can leverage USB flash drives, bluetooth technology, and distribution hubs to pass along political information and organize events. While cost barriers and signal strength generate inequalities in who has access to smartphone

[32] www.codeoghana.org/news-details.php?story=584C020FE5AF4.

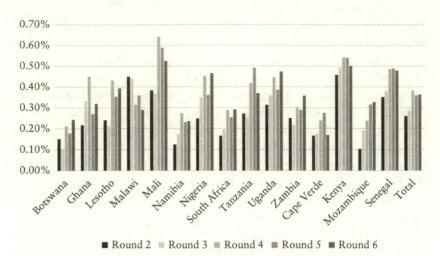

technology, it is important to highlight the ways in which phones can also help citizens to engage with politics in new ways.

Greater access to information and technology coincides with an increase in associational membership over time. Using Afrobarometer data, Figure 7.4 shows respondents who are members of self-help groups. The growing connectedness is a hopeful sign for civil society and for increasing political information and participation.

While the opportunities for civil society actors are considerably greater they were than before the 1990s, the past decade has been characterized by tremendous variation in trajectories of political freedom across Africa. In some countries, such as Burundi, Gambia, Ethiopia, South Africa, and Uganda, political learning by elites has translated into fewer freedoms for civil society; governments use legislation to regulate and control the activities of nongovernmental organizations (NGOs), the media, and other parts of civil society (Tripp, 2017, pp. 89–91). Tripp (2017, p. 91) provides examples of tightening restrictions in Uganda, including the 2006 NGO Act, which limited advocacy work and public policy outreach, and the 2013 Public Order Management Act, which allowed the police to pick venues for public meetings and to ban those meetings if need be. Most recently, the Ugandan government passed the 2015 NGO Act, which allowed the government to refuse registration of NGOs, to restrict foreign employees, and to prohibit public meetings, and the 2016

NGO Act, by which individuals found guilty of "vague offences" related to failure to comply with an inspector from the NGO Bureau can face three years of imprisonment and/or a fine of $432 (Tripp, 2017, p. 91). In Angola, Burundi, and the Democratic Republic of the Congo, governments make it very difficult to register NGOs. Equatorial Guinea forbids NGOs from "promoting, monitoring, or engaging in human rights activities" (Tripp, 2017, p. 95). In 2014, the Ethiopian government passed a law mandating that NGOs could receive no more than 10 percent of their funding from foreign sources if they wanted to participate in human rights and advocacy work (Tripp, 2017, p. 95).

7.5.2 Urbanization and Participation

Increasing rates of urbanization might initially lead to lower rates of electoral participation, since partisanship and turnout currently are typically higher in rural areas (Ishiyama and Fox, 2006). However, this trend also opens up interesting possibilities as voters move away from collective mobilization to autonomous voting. It could also mean greater chances for opposition candidates to make inroads, since we have already observed that the opposition has been able to dominate capital cities in countries with high population density and a strong history of trade unions (Larmer, 2011; Resnick, 2012; Cheeseman and Larmer, 2015).

As urbanization and flows of information increase, we may see a decline in the salience of ethnic cues. Green (2013) argues that urbanization trends across the continent make ethnicity less salient as a homogenization effect take place. However, this probably depends on the dynamics within urban communities. Bates (1974) posited that competition for jobs in urban areas was likely to exacerbate ethnic competition. In some instances, movement from rural to urban areas might change citizens' relationship with these vertical networks as migration disrupt traditional channels of mobilization. For instance, McCauley (2012) discusses the growing strength of Pentecostal networks in Ghana in the context of state weakness and urbanization. Pentecostal networks urge followers to break with existing ethnic or hometown-based affiliations and to reform their sense of community around the church. Migration to urban zones fractures ties with ethnoregional patrons as well as social sanctioning mechanisms within coethnic kinship networks, creating opportunities for the formation of new types of communities of support (McCauley, 2012). Thus urban migration may change dynamics of political mobilization.

Greater access to information could lessen the need for an ethnic heuristic. Even in countries with ethnic parties, voters can move from ethnoregional allegiances to vote choice based on performance evaluation (Youde, 2005; Fridy, 2007; Lindberg and Morrison, 2008; Ferree and Horowitz, 2010; Ishiyama, 2010). Some recent empirical work shows that voters are more willing to vote for a non-coethnic as they gain information about candidates. For instance, Conroy-Krutz's (2013) experiment in Uganda found that with no additional information, the vast majority of voters preferred a coethnic candidate but that 97 percent of respondents were willing to support a non-coethnic who had better performance in office than a coethnic.

7.5.3 Media Increases and Multiple Election Cycles

Some research suggests that campaigns are effective in generating political knowledge around key issues, particularly among more marginalized populations (Conroy-Krutz, 2016). However, as Conroy-Krutz (2016) found in Uganda, increases in knowledge are generally correlated with greater criticism of institutions but not with more participation. As media sources become more numerous and available, citizens are less likely to believe state propaganda that reinforces status quo powers. In one-sided media environments, citizens' level of knowledge can be limited by their informational environment. For instance, in Cameroon, citizens in low information environments are the strongest supporters of President Paul Biya because his party can single-handedly shape the political narrative (Letsa, 2017).

Figures 7.5 and 7.6 confirm that, while there is still tremendous cross-country variation in terms of citizens' exposure to television and Internet media, exposure to these sources is increasing over time.

In Figures 7.7 and 7.8, we draw on self-reported interest in politics and political discussion to assess the media's impact on citizens' engagement with the political world. In most countries, political interest appears to peak when it is first measured in Round 2 of Afrobarometer in 2002, but then stabilizes. Political discussion also appears relatively stable over time, contrasting with predictions that interest might peak after political transitions and then decrease over time as citizens become more skeptical and disengaged (Carothers, 2002).

Do more access to information and steady political interest result in greater political knowledge? Recent studies in other contexts show an ambiguous relationship between greater access to the Internet and

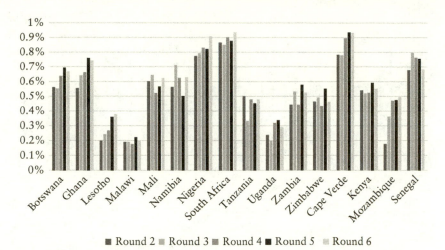

FIGURE 7.5. *Percentage of respondents who watch TV at least once a month*

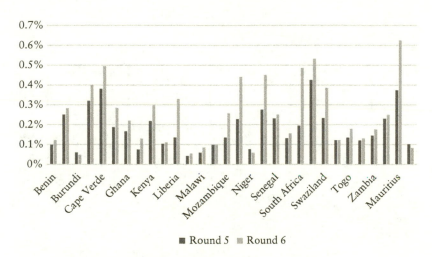

FIGURE 7.6. *Percentage of respondents who use the Internet at least once a month*

political knowledge, unlike earlier studies that showed a strong correlation between newspaper readership and political knowledge and efficacy (Scheufele and Nisbe, 2002; Kim, 2008). Dimitrova et al.'s (2014) study of the 2010 Swedish election finds that higher social media usage during electoral campaigns increased political participation offline but had no impact on political knowledge. In the US context, Prior (2005)

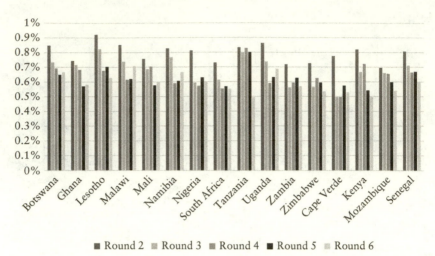

FIGURE 7.7. *Respondents who are somewhat or very interested in politics*

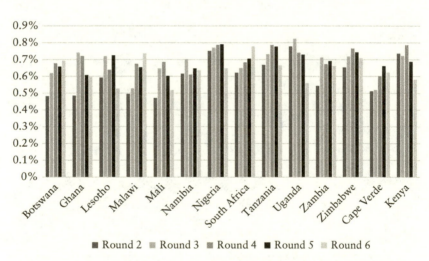

FIGURE 7.8. *Respondents who claim to discuss political matters with friends*

argues that we have not observed increases in political knowledge that are consistent with greater access to information through the Internet and cable news resulting from the audience's ability to choose content. Consumers can choose entertainment over news and, in doing so, exhibit a knowledge deficit in comparison with consumers who are choosing news media.

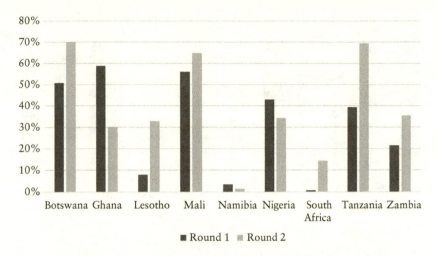

FIGURE 7.9. *Respondents' ability to name their local councilor*

Do we see a relationship between access to new forms of media and political knowledge? The preponderance of political rants and political rumors on Facebook and WhatsApp suggests that the Internet could play an important role in generating political knowledge in sub-Saharan Africa, particularly in countries where state media is heavily biased.

Figures 7.9 and 7.10 show Afrobarometer data on citizens' knowledge of various elected officials over time.[33] They demonstrate significant variation across countries. For instance, more than half of Malians can name their mayor, in contrast to fewer than 5 percent of Namibians. In six of nine countries, citizens appeared more knowledgeable about their local councilors by Round 2 of the Afrobarometer (a year after Round 1). In eight of ten countries, more citizens were able to name their member of parliament (MP) in Round 3 than in Round 1. Political learning about the finance minister seems less clear. In only five of eleven countries were higher percentages of respondents able to name the finance minister in Round 4 (2008) than in Round 1 (2001–2). While there is not a clearly positive trend in every country for naming their local councilor or MP, the rough general trend appears to be that political knowledge is increasing over time, at least when we compare Round 1 to later rounds.

---

[33] The question for the data in Figure 7.10 was as follows: "Now let us speak about the political system in this country. First of all, can you tell me who presently holds the following positions: A member of parliament who has been assigned to represent this area?".

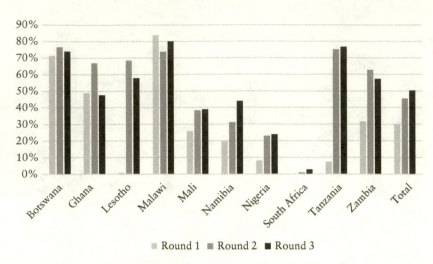

FIGURE 7.10. *Respondents' knowledge of their member of parliament*

These aggregate data provide a very rough proxy for assessing the effect of access to social media on political knowledge. Given the dramatic changes in access and connectivity of the past two decades, there is important future research to be done to better understand African's news consumption and political mobilization using online and phone platforms.

The average age of African voters continues to drop, presenting important challenges for political incorporation. The growing number of unemployed recent diploma holders should be a source of concern, as these individuals too often are unable to find satisfactory jobs and feel marginalized from the economic and political systems. Perhaps entrepreneurial opposition parties will prove able to capture some of this demographic with campaigns that leverage new types of media and make strong programmatic appeals to young people. Otherwise, they might increasingly withdraw from voting and turn to nonconventional means of participation, such as protest and political violence.

7.5.4 Difficult Conventional Participation and Contentious Politics

While elections tend to generate worldwide attentions for African political systems and are an important threshold condition for democracy, voting is only one type of political participation. Voting falls squarely within a spectrum of formal political participation – participation that is sanctioned and supported by political institutions. However, there are many other types of formal participation, including more difficult political acts[34] and contentious political behavior,[35] such as protests and boycotts. We cannot address these important forms of participation adequately in this book. Future research is needed to better understand the relationship between difficult and contentious forms of participation and other forms of participation. In this concluding section, we offer some initial thoughts about trends related to contentious politics.

Research in the US context has shown that when citizens have low expectations about their political system's accountability or responsiveness (such as low external efficacy), they tend to focus on more difficult kinds of formal participation as well as contentious politics (see Fraser, 1970; Craig, 1980; Craig and Maggiotto, 1982). Given that more than 60 percent of African citizens feel that their voices go unheard between election cycles (Logan, 2010), it is important to investigate patterns of contentious participation as well as patterns of voting. After all, many transitions to democracy were initiated by popular protests against the former authoritarian regimes (Bratton and van de Walle, 1997). In Chapter 6, we argued that some of the most salient and controversial issues that African citizens care about are addressed in these types of participation because political parties have been slow to pick up these issues.

What is the legacy of contentious politics in the wake of transitions to democracy? Do protests and strikes complement or substitute for formal political participation?[36] Are citizens who undertake the former more or less likely to perform the latter? African political history is characterized by a resilient pattern of taking to the streets. Both the independence era and the period just before transitions to democracy were characterized by widespread protests (Branch and Mampilly, 2015; Mueller, 2018). Protests aimed at the colonial authorities activated various sectors of

---

[34] Nie et al. (1996) categorize voting along with partisan identification as "easy" political behavior in contrast to "difficult" participation, such as running for office, campaigning, or contacting a government official, which require greater sets of skills. Other researchers refer to synonymous acts as "high initiative" participation.

[35] Tilly and Tarrow (2006, p. 4) describe contentious political participation as "interactions in which actors make claims bearing on someone else's interests, leading to coordinated efforts on behalf of shared interests or programs, in which governments are involved as targets, initiators of claims, or third parties."

[36] For instance, Brownlee (2011) argues that in Egypt, the very low voter turnout rate (22 percent) is due to substitution effects of mass protest, which had more political salience to potential voters.

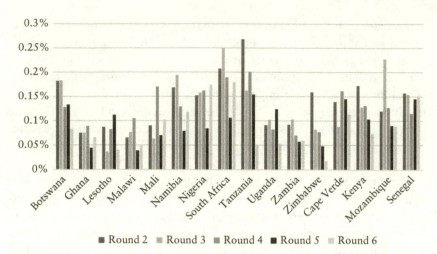

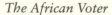

FIGURE 7.11. *Percentage of Afrobarometer respondents who claim to have attended a demonstration*

civil society, including trade unions, cooperatives, and social clubs, which united to protest the "loss of dignity and respect at the hands of colonial officials" rather than pursuing specific grievances (Hyden, 2011, p. 113). In transitions in the 1990s, many member of civil society who had been in the streets exploited a more open political environment to create formal associations, which became the basis of civil society in the multiparty electoral era.

Mueller (2013, 2018) suggests that membership in associations, which we suggest is increasing, as shown in Figure 7.4, is associated with a greater likelihood of participation in protests. This is due to groups' ability to mobilize members. She argues that participation protests in Niger were largely due to economic grievances but that the prodemocracy protests gave citizens a chance to express those grievances (Mueller, 2013).

The Afrobarometer provides self-reported participation data by country, which we can also utilize to identify participation trends.[37] Figure 7.11 documents self-reported protest attendance among Afrobarometer respondents. There are no clear trends over time. Protests in some countries, such as Botswana, Kenya, Malawi, Namibia, Tanzania, Uganda, Zambia, and Zimbabwe, may be decreasing over time. In some countries, this could be the result of repression and crackdowns on civil society.

---

[37] Self-reported electoral participation is typically inflated (Isaksson et al., 2014); in contrast, respondents are probably likely to underreport protest behavior.

In other countries, reports of protest vary greatly across the different rounds of the Afrobarometer survey; this may be due to the salience of different political issues over time. It is also likely that protest behavior is related to associational membership. For instance, Scacco (2010) found that Nigerians who attend community meetings are more likely to engage in ethnic riots; she argues that social networks can "pull" people into the streets to participate in protests.

It may be that citizens' decisions to protest reflect their evaluation of their potential success. While the protests anticipating the removal of Compaore in Burkina Faso and the term limit protests in Burundi may have inspired other people to take to the streets, opposition figures who try to mobilize citizens to protest against what they consider to be rigged elections often are less successful. This may be due to the international community's tendency to rubber stamp electoral outcomes,[38] in contrast to past success of different countries' attempts to block term limits throughout Africa.[39] Despite serious restrictions on freedom of the press during the 2016 Zambian election, the opposition party lost its appeal to the electoral commission and found little international backing after this outcome was announced.

In some instances, protests are met by tremendous use of force by governments but are effective in politicizing electoral results. Straus and Taylor (2009) found that that postelectoral violence in Africa has overwhelmingly been the result of opposition protests against incumbent efforts to manipulate the electoral process. For instance, in Togo, nearly every presidential election has been followed by street protests, some of which (as in the 2005 reelection of Gnassingbé) turned into violent confrontations with state security forces (Ahlin et al., 2015).

At a minimum, we observe that protests are not displacing electoral engagement. Instead, they are likely to be used as a supplementary form of political participation. Protests give civil society an ability to signal their political preferences to political parties and in some instances shape the platform. This type of signaling is particularly important given high levels of uncertainty about voter preferences. It also demonstrates groups' organizational capacity to effectively get voters to the polls. This can happens at the national level, as shown by the example of Mali, where an information campaign led by popular talk show host Ras Bath that led to

---

[38] See Pfeiffer and Englebert (2012) on the tendency of the international community to endorse electoral results.

[39] See McKie (2012) on the success of citizen movements in blocking term limits in Africa.

mass protests made constitutional reform into a central political issue.⁴⁰ However, protests also occur at the municipal level, where constituents frequently use them to express displeasure with the mayor's office and threaten to vote the mayor out of office in the next election. In regimes in which leaders do not have the capacity to suppress them, these types of protests can effectively generate accountability and responsiveness from the government (Bleck and Logveninko, 2018). As we discuss throughout the book, the vigorous debates and protests around executive term limits have, in some instances, resulted in executive turnover.

This chapter has argued that political participation in Africa is very context dependent. Citizens respond to the incentives and power structures around them. Even within the same countries, rural and urban voters can come to the polls through very different forms of mobilization. We observe that the regularization of elections has not generated a withdrawal from electoral participation or surge in protest behavior in light of democratic dissatisfaction. Instead, country-level participation rates have remained relatively stable. Despite presidentialism, African voters turn out at a relatively high rate for legislative and municipal elections, which suggests that these races contain their own incentives and dynamics. The last two decades has generated unprecedented access to information for voters through cell phone, digital, and online networks. This increase in information has coincided with the growth of associational membership and urbanization. These dynamics, which may mean a general strengthening of civil society in the longer term, are worthy of future exploration.

⁴⁰ http://maliactu.net/mali-revision-constitutionnelle-les-raisons-du-non-de-ras-bath-leader-dopinion-video.

8

Do African Elections Matter?

A decade or so ago, one of the authors of this book was doing field research in the eastern region of Uganda, near the district seat of Mbale. In the course of a couple days, in a succession of rural villages, the talk was about the ministerial party that had just visited the village or whose visit was being prepared. Villagers made it clear that the minister and his colleagues were in the region to take credit on behalf of the government for a number of recent infrastructural investments in schools, clinics, and water wells in the region – albeit often funded by foreign donors – as could be discerned from well-placed placards and notices on or near the new installations. Villagers seemed to understand intuitively that the visit was not unrelated to the presidential elections that were scheduled for some ten weeks later.

On the other side of the continent, in the Mopti region of Mali several years later, the other author of this book observed that rural citizens were frustrated that a military coup had disrupted the 2012 presidential electoral campaign. Politicians and parties made the pilgrimage to these remote areas – more than an hour's drive from any paved road – only during campaign time. Citizens felt that this was their moment to be heard and to extract resources from the politicians who hoped to govern their country. The villagers had been looking forward to parties' competition for their vote, as it would likely translate into substantial transfers in resources. One party had promised televisions and solar batteries so that the villagers could watch the Africa's Cup; another had promised cataract surgeries for heads of household. Now, with the junta in power, the parties were unlikely to deliver on these promises.[1]

These two anecdotes suggest that regular multiparty elections in Africa have altered the relationship between citizens and political elites. The first anecdote suggests that politicians want voters to give them electoral credit for developmental outcomes and reveals the expectations citizens hold about what the state can and should deliver to them. The second anecdote similarly describes patterns of redistribution embedded in the political business cycle and citizen discontent that the junta had interrupted the lucrative campaigning period. In Uganda and Mali, the subsequent elections did little to change formal institutional accountability to rural populations or policy affecting the government's engagement with the countryside, in which individual poverty and public inconstancy remain the norm. However, even in these contexts, elections are now anticipated and expected events, suggesting that they matter to citizens.

In this chapter, we examine the impact of a quarter-century of competitive multiparty elections in sub-Saharan Africa. In previous chapters, we argued that such elections constitute a necessary but insufficient institution for creating more accountable and responsive government. We stressed the diversity of national experiences in African elections. Although they have become routine across the region, competitive multiparty elections have accompanied democratic deepening in only a minority of the region's political systems. They provide windows of opportunity for flux, but these political moments do not always lead to positive change. Although our analysis is cautious and we conclude that much progress remains to be achieved, we also argue that a quarter-century of electoral politics has generated evidence that offers many reasons for cautious optimism about the future, in large part because of the changes we see in African societies. We have documented the variation in electoral results, their evolution over time, and the emergence of specific patterns, whether in the party systems that have emerged or in the degree of political alternation. We have examined the issues that dominate the discourse of electoral campaigns, and we have presented evidence that most political discourse focuses on key valence issues that matter to African voters, including politicians' commitments to development and democracy.

In this chapter, we conclude our analysis by asking whether the regular convening of multiparty elections has generated any difference in substantive outcomes for citizens. We examine the actual political and

---

[1] These accounts are based on fieldwork from Bleck and Michelitch (2015).

socioeconomic impact of the turn to regular multiparty electoral competition since 1990. We explore the effect of elections on the issues that citizens seem to care most about: good governance, development, natural resource distribution, sovereignty, security, and citizenship. Chapter 6 revealed that these were the issues that politicians mostly champion in their electoral campaigns. Here, we ask whether that discourse translates into any positive change for the lives of Africans.

We caution that the introduction of regular multiparty elections has been coterminous with other substantial recent socioeconomic changes in the region: strong economic growth rates, urbanization, the communications revolution, social media expansion, and the growth of civil society. Ultimately, it is difficult to disentangle the impact of a regularized electoral calendar from these broader changes. We also need to consider how elections are affected by greater Internet connectivity and greater citizen-level information and monitoring, which result in greater costs for political leaders. These structural changes have created a new type of "mass public" that is partly, but not entirely, related to regime change. In these ways, leaders of any government may be more wary of how their policy choices are perceived and evaluated by citizens. We try to emphasize the specific role that elections play in this context.

Elections vary in their fairness and in whether or not they are conducted on a level playing field (Levitsky and Way, 2010). The degree of competitiveness, the capacity and resources of political parties, and media coverage also vary across the region. These factors mediate the ways in which elections affect citizens; however, even in less competitive or dominant-party systems, in which opposition parties are quite disadvantaged, elections might generate different policy outcomes. In states where the incumbent continues to manipulate electoral environments and outcomes, the regular convening of elections cannot be equated with improvements in governance. Regular elections can coexist for quite a long time with highly undemocratic institutions. However, even highly repressive regimes need to put some effort into electoral campaigns, since the election cycle shines a spotlight on government performance. Even in repressive regimes and those characterized by a tremendous incumbency advantage, there are some elements of regularized elections that we might anticipate to improve localized government service and goods provision. It is particularly important to explore opportunities and effects at the subnational and local levels that might be generated through the election cycle. For instance, some existing evidence, which we presented in Chapter 5, suggests that at the legislative or municipal level, many incumbents choose not to run or face a disadvantage when they do run, even where the president wins by an overwhelming margin at the national level. These incumbents choose not to run or are being voted out of office because they are not meeting citizens' expectations. Even if their seats are maintained by a dominant party, the turnover in governing personnel raises questions about the effects on policy.

Outside of the distribution associated with the election campaign cycle, in many instances these elections will not generate more accountable and responsive governance. However, in nearly all cases, elections – regardless of quality – generate opportunities for information dissemination and political learning and for interactions between candidates and constituencies, as well as new constellations of collaboration or competition between sets of competing politicians both within and across parties.

8.2 THE IMPACT OF ELECTIONS ON THE QUALITY OF GOVERNANCE

Does experience with regular elections generate better governance outcomes for citizens? Or do redistributive pressures associated with multiparty elections worsen policy performance by putting increasing pressure on politicians to engage in more clientelism and corruption to garner electoral support and finance their campaigns? Claims have been made that the turn to competitive elections has fueled a surge in corruption (Szeftel, 1998; Khan, 2012; Booth and Cammack, 2013). Boone (2009) argues that the increase in conflicts around land in Africa is in part caused by the need for politicians to find new assets to use in clientelist deal making. Collier (2011) and Chua (2004) have argued that elections in low-income countries engender more civil conflict and ethnic strife, with negative effects on governance.

In Chapter 3, we rejected the extreme arguments concerning the political effects of elections, both the optimistic view that elections promote democratic deepening (Lindberg, 2006) and the pessimistic view that elections are irrelevant or even negative in their political effect (Karl, 1995; Chabal and Daloz, 1999; Collier, 2011). But how do these systemic effects translate to the citizen level? What do the data reveal about the effects of regular multiparty elections on the everyday lives of African citizens? That is the focus of this chapter.

On the one hand, it is clear that regular elections have not eliminated poor governance and that corruption and abuses of power remain significant, particularly in the less democratic countries that now convene elections. On the other hand, the argument that governance has worsened in the democratic era is less convincing. First, regardless of quality, elections can serve as a forum for citizens to evaluate national governance norms. The survey literature is fairly clear that African citizens are good judges of whether or not an election was free and fair (see, for instance, Greenberg and Mattes, 2013). Support for democracy tends to go up after elections that are perceived as free and fair, while elections that are perceived as unfair decrease satisfaction with democracy. Citizens in countries with free and fair elections are also more likely to increase their demands for democracy (Mattes and Bratton, 2016). Citizens in the Afrobarometer countries with unfair elections were more systematically skeptical about the performance of their governments. Vote rigging, voter suppression, and jailing opposition leaders all negatively affect citizens' perceptions of the regime. In countries with truly free and fair elections, there appears to be a self-reinforcing relationship between the quality of elections and citizens' support of government authority (Greenberg and Mattes, 2013). Cho and Logan (2013) found that election quality, rather than the number of elections, is correlated with perceptions of the durability of democracy. Improvements in civil liberties and political rights are also significantly correlated with positive impacts of democratic durability (Cho and Logan, 2013). Research has shown that years lived under democratic regimes translates into greater support for democracy (Aquino, 2015). Alternation in power can spark hope that democracy will endure (Cho and Logan, 2013), positively affects assessments of the state of democracy (Bratton, 2004), and generates shared perceptions of system legitimacy by winners and losers, thus moderating polarization (Moehler and Lindberg, 2009). Conversely, lack of alternation can undermine citizens' confidence in that democracy will be durable (Cho and Logan, 2013).

Second, survey data unambiguously suggest that citizens associate free and fair elections with good governance. Bratton (2013) finds a fairly strong correlation between free and fair elections and positive citizen attitudes about the control of corruption by the government and the broader legitimacy of the government. Countries that manage to hold truly free and fair elections generate a positive feedback cycle of greater participation and greater government accountability. Citizens' belief that elections serve a good proxy for broader governance seems to have some basis in fact. Democracy indicators and the presence of free and fair elections correlate with a wide variety of the World Bank's World Development Indicators (WDI) governance indicators, from rule of law to control of corruption and government effectiveness (Radelet, 2010). Scholars have found that elections generate greater service delivery (Stasavage, 2005; Harding and Stasavage, 2013), and receipt of these services may provide incentives for citizens to participate in future elections through a policy feedback effect (MacLean, 2011b; Bleck, 2015; Hern, 2017), thus generating a positive cycle of participation.

Regardless of a country's level of democracy, the electoral period is characterized by government outreach to rural constituencies (Jourde, 2005), increased financing and support to democracy assistance including electoral institutions, increased press coverage of government activities and actors, and increased citizen attention to politics (Michelitch and Utych, 2014). Electoral episodes force politicians to interact with more marginalized sections of the population, whom they might otherwise ignore. This heightened interaction and information flow around government performance have the potential to transform citizens' expectations and demands. Elections also create focal points for local media and other electoral observers, including watchdog organizations within civil society. Comparative literature suggests that greater access to information through local media can increase voters' political knowledge (Prat and Strömberg, 2005; Snyder and Strömberg, 2010) and voters' sanctioning of politicians (Ferraz and Finan, 2008).

Radio sensitization campaigns can make voters more aware of trade-offs between targeted patronage and public goods provision. Keefer and Khemani (2014) found that access to community radio in Benin makes respondents less likely to support patronage jobs that reduce likelihood of access to public health or education projects. The unprecedented expansion of telephone and Internet availability provides voters with tools such as Facebook, WhatsApp, Instagram, and Twitter from which they can gain political information. Elections can generate reflection and opportunities for political activism. Social media enable voters to share their ideas and organize political activities, including protest in the context of economic downturn (Manacorda and Tesei, 2016). Elections and campaigns provide focal points for this kind of information diffusion and coordination.

Finally, elections map onto the local political context. Local races have the ability to generate greater responsiveness and accountability to local populations or to exacerbate local-level corruption and power relationships. Contrasting examples from Botswana and Tanzania illustrate this variation. Writing about land management around the Serengeti, Ngoitiko et al. (2010) offer an optimistic view of the ability of elections to generate better governance outcomes. Elections are a focus of local politics, campaigns, and collective engagement with the potential to create meaningful change in the performance of elected officials and therefore of local collective action in relation to contested lands and resources. Constituencies judge their elected representatives constituency in large part on the basis of how well they represent villagers' land and resource claims and help to prevent higher-level appropriations from taking place. Struggles over natural resource governance lie at the center of democratic contests, and local democratic institutions and processes are increasingly relevant and influential avenues as local communities organize to pursue and defend their own interests (Ngoitiko et al., 2010).

However, in the same edited volume, Rihoy and Maguranyanga (2010) describe a brokerage strategy in Botswana's 2004 parliamentary elections in which a ruling party's politicians used a wildlife quota as patronage for local elites, overlooking the local development trust's failure to produce financial audits for the last three years; previously, the trust's appeal to the audit charge had been denied, but in the context of the elections, this was overturned.

These examples show some ways in which elections interact with local power configuration as well as the linkages between parties and communities. These contextual factors can create very different governance outcomes, even in the context of dominant-party systems.

Relatedly, there is some evidence that when legislators have sufficient autonomy and access to resources, they seek to "deliver the goods" to their constituencies in a strategy to win reelection. Opalo's (2017) study of legislatures offers some evidence that the introduction of multiparty elections has strengthened linkages of accountability between legislators and constituencies in some countries. He argues that legislators in Kenya were able to gain greater remuneration and autonomy. Access to greater resources, including constituency development funds, enabled legislators to begin to deliver services to their constituencies. This gave them a slight incumbency advantage that was not present before 1991 (Opalo, 2017).

8.3 ELECTIONS AND DEVELOPMENT

In Chapters 5 and 6, we showed that citizens' number one policy priority was economic development, which is broadly defined as economic growth, access to services, and employment. Do competitive elections encourage politicians and governments to be more attentive to these concerns? Even if politicians are highly motivated, the correlation between the introduction of elections and better economic outcomes is complicated both by politicians' limited access to resources and by the level of prevailing state capacity. Although politicians know that service delivery to their home constituencies is key to their reelection, they do not all have access to independent budgets and too often rely on the executive for funding, which limits their ability to advocate for reform outside the existing political configuration (Barkan, 2008). Additionally, the quality of service delivery is mediated by state resources and capacity. In some of the poorer countries, the state has historically delivered very few effective services and public goods, particularly outside the main cities. Even when politicians have the best intentions and there is true political will, poor states often have difficulty fully funding and implementing initiatives without the support of outside actors. Reliance on external support, through international institutions or foreign donors, curtails government's political autonomy. Over the last few decades, incumbents have enjoyed budgets buoyed by high commodity prices, but declining oil prices will create new challenges for incumbents.

Some evidence suggests that electoral democracies are actually engaging in smarter governance, which translates to better economic and social provision outcomes. For instance, Masaki and van de Walle (2014) found not only that democracy is positively associated with faster economic growth, but also that the "democratic advantage" in Africa increases the longevity of a country's democracy. Relatedly, in a three-country case study, Grepin and Dionne (2013) show how Ghanaian policy makers implemented health sector reforms to cover broader portions of the population as compared to less democratic Senegal and Kenya. In other words, the quality of democracy affects the inclusiveness of policy outcomes.

Emerging evidence suggests that democracies around the world tend to outperform nondemocracies in access to services, infrastructure, and development outcomes (Baum and Lake, 2003; Kudamatsu, 2012; Golden and Min, 2013). This superior performance must be at least in part due to the higher levels of vertical accountability brought about by even flawed regular elections. Moreover, evidence from Africa suggests that candidates respond to constituents' demands for access to services and that provision of public goods increases with electoral politics, even if the improvements are halting and imperfect (Stasavage, 2005; Harding, 2015; Kjaer and Therkildsen, 2013; Harding and Stasavage, 2013). Even in dominant-party systems, increases in competition in electoral districts are associated with greater public goods provision as the government targets more competitive districts with more government resources (Rosenzweig, 2015). The very presence of multiparty elections makes dominant parties nervous and triggers greater efforts at publicity and gift giving.[2] This may be in part because many parties continue to rely on charismatic leaders and election cycles present a venue in which they can attempt to build a party brand beyond these figureheads.

In a cross-national analysis, Miller (2015) argues that contested autocratic elections improve state accountability and capacity and, in turn, promote human development. Multiparty elections are associated with better outcomes on measures of infant mortality, literacy, and gender balance in schooling than are seen in countries that either do not hold elections or hold only single-party elections. Harding (2018) argues that the introduction of elections in Africa has reduced infant mortality and increased school attendance as politicians seek to satisfy rural voters. In the context of Ghana, Harding (2015) shows that electoral support is contingent upon improvements in the quality of local roads. Thus, citizens are using their electoral support strategically to reward parties that provide them with the goods that they want.

There are two clear exceptions to this generalization. Recent state-led development efforts in two authoritarian regimes, Ethiopia and Rwanda, have generated excellent results. In Rwanda, during President Paul Kagame's tenure in office, economic growth rates have soared, and development indicators in the health and education sectors have improved significantly, at least if the official statistics are to be believed.[3] Ethiopia has probably had the fastest-growing economy in Africa for the last two decades. Both countries have, as a result, been lauded as developmental states in the East Asian mold and as potential models for the rest of Africa (see, for example, Kelsall, 2013b; Noman et al., 2012). However, much of the growth in both Ethiopia and Rwanda is related to postconflict reconstruction and has arisen from a very low base; in 2013, despite much

---

[2] For a description of this phenomena during the 2016 Ugandan elections, see Nic Cheeseman, Gabrielle Lynch, Justin Willis, The Man Who Overstayed. February 16, 2016, 11:22 AM Foreign Policy. Accessed June 8 2016 http://foreignpolicy.com/2016/02/16/the-man-who-overstayed-uganda-museveni.

[3] Independent researchers have recently called into question some of the government's developmental claims. See, for instance, Margo Leegwater et al., "Rwanda's Agricultural Revolution Is Not the Success It Claims to Be," *The Conversation*, December 13, 2017, accessed at https://theconversation.com/rwandas-agricultural-revolution-is-not-the-success-it-claims-to-be-86712; and "Faking it: The Rwandan GDP Growth Myth," *The Review of African Political Economy*, July 26, 2017, accessed at http://roape.net/2017/07/26/faking-rwandan-gdp-growth-myth.

progress, Rwanda's Human Development Index rank was still only 159 out of 188 countries in 2016, while Ethiopia was ranked 174th. Whether either country can transform its recent progress into sustainable intensive growth remains to be seen. Moreover, the record in other authoritarian states in the region is generally much worse, suggesting that it is less the absence of electoral democracy that explains Ethiopia's and Rwanda's developmental success than other, country-specific factors.

In competitive electoral regimes, the focus of governments is more likely to be on visible policy outputs in order to generate electoral returns (Harding and Stasavage, 2013). Voters can reward politicians and parties for better service provision (Weghorst and Lindberg, 2013). However, the receipt of services does not generate blind support from citizens. In a recent study of elections in Southern Africa, de Kadt and Lieberman (2015) showed that citizens who receive the most services are actually less likely to support the incumbent; citizens who have greater exposure to services are also more likely to perceive corruption in the African National Congress (ANC). More research is needed to understand how access to service provision increases participation but also generates a class of more skeptical and discerning citizens (Moehler, 2006).

Since 2013, Africa has appeared to be in a downward economic cycle, with a decline in commodity prices and slower global economic growth. It remains to be seen whether regimes with multiparty elections will adopt better economic policy responses to this new situation than their authoritarian peers do. Current economic forecasting for the region emphasizes the impact of low oil and mineral prices, but at least some non–oil producers are expected to maintain growth rates above 5 percent (IMF Regional Outlook, 2015, 2016). While non-oil producers tend to be more democratic than oil-producing regimes, it is difficult to disentangle democratic policy making from resource endowments.

In this book, we have portrayed development primarily as a valence issue, but in the future, we may see the emergence of different types of position debates rooted in new beliefs about political economy and electoral participation. Older citizens' attachments to socialism are being replaced by the newer generation's belief in the private sector. Sparked by high growth rates over the last decade, most parties are embracing a form of liberalism[4] and advocating the "equal opportunity of citizens to earn money." Support for the private sector may grow as shrinking civil

[4] Obeng-Odoom (2013) describes the common strand of economic liberalism in Ghana's 2012 elections.

service recruitment has excluded many bright young Africans from public sector employment.

8.3.1 Development in Rural Areas?

Despite the high speed of urbanization, most Africans live in rural areas, where many citizens trail far behind their urban counterparts in access to basic services (Bleck and Michelitch, 2015). Does the turn to electoral politics shape the relative weights of urban and rural populations? Bates (1991) famously demonstrated that much of African public policy in the decades after independence was characterized by a great deal of urban bias, because urban constituencies were more politically influential in the post independence authoritarian regimes that dominated the region. Are rural populations better off under the current electoral regimes? Answering this question is complicated by the fact that extremely rapid urbanization means that this issue is in constant flux and varies by country.

The nature of political participation in the countryside is different from that in urban areas, regardless of similarities in broad aggregate statistics such as voting turnout. Rural turnout rates and partisanship typically exceed or rival participation in cities (Ishiyama and Fox, 2006; Isaksson et al., 2014). In fact, turnout in the countryside is widely associated with brokerage mechanisms (Koter, 2016) that call into question the autonomy of many rural voters. Are rural populations better able to extract resources from the state under democracy? Evidence suggests that politicians treat rural and urban populations differently, in a manner that ultimately will increase the rural–urban development gap. For instance, Resnick (2012) shows that politicians in Zambia and Senegal pursue different strategies to attract urban and rural populations, focusing more on public goods for the former and private goods for the latter. Such an urban bias will probably continue to hold sway in many countries.

On the other hand, Harding's (2018) work indicates that politicians are courting voters with provision of services that voters care about. In an analysis of thirty African countries, he found a rural bias in service provision: Democratic elections increase access to primary education and reduce infant mortality exclusively in rural areas. Similarly, Bates and Block (2013) found that competitive elections in Africa have led to better agricultural policies, something that rural voters care about.

The evidence suggests that popular participation varies across rural and urban areas, with a much broader role played by brokers and traditional authorities in rural areas, particularly poor ones (Baldwin, 2015; Wahman and Boone, 2018; Koter, 2016). Baldwin (2015) argues that traditional chiefs have served as effective intermediaries for their constituents in bringing social services to the countryside. In this model, brokerage serves to empower voters. Other observers are less sanguine, suggesting that traditional brokers are more likely to be placated by clientelist goods and that their brokerage plays a conservative function, often in support of incumbents (Boone and Wahman, 2015). In addition, the salience and authority of traditional leaders vary widely, as does their capacity to mobilize constituents out to the polls, and parties will typically seek out and court the most effective brokers (Larreguy and Gottlieb, 2016). These factors are likely to shape the relationship between elections, rural participation, and service provision across different countries.

8.3.2 Development and Redistribution Independent of Electoral Quality

Finally, we ask whether the electoral calendar itself has a positive or negative impact on citizens. This question is important because elections represent a focal point for citizens, regardless of the quality of the elections or the regime context. First, we note that the election cycle itself creates opportunities for redistribution and patronage. Public spending typically increases during the election cycle (Block, 2002; Block et al., 2003). A cross-national analysis of political budget cycles found that younger political parties spend disproportionately more money during election years (Hanusch and Keefer, 2014). For instance, in the run-up to the 2012 election in Ghana, the government doubled spending on civil servants' wages, ended up doubling its budget deficit, and subsequently turned to the IMF for funding support.[5] The government of Edgar Lungu in Zambia explicitly held off from an IMF bailout – and enacting the associated austerity measures – until after the 2016 election cycle was over.[6]

As we discussed in Chapter 5, pre-election distribution of goods is a staple campaign practice. Candidates need to prove their ability to provide for constituencies at a later date by providing them with some support up front as a type of credible commitment (Jourde, 2005; Lindberg, 2010; Lindberg, 2013; Kramon, 2016; Paller, 2014a). A common refrain is that one need to show that one has money before becoming a politician to prove that one isn't in the game just to steal money from the state. At

[5] www.reuters.com/article/ghana-imf-idUSL4N19L4JY.
[6] www.lusakatimes.com/2016/04/17/no-imf-bailout-zambia-august-elections-imf.

the candidate level, office seekers feel pressure to distribute public or club goods to prove their credibility as elected officials. Many voters see the campaign period as their window of opportunity to extract resources from parties or the government (Bleck, 2015). Voters can make very personal demands[7] on campaign staff even when the staff does not have the ability to monitor how these individuals vote beyond looking at polling station results. Research demonstrates that voters often accept money from multiple parties but then vote according to other criteria (Banégas, 2003). Across seventeen Afrobarometer countries, 19 percent of respondents report having been offered a gift in during the previous election campaign (Cruz et al., 2015). Accepting electoral gifts does not usually translate into a predetermined vote at the ballot box when the secrecy of the ballot is ensured; rather, it translates into mass resource distribution.

In most imperfect democracies, attempts at vote buying and the distribution of gifts are persistent. van Hamm and Lindberg (2015) found that increases in democratization make certain forms of electoral manipulation, such as voter intimidation or manipulation of the results at the polling stations, less viable, so candidates increase the use of vote buying. Drawing on V-Dem data, van Hamm and Lindberg (2015) found that as manipulation of election administration declines, vote buying increases; however, at the highest levels of democratization, vote buying no longer increases with the decline in other forms of manipulation.

From a citizen's perspective, these cycles of redistribution are important. While a villager might not be able to count on a politician to pass policy that ensures service provision or even to make good on a clientelist offer to provide jobs, the villager can count on redistribution in the context of party competition in the run-up to elections. Historically, rural constituencies have been satiated with bags of sugar and salt, but as the anecdotes at the beginning of this chapter suggest, expectations may be changing. Certainly, citizens understand that elections give them a novel amount of leverage, albeit a relatively temporary one. In political systems that have historically been marked by limited attentiveness to the welfare of citizens, this is significant progress, no matter how imperfect.

8.4 OTHER ISSUE AREAS

In addition to the key areas of democracy and development, in Chapter 7 we identified four other persistent issue areas in African campaigns.

---

[7] Rauschenberg (2015) documents requests for fishing nets and school fees in Ghana.

Below, we explore whether elections have substantial repercussions in these areas.

8.4.1 Citizenship, Identity, and Tradition

Politicians' responsiveness to the popular will is not always linked to public goods provision and other "positive" development outcomes. Like politicians in electoral races in the rest of the world, African politicians respond to issues of identity, religion, and sovereignty that resonate with the popular masses and have implications for how African voters conceive of and debate citizenship. First, active debates about citizenship rights continue to mark a number of African countries (Dorman et al., 2007; Manby, 2013). The citizenship of ethnic and racial minorities has been contested in several countries, such as Tanzania (Aminzade, 2013) and Ethiopia (Smith, 2013). In other countries, large-scale movements of population, which in some cases go back decades, have become contentious matters in recent years, owing in part to growing land scarcity and the demagoguery of some politicians (Dorman et al., 2007). In yet other countries, voting rights for citizens in the diaspora have been meaningfully discussed, leading to incorporation of voters abroad in three-fourths of all African countries (Hartmann, 2015). These policy changes have consequences for electoral outcomes. In Cape Verde, diaspora voters may have determined victories for the opposition party in 2001 and helped it to another victory in 2006 (Baker, 2006).

Some scholars have noted a rise in citizenship-related conflict since the transition to multiparty elections in the 1990 (Whitaker, 2005; Bøås and Dunn, 2007; Geschiere and Jackson, 2006; Geschiere, 2009). Populist electoral rhetoric can also rely on xenophobic appeals that distinguish indigenous citizens from outsiders. In some cases, this can generate societal division and violence. In Cote d'Ivoire, Laurent Gbagbo forcefully instrumentalized Henri Konan Bédié's language of "Ivoirité" for his electoral bid (Banégas and Losch, 2002; Akindès, 2003; Whitaker, 2015). In South Africa, politicians stoke fears of immigrants in attempts to generate electoral support; for example, the newly formed South African First Party aims to "drive foreign nationals out of South Africa."[6] While politicians in any system can use strategies to divide and rule or to stigmatize economically powerful immigrant groups (Honig, 2016), these attempts often intensify around election time. Drawing on case studies of Ghana and Cote d'Ivoire, Whitaker (2015) argues that these strategies are particularly attractive for opposition parties, which want to divide the incumbent coalition by accusing the ruling party of pro-immigrant policy positions when key constituents bear concentrated costs of immigration and/or when anti-immigrant rhetoric will build an electoral coalition.

Women make up more than half of the population of sub-Saharan Africa, and since the transition to regular multiparty elections, women's voices have been increasingly heard, advocating for greater rights and positions in government. The advent of regularized elections has been accompanied by increases in women's rights. Since transitions to multi-party democracy, a number of countries have added nondiscrimination provisions to the constitution that prohibit customary practices if they undermine the status of women; these countries include Burundi, Ethiopia, Malawi, Namibia, Rwanda, South Africa, Swaziland, and Uganda (Tripp, 2017). In Chapter 3, we noted the increases in women's representation over the past three decades. Some research suggests that the presence of more women in parliament generates greater political engagement among women (Barnes and Burchard, 2013) and creates an environment that enables the passage of more pro-woman legislation (Browne, 2014), including legislation against gender-based violence (Tripp, 2015). Tripp argues that women in many countries have had a fundamental role in shaping legislation that improves their land rights (Tripp, 2017).

However, there is still a pervasive gender gap in political participation and knowledge in sub-Saharan Africa (Logan and Bratton, 2006; Coffe and Bolzendahl, 2011; Isaksson et al., 2014), and women parliamentarians still struggle to have their voices heard (Clayton et al., 2014). Women elected at the local level often face pushback from traditional authorities (Bazugba, 2014; Clayton, 2015). Women's rights advocates have had successes and setbacks (Kang, 2015). More research is needed to understand the relationships between female politicians, female voters, and traditional authorities.

Government responses to these debates can have serious policy consequences. For instance, Grossman (2015) draws on the rise of anti-gay legislation across Africa to demonstrate that increasing competitiveness in elections was associated with a rise of morality politics as a valence issue in order to cater to religiously inclined constituents. Grossman (2015) focuses on evangelical churches as conduits for heightening the salience of these moral issues, but politicians in Muslim-majority countries have made similar attempts to capture the religious preferences of the masses by blocking women's rights legislation (Wing, 2012; Kang, 2015). In each of these countries, as we posited in Chapter 6, religious institutions, rather than parties, play a major role in pushing contentious religious issues into the electoral and legislative spotlight. The powerful role of religious actors in democratic debates underscores the importance of understanding what the content of democracy looks like for voting populations. For instance, Kendhammer (2013) shows how Nigerian proponents of sharia law used democracy as a justification for its implementation, arguing that Islamic courts would be better able to adjudicate and resolve citizens' concerns. While Islamist parties have yet to emerge in Africa,[8] religious elites can play very powerful roles behind the scenes.

Multiparty elections have changed the power of traditional and religious elites. Increasingly, traditional authorities compete to prove their credibility in being able to deliver the votes of their constituents; parties look for leaders who consistently bring people to the polls (Gottlieb and Larreguy, 2016). The fortunes of traditional and religious leaders vary by country context, including precolonial concentrations of power (Wilfahrt, 2015), and in their levels of organization, coordination, and centralization (Beck, 2008). Many local rulers had more autonomy under dictatorships because they did not have to compete with local elected leaders for power and influence, which was often bestowed on traditional rulers by authoritarian governments eager for their support.

In some cases, the introduction of elections for traditional authority positions has further weakened these leaders by giving others a chance to rule at the local level. Still, many traditional leaders continue to play strong roles in elections at all levels (Logan, 2013), especially when they are well integrated as party brokers. Religious leaders also continue to play strong roles in the multiparty era. In Senegal, the Mourides play an indispensable political role advising on politics; in Mali, the High Council of Islam enjoys enormous political influence. These groups play important roles in determining what citizenship should look like. Moving forward, perhaps it is more important to understand what types of electoral regimes will look like. To do so, it is important to understand what the content of electoral regimes looks like for voting populations and how it maps onto their broader conceptions and expectations of democracy.

8.4.2 Natural Resource Redistribution

Historically, the concern about distributional politics in the context of multiparty elections is that it leads to ethnic favoritism or the privileging

---

[8] The exception is Tewassoul, the leading opposition party in Mauritania, which had electoral success in the 2013 legislative elections.

of other specific groups of the population. Some research has shown that electoral politics heighten favoritism toward copartisans and coethnics (Burgess et al., 2015). However, redistribution to one's own constituency while neglecting the rest of the population appears to be relatively rare. In their study of Kenya, Malawi, and Zambia, Kramon and Posner (2013), found that examples of favoritism often concern a single policy program but do not reveal the overall patterns of public redistribution. Public goods provision programs that favor coethnics tend to be complemented by other broader redistribution mechanisms for the entire population; in only one country in their study, Malawi, were coethnics of presidents more likely to receive all types of state support: infant mortality, childhood vaccinations, educational attainment, access to improved water sources, and household electrification. In work looking at educational attainment in Kenya since the 1960s, Kramon and Posner (2016) found that coethnics of the president achieve higher schooling attainment, a result that has not been changed by the introduction of multiparty elections in that country.

Africa is generally viewed as a region where inequality levels are not changing much (unlike, say, the countries of the Organisation for Economic Co-operation and Development, where inequality levels are viewed as increasing). Cross-national analysis, including countries outside of Africa, suggests that governing institutions do little to mitigate between-group inequality in countries with lower levels of democracy (Baldwin and Huber, 2010). Regime type does not predict levels of inequality. Regional differences and historical factors appear to be more directly correlated with inequality. Thus, for instance, the former settler colonies of Southern African have long exhibited the highest levels of inequality (Acemoglu et al., 2001) across several regime changes.

8.4.3 Security and Sovereignty

Rhetoric about security and sovereignty is common in elections and may influence policy, but it is less clear that elections generate positive policy outcomes in practice in this area. Nigerian President Muhammadu Buhari, elected in 2015 in part thanks to his platform of greater security, has had some limited victories in fighting Boko Haram, but it is harder to claim that the evolution to regular elections in Nigeria after 1999 can be associated with broad security reform in a country in which insecurity remains chronic. Similarly, while many candidates have used anti-West or anti-China rhetoric on the campaign trail, it is unclear that this has translated into changes in foreign relations with the targeted states or greater autonomy in policy making.

However, there are also examples of policy response to public opinion, particularly in the area of sovereignty concerns. Civil society watchdog groups have been effective in thwarting United States Africa Command (AFRICOM) from relocating its base to the continent, largely on the basis of arguments about national sovereignty.[9] The South African Development Community members, Nigeria, and Ghana have all rejected requests to host the US military base, largely as a result of the popular pressure. Similarly, the installation of the US and French bases in Niger has stimulated a lively political debate in Niger, where many commentators have been critical of President Mahamadou Issoufou, who had rejected the idea of foreign bases during his campaign.[10] In other contexts, politicians seek to avoid the political backlash for compromising on sovereignty. Chinese and Western involvement in mining in the former Katanga region has generated substantial debate in provincial assemblies and has led to significant policy reform for foreign companies operating in the mining sector.[11] Such examples could be multiplied.

What is clear is that politicians increasingly need to pay attention to popular positions on issues of sovereignty and security. While it will be difficult to translate campaign promises to policy if those promises require substantial structural change, we expect that politicians will increasingly be held accountable for campaign promises. For instance, in the 2018 Malian elections, President Ibrahim Boubacar Keïta will need to address popular discontent with his management of insecurity, given his campaign promises to reestablish peace and security.

Two authoritarian-leaning regimes, Ethiopia and Rwanda, have been among the most effective regimes in pursuing their own policy vision without donor constraint but also in leveraging the issue of sovereignty to build the legitimacy of incumbents. For instance, Ethiopia has nearly completed the $5 billion Grand Renaissance Dam project even though most donors did not want to get involved. Ethiopia was successfully able to raise its own domestic capital and leverage Chinese support. Rwanda added English as one of its official languages after the Rwandan Patriotic Front took power in 1994 and later boldly replaced French with English

---

[9] www.globalsecurity.org/military/facility/africom.htm.

[10] www.actuniger.com/tribune-opinion/11079-issoufou-mahamadou-a-trahi-les-nigériens-le-niger-à-l-aube-de-la-reconquête-coloniale-des-pays-du-sahel.html.

[11] www.businesslive.co.za/bd/world/africa/2017-04-25-democratic-republic-of-congo-tells-mining-companies-to-relocate.

as the language of instruction in its education system.[12] Both Ethiopia and Rwanda have been able to attract large amounts of donor funding without tremendous constraints on the policies that they can implement. If donors relax conditionalities for countries with strategic security interests, we may see even more of this kind of discourse.

8.5 CONTINUITY OR CHANGE?: THE FUTURE OF ELECTIONS

Could a final impact of regular elections be their permanence? Will the current ubiquity of elections be sustained? Or will we see a return to traditional authoritarian governments, which eschew competitive elections?

Certainly, international support for electoral competition has become more ambiguous in the international community over the last twenty years. New international actors in the region, most notably China, have been openly dismissive of the benefits of democracy. Western support for democracy increasingly takes a back seat to concerns about security, terrorism, and illegal immigration issues (Carothers and Brechenmacher, 2014; van de Walle, 2016). As a result, funding both for governance programs and, more specifically, for international election observers has declined in recent years. The high-profile international efforts of the past have increasingly been replaced by less well-funded and often lenient regionally based observers.

A continuing decline in international pressure for good electoral quality seems likely for the foreseeable future. As a result, the responsibility for sustaining the progress in electoral quality is likely to fall on domestic electoral institutions and broader civil society. We opened this book by describing the divergence in outcomes in electoral quality in the Zambian and Ghanaian elections of 2016. Many of those differences in outcome had to do with the quality of the electoral commission in Ghana as well as the organizing power of Ghanaian civil society. The Ghanaian Electoral Commission has emerged as a key factor in Ghana's democratic deepening. Furthermore, in countries such as Ghana, where domestic civil society can organize and coordinate observation, local groups can play a tremendous role; however, many countries lack credible, competent, and organized observer teams. The recent African Union Intervention in the Gambia set a new precedent for regional organizations' willingness to enforce electoral results. Although it is unlikely that democratic

---

[12] www.theguardian.com/education/2009/jan/16/rwanda-english-genocide.

deepening will occur without key actors and institutions committed to democratic progress, these trends suggest that elections will continue to provide moments of opportunity for political change and democratic improvement.

We have argued that multiparty competitive elections do not necessarily bring about improvements in governance or policy. If elections do not improve the welfare of citizens, will African electorates eventually grow tired of casting ballots? Where political elites are viewed as unresponsive and self-interested, citizens are more likely to become skeptical of the electoral process. Even in environments where elected officials have strong political will, limited state budgets or capacity might limit officials' ability to meet voters' expectations and could generate skepticism. Electoral skepticism could translate into withdrawal from participation (Moehler, 2008) or even regime change. According to Round 3 Afrobarometer data, only a little fewer than half of all respondents – ranging from 42 percent in Malawi to 70 percent in Ghana – thought that their country would remain democratic (Cho and Logan, 2013).

Still, while it is important to acknowledge democracies' imperfections, it seems likely that regularized elections are here to stay. Using the newest round of Afrobarometer data, Mattes and Bratton (2016) found that, on average, 78 percent of citizens reject presidential dictatorship and 73 percent reject military rule as viable options for governing their countries. In comparison, just a few years after independence and often after a single election, the citizenry in most countries of the region did not openly protest the descent into authoritarian rule. The continuing strong support for electoral politics, after a quarter-century and typically half a dozen electoral cycles, is surely one of the real achievement of this second electoral era. Today, public opinion research shows that this popular attachment to multiparty elections is tied to aspirations of responsive and accountable governance rather than only to the delivery of economic goods (Bratton et al., 2005; Mattes and Bratton, 2007).

Citizens' support for democracy seems resilient (Bratton et al., 2005), although for many African citizens, support for democracy is often justifiably coupled with skepticism about the state of democracy in their own country. Various studies have shown that individual support for democracy has a positive influence on participation (Kuenzi and Lambright, 2007, 2011). For instance, despite Mali's recent democratic breakdown, citizens remain strongly wedded to the idea of democracy and supportive of elections as the only way out of the crisis (Coulibaly and Bratton, 2013). A recent Afrobarometer survey (2014–15) suggests that citizens' attachment to multiple parties, affirmed by about two-thirds of respondents, has remained relatively constant over time (Bratton and Logan, 2015). Afrobarometer data show that Muslims are just as supportive of democracy as other citizens are (Bratton, 2003). The strongest factor associated with citizens' support for democracy and rejection of nondemocratic rule may be level of education (Evans and Rose, 2012), which continues to rise across Africa.

Perhaps the clearest proof of voters' attachment to democratic alternation can be found in the strong support for the idea of term limits even in countries where such limits are not present (Dulani, 2015).[13] Attempts to abolish or bypass term limits have been met by substantial protests and unrest in Burkina Faso, Congo, Niger, Senegal, and Togo. In describing protests against President Denis Sassou Nguesso's proposed referendum to extend term limits in the Republic of the Congo, opposition leaders directly cited the Burkinabe movement Balai Citoyen. In some instances, resistance to these movements has generated violent reprisal by the state, but this kind of learning demonstrates the possibilities for regional contamination as voters realize the efficacy of this brand of contentious politics.[14]

Recurrent cycles of backsliding and recovery in countries such as Kenya, Madagascar, and Mali have created important tests of democratic sustainability in recent years. However, as we discussed in Chapter 7, even though short-term support exists for power grabs, longer-term trends point to citizens' support for elections. Mali's experience in 2012 illustrates this pattern. When a young junta seized control of the presidential palace in 2012, many people in the capital initially supported them (Guindo, 2012). However, over time, Malians told survey conductors that elections were the only acceptable solution and way out of the crisis.[15]

---

[13] Support for Paul Kagame's bid for a third term as president of Rwanda contrasts with these strong preferences for democratic alternation. Voters' support for Kagame might reflect his position as the only credible candidate in the foreseeable future as well as Rwanda's strong economic growth rate during his tenure (see http://venturesafrica.com/paul-kagame-and-rwanda-an-economic-model-for-africa).

[14] www.voanews.com/content/congo-brazzaville-opposition-to-protest-president-third-term-bid/2976658.html.

[15] See data in Coulibaly and Bratton (2013), which show that more than 80 percent of Malians remaining attached to elections. More than 90 percent of displaced persons surveyed by Bleck et al. (2016) wanted to stick to a strict electoral calendar despite the fact that much of the country's north remained insecure and many Malians were displaced.

In a recent phenomenon, military actors are intervening in civilian affairs as "watchdogs of democracy," largely in response to citizen sentiment. In Burkina Faso and Niger, popularly supported coup d'états deposed leaders who were attempting to defy constitutionally mandated term limits. Ultimately, these leaders were able to hand control back to civilians, and democratic debates and discourse have become much richer as a result. In Mali, the junta proved militarily impotent, but it raised populist issues that the political class had been unwilling to touch, such as inequality and the decline of the education sector. The interim government introduced local language discourse into major speeches and news broadcasts, a trend that has stuck through the newly elected regime (Bleck and Michelitch, 2017).

We are reasonably confident that societal forces are likely to promote the continuation of the current electoral regimes that we have observed for the last quarter-century and to continue the timid and inconstant democratization that began in the early 1990s. What about political society and the prospects for more profound political change? In this book, we have argued that the persistence of presidentialism has generated a tremendous incumbency advantage for African executives. Additionally, the recent introduction of the multiparty politics means that opposition parties and candidates have had a limited window in which to gain experience and support from voters. To date, these factors have contributed to the striking continuity from the pretransition era to today. Many of the same elites dominate political systems, and despite the regularization of elections, in most cases we do not observe increases in horizontal accountability or strengthening of other branches of government (such as the judiciary and legislature).

But there are reasons to think that these incumbency advantages may decline in the future. First, African governments that have been ruled by a single executive for decades, without the complementary emergence of strong parties, face tremendous uncertainty when the president leaves office. Because of the personalist nature of most systems, it will be difficult for a successor, including kin, to claim the same valence characteristics as someone who is been the central node of power for many years. In short, the introduction of any new leader, even from the same elite family, will result in greater uncertainty. In countries such as Togo and Gabon, we have seen presidents' sons struggle to control politics with the skill and authority of their fathers. This is in part because successors are new to office and need to learn how to manage power, but it is also due to the tremendous uncertainty generated by turnover. It leaves questions in the minds of the political establishment as well as voters. Will the new leader be able to adeptly manage political coalitions and international partners? Does the new leader have the backing of the party members? Will the new leader disrupt traditional power structures in favor of his or her own allies and networks? Over time, the introduction of this uncertainty in the context of Africans' desires for multiparty democracy described earlier in this chapter might very well mean a declining incumbency advantage and greater turnover.

Furthermore, as new candidates and parties gain experience in electoral campaigns and in office, they gain credibility as "issue owners," learn more about their constituencies, and will need to innovate as they face increasingly competitive electoral environments. This may lead to the emergence of more credible candidates and parties benefiting from greater partisan attachments. This should help members of opposition parties to overcome some of the valence gap they face in races against incumbent candidates. Over time, we may see parties associated with different policies as issue owners. In Chapter 7, we argued that many African voters use performance-based criteria in candidate selection, and we discussed the presence of swing voters. While it is unlikely that we will see a shift to the left-right economic spectrum in Africa, we already observe some citizens' supporting parties on the basis of criteria other than ethnic heuristics and this trend may grow. This will be harder in places where brokerage mechanisms link candidates to specific communities of ethnic elites, but as we described in Chapter 5, we already see populist issue-based campaigns in urban areas targeting disenfranchised voters.

These processes are already in motion at the legislative and municipal levels, where many voters consider candidates' ability to "deliver the goods" irrespective of their party or their status as an incumbent. Because public goods outcomes are relatively visible, it is fairly easy for voters to evaluate the performance of local officials. This leads to high rates of turnover in these offices. Given the rapid adoption of cellphone and Internet technology across many parts of Africa, candidates will have to compete in environments of unprecedented information flows. Thus, although it is unlikely that the existing power asymmetry in favor of the executive branch will erode in the near future, we may observe voters being increasingly willing to vote underperforming executives out of office.

References

Aalen, L., & Tronvoll, K. (2009). The end of democracy? Curtailing political and civil rights in Ethiopia. *Review of African Political Economy*, 36(120), 193–207.

Abney, R., Adams, J., Clark, M., et al. (2011). When does valence matter? Heightened valence effects for governing parties during electoral campaigns. *Party Politics*, 19(1), 61–82.

Abrahamsen, R., & Bareebe, G. (2016). Uganda's 2016 elections: Not even faking it anymore. *African Affairs*, 115(461), 751–765.

Acemoglu, D., Johnson, S., & Robinson, J. A. (2001). The colonial origins of comparative development: An empirical investigation. *American Economic Review*, 91(5), 1369–1401.

Adida, C., Combes, N., Lo, A., & Vernik, A. (2016). The spousal bump: Do cross-ethnic marriages increase political support in multiethnic democracies? *Comparative Political Studies*, 49(5), 635–661.

Adamolekun, L., & Laleye, M. (2009). Benin: Legislative development in Africa's first democratizer'. In Joel D. Barkan eds., *Legislative Power in Emerging African Democracies*. Boulder, CO: Lynne Rienner Publishers, 109–146.

Adejumobi, S. (2009). *Political Parties in West Africa: The Challenge of Democratization in Fragile States*. International IDEA.

Ahlin, E., Dionne, K. Y., & Roberts, T. (2015). The 2015 presidential election in Togo. *Electoral Studies*, 39, 168–173.

Ake, C. (1991). Rethinking African democracy. *Journal of Democracy*, 2(1), 32–44.

(1996). *Is Africa Democratizing?*. No. 5. Malthouse Pr, 1996.

(2000). *The Feasibility of Democracy in Africa*. Dakar: Council for the Development of Social Science Research in Africa.

Aker, J. C., Collier, P., & Vicente, P. C. (2017). Is information power? Using mobile phones and free newspapers during an election in Mozambique. *Review of Economics and Statistics*, 99(2), 185–200. DOI:10.1162/REST_a_00611.

Akindes, F. (2003). Cote d'Ivoire: Socio-political crises, "Ivoirite" and the course of history. *African Sociological Review*, 7(2), 11–28.

Albaugh, E. (2007). Language choice in education: A politics of persuasion. *The Journal of Modern African Studies*, 45(1), 1–32.

Albaugh, E. A. (2009). The colonial image reversed: Language preferences and policy outcomes in African education. *International Studies Quarterly*, 53 (2), 389–420.

Albaugh, E. (2011). An autocrat's toolkit: Adaptation and manipulation in "democratic" Cameroon. *Democratization*, 18(2), 388–414.

Alexander, J., & McGregor, J. (2001). Elections, land and the politics of opposition in Matabeleland. *Journal of Agrarian Change*, 1(4), 510–33.

Alou, T., & Adamou, M. (2015). Au Niger, le soutien est fort mais pas unanime pour l'adoption de la sharia dans la Constitution *Afrobarometer Briefing Paper 156*.

Alves de Aquino, J. (2015). The effect of exposure to political institutions and economic events on demand for democracy in Africa. *Afrobarometer*, Working Paper 160.

Aminzade, R. (2013). *Race, Nation, and Citizenship in Post-colonial Africa: The Case of Tanzania*. Cambridge: Cambridge University Press.

Amselle, J.-L. (1985). Le Wahabisme à Bamako (1945–1985). *Canadian Journal of African Studies/La Revue canadienne des études africaines*, 19(2), 345–57.

Andersen, P. A., & Kibler, R. J. (1978). Candidate valence as a predictor of voter preference. *Human Communication Research*, 5(1), 4–14.

Anderson, D. (2005). Yours in Struggle for Majimbo. Nationalism and the party politics of decolonization in Kenya, 1955–64. *Journal of Contemporary History*, 40(3), 547–564.

Anderson, J. N. D. (2013). *Islamic Law in Africa (No. 3)*. Routledge.

Andersen, R., Tilley, J., & Heath, A. (2005). Political knowledge and enlightened preferences: Party choice through the electoral cycle. *British Journal of Political Science*, 35(2), 285–302.

Arriola, L. (2009). Patronage and political stability in Africa. *Comparative Political Studies*, 42(10), 1362–1399.

   (2012). *Multi-ethnic Coalitions in Africa: Business Financing of Opposition Election Campaigns*. Cambridge University Press.

   (2013). Capital and opposition in Africa: Coalition building in multiethnic societies. *World Politics*, 65(2), 233–272.

Arriola, L. R., Choi, D. D., & Gichohi, M. (2016). Political endorsements and cross-ethnic voting. Working Paper.

Arriola, L. R., & Johnson, M. C. (2014). Ethnic politics and women's empowerment in Africa: Ministerial appointments to executive cabinets. *American Journal of Political Science*, 58(2), 495–510.

Aquino, J. A. (2015). Do democratic institutions forge a demand for democracy? An investigation of Latin American citizens' attitudes. *73rd Annual Midwest Political Science Association Conference*. Midwest Political Science Association, Chicago.

Auerbach, A., & Thachil, T. (2016). Who Do Brokers Serve? Experimental Evidence from Informal Leaders in India's Slums. *Annual Meeting of the American Political Science Association*.

Ayee, J. R. A. (1990). The implementation of the 1988/89 district assembly (local government) elections in Ghana. *Africa Insight*, 20(3), 169–175.

Ba, Oumar Issiaka. (2009). *Une histoire de l'enseignement au Mali: Entre réforme et réticences*. Paris: L'Harmattan.

Bakary, T. D. (1993). Systèmes éducatifs, stratification sociale et construction de l'État. D. Bach et A. Kirk-Greene (sous la dir.), *États et sociétés en Afrique noire*. Paris: Economica, 71–88.

Baker, B. (1998). The class of 1990: How have the autocratic leaders of sub-Saharan Africa fared under democratisation? *Third World Quarterly*, 19(1), 115–127.

(2002). Outstaying one's welcome: The presidential third-term debate in Africa. *Contemporary Politics*, 8(4), 285–301.

(2006). Cape Verde: The most democratic nation in Africa? *Journal of Modern African Studies*, 44(4), 493–511.

Baldwin, K. (2013). Why vote with the chief? Political connections and public goods provision in Zambia. *American Journal of Political Science*, 57(4), 794–809.

(2015). *The Paradox of Traditional Chiefs in Democratic Africa*. New Haven, CT: Yale University Press.

(2016). *The Paradox of Traditional Chiefs in Democratic Africa*. Cambridge University Press.

Baldwin, K., & Huber, J. (2010). Economic versus cultural differences: Forms of ethnic diversity and public goods provision. *American Political Science Review*, 104(4), 644–662.

Baller, S. (2014). Urban football performances: Playing for the neighbourhood in Senegal, 1950s–2000s. *Africa*, 84(1), 17–35.

Banégas, R. (1998). Marchandisation du vote, citoyenneté et consolidation démocratique au Bénin. *Politique Africaine*, 69, 75–88.

(2003). *La démocratie à pas de caméléon: Transition et imaginaires politiques au Bénin*. Karthala Editions.

(2015). Putsch et politique de la rue au Burkina Faso: Quand les étudiants débattent du Régime de sécurité présidentielle. *Politique africaine* 3(139), 147–170.

Banégas, R., & Losch, B. (2002). La Côte d'Ivoire au bord de l'implosion. *Politique Africaine*, 87, 139–161.

Barkan, J. D. (1995). I. Elections in Agrarian Societies. *Journal of Democracy*, 6(4), 106–116.

(2008). Legislatures on the rise. *Journal of Democracy*, 19(2), 124–137.

(2009). *Legislative Power in Emerging African Democracies*. Boulder, CO: Lynne Rienner.

Barkan, J. D., & Ng'ethe, N. (1998). Kenya tries again. *Journal of Democracy*, 9(2), 32–48.

Barkan, J. D., & Okumu, J. J. (1978). Semi-Competitive elections, clientelism, and political recruitment in a no-party state: The Kenyan experience. In Guy Hermet, Richard Rose, and Alain Rouqié (eds.) *Elections without Choice*. UK: Palgrave Macmillan, 88–107.

Barnes, T. D., & Burchard, S. M. (2013). "Engendering" politics: The impact of descriptive representation on women's political engagement in sub-Saharan Africa. *Comparative Political Studies*, 46(7), 767–790.

(2013). 'Engendering' Politics: The Impact of Descriptive Representation on Women's Political Engagement in Sub-Saharan Africa. *Comparative Political Studies*, 46 (7), 767–90.

Basedau, M., Erdmann, G., Lay, J., & Stroh, A. (2011). Ethnicity and party preference in sub-Saharan Africa. *Democratization*, 18(2), 462–489.

Basedau, M., Erdmann, G., & Mehler, A. (2007). *Votes, Money and Violence: Political Parties and Elections in Sub-Saharan Africa*. Scottsville, South Africa: University of Kwazulu-Natal Press.

Basedau, M., & Stroh, A. (2009). Ethnicity and party systems in francophone sub-Saharan Africa. GIGA Research Programme: Institute of African Affairs. Working Paper, No 100.

Bates, R. (1981). *States and Markets in TropicalAfrica: The Political Basis of Agricultural Policy*. Berkeley, CA: University of California Press, series on social choice and political economy.

Bates, R. H. (1974). Ethnic competition and modernization in contemporary Africa. *Comparative Political Studies*, 6(4) 457–84.

Bates, R. H., & Block, S. A. (2013). Revisiting African agriculture: Institutional change and productivity growth. *Journal of Politics*, 75(2), 372–384.

Baudais, V., & Chauzal, G. (2006). Les partis politiques et l'indépendance partisane d'Amadou Toumani Touré. *Politique Africaine*, 104, 61–80.

(2011). The 2010 coup d'état in Niger: A praetorian regulation of politics?. *African Affairs*, 110 (439), 295–304.

Bauer, G., & Burnet, J. E. (2013). Gender quotas, democracy and women's representation in Africa: Some insights from democratic Botswana and autocratic Rwanda. *Anthropology Faculty Publications*, Paper 2.

Baum, M. A., & Lake, D. A. (2003). The political economy of growth: Democracy and human consolidation. *Review of African Political Economy*, 24(71), 113–128.

Bayart, J.-F. (1993). *The State in Africa: The Politics of the Belly*. London: Longman.

Baylies, C., & Szeftel, M. (1997). The 1996 Zambian elections: Still awaiting democratic consolidation. *Review of African Political Economy*, 24(71), 113–128.

Bazenguissa-Ganga, R. (1996). Milices politiques et bandes armées à Brazzaville. *Les Cahiers du CERI* 13.

(1999). The spread of political violence in Congo-Brazzaville. *African Affairs*, 98(390), 37–54.

Bazugba, A. (2014). *The Politics of Gender Quotas: What Accounts for the Relative Success of Gender Quotas in the First South Sudanese Elections*. PhD Thesis, University of Edinburgh.

Beardsworth, N. (2018, unpublished). From a 'Regional Party' to the Gates of State House: The resurgence of the UPND Warwick University.

Beck, L. (2008). *Brokering Democracy in Africa: The Rise of Clientelist Democracy in Senegal*. New York, NY: Palgrave Macmillan.

Bekoe, D. A. (2012). *Voting in Fear: Electoral Violence in Sub-Saharan Africa*. Washington, DC: United States Institute of Peace.

Bekoe, D. A., & Burchard, S. M. (2017). The contradictions of pre-election violence: The effects of violence on voter turnout in Sub-Saharan Africa. *African Studies Review*, 60(2), 73–92.

Bellows, J., & Miguel, E. (2006). War and institutions: New evidence from Sierra Leone. *American Economic Association: Papers and Proceedings*, 96(2), 394–399.

Benavot, A, & Riddle, P. (1988). The expansion of primary education, 1870–1940: Trends and issues. *Sociology of Education*, 61(93), 191–210.

Bermeo, N. (2016). On democratic backsliding. *Journal of Democracy*, 27(1), 5–19.

Bienen, H. (1970a). *Kenya: The Politics of Participation and Control*. Princeton, NJ: Princeton University Press.

(1970b). *Tanzania: Party Transformation and Economic Development*. Princeton, NJ: Princeton University Press.

(1974). Military and society in East Africa: Thinking again about praetorianism. *Comparative Politics*, 6(4), 489–517.

(1978). *Armies and Parties in Africa*, Holmes & Meier Pub.

(1983). The state and ethnicity: Integrative formulas in Africa. In Donald Rothchild, & Victor Olorunsola, eds., *State versus Ethnic Claims: African Policy Dilemmas*. Westview Press, 100–126.

Bierschenk, T. (2006). The local appropriation of democracy: an analysis of the municipal elections in Parakou, Republic of Benin, 2002–03. *The Journal of Modern African Studies*, 44(4), 543–571.

Biersteker, T. J. (2014). *Multinationals, the State and Control of the Nigerian Economy*. Princeton University Press.

Blattman, C. (2009). From violence to voting: War and political participation in Uganda. *American Political Science Review*, 103(2), 231–247.

Bleck, J. (2013). Do Francophone and Islamic schooling communities participate differently? Disaggregating parents' political behaviour in Mali. *The Journal of Modern African Studies*, 51(3), 377–408.

(2015). *Education and Empowered Citizenship in Mali*, Baltimore, MD: Johns Hopkins.

Bleck, J., Dembele, A. & Guindo, S. (2016). Malian crisis and the lingering problem of good governance. *Stability: International Journal of Security and Development*, 5(1). https://stabilityjournal.org/articles/10.5334/sta.457/

Bleck, J., & Logveninko, I. (2016). Democracy in unlikely places: Lessons from Mali and Kyrgyzstan. Working Paper.

(2018). Weak states and uneven pluralism: lessons from Mali and Kyrgyzstan. *Democratization*, 25(5), 804–823.

Bleck, J., & Michelitch, K. (2015). The 2012 crisis in Mali: Ongoing empirical state failure. *African Affairs*, 114(457), 598–623.

(2017). Capturing the Airwaves, Capturing the Nation? A Field Experiment on State-Run Media Effects in the Wake of a Coup. *The Journal of Politics*, 79(3), 873–89.

(2018). Is women's empowerment associated with political knowledge and opinions? Evidence from rural Mali. *World Development*, 106, 299–323.

Bleck, J., & Patel, D. (2015). Out of Africa: Why Islamists do not (yet) participate in African elections. Working Paper.

(2018). Out of Africa: Electoral Failure and the Future of Political Islam in Africa. Working Paper.

Bleck, J., & Van de Walle, N. (2011). Parties and issues in Francophone West Africa: Towards a theory of non-mobilization. *Democratization*, 18(5), 1125–1145.

(2013). Valence issues in African elections navigating uncertainty and the weight of the past. *Comparative Political Studies*, 46(11), 1394–1421.

Block, S. (2002). Political business cycles, democratization, and economic reform: The case of Africa. *Journal of Development Economics*, 67, 205–208.

Block, S. A., Ferree, K. E., & Singh, S. (2003). Multiparty competition, founding elections and political business cycles in Africa. *Journal of African Economies*, 12(3), 444–468.

Bøås, M., & Dunn, K. C. eds. (2007). *African Guerrillas: raging against the machine*. Boulder, CO: Lynne Rienner.

(2013). *Politics of Origin in Africa: Autochthony, Citizenship and Conflict*. London: Zed Books.

Bob-Milliar, G. M. (2012). Party factions and power blocs in Ghana: A case study of power politics in the National Democratic Congress. *The Journal of Modern African Studies*, 50(4), 573–601.

Bogaards, M. (2000). Crafting competitive party systems: Electoral laws and the opposition in Africa. *Democratization*, 7(4), 163–190.

(2004). Counting parties and identifying dominant party systems in Africa. pliability of "normative" democracy. *European Journal of Political Research*, 43(2), 173–97.

(2007). Measuring democracy through election outcomes: A critique with African data. *Comparative Political Studies*, 40(10), 1211–1237.

(2008). Dominant party systems and electoral volatility in Africa: A comment on Mozaffar and Scarritt. *Party Politics*, 14(1), 113–130.

(2013). Reexamining African elections. *Journal of Democracy*, 24(4), 151–160.

Bolten, C. (2016). I will vote what is in my heart: Sierra Leone's 2012 Elections and the pliability of "normative" democracy. *Anthropological Quarterly*, 89(4), 1017–1046.

Bonnecase, V. (2015). Sur la chute de Blaise Compaoré. Autorité et colère dans les derniers jours d'un régime. *Politique Africaine*, 1, 151–168.

Boone, C. (1993). Commerce in Cote d'Ivoire: Ivoirianisation without Ivoirian traders. *The Journal of Modern African Studies*, 31(1), 67–92.

(2003). *Political Topographies of the African State: Territorial Authority and Institutional Choice*. Cambridge: Cambridge University Press.

(2009). Electoral populism where property rights are weak: Land politics in contemporary sub-Saharan Africa. *Comparative Politics*, 41(2), 183–201.

(2011). Politically allocated land rights and the geography of electoral violence: The case of Kenya in the 1990s. *Comparative Political Studies*, 44(10), 1311–1342.

Boone, C., & Wahman, M. (2015). Captured countryside? Stability and change in sub-national support for African incumbent parties. London School of Economics, Working Paper, 15–172.

Booth, D. (2012). *Development as a Collective-Action Problem. Addressing the Real Challenges of African Governance.* London: ODI.

Booth, D., & Cammack, D. R. (2013). *Governance for Development in Africa: Solving Collective Action Problems.* London: Zed Books.

Brambor, T., Clark, W. R., & Golder, M. (2007). Are African party systems different? *Electoral Studies,* 26(2), 315–323.

Branch, A., & Mampilly, Z. (2015). *Africa Uprising: Popular Protest and Political Change.* Zed Books Ltd.

Branch, B., Cheeseman, N., & Gardner, L. (2010). *Our Turn to Eat: Politics in Kenya Since 1950.* Berlin: Lit Verlag.

Brazys, S., Heaney, P., & Walsh, P. P. (2015). Fertilizer and votes: Does strategic economic policy explain the 2009 Malawi election? *Electoral Studies,* 39, 39–55.

Bratton, M. (1989). Beyond the state: Civil society and associational life in Africa. *World Politics,* 41(3), 407–430.

(2003). Briefing: Islam, democracy and public opinion in Africa. *African Affairs,* 102(408), 493–501.

(2004). The alteration effect in Africa. *Journal of Democracy,* 15(4), 147–158.

(2008). Vote buying and violence in Nigerian election campaigns. *Electoral Studies,* 27(4), 621–632.

ed. (2013). *Voting and Democratic Citizenship in Africa.* Boulder, CO: Lynne Rienner Press.

(2013). Where do elections lead in Africa. In Michael Bratton, ed., *Voting and Democratic Citizenship in Africa.* Boulder, CO: Lynne Rienner Publishers, 17–40.

Bratton, M., Alderfer, P., Bowser, G., & Temba, J. (1999). The effects of civic education on political culture: Evidence from Zambia. *World Development,* 27(5), 807–824.

Bratton, M., Bhavani, R. & Chen, T.-H. (2011). Voting Intentions in Africa: Ethnic, Economic or Partisan? *Afrobarometer,* Working Paper No. 127.

Bratton, M., Bhavani, R., & Chen, T. (2012). Voting intentions in Africa: Ethnic, economic or partisan? *Commonwealth and Comparative Politics,* 50(1), 27–52.

Bratton, M., Chikwana, A., & Sithole, T. (2005). Propaganda and public opinion in Zimbabwe. *Journal of Contemporary African Studies,* 23(1), 77–108.

Bratton, M., & Kimenyi, M. S. (2008). Voting in Kenya: Putting ethnicity in perspective. *Journal of Eastern African Studies,* 2(2), 272–289.

Bratton, M., & Logan, C. (2015). The Viability of Political Opposition in Africa: Popular Views. *Afrobarometer Policy Paper,* 26.

Bratton, M., & Mattes, R. (2001). Africans' surprising universalism. *Journal of Democracy,* 12(1), 107–121.

Bratton, M., Mattes, R., & Gyimah-Boadi, E. (2005). *Public Opinion, Democracy and Market Reform in Africa.* Cambridge: Cambridge University Press.

Bratton, M., & van de Walle, N. (1997). *Democratic Experiments in Africa: Regime Transitions in Comparative Perspective.* Cambridge: Cambridge University Press.

Brenner, L. (2001). *Controlling Knowledge: Religion, Power, and Schooling in a West African Muslim Society.* Bloomington: Indiana University Press.

Briggs, R. C. (2012). Electrifying the base? Aid and incumbent advantage in Ghana. *The Journal of Modern African Studies*, 50(4), 603–624.

(2014). Aiding and abetting: Project aid and ethnic politics in Kenya. *World Development*, 64, 194–205.

(2017). Explaining case selection in African politics research. *Journal of Contemporary African Studies*, 35(4), 1–8.

Brossier, M., & Dorronsoro, G. (2016). Le paradoxe de la transmission familiale du pouvoir. *Critique internationale*, (4), 9–17.

Brown, D. S. (2000). Democracy, colonization, and human capital in sub-Saharan Africa. *Studies in Comparative International Development*, 35(1), 20–40.

Brown, S. (2011). "Well, what can you expect?": Donor officials' apologetics for hybrid regimes in Africa. *Democratization*, 18(2), 512–534.

Browne, E. (2014). Elected women's effectiveness at representing women's interests. *Applied Knowledge Services*.

Brownlee, J. (2007) *Authoritarianism in an Age of Democratization*. New York: Cambridge University Press.

(2011). Executive elections in the Arab world: When and how do they matter? *Comparative Political Studies*, 44(7), 807–828.

Bunce, V. J., & Wolchik, S. L. (2011). *Defeating Authoritarian Leaders in Postcommunist Countries*. Cambridge: Cambridge University Press.

Burgess, R., Jedwab, R., Miguel, E., Morjaria, A., & Miquel, G. P. (2015). The value of democracy: Evidence form road building in Kenya. *American Economic Review*, 105(6), 1817–1851.

Burnell, P. (1997). Whither Zambia? The Zambian presidential and parliamentary elections of November 1996. *Electoral Studies*, 16(3), 407–416.

(2001). The party system and party politics in Zambia: Continuities past, present and future. *African Affairs*, 100(399), 239–263.

Camara, S. (2014). Political Islam and the negotiation of political roles among peripheral Sufi leaders in Senegal. *International Journal of Political Science*, 2(6): 105–116.

Capoccia, G., & Kelemen, R. D. (2007). The study of critical junctures: Theory, narrative, and counterfactuals in historical institutionalism. *World Politics*, 59(3), 341–369.

Carothers, T., (2002). The end of the transition paradigm. *Journal of democracy*, 13(1), 5–21

Carbone, G. M. (2007). Political parties and party systems in Africa: Themes and research perspectives. *World Political Science Review*, 3(3), 1–29.

Carlson, E. (2015). Ethnic voting and accountability in Africa: A choice experiment in Uganda. *World Politics*, 67(2), 353–385.

Carothers, T. (2002). The end of the transition paradigm. *Journal of Democracy*, 13(1), 5–21.

Carothers, T., & Brechenmacher, S. (2014). *Closing Space: Democracy and Human Rights Support Under Fire*. Carnegie Endowment for International Peace.

Chabal, P. (1998). A few considerations on democracy in Africa. *International Affairs*, 74(2), 289–303.

(2009). *The Politics of Suffering and Smiling*. London: Zed Books.

Chabal, P., & Daloz, J. P. (1999). *Africa Works: Disorder as Political Instrument*. London: International African Institute.

Chattopadhyay, R., & Duflo, E. (2004). Women as policy makers: Evidence from a randomized policy experiment in India. *Econometrica*, 72(5), 1409–1443.

Chazan, N. (1982). The new politics of participation in tropical Africa. *Comparative Politics*, 14(2), 169–189.

Cheeseman, N. (2008). The Kenyan elections of 2007: An introduction. *Journal of Eastern African Studies*, 2(2), 166–184.

(2010). African elections as vehicles for change. *Journal of Democracy*, 21(4), 139–153.

(2014). Does the African middle class defend democracy? Evidence from Kenya. *Afrobarometer*, Working Paper 150.

(2015a). *Democracy in Africa: Successes, Failures, and the Struggle for Political Reform*. Vol. 9. Cambridge University Press.

(2015b). 'No bourgeoisie, no democracy'? The political attitudes of the Kenyan middle class. *Journal of International Development*, 27(5), 647–664.

Cheeseman, N., & Ford, R. (May 2007). Ethnicity as a political cleavage. In *Afrobarometer Conference on 'The Micro-Foundations of Mass Politics in Africa', East Lansing* (Vol. 12, No. 13.05).

Cheeseman, N., & Larmer, M. (2015). Ethnopopulism in Africa: Opposition mobilization in diverse and unequal societies. *Democratization*, 22(1), 22–50.

Cheibub, J. A., Przeworski, A., Limongi Neto, F. P., & Alvarez, M. M. (1996). What makes democracies endure? *Journal of Democracy*, 7(1), 39–55.

Cho, W., & Logan, C. (2013). Looking toward the future: Alternations in power and popular perspectives on democratic durability in Africa. *Comparative Political Studies*. 47(1), 30–54.

Chua, A. (2004). *World on Fire: How Exporting Free Market Democracy Breeds Ethnic Hatred and Global Instability*. New York: Anchor.

Clapham, C. (1997). Opposition in tropical Africa. *Government and Opposition*, 32(4), 541–556.

Clark, J. (1997). Petro-politics in Congo. *Journal of Democracy*, 8(3), 62–76.

Clark, J. F. (2002). The neo-colonial context of the democratic experiment of Congo-Brazzaville. *African Affairs*, 101(403), 171–192.

(2008). *The Failure of Democracy in the Republic of Congo*. Lynne Rienner Publishers.

Clark, J. F., & Gardinier, D. E., eds. (1997). *Political Reform in Francophone Africa*. Boulder, CO: Westivew Press.

Clayton, A. (2014). Electoral gender quotas and attitudes toward traditional leaders: A policy experiment in Lesotho. *Journal of Policy Analysis and Management*, 33(4), 1007–1026.

Clayton, A., Josefsson, C., & Wang, V. (2014). Present without presence? Gender, quotas and debate recognition in the Ugandan parliament. *Representation*, 50(3), 379–392.

Clayton, A. B. (2015). Electoral gender quotas, female leadership, and women's political engagement: Evidence from a randomized policy experiment. *Comparative Political Studies*, 48(3), 333–369.

Coffe, H., & Bolzendahl, C. (2011). Gender gaps in political participation across sub-Saharan African nations. *Social Indicators Research*, 102(2), 245–264.

Collier, D., & Levitsky, S. (1997). Democracy with adjectives: Conceptual innovation in comparative research. *World Politics*, 49(3), 430–451.

Collier, P. (2011). *Wars, Guns and Votes: Democracy in Dangerous Places*. Random House.

Collier, P., & Vicente, P. C. (2014). Votes and violence: Evidence from a field experiment in Nigeria. *The Economic Journal*, 124(574), F327–F355.

Collier, R. B. (1978). Parties, coups, and authoritarian rule: Patterns of political change in tropical Africa. *Comparative Political Studies*, 11(1), 62–93.

   (1982). *Regimes in Tropical Africa: Changing Forms of Supremacy, 1945–1975*. Berkeley, CA: University of California Press.

Collier, R. W. (1972). The evolution of regional districts. *BC Studies: The British Columbian Quarterly*, (15), 29–39.

Conroy-Krutz, J. (2006). African Cities and Incumbent Hostility: Explaining Opposition Success in Urban Areas. In *annual meeting of the African Studies Association, San Francisco*.

   (2013). Information and ethnic politics in Africa. *British Journal of Political Science*, 43(2), 345–373.

   (2016). Electoral campaigns as learning opportunities: Lessons from Uganda. *African Affairs*, 115(460), 516–540.

   (2017). Loyalty premiums: Vote prices and political support in a dominant-party regime. *Comparative Politics*, 50(1), 1–35.

Conroy-Krutz, J., & Kerr, N. (2015). Dynamics of democratic satisfaction in transitional settings: Evidence from a panel study in Uganda. *Political Research Quarterly*, 68(3), 593–606.

Conroy-Krutz, J., & Lewis, D. (2011). *Mapping Ideologies in African Landscapes*. Institute for Democracy in South Africa.

Conroy-Krutz, J., & Logan, C. (2012). Museveni and the 2011 Ugandan election: Did the money matter? *The Journal of Modern African Studies*, 50(4), 625–655.

Conroy-Krutz, J., & Moehler, D. (2014). Ethnic cues and ballot design. Working Paper, University of Pennsylvania (January 3, 2014).

Conroy-Krutz, J., & Moehler, D. C. (2015). Moderation from bias: A field experiment on partisan media in a new democracy. *Journal of Politics*, 77(2), 575–587.

Conroy-Krutz, J., Moehler, D. C., & Aguilar, R. (2016). Partisan cues and vote choice in new multiparty systems. *Comparative Political Studies*, 49(1), 3–35.

Converse, P. E. (1972). Change in the American electorate. In Angus Campbell, & Philip E. Converse, eds., *The Human Meaning of Social Change*. New York, NY: Russell Sage Foundation.

Cooper, F. (1996). *Decolonization and African Society: The Labor Question in French and British Africa*. Vol. 89. Cambridge University Press.

   (2002). *Africa since 1940: The Past of the Present*, Vol. 1. Cambridge University Press.

Coppedge, M., Gerring, J., Lindberg, S. I. et al. (2017). V-Dem Codebook v7. Varieties of Democracy (V-Dem) Project.

Coulibaly, M., & Bratton, M. (2013). Crisis in Mali: Ambivalent popular attitudes on the way forward. *Stability: International Journal of Security and Development*, 2(31), 1–10.

Crawford, G., & Lynch, G. (2011). Democratization in Africa 1990–2010: An assessment. *Democratization*, 18(2), 275–310.

ed. (2012). *Democratization in Africa: Challenges and Prospects (Democratization Special Issues)*. New York, NY: Routledge.

Craig, S. C. (1980). The mobilization of political discontent. *Political Behavior*, 2(2), 189–209.

Craig, S. C., & Maggiotto, M. A. (1982). Measuring political efficacy. *Political Methodology*, 85–109.

Criminal Politics: Violence (2007). "Godfathers" and Corruption in Nigeria. Human Rights Watch October 2007 19(16A). https://www.hrw.org/reports/2007/nigeria1007/

Croke, K., Grossman, G., Larreguy, H., & Marshall, J. (2015). Deliberate disengagement: How education decreases participation in electoral authoritarian regimes. *Afrobarometer*. Working Paper 156.

Crook, R. C. (1997). Winning coalitions and ethno-regional politics: The failure of the opposition in the 1990 and 1995 elections in Côte D'Ivoire. *African Affairs*, 96(April), 215–242.

Crook, R. C., & Manor, J. (1998). *Democracy and Decentralisation in South Asia and West Africa: Participation, Accountability and Performance*. Cambridge University Press.

Crowder, M. (1987). Whose dream was it anyway? Twenty-five years of African independence. *African Affairs*, 86(342), 7–24.

Cruz, C., Keefer, P., & Labonne, J. (2015). Incumbent advantage, voter information, and vote buying. Working Paper.

Dahl, R. (1971). *Polyarchy: Participation and Opposition*. New Haven, CT: Yale University Press.

Daloz, J. P., (1998). *Le(non-) renouvellement des élites en Afrique subsaharienne*. Bordeaux: CEAN.

Daloz, J. P., & Quantin, P., eds. (1997). *Transitions démocratiques africaines: Dynamiques et contraintes (1990–1994)*. KARTHALA Editions.

Dalton, R. (2007). Partisan mobilization, cognitive mobilization, and the changing American electorate. *Electoral Studies*, 26(2), 274–286.

(2008). Citizenship norms and the expansion of political participation. *Political Studies*, 56, 76–98.

Dalton, R., Flanagan, S., & Beck, P. A., eds. (1984). *Electoral Change in Advanced Industrial Democracies*. Princeton, NJ: Princeton University Press.

Debrah, E. (2011). "Measuring governance institutions' success in Ghana: the case of the electoral commission, 1993–2008." *African Studies* 70(1), 25–45.

Decalo, S. (1976). *Coups and Army Rule in Africa: Studies in Military Style*. New Haven, CT: Yale University Press.

Decoudras, P.-M., & Gazibo, M. (1997). Niger: démocratie ambiguë: chronique d'un coup d'État annoncé. *L'Afrique politique*, 155–189.

Deets, M. (2016). "Grown-Ups on White Plastic Chairs": Soccer and separatism in Senegal, 1969–2012. *History in Africa*, 43, 347–374.

Dendere, C. (2015). *The Impact of Voter Exit on Party Survival: Evidence from Zimbabwe's ZANU-PF*. (Doctoral dissertation, Georgia State University).

(2016). "The impact of Money on African Politics. Conference Presentation." The African Studies Association Conference, Washington, DC, November 2016.

De Leon, C., Desai, M., & Tuğal, C. (2009). Political articulation: Parties and the constitution of cleavages in the United States, India, and Turkey. *Sociological Theory*, 27(3), 193–219.

De Oliveira, R. S. (2015) *Magnificent and Beggar Land: Angola since the Civil War*. Oxford University Press.

Diamond, L. (2015). Facing up to the democratic recession. *Journal of Democracy*, 26(1), 141–155.

Diamond, L. J. (1994). Toward democratic consolidation. *Journal of Democracy*, 5(3), 4–17.

Diescho, J. (1996). Government and opposition in post-independence Namibia: Perceptions and performance. In *Building Democracy: Perceptions and Performance of Government and Opposition in Namibia*. Windhoek: Namibia Institute for Democracy and Konrad- Adenauer-Stiftung, 4–25.

Dimitrova, D. V., Shehata, A., Strömbäck, J., & Nord, L. W. (2014). The effects of digital media on political knowledge and participation in election campaigns: Evidence from panel data. *Communication Research*, 41(1), 95–118.

Dionne, K., Yi, Inman, K. L., & Montinolao, G. R. (2014). Another resource curse? The impact of remittances on political participation. *Afrobarometer*, Working Paper 145.

Diop, M. (2006). Le Sénégal à la croisée des chemins. *Politique Africaine*, 4, 103–126.

Diwakar, R. (2008). Voter turnout in the Indian states: An empirical analysis. *Journal of Elections, Public Opinion and Parties*, 18(1), 75–100.

Dome, M. (2015). A window on policy priorities: Evidence from the citizens of 34 African countries'. *Afrobarometer Policy Paper* (18).

Doorenspleet, R., & Nijzink, L. (2013). *One Party Dominance in African Democracies*. Boulder, CO: Lynne Rienner.

Dorman, S. R. (2016a). 'We have not made anybody homeless': Regulation and control of urban life in Zimbabwe. *Citizenship Studies*, 20(1), 84–98.

(2016b). *Understanding Zimbabwe: From Liberation to Authoritarianism*. Oxford: Oxford University Press.

Dorman, S. R., Hammett, D. P., & Nugent, P., eds. (2007). *Making Nations, Creating Strangers: States and Citizenship in Africa*, Vol. 16. Brill.

Dowd, R. A., & Driessen, M. (2008). Ethnically dominated party systems and the quality of democracy: Evidence from sub-Saharan Africa. *Afrobarometer*, Working Paper 92.

Downs, A. (1957). An economic theory of political action in a democracy. *Journal of Political Economy*, 65(2), 135–150.

Dulani, B. (2015). African publics strongly support term limits, resist leaders' efforts to extend their tenure. *Afrobarometer Dispatche*, 30.

Dulani, B., & Dionne, K. Y. (2014). Presidential, parliamentary, and local government elections in Malawi. *Electoral Studies*, 36, 210–239.

Dumont, R. (1966). *False Start in Africa*. New York, NY: Praeger Publishers.

Dunning, T., & Harrison, L. (2010). Cross-cutting cleavages and ethnic voting: An experimental study of cousinage in Mali. *American Political Science Review*, 104(1), 21–39.

Ebeke, C., & Yogo, T. (2013). Remittances and the voter turnout in sub-Saharan Africa: Evidence from macro and micro level data. African Development Bank Group, Working Paper 185.

Edgell, A. B., Mechkova, V., Altman, D., Bernhard, M., & Lindberg, S. I. (2017). When and where do elections matter? A global test of the democratization by elections hypothesis, 1900–2010. *Democratization*, 1–23.

Egan, P. J. (2008). Issue ownership and representation: A theory of legislative responsiveness to constituency opinion. Available at SSRN: 1239464.

Eifert, B., Miguel, E., & Posner, D. N. (2010). Political competition and ethnic identification in Africa. *American Journal of Political Science*, 54(2), 494–510.

Ellis, E. (2014). A vote of confidence: Retrospective voting in Africa. *Afrobarometer*, Working Paper 147.

Ellis, S., & Ter Haar, G. (2004). *Worlds of Power: Religious Thought and Political Practice in Africa*, Vol. 1. New York: Oxford University Press.

Elischer, S. (2013). *Political Parties in Africa: Ethnicity and Party Formation*. Cambridge University Press.

Ejdemyr, S., Kramon, E., & Robinson, A. L. (2017). Segregation, ethnic favoritism, and the strategic targeting of local public goods. *Comparative Political Studies*: 1–33.

Ekeh, P. (1975). Colonialism and the two publics in Africa: A theoretical statement. *Comparative Studies in Society and History*, 17(1), 91–112.

Ekine, S. (2010). *SMS Uprising: Mobile Activism in Africa*. Capetown: Pambazuka Press.

Elgie, R., & Sophia, M., eds. (2007). *Semi-Presidentialism Outside Europe: A Comparative Study*. Routledge.

Embaló, B. (2012). Civil–military relations and political order in Guinea-Bissau. *The Journal of Modern African Studies*, 50(2), 253–281.

Englebert, P. (1996). *Burkina Faso: Unsteady Statehood in West Africa*. Westview Press.

(2000). Pre-colonial institutions, post-colonial states, and economic development in tropical Africa. *Political Research Quarterly*, 53(1), 7–36.

Erdmann, G. (2004). Party research: Western European bias and the African labyrinth. *Democratization*, 3(11), 63–87.

Erdmann, G., & Basedau, M. (2013). An overview of African party systems. In Renske Doorenspleet, & Lia Nijzink, eds., *One Party Dominance in African Democracies*. Boulder, CO: Lynne Rienner, 25–48.

Evans, G., & Rose, P. (2007). Education and support for democracy in sub-Saharan Africa: Testing mechanisms of influence. *Afrobarometer*, Working Paper 75.

(2012). Understanding education's influence on support for democracy in Sub-Saharan Africa. *Journal of Development Studies*, 48(4), 498–515.

Falola, T., & Ihonybere, J. O. (1985). *The Rise and Fall of Nigeria's Second Republic, 1979–1984*. London: Zed Books.

Faure, Y. (1993). Democracy and realism: Reflections on the case of Cote d'Ivoire. *Africa*, 63(3), 313–329.

Fauré, Y.-A., & Médard, J.-F. (1982). *État et bourgeoisie en Côte d'Ivoire*. Paris: Éditions Karthala.

Fauvelle-Aymar, C. (2008). Electoral turnout in Johannesburg: Socio-economic and political determinants. *Transformation: Critical Perspectives on Southern Africa*, 66(1), 142–167.

Fearon, J. D., & Laitin, D. D. (1996). Explaining interethnic cooperation. *American Political Science Review*, 90(4), 715–735.

Fenno, R. F. (1978). *Home Style*. Boston, MA: Little Brown.

Fenno, R. F., & Fenno, R. F., Jr. (1978). *Home Style: House Members in Their Districts*. HarperCollins.

Fernandez, K. E., & Kuenzi, M. (2006). Crime and support for democracy: Revisiting modernization theory. *Afrobarometer*, Working Paper 64.

Ferraz, C., & Finan, F. (2008). Exposing corrupt politicians: The effects of Brazil's publicly released audits on electoral outcomes. *The Quarterly Journal of Economics*, 123(2), 703–745.

Ferree, K. E. (2006). Explaining South Africa's racial census. *Journal of Politics*, 68(4), 803–815.

(2010). *Framing the Race in South Africa: The Political Origins of Racial Census Elections*. New York: Cambridge University Press.

(2013). *Framing the Race in South Africa: The Political Origins of Racial Census Elections*. Cambridge: Cambridge University Press.

Ferree, K. E, & Horowitz, J. (2010). Ties that bind? The rise and decline of ethnoregional partisanship in Malawi, 1994–2009. *Democratization*, 17(3), 534–563.

Ferree, K. E., & Long, J. D. (2016). Gifts, threats, and perceptions of ballot secrecy in African elections. *African Affairs*, 115(461), 621–645.

Finkel, S. E., Horowitz, J., & Rojo-Mendoza, R. T. (2012). Civic education and democratic backsliding in the wake of Kenya's post-2007 election violence. *The Journal of Politics*, 74(1), 52–65.

Finkel, S. E., & Smith, A. E. (2011). Civic education, political discussion, and the social transmission of democratic knowledge and values in a new democracy: Kenya 2002. *American Journal of Political Science*, 55(2), 417–435.

Fiorina, M. P. (1981). *Retrospective Voting in American National Elections* New Haven: Yale University Press.

Flores, T. E., & Nooruddin, I. (2016). *Elections in Hard Times: Building Stronger Democracies in the 21st Century*. Cambridge: Cambridge University Press.

Fornos, C. A., Power, T. J., & Garand, J. C. (2004). Explaining voter turnout in Latin America, 1980 to 2000. *Comparative Political Studies*, 37(8), 909–940.

Frankema, E. H. P. (2012). The origins of formal education in sub-Saharan Africa: Was British rule more benign? *European Review of Economic History*, 16, 335–355.

Fraser, A. (2017). Post-populism in Zambia: Michael Sata's rise, demise and legacy. *International Political Science Review*, 38(4), 456–472.

Fraser, J. (1970). The mistrustful-efficacious hypothesis and political participation. *Journal of Politics*, 32(2), 444–449.

Freire, M., Lall, S., & Leipziger, D. (2015). Africa's urbanization: Challenges and opportunities. In C. Monga and J. Y. Lin eds. *The Oxford Handbook of Africa and Economics: Volume 1: Context and Concepts.* Oxford: Oxford University Press.

Fréchette, G. R., Maniquet, F., & Morelli, M. (2008). Incumbents' interests and gender quotas. *American Journal of Political Science*, 52(4), 891–909.

Friesen, P. (2017). *The State of Political Parties in Southern Africa: Ideology, Legitimacy, and Coercion.* Working Paper.

Fridy, K. S. (2007). *We only vote but do not know: The social foundations of partisanship in Ghana* (Doctoral dissertation, University of Florida).

(2009). Africa's disappearing election results: Why announcing the winner is simply not enough. *Journal of African Elections*, 8(2), 88–101.

Fukuyama, F. (2015). Why is democracy performing so poorly? *Journal of Democracy*, 26(1), 11–20.

Gandhi, J. (2008). *Political Institutions under Dictatorship.* New York: Cambridge University Press.

Gandhi, J., & Lust-Okar, E. (2009). Elections under authoritarianism. *Annual Review of Political Science*, 12, 403–422.

Gandhi, J., & Przeworski, A. (2007). Authoritarian institutions and the survival of autocrats. *Comparative Political Studies*, 40(11), 1279–1301.

Garand, J. C., & Sharpe, C. L. (2000). Turnout, economic conditions, and government spending in the American states: A pooled analysis, 1960–1996. *Annual meeting of the Southern Political Science Association, Atlanta, GA.*

Gazibo, M. (2005). *Les paradoxes de la démocratisation en Afrique: analyse institutionnelle et stratégique.* Les Presses de l'Université de Montréal.

(2006). The forging of institutional autonomy: a comparative study of electoral management commissions in Africa. *Canadian Journal of Political Science/ Revue canadienne de science politique*, 39(3), 611–633.

Geddes, B. (2005). Why parties and elections in authoritarian regimes?. In *Annual meeting of the American Political Science Association*, pp. 456–471.

Gellar, S. (2005). *Democracy in Senegal: Tocquevillian Analytics in Africa.* Bloomington, IN: Indiana University Press.

Gertzel, C. J., & Szeftel, M., eds. (1984). *The Dynamics of the One-Party State in Zambia.* Manchester: Manchester University Press.

Geschiere, P. (2009). *The Perils of Belonging: Autochthony, Citizenship, and Exclusion in Africa and Europe.* Chicago, IL: University of Chicago Press.

Geschiere, P., & Jackson, S. (2006). Autochthony and the crisis of citizenship: Democratization, decentralization, and the politics of belonging. *African Studies Review*, 49(2), 1–7.

Geys, B. (2006). Explaining voter turnout: A review of aggregate-level research. *Electoral Studies*, 25(4), 637–663.

Giannini, P., Pavao, N., & Bleck, J. (2017). Campaign Images and Citizen-Politician Linkages: Exploring Visual Appeals in Presidential Campaigns in Sub Saharan Africa and Latin America, *Working Paper.*

Gibson, J. L. (2009). *Overcoming Historical Injustices: Land Reconciliation in South Africa.* New York: Cambridge University Press.

Gifford, P. (1998). *African Christianity: Its Public Role*. Bloomington: Indiana University Press.

(2004). *Ghana's New Christianity: Pentecostalism in a Globalising African Economy*. London: C. Hurst & Co. Publishers.

Glennerster, R., Miguel, E., & Rothenberg, A. D. (2013). Collective action in diverse Sierra Leone communities. *The Economic Journal*, 123(568), 285–316.

Goetz, A. M., & Hassim, S., eds. (2003). *No Shortcuts to Power: African Women in Politics and Policymaking*. New York, NY: Zed Books.

Goeke, M., & Hartmann, C. (2011). The regulation of party-switching in Africa. *Journal of Contemporary African Studies*, 29(3), 263–280.

Golden, M., & Min, B. (2013). Distributive politics around the world. *Annual Review of Political Science*, 16, 73–99.

Goldsmith, A. A. (2010). Mixed regimes and political violence in Africa. *The Journal of Modern African Studies*, 48(3), 413–433.

Good, K. (2009). The presidency of General Ian Khama: The militarization of the Botswana "miracle". *African Affairs*, 109(435), 315–324.

Gottlieb, J. (2015). The logic of party collusion in a democracy: Evidence from Mali. *World Politics*, 67(1), 1–36.

Gottlieb, J., Grossman, G., & Robinson, A. L. (2015). Do men and women have different policy preferences, and if so, why? *Afrobarometer WP153*.

Gottlieb, J., & Larreguy, H. (2016). An Informational Theory of Electoral Targeting in Young Clientelistic Democracies: Evidence from Senegal. URL: www.dropbox.com/s/7zwr9io5lcpghuf/GL_SenegalElectoralBehavior_Website.pdf.

Gottlieb, J., & Robinson, A. L. (April 2016). The effects of matrilineality on gender differences in political behavior across Africa. In *April 2016 Meeting of Working Group on African Political Economy in Washington, DC*.

Green, K. F. (2007). *Why Dominant Parties Lose: Mexico's Democratiztion in Comparative Perspective*. New York, NY: Cambridge University Press.

(2010). 9 A resource theory of single-party dominance. In Bogaards, & Boucek, eds., *Dominant Political Parties and Democracy: Concepts, Measures, Cases and Comparisons*, 155–174.

Green, E. D. (2013). Explaining African ethnic diversity. *International Political Science Review*, 34(3), 235–253. ISSN 0192-5121.

Greenberg, A., & Mattes, R. (2013). Does the quality of elections affect the consolidation of democracy? In *Voting and Democratic Citizenship in Africa*, 239–252.

Grepin, K., & Dionne, K. Y. (2013). Democratization and universal health coverage: A case comparison of Ghana, Kenya, and Senegal. *Global Health Governance*, 4(2), 1–27.

Grose, C. R., & Husser, J. A. (2008). The valence advantage of presidential persuasion: Do presidential candidates use oratory to persuade citizens to vote contrary to ideological preferences?

Groseclose, T. (2001). A model of candidate location when one candidate has a valence advantage. *American Journal of Political Science*, 45(4), 862–886.

Grossman, G. (2015). Renewalist Christianity and the political saliency of LGBTs: Theory and evidence from sub-Saharan Africa. *Journal of Politics*, 77(2), 337–351.

Grossman, G., Humphreys, M., & Sacramone-Lutz, G. (2014). 'I wld like u WMP to extend electricity 2 our village: On Information Technology and Interest Articulation. *American Political Science Review*, 108(3), 688–705.

Grossman, G., Michelitch, K., & Santamaria, M. (2016). Texting complaints to politicians: Name personalization and politicians' encouragement in citizen mobilization. *Comparative Political Studies*, 50(10), 1325–1357.

(2017). Texting complaints to politicians: Name personalization and politicians' encouragement in citizen mobilization. *Comparative Political Studies*, 50(10), 1325–1357.

Guindo, S. (2012). 'Analyse des résultats de l'enquête d'opinion sur la crise Malienne', *Working Paper* available at http://www.gisse.org

Gyimah-Boadi, E. (2009). "Another step forward for Ghana." *Journal of Democracy*, 20(2), 138–152.

(2015). Africa's waning democratic commitment. *Journal of Democracy*, 26(1), 101–113.

Habyarimana, J., Humphreys, M., Posner, D. N., & Weinstein, J. M. (2007). Why does ethnic diversity undermine public goods provision? *American Political Science Review*, 101(4), 709–725.

Hadenius, A., & Teorell, J. (2007). Pathways from authoritarianism. *Journal of democracy*, 18(1), 143–157.

Hafner-Burton, E. M., Hyde, S. D., & Jablonski, R. S. (2014). When do governments resort to election violence? *British Journal of Political Science*, 44(1), 149–179.

Hajnal, Z., & Lewis, P. G. (2003). Muncipal institutions and voter turnout in local elections. *Urban Affairs Review*, 38(5), 645–668.

Hanusch, M., & Keefer, P. (2014). Younger parties, bigger spenders? Party age and political budget cycles. *European Economic Review*, 72, 1–18.

Harding, R. (2010). Democracy, urbanization, and rural bias: Explaining urban/rural differences in incumbent support across Africa (No. 120). *Afrobarometer*, Working Paper.

(2015). Attribution and accountability: Voting for roads in Ghana. *World Politics*, 67(4), 656–689.

(2018). Who is Democracy Good For? African Elections and Rural Bias in the Provision of Basic Services Working paper, Oxford University.

Harding, R., & Michelitch, K. (2017). Partisanship in sub-Saharan Africa: The nexus between contextual and individual determinants. Working Paper.

Harding, R., & Stasavage, D. (2013). What democracy does (and doesn't do) for basic services: School fees, school inputs, and African elections. *The Journal of Politics*, 76(1), 229–245.

Hartmann, C. (2007). Paths of electoral reform in Africa. In Matthias Basedau, Gero Erdmann, & Andreas Mehler, eds., *Votes, Money and Violence: Political Parties and Elections in Sub-Saharan Africa*, 144–167.

(2015). Expatriates as voters? The new dynamics of external voting in Sub-Saharan Africa. *Democratization*, 22(5), 906–926.

Haynes, J. (1996). *Religion and Politics in Africa*. Zed Books.

Hayward, F. M, ed. (1987). *Elections in Independent Africa*. Westview Press.

Heilbrunn, J. R. (1993). Social origins of national conferences in Benin and Togo. *The Journal of Modern African Studies*, 31(2), 277–299.

Hellwig, T. (2012). Constructing accountability: Party position taking and economic voting. *Comparative Political Studies*, 45(1), 91–118.

Herbst, J. (1990). Migration, the politics of protest, and state consolidation in Africa. *African Affairs*. 89(355), 183–203.

(2014). *States and Power in Africa: Comparative Lessons in Authority and Control*. Princeton: Princeton University Press.

Hermet, G., Rose, R., & Rouquié, A., eds. (1978). *Elections without Choice*. UK: Palgrave Macmillan.

Hern, E. A. (2017). Better than nothing: How policies influence political participation in low-capacity democracies. *Governance*, 30(4), 583–600.

Herskovits, J. (2007). Nigeria's rigged democracy. *Foreign Affairs*, 115–130.

Hibbs, D. A., Rivers, R. D., & Vasilatos, N. (1982). On the demand for economic outcomes: Macroeconomic performance and mass political support in the United States, Great Britain, and Germany. *The Journal of Politics*, 44(2), 426–462.

Hicken, A. (2009). *Building Party Systems in Developing Democracies*. New York, NY: Cambridge University Press.

(2011). Clientelism. *Annual Review of Political Science*, 14, 289–310.

Hickman, J. (2009). Is electoral violence effective? Evidence from Sri Lanka's 2005 presidential election. *Contemporary South Asia*, 17 (4), 429–435.

Hill, M. (2016). Zambia's Lungu appoints Felix Mutati as his finance minister. In *Bloomberg Markets*.

Hoffman, B., & Robinson, L. (2009). Tanzania's missing opposition. *Journal of Democracy*, 20(4), 123–136.

Holm, J. D., Molutsi, P. P., & Somolekae, G. (1996). The development of civil society in a democratic state: The Botswana model. *African Studies Review*, 39(2), 43–69.

Honig, L. (2016). Immigrant political economies and exclusionary policy in Africa. *Comparative Politics*, 48(4), 517–537.

Horowitz, D. L. (1985). *Ethnic Groups in Conflict*. University of California Press.

Horowitz, J. (2012). *Campaigns and Ethnic Polarization in Kenya*. Dissertation.

(2016). The ethnic logic of campaign strategy in diverse societies: Theory and evidence From Kenya. *Comparative Political Studies*, 49(3), 324–356.

(2017). Ethnicity and the swing vote in Africa's emerging democracies: Evidence from Kenya. *British Journal of Political Science*, 1–21.

Horowitz, J., & Dionne, K. Y. (2016). The political effects of agricultural subsidies in Africa: Evidence from Malawi. *World Development*, 87, 215–226.

Horowitz, J., & Long, J. (2016). Strategic voting, information, and ethnicity in emerging democracies: Evidence from Kenya. *Electoral Studies*, 44, 351–361.

Houngnikpo, M. C., N'Diaye, B., & Saine, A. S., eds. (2011). *Elections and Democratization in West Africa, 1990–2009*. Trenton: Africa World Press.

Howard, M. M., & Roessler, P. G. (2006). Liberalizing electoral outcomes in competitive authoritarian regimes. *American Journal of Political Science*, 50(2), 365–381.

Huntington, S. P. (1984). Will more countries become democratic? *Political Science Quarterly*, 99(2), 193–218.

(1991). *The Third Wave: Democratization in the Late Twentieth Century*. Norman: University of Oklahoma Press.

Huntington, S. P., & Nelson, J. M. (1976). *No Easy Choice: Political Participation in Developing Countries*, Vol. 3. Cambridge: Harvard University Press.

Hyden, G. (2006). *Big Man Rule. African Politics in Comparative Perspective*. Cambridge: Cambridge University Press.

(2011). Barriers to party systems in Africa: The movement legacy. *Africa Review*, 3(2), 103–122.

Hyden, G., Leslie, M., & Ogundimu, F., eds. (2003). *Media and Democracy in Africa*. Transaction.

Ichino, N., & Nathan, N. L. (2013a). Crossing the line: Local ethnic geography and voting in Ghana. *American Political Science Review*, 107(2), 344–361.

(2013b). Do primaries improve electoral performance? Evidence from Ghana. *American Journal of Political Science*, 57(2), 428–441.

Ichino, N., & Schündeln, M. (2012). Deterring or displacing electoral irregularities? Spillover effects of observers in a randomized field experiment in Ghana. *Journal of Politics*, 74(1), 292–307.

Idrissa, A. (2008). *The Invention of Order: Republican Codes and Islamic Law in Niger*. PhD Dissertation, University of Florida.

Ihonvbere, J. O. (1996). Are things falling apart? The military and the crisis of democratisation in Nigeria. *The Journal of Modern African Studies*, 34(2), 193–225.

Isaksson, A. S. (2010). Political participation in Africa: Participatory inequalities and the role of resources. *Afrobarometer*, Working Paper 121: http://afrobarometer .org/publications/wp121-political-participation-africa-participatory-inequalities -and-role-resources.

(2014). Political participation in Africa: The role of individual Resources. *Electoral Studies*, 34, 244–260.

Isaksson, A. S., Kotsadam, A., & Nerman, M. (2014). The gender gap in African political participation: Testing theories of individual and contextual determinants. *Journal of Development Studies*, 1–17.

Ishiyama, J. (2010). Ethnic partisanship in Ethiopia. *Nationalism and Ethnic Politics*, 16(3–4), 290–310.

Ishiyama, J., & Fox, K. (2006). What affects the strength of partisan identity in sub-Saharan Africa? *Politics and Policy*, 34(4), 748–773.

Jackson, R. H., & Rosberg, C. G. (1982). *Personal Rule in Black Africa: Prince, Autocrat, Prophet, Tyrant*. Berkeley, CA: University of California Press.

(1991). Personal Rule in Black Africa: Prince, Autocrat, Prophet, Tyrant (Berkeley, CA, 1982). *Jackson6Personal Rule in Black Africa: Prince, Autocrat, Prophet, Tyrant1982*.

Jacobson, G. C. (2000). *The Politics of Congressional Elections*. Reading, MA: Addison-Wesley.

Jentzsch, C. (2014). How Frelimo rehabilitated Renamo in time for Mozambique's Elections. Interview with Domingo Manuel de Rosário, Africa is a Country: https://africasacountry.com/2014/11/how-frelimo-rehabilitated- renamo-in-time-for-mozambiques-elections/

Joseph, R. A. (1998). Africa, 1990–1997: From abertura to closure. *Journal of Democracy*, 9(2), 3–17.

Jourde, C. (2005). "The President Is Coming to Visit!": Dramas and the hijack of democratization in the Islamic Republic of Mauritania. *Comparative Politics*, 37(4), 421–440.

de Kadt, D., & Lieberman, E. S. (2015). Do citizens reward good service? Voter responses to basic service provision in southern Africa. *Afrobarometer*, Working Paper 161.

Kamaté, A., & Banégas, R. (2010). Football, clivages identitaires et conflit politique en Côte d'Ivoire. *Politique Africaine*, 2, 85–102.

Kang, A. (2015). *Bargaining for Women's Rights: Activism in an Aspiring Muslim Democracy*. Minneapolis, MN: University of Minnesota Press.

Karl, T. L. (1986). Imposing consent? Electoralism vs. democratization in El Salvador. In Paul Drake, & Eduardo Silva, eds., *Elections in Latin America*. San Diego, CA: University of California.

(1995). The hybrid regimes of Central America. *Journal of Democracy*, 6(3), 72–86.

Kartik, N., & McAfee, R. P. (2007). Signaling character in electoral competition. *The American Economic Review*, 97(3), 852–870.

Kasara, K. (2007). Tax me if you can: Ethnic geography, democracy, and the taxation of agriculture in Africa. *American Political Science Review*, 101(1), 159–172.

Kasara, K., & Suryanarayan, P. (2014). When do the rich vote less than the poor and why? Explaining turnout inequality across the world. *American Journal of Political Science*, 59(3), 613–627.

Kasenally, R. (2011). Mauritius: The not so perfect democracy. *Journal of African Elections*, 10(1), 33–47.

Kasfir, N. (1974). Departicipation and political development in black African politics. *Studies in Comparative International Development (SCID)*, 9(3), 3–25.

(1976). *The Shrinking Political Arena: Participation and Ethnicity in African Politics, with a Case Study of Uganda*. University of California Press.

Kasfir, N., & Twebaze, S. H. (2009). The rise and ebb of Uganda's no-party parliament. In Joel Barkan, ed., *Legislative power in emerging African democracies*, 73–108.

Kavuma, R. M. (2016). Ugandan elections marred by shambolic polls and claims of fraud. *The Guardian*. February 22, 2016. https://www.theguardian.com/global-development/2016/feb/22/ugandan-elections-polls-fraud-yoweri-museveni.

Keefer, P. (2015). Incumbent advantage, voter information, and vote buying incumbent advantage, voter information and vote buying.

Keefer, P., & Khemani, S. (2014). Radio's impact on preferences for patronage benefits. *World Bank Policy Research*, Working Paper 6932.

Keller, E. J. (2014). *Identity, Citizenship, and Political Conflict in Africa*. Bloomington: Indiana University Press.

Kelly, C. (2018). Party proliferation and trajectories of opposition in Africa, *Comparative Politics*, 50(2), 1–21.

Kelly, C. L. (2015). *Why (the Proliferation) Parties? Competitive Authoritarianism and Party Building in Senegal*. Unpublished manuscript, Washington University of St. Louis.

Kelsall, T. (2008). Going with the grain in African development? *Development Policy Review*, 26(6), 627–655.

(2013a). *Business, Politics, and the State in Africa: Challenging the Orthodoxies on Growth and Transformation*. Zed Books.

(2013b). Economic growth and political succession: A study of two regions. *Developmental Regimes in Africa*, Working Paper.

Kendhammer, B. (2013). The sharia controversy in northern Nigeria and the politics of Islamic law in new and uncertain democracies. *Comparative Politics*, 45(3), 291–311.

(2016). *Muslims Talking Politics: Framing Islam, Democracy, and Law in Northern Nigeria*. University of Chicago Press.

Key, V. O. (1942). *Politics, Parties, and Pressure Groups*. Crowell.

Khan, M. (2010). *Political Settlements and the Governance of Growth-Enhancing Institutions*. London: SOAS.

(2012). Governance and growth challenges in Africa. In Akbar Noman, ed., *Good Growth and Governance in Africa: Rethinking Development Strategies*. Oxford University Press, 114–139.

(2014). Governance and Growth Challenges for Africa. In A. Noman, K. Botchwey, H. Stein, and J. E. Stiglitz eds., *Good Growth and Governance in Africa: Rethinking Development Strategies*. New York: Oxford University Press. pp. 51–79.

Kim, S. H. (2008). Testing the knowledge gap hypothesis in South Korea: Traditional news media, the Internet, and political learning. *International Journal of Public Opinion Research*, 20(2), 193–210.

King, G. (1991). Constituency service and incumbency advantage. *British Journal of Political Science*, 21(1), 119–128.

Kiwuwa, D. E. (2013). Democracy and the politics of power alternation in Africa. *Contemporary Politics*, 19(3), 262–278.

Kitschelt, H., & Kselman, D. M. (2010). The organizational foundations of democratic accountability: Organizational form and the choice of electoral linkage strategy.

Kitschelt, H., & Wilkinson, S. I. (2007). *Patrons, Clients and Policies: Patterns of Democratic Accountability and Political Competition*. Cambridge University Press.

Kjaer, A. M., & Therkildsen, Ole. (2013). Elections and landmark policies in Tanzania and Uganda. *Democratization*, 20(4), 592–614.

Klopp, J. (2000). Pilfering the public: The problem of land grabbing in contemporary Kenya. *Africa Today*, 47(1), 7–26.

Klaus, K., & Mitchell, M. I. (2015). Land grievances and the mobilization of electoral violence Evidence from Côte d'Ivoire and Kenya. *Journal of Peace Research*, 52(5), 622–635.

Koter, D. (2013). Urban and rural voting patterns in Senegal: The spatial aspects of incumbency, c. 1978–2012. *The Journal of Modern African Studies*, 51(4), 653–679.

(2016). *Beyond Ethnic Politics in Africa*. Cambridge University Press.

Krieger, M. (1994). Cameroon's democratic crossroads, 1990–4. *The Journal of Modern African Studies*, 32(4), 605–628.

Kramon, E. (2010). Vote-Buying and Political Behavior: Estimating and Explaining Vote-Buying's Effect on Turnout in Kenya. Presented at Annual Meeting of Midwest Political Science Association, Chicago.

(2016). Electoral handouts as information: Explaining unmonitored vote buying. *World Politics*, 68(3), 454–498.

Kramon, E., & Posner, D. N. (2013). Who benefits from distributive politics? How the outcome one studies affects the answer one gets. *Perspectives on Politics*, 11(2), 461–474.

(2016). Ethnic favoritism in Education in Kenya. *Quarterly Journal of Political Science*, 11(1), 1–58.

Krieger, M. (1994). Cameroon's democratic crossroads, 1990–4. *The Journal of Modern African Studies*, 32(4), 605–628.

Kriger, N. (2005). ZANU (PF) strategies in general elections, 1980–2000: Discourse and coercion. *African Affairs*, 104 (414), 1–34.

Kron, J. (2016). Yoweri Museveni, Uganda's President, Wins a Widely Criticized Election. New York Times.

Kuenzi, M. (2006). Nonformal education, political participation, and democracy: Findings from Senegal. *Political Behavior*, 28(1), 1–31.

Kuenzi, M., & Lambright, G. (2001). Party system institutionalization in 30 African countries. *Party Politics*, 7(4), 437–468.

(2005). Party systems and democratic consolidation in Africa's electoral regimes. *Party Politics*, 11, 423–446.

Kuenzi, M., & Lambright, G. M. S. (2007). Voter turnout in Africa's multiparty regimes. *Comparative Political Studies*, 40(6), 665–690.

(2011). Who votes in Africa? An examination of electoral participation in 10 African countries. *Party Politics*, 17(6), 767–799.

Kudamatsu, M. (2012). Has democratization reduced infant mortality in sub-Saharan Africa? Evidence from micro data. *Journal of the European Economic Association*, 10(6), 1294–1317.

Laitin, D. (1992). *Language Repertoires and State Construction in Africa*. Cambridge: Cambridge University Press.

Lake, D. A., & Baum, M. A. (2001). The invisible hand of democracy: Political control and the provision of public services. *Comparative Political Studies*, 34(6), 587.

Larmer, M. (2011). *Rethinking African Politics: A History of Opposition in Zambia*. Farnham: Ashgate.

Larmer, M., & Fraser, A. (2007). Of cabbages and Kɪng Cobra: populist politics and Zambia's 2006 election. *African Affairs*, 106(425), 611–637.

Larreguy, H., & Marshall, J. (2014). The effect of education on political engagement in non-consolidated democracies: Evidence from Nigeria. Working Paper.

(2017). The effect of education on civic and political engagement in nonconsolidated democracies: Evidence from Nigeria. *Review of Economics and Statistics*, 99(3), 387–401.

LeBas, A. (2011). *From Protest to Parties: Party-Building and Democratization in Africa*. Oxford: Oxford University Press.

(2013a). *From Protest to Parties: Party-Building and Democratization in Africa*. Oxford, MS: Oxford University Press.

(2013b). Violence and urban order in Nairobi, Kenya and Lagos, Nigeria. *Studies in Comparative International Development*, 48(3), 240–262.

(2016). *The Survival of Authoritarian Successor Parties in Africa: Organizational Legacies or Competitive Landscape?* Unpublished manuscript, American University.

Lehman, H. P. (2007). Deepening democracy?: Demarcation, traditional authorities, and municipal elections in South Africa. *The Social Science Journal*, 44(2), 301–317.

Lemarchand, R. (1972). Political clientelism and ethnicity in tropical Africa: Competing solidarities in nation-building. *American Political Science Review*, 66(1), 68–90.

Lemarchand, R., & Legg, K. (1972). Political clientelism and development: A preliminary analysis. *Comparative Politics*, 4(2), 149–178.

Leo, B., Morello, R., Mellon, J., Peixoto, T., & Davenport, S. T. (2015). Do mobile phone surveys work in poor countries?

Leonard, D. K. (2009). Elections and conflict in Africa: An introduction. *Journal of African Elections*, 8(1), 1–13.

Lerner, D. (1958). *The Passing of Traditional Society: Modernizing the Middle East*. New York: Free Press.

Letsa, N. W. (2015). Voting in Autocratic Elections: Explaining Who Votes and Why with Evidence from Cameroon. Presented at the *African Studies Association Conference*, November 2015.

(2017). "The people's choice": Popular (il) legitimacy in autocratic Cameroon. *The Journal of Modern African Studies*, 55(4), 647–679.

Le Vine, V. T. (1997). The fall and rise of constitutionalism in West Africa. *The Journal of Modern African Studies*, 35(2), 181–206.

Levine, V. T. (2004). *Politics in Francophone Africa*. Boulder: Lynne Rienner Publishers.

Levitsky, S., Loxton, J., Van Dyck, B., & Domínguez, J. I. eds. (2016). *Challenges of Party-Building in Latin America*. Cambridge University Press.

Levitsky, S., & Way, L. (2010). Why democracy needs a level playing field. *Journal of Democracy*, 21(1), 57–68.

(2015). The myth of democratic recession. *Journal of Democracy*, 26(1), 45–58.

Levitt, S. D., & Wolfram, C. D. (1997). Decomposing the sources of incumbency advantage in the US House. *Legislative Studies Quarterly*, 45–60.

Lewis, P. M. (2009). Rules and rents in Nigeria's National Assembly., In Joel D. Barkan, ed., *Legislative Power in Emerging African Democracies*. Boulder, CO: Lynne Rienner, 177–204.

(1994). Endgame in Nigeria? The politics of a failed democratic transition. *African Affairs*, 93(372), 323–340.

Lewis-Beck, M. S. (1990). *Economics and Elections: The Major Western Democracies*. University of Michigan Press.

Lewis-Beck, M. S., & Rice, T. W. (1982). Presidential popularity and presidential vote. *Public Opinion Quarterly*, 46(4), 534–537.

Lindberg, S. I. (2006). *Democracy and Elections in Africa*. Johns Hopkins University Press.

(2007). Institutionalization of party systems? Stability and fluidity among legislative parties in Africa's democracies. *Government and Opposition*, 42(2), 215–241.

ed. (2009). *Democratization by Elections: A New Mode of Transition*. Johns Hopkins University Press.

(2010a). 'The demand-side of political clientelism: Campaign spending in Ghana's 2008 election', APP working paper series, London: Overseas Development Institute, African Power and Politics Programme.

(2010b). What accountability pressures do MPs in Africa face and how do they respond? Evidence from Ghana. *The Journal of Modern African Studies*, 48(1), 117–142.

(2013). Have the cake and eat it: The rational voter in Africa. *Party Politics*, 19(6), 945–961.

Lindberg, S. I., & Clark, J. F. (2008). Does democratization reduce the risk of military interventions in politics in Africa? *Democratisation*, 15(1), 86–105.

Lindberg, S. I., & Morrison, M. K. (2008). Are African voters really ethnic or clientelistic? Survey evidence from Ghana. *Political Science Quarterly*, 123(1), 95–122.

Lindberg, S. I., & Morrison, M. K. C. (2005). Exploring voter alignments in Africa: Core and swing voters in Ghana. *The Journal of Modern African Studies*, 43(4), 565–586.

Lindberg, S., & Zhou, Y. (2009). Co-optation despite democratization in Ghana. In Joel D. Barkan, ed., *Legislative Power in Emerging African Democracies*. Boulder, CO: Lynne Rienner, 147–176.

Linz, J. J., & Stepan, A. C. (1996). Toward consolidated democracies. *Journal of Democracy*, 7(2), 14–33.

Lipset, S. M. (1959). Democracy and working-class authoritarianism. *American Sociological Review*, 482–501.

Lipset, S. M., & Rokkan, S. (1967). Cleavage structures, party systems, and voter alignments: An introduction. In Lipset, S. M., and Rokkan, S. eds. Party systems and voter alignments: Cross-national perspectives. Vol. 7. New York: Free press.

Little, E., & Logan, C. (2008). The Quality of Democracy and Governance in Africa: New Results from Afrobarometer Round 4: A Compendium of Public Opinion Findings from 19 African Countries, 2008. Institute for Democracy in South Africa (IDASA), 2008.

Logan, C. (2008). Rejecting the disloyal opposition? The trust gap in mass attitudes toward ruling and opposition parties inAfrica. *East Lansing: Michigan State University, Afrobarometer*, Working Paper 92.

(2009). Selected chiefs, elected councillors and hybrid democrats: Popular perspectives on the co-existence of democracy and traditional authority. *The Journal of Modern African Studies*, 47(1), 101–128.

(2010). Citizens or Subjects? How Individuals Relate to the Local State in Democratizing Africa. Presented at the *African Studies Association Annual Conference*, San Francisco.

(2013). The roots of resilience: Exploring popular support for African traditional authorities. *African Affairs*, 112(448), 353–376.

Logan, C., & Bratton, M. (2006). The political gender gap in Africa: Similar attitudes, different behaviors.

Logan, J. (2009). *Beyond the City Limits: Urban Policy and Economic Restructuring in Comparative Perspective*. Temple University Press.

Loxton, J. (2015). Authoritarian successor parties. *Journal of Democracy*, 26(3), 157–170.

Lucardi, A. (2015). Making authoritarian elections competitive: The origins of ruling party defections and opposition coalitions in competitive authoritarian regimes. Working Paper.

Lust-Okar, E. (2006). "Elections under authoritarianism: Preliminary lessons from Jordan." *Democratization* 13(3), 456–471.

Lynch, G. (2011). *I Say to You: Ethnic Politics and the Kalenjin in Kenya*. Chicago: University of Chicago Press.

Lynch, G., & Crawford, G. (2011). Democratization in Africa 1990–2010: An assessment. *Democratization*, 18(2), 275–310.

Macdonald, B. (2014). Incumbency disadvantages in African politics? Regression discontinuity evidence from Zambian elections. *Regression Discontinuity Evidence from Zambian Elections* (January 2014).

MacLean, L. M. (2011a). Exhaustion and exclusion in the African village: State legacies and non-state social welfare in Ghana and Cote d'Ivoire. *Studies in Comparative and International Development*, 46(1), 118–36.

(2011b). State retrenchment and the exercise of citizenship in Africa. *Comparative Political Studies*, 44(9), 1238–1266.

Magaloni, B. (2006). Voting for autocracy: Hegemonic party survival and its demise in Mexico.

Mainwaring, S. (1989). *Transitions to Democracy and Democratic Consolidation: Theoretical and Comparative Issues*, Vol. 130. University of Notre Dame, Helen Kellogg Institute for International Studies.

(1999). *Rethinking Party Systems in the Third Wave of Democratization: The Case of Brazil*. Stanford, CA: Stanford University Press.

Mainwaring, S., & Scully, T., eds. (1995). *Building Democratic Institutions: Party Systems in Latin America*. Stanford, CA: Stanford University Press, 1.

Mäkinen, M., & Kuira, M. W. (2008). Social media and postelection crisis in Kenya. *The International Journal of Press/Politics*, 13(3), 328–335.

Manacorda, M., & Tesei, A. (2016). Liberation technology: Mobile phones and political mobilization in Africa.

Manby, B. (2013). *Struggles for Citizenship in Africa*. London: Zed Books.

Manirakiza, D. (2010). Football amateur au Cameroun: Entre clientélisme politique et échanges mutuels. *Politique Africaine*, 2, 103–122.

Manning, C. (2005). Assessing African party systems after the third wave. *Party Politics*, 11(6), 707–727.

Mansfield, E. D., & Snyder, J. (2002). Democratic transitions, institutional strength, and war. *International Organization*, 56(2), 297–337.

Marcus, R. R., & Ratsimbaharison, A. M. (2005). Political parties in Madagascar neopatrimonial: Tools or democratic instruments? *Party Politics*, 11(4), 495–512.

Mares, I. (2015). *From Open Secrets to Secret Voting: Democratic Electoral Reforms and Voter Autonomy*. New York: Cambridge University Press.

Mares, I., & Young, L. (2016). Buying, expropriating, and stealing votes. *Annual Review of Political Science*, 19, 267–288.

Maring, G. H. (1978). Freire, Gray, and Robinson on reading. *Journal of Reading*, 21(5), 421–425.

Markakis, J. (1974). *Ethiopia: Anatomy of a Traditional Polity*. New York: Oxford University Press.

Marshall, R. (2009). *Political Spiritualties: The Pentecostal Revolution in Nigeria*. University of Chicago Press.

Masaki, T. (2016). Coups d'état and foreign aid. *World Development*, 79, 51–68.

Masaki, T., & Van de Walle, N. (2014). The impact of democracy on economic growth in sub-Saharan Africa, 1982–2012. Working Paper.

Mason, N. M., Jayne, T. S., & van de Walle, N. (2017). The political economy of fertilizer subsidy programs in Africa: Evidence from Zambia. *American Journal of Agricultural Economics*, 99(3), 705–731.

Mattes, R., & Bratton, M. (2007). Learning about democracy in Africa: Awareness, performance, and experience. *American Journal of Political Science*, 51(1), 192–217.

(2016). Do Africans still want democracy? *Afrobarometer*, Policy Paper No. 36.

Mattes, R., & Mughogho, D. (2009). The limited impacts of formal education on democratic citizenship in Africa. *Afrobarometer*, Working Paper 109.

Mattes, R., & Shenga, C. (2007). Uncritical citizenship' in a "Low-Information" society: Mozambicans in comparative perspective. *Afrobarometer*.

Maxwell, D. (1998). Delivered from the spirit of poverty? Pentecostalism, prosperity, and modernity in Zimbabwe. *Journal of Religion in Africa*, 28(3), 350–373.

Mayrargue, C. (2006). Yayi Boni, Un President Inattendu? Construction de la figure du Candidat et Dynamiques Electorales au Benin. *Politique Africaine*, 102, 155–172.

McCauley, J. F. (2012). Africa's new big man rule? Pentecostalism and patronage in Ghana. *African Affairs*, 112(446), 1–21.

McGraw, S. (2008). Managing change: Party competition in the New Ireland. *Irish Political Studies*, 23(4), 627–648.

McGuire, W. J. (1969). The nature of attitudes and attitude change, In G. Lindzey and E. Aronson eds., *The Handbook of Social Psychology*, Second edition, Vol. 3. Reading, MA: Addison-Wesley, 136–314.

McKie, K. (2012). How to be a President for Life: Party Competition and Executive Term Limit Enforcement across Sub-Saharan Africa. Working Paper presented at the *African Studies Association Conference*, Philadelphia, November 2012.

(2013). Uncertain incumbents: The politics of executive term limit adoption across sub-Saharan Africa. *ASA 2013*. Annual Meeting Paper.

(2016). Comparative *Continuismo*: Presidential term limit adherence across developing democracies, Kellogg Institute Working Paper Series, University of Notre Dame.

McGowan, P. J. (2003). African military coups d'état, 1956–2001: Frequency, trends and distribution. *The Journal of Modern African Studies*, 41(3), 339–370.

Médard, J. F. (1991). *États d'Afrique noire: formation, mécanismes et crise*. Karthala.

Melber, H. (2003). 'Namibia, Land of the Brave': Selective Memories on War and Violence Within Nation Building. *Rethinking Resistance: Revolt and Violence in African History*, 305–327.

(2010). Namibia's national assembly and presidential elections 2009: Did democracy win? *Journal of Contemporary African Studies*, 28(2), 203–214.

(2013a). Africa and the middle class (es). *Africa Spectrum*, 48(3), 111–120

(2013b). Namibia: Cultivating the liberation gospel. In Renske Doorenspleet, & Lia Nijzink, eds., *One Party Dominance in African Democracies*. Boulder, CO: Lynne Rienner, 49–72.

Michelitch, K. (2015). Does electoral competition exacerbate interethnic or interpartisan economic discrimination? Evidence from a field experiment in market price bargaining. *American Political Science Review*, 109(1), 43–61.

Michelitch, K., & Utych, S. (2018). Electoral cycle fluctuations in partisanship: Global evidence from eighty-six countries. *The Journal of Politics*, 80(2), 412–427.

(2014). Electoral cycle fluctuations in partisanship salience: Global evidence. Presented at the Annual Meeting of the European Political Science Association.

Michelitch, K., & Weghorst, K. R. (2013). *Islam, Christianity, and Attitudes Toward Women's Political Equality: Evidences from Sub-Saharan Africa*. Helen Kellogg Institute for International Studies.

Mihyo, P. B. (2003). Chama Cha Mapinduzi (CCM): A revolutionary party in transition, Tanzania. In Mohamed Salih, ed., *African Political Parties: Evolution, Institutionalism and Governance*. Pluto Press, 66–93.

Miles, W. F. S., ed. (2007). *Political Islam in West Africa*. Lynne Rienner Press.

Miller, M. K. (2015). Elections, information, and policy responsiveness in autocratic regimes. *Comparative Political Studies*, 48(6), 691–727.

Mkandawire, T. (1999). Social sciences and democracy: Debates in Africa. *African Sociological Review/Revue Africaine de Sociologie*, 3(1), 20–34.

Moehler, D. C. (2006). Participation and support for the constitution in Uganda. *Journal of Modern African Studies*, 44(2), 275–308.

(2008). *Distrusting Democrats: Outcomes of Participatory Constitution-Making*. Ann Arbor, MI: University of Michigan Press.

Moehler, D. C., & Conroy-Krutz, J. (2016). Partisan media and engagement: A field experiment in a newly liberalized system. *Political Communication*, 33(3), 414–432.

Moehler, D. C., & Lindberg, S. (2009). Narrowing the legitimacy gap: Turnovers as a cause of democratic consolidation. *Journal of Politics*, 71(4), 1448–1466.

Moehler, D. C., & Singh, N. (2011). Whose news do you trust? Explaining trust in private versus public media in Africa. *Political Research Quarterly*, 64(2), 276–292.

Moehler, D. C., & Staffan, I. L. (2009). Narrowing the legitimacy gap: Turnovers as a cause of democratic consolidation. *The Journal of Politics*, 71(4), 1448–1466.

Moestrup, S. (1999). The role of actors and institutions: The difficulties of democratic survival in Mali and Niger. *Democratization*, 6(2), 171–186.

Molomo, M. G. (2000). Understanding government and opposition parties in Botswana. *Journal of Commonwealth & Comparative Politics*, 38(1), 65–92.

Momba, J. C. (2003). Democratic transition and the crisis of an African Nationalist Party: UNIP, Zambia. In Mohamed Salih, ed., *African Political Parties: Evolution, Institutionalism and Governance*. Pluto Press, 37–65.

Monga, C. (1997). Eight problems with African politics. *Journal of Democracy*, 8(3), 156–170.

Morgenthau, R. (1963). African socialism: Declaration of ideological independence. *Africa Report*, 8(5), 3.

   (1971). Old cleavages among new West African states: The heritage of French rule. *Africa Today*, 18(2), 6–16.

Morlan, R. (1984). Municipal vs. national election voter turnout: Europe and the United States. *Political Science Quarterly*, 99(3), 457–470.

Morrison, K. M. (2014). *Nontaxation and Representation*. Cambridge University Press. Morrison 2013: date should be 2014

Morse, Y. L. (2011). In the Shadow of the Party: Electoral Hegemony in Modern Day Tanzania.

   (2014). Party matters: The institutional origins of competitive hegemony in Tanzania. *Democratization*, 21(4), 655–677.

   (2015). From single-party to electoral authoritarian regimes: The institutional origins of competitiveness in post-Cold War Africa. *Comparative Politics*, 48(1), 126–151.

Moss, T. J., Pettersson Gelander, G., & Van de Walle, N. (2008). An aid-institutions paradox? A review essay on aid dependency and state building in sub-Saharan Africa. In Easterly, W. eds., *Reinventing Foreign Aid* (Vol. 1). Boston: The MIT Press, 255–282.

Motlogelwa, T. (2009). The symbolism of Khama in Naledi. *Mmegi Online*. Accessed September 12, 2016. www.mmegi.bw/index.php?sid=6&aid=198&dir=2009/October/Friday23

Mozaffar, S., &. Scarritt, J. R. (2005). The puzzle of African party systems. *Party Politics*, 11(4), 399–421.

Mozaffar, S., Scarrit, J. R., & Galaich, G. (2003). Electoral institutions, ethnopolitical cleavages, and party systems in Africa's emerging democracies. *American Political Science Review*, 97(3), 379–390.

Mueller, L. (2013). Democratic revolutionaries or pocketbook protesters? The roots of the 2009–2010 uprisings in Niger. *African Affairs*, 112(448), 398–420.

   (2018). Personal politics without clientelism? Interpreting citizen-politician contact in Africa. *African Studies Review*, 61(2), 28–54.

   (2018). *Political Protest in Contemporary Africa*. New York, NY: Cambridge University Press.

Muriaas, R. L., & Wang, V. (2012). Executive dominance and the politics of quota representation in Uganda. *The Journal of Modern African Studies*, 50(2), 309–338.

Mwanawasa, C-M, Hamukoma, N., and McNamee, T. (2017). *Elections in Africa: Preparing a democratic playbook*. The Brenthurst Foundation, Johannesburg, South Africa.

Ndletyana, M. (2007). Muncipal elections 2006: Protests, independent candidates, and cross-border municipalities. In Sakhela Buhlungu, John Daniel, & Roger Southall, eds., *State of the Nation: South Africa 2007*. HSRC Press.

Ngayap, P. (1983). *Cameroun, qui gouverne?: De Ahidjo à Biya: l'héritage et l'enjeu*. Editions L'Harmattan.

Ngoitiko, M., Sinandei, M., Meitaya, P., & Nelson, F. (2010). Pastoral activists: Negotiating power imbalances in the Tanzanian Serengeti. In Nelson, F., ed., *Community Rights, Conservation and Contested Land: The Politics of Natural Resource Governance in Africa*, 269.

Ngayap, P. F. (1999). *L'opposition au Cameroun: les années de braise: villes mortes et Tripartite*. Editions L'Harmattan.

Nichter, S. (2008). Vote buying or turnout buying? Machine politics and the secret ballot. *American Political Science Review*, 102(1), 19–31.

Nie, N., Junn, J., & Barry, K. S. (1996). *Education and Democratic Citizenship in America*. Chicago, IL: University of Chicago Press.

Ninsin, K. A. (1991). *The Informal Sector in Ghana's Political Economy*. Middlebury: Freedom Publications.

(1993). Some problems in Ghana's transition to democratic governance. *Africa Development/Afrique et Développement*, 5–22.

Noman, A. (2012). *Good Growth and Governance in Africa: Rethinking Development Strategies*. Oxford University Press.

Noman, A., Botchwey, K., Stiglitz, J. & Stein, H. (2012). *Good growth and governance in Africa: Rethinking development strategies*. New York: Oxford University Press.

Nordhaus, W. D. (1975). The political business cycle. *The Review of Economic Studies*, 42(2), 169–190.

North, D. C., Wallis, J. J., Webb, S. B., & Weingast, B. R. eds. (2013). *In the Shadow of Violence: Politics, Economics, and the Problems of Development*. Cambridge University Press.

North, D. C., Wallis, J. J., & Weingast, B. R. (2009). *Violence and Social Orders: A Conceptual Framework for Interpreting Recorded Human History*. New York Cambridge University Press.

Nugent, P. (2001). Winners, losers and also rans: Money, moral authority and voting patterns in the Ghana 2000 elections. *African Affairs*, 100, 405–428.

(2007). Banknotes and symbolic capital. In Matthias Basedau, Gero Erdmann, & Andreas Mehler, eds., *Votes, Money and Violence: Political Parties and Elections in Sub Saharan Africa*. Sweden: Nordiska Afrikainstitutet, 252–275.

Nuvunga, A., & Adalima, J. (2011). *Mozambique Democratic Movement (MDM): An Analysis of a New Opposition Party in Mozambique. Studies on Political Parties and Democracies*. Friedrich Ebert Stiftung.

Nyerere, J. K. (1967). *Freedom and unity: Uhuru na umoja; a selection from writings and speeches, 1952–65.* London; Nairobi [etc.]: Oxford University Press.

Nyong'o, P. A., ed. (1987). *Popular Struggles for Democracy in Africa.* Tokyo, Japan: United Nations University; Atlantic Highlands, NJ: Zed Books.

Obeng-Odoom, F. (2013). The nature of ideology in Ghana's 2012 elections. *Journal of African Elections: Ghana's 2012 Elections,* 12(2), 75–95.

O'Donnell, G., Schmitter, P. C. and Whitehead, L. eds. (1986). *Transitions from Authoritarian Rule: comparative perspectives,* vol. 3. Johns Hopkins University Press.

Olken, B. A. (2009). Do television and radio destroy social capital? Evidence from Indonesian villages. *American Economic Journal: Applied Economics,* 1(4), 1–33.

  (2010). Direct democracy and local public goods: Evidence from a field experiment in Indonesia. *American Political Science Review,* 104(2), 243–267.

Omgba, L. D. (2009). On the duration of political power in Africa: The role of oil rents. *Comparative Political Studies,* 42(3), 416–436.

Opalo, K. O. (2012). African elections: Two divergent trends. *Journal of Democracy* 23(3), 80–93.

  (2014). The long road to institutionalization: The Kenyan parliament and the 2013 elections. *Journal of Eastern African Studies,* 8(1), 63–77.

  (2015). *Institutions and Political Change: The Case of African Legislatures.* Doctoral Dissertation, Stanford University.

  (2017a). Institutional origins of incumbency advantage: Evidence from legislative elections.

  (2017b). Legislative Independence and Incumbent Electoral Advantage: Evidence from Parliamentary Elections in Kenya (December 20, 2017). Available at SSRN: https://ssrn.com/abstract=2906382 or http://dx.doi.org/10.2139/ssrn.2906382

Osei, A. (2012). *Party-Voter Linkage in Africa: Ghana and Senegal in Comparative Perspective.* Springer Science & Business Media.

  (2015). Elites and democracy in Ghana: A social network approach. *African Affairs (London),* 114(457), 529–554.

  (2016). Formal party organisation and informal relations in African parties: Evidence from Ghana. *The Journal of Modern African Studies,* 54(1), 37–66.

Osei-Hwedie, B. Z. (2013). 10 The quest for gender parity in southern African politics. *Regime Change and Succession Politics in Africa: Five Decades of Misrule,* 9, 157.

Paget, D. (2017a). Dancers, branches, stereos and choppers: Party finance and capital-intensive campaigning in Tanzania. Working Paper Presented at the African Studies Association Chicago, November 2017.

  (2017b). Tanzania: Shrinking space and opposition protest. *Journal of Democracy,* 28(3), 153–167.

Paller, J. W. (2014a). African Slums: Constructing Democracy in Unexpected Places. PhD diss., University of Wisconsin-Madison.

  (2014b). Informal institutions and personal rule in urban Ghana. *African Studies Review,* 57(3), 123–142.

Pande, R. (2011). Can informed voters enforce better governance? Experiments in low-income democracies. *Annual Review of Economics,* 3, 215–237.

Panebianco, A. (1988). *Political Parties: Organization and Power*. Cambridge University Press.

Peters, P. (2004). Inequality and social conflict over land in Africa. *Journal of Agrarian Change*, 4(3), 269–314.

Petrocik, J. R. (1996). Issue ownership in presidential elections, with a 1980 case study. *American Journal of Political Science*, 40(3), 825–850.

Pfeiffer, C., & Englebert, P. (2012). Extraversion, vulnerability to donors, and political liberalization in Africa. *African Affairs*, 111(444), 355–378.

Pigeaud, F. (2011). *Au Cameroun de Paul Biya*. KARTHALA Editions.

Pitcher, M. A. (2012). *Party Politics and Economic Reform in Africa's Democracies*. Cambridge University Press.

(2017). Party system competition and private sector development in Africa. *The Journal of Development Studies*, 53(1), 1–17.

Posner, D. (2004). Measuring ethnic fractionalization in Africa. *American Journal of Political Science*, 48(4), 849–863.

(2005). *Institutions and Ethnic Politics in Africa*. Cambridge: Cambridge University Press.

Posner, D. N., & Simon, R. J. (2002). Economic conditions and incumbent support in Africa's new democracies: Evidence from Zambia. *Comparative Political Studies*, 35(3), 313–336.

Posner, D. N., & Young, D. J. (2007). The institutionalization of political power in Africa. *Journal of Democracy*, 18(3), 126–140.

Poteete, A. R., & Ribot, J. C. (2011). Repertoires of domination: decentralization as process in Botswana and Senegal. *World Development*, 39(3), 439–449.

Pottie, D. (2003). Party finance and the politics of money in southern Africa. *Journal of Contemporary African Studies*, 21, 5–28.

Prat, A., & Strömberg, D. (2005). Commercial television and voter information. Working Paper: www.gsb.columbia.edu/faculty/aprat/papers/statetv.pdf

Prempeh, H. K. (2007). Presidential power in comparative perspective: The puzzling persistence of imperial presidency in post-authoritarian Africa. *Hastings Constitutional Law Quarterly*, 35, 761.

Prior, M. (2005). News vs. entertainment: How increasing media choice widens gaps in political knowledge and turnout. American Journal of Political Science, 49(3), 577–592.

Przeworski, A. (2015). Acquiring the habit of changing governments through elections. *Comparative Political Studies*, 48(1), 101–129.

Przeworski, A., Cheibub, J. A., Limongi Neto, F. P., & Alvarez, M. M., et al. (1996). What makes democracies endure? *Journal of Democracy*, 7(1), 39–55.

Puddington, A., & Roylance, T. (2017). The dual threat of populists and autocrats. *Journal of Democracy*, 28(2), 105–119.

Quantin, P. (1995). Les élites politiques face aux transitions démocratiques. *L'Afrique Politique*, 2, 277–285.

(1997). Congo: Transition démocratique et conjoncture critique. In Jean Pacal Daloz, & Patrick Quantin, eds., *Transitions démocratiques africaines: Dynamiques et contraintes (1990–1994)*. Paris: Karthala, 139–191.

Radelet, S. C. (2010). *Emerging Africa: How Seventeen Countries Are Leading the Way*. CGD Books.

Rakner, L., & van de Walle, N. (2007). Opposition parties in sub-Saharan Africa. In Siri Gloppen and Lise Rakner eds. *Globalization and Democratization: Challenges for Political Parties.* Oslo: Fagbokforlaget, 91–110.

(2009). Opposition weakness in Africa. *Journal of Democracy*, 20(3), 108–121.

Randall, V., & Svåsand, L. (2002). Political parties and democratic consolidation in Africa. *Democratization*, 9(3), 30–52.

Ranger, T. (2004). Nationalist historiography, patriotic history and the history of the nation: The struggle over the past in Zimbabwe. *Journal of Southern African Studies*, 30(2), 215–234.

Ranger, T. O., ed. (2008). *Evangelical Christianity and Democracy in Africa.* Oxford University Press.

Rauschenbach, M. (2015). *The Importance of Preaching to the Converted: The Strategic Use of Campaign Rallies, Campaign Promises, Clientelism, and Violence in African Elections.* PhD Dissertation, University of Mannheim.

(2017). Mobilizing Party Supporters: The Allocation of Campaign Rallies in Ghana's 2012 Elections. Presented at the *African Studies Association Conference*, Chicago, November 2017.

Rawlence, B., & Albin-Lackey, C. (2007). Briefing: Nigeria's 2007 general elections: Democracy in retreat. *African Affairs*, 106(424), 497–506.

Resnick, D. (2012). Opposition parties and the urban poor in African democracies. *Comparative Political Studies*, 45(11), 1351–1378.

(2013a). Do electoral coalitions facilitate democratic consolidation in Africa?. *Party Politics*, 19(5), 735–757.

(2013b). Continuity and change in Senegalese party politics: Lessons from the 2012 elections. *African Affairs*, 112(449), 623–645.

(2014). *Urban Poverty and Party Populism in African Democracies.* Cambridge University Press.

(2015). Varieties of African populism in the comparative perspective. In Carlos de la Torre, ed., *The Promise and Perils of Populism: Global Perspectives.* Lexington: University of Kentucky Press, 317–348.

(2017). Democracy, decentralization, and district proliferation: The case of Ghana. *Political Geography*, 59, 47–60.

Resnick, D., & Casale, D. (2011). The political participation of Africa's youth turnout, partisanship, and protest. *World* (136). Working Paper No. 2011/56.

Resnick, D., & van de Walle, N. (2013). *Democratic Trajectories in Africa Unravelling the Impact of Foreign Aid.* Oxford: Oxford University Press.

Resnick, D., & Casale, D. (2014). Young populations in young democracies: Generational voting behaviour in sub-Saharan Africa. *Democratization*, 21(6), 1172–1194.

Reynolds, A., & Steenbergen, M. (2006). How the world votes: The political consequences of ballot design, innovation and manipulation. *Electoral Studies*, 25(3), 570–598.

Reyntjens, F. (2016). Reimagining a reluctant post-genocide society: The Rwandan Patriotic Front's ideology and practice. *Journal of Genocide Research*, 18(1), 61–81.

Ribot, J. C. (2003). Democratic decentralisation of natural resources: Institutional choice and discretionary power transfers in sub-Saharan Africa. *Public Administration and Development*, 23(1), 53–65.

Riedl, R. B. (2012). Transforming politics, dynamic religion: Religion's political impact in contemporary Africa. *African Conflict & Peacebuilding Review*, 2(2), 29–50.

(2014). *Authoritarian Origins of Democratic Party Systems in Africa*. Cambridge University Press.

Riedl, R. B., & Dickovick, J. T. (2014). Party systems and decentralization in Africa. *Studies in Comparative International Development*, 49(3), 321–142.

Riedl, R. B., & McClendon, G. (2015). Religion as a stimulant of political participation: Evidence from an experiment in Nairobi, Kenya. *Journal of Politics*, 77(4), 1045–1057.

Rihoy, L., & Maguranyanga, B. (2010). The politics of community-based natural resource management in Botswana. In Fred Nelson eds. *Community Rights, Conservation and Contested Land: The Politics of Natural Resource Governance in Africa*. London: Earthscan, 55–78.

Riker, W. (1986). *The Art of Political Manipulation*. New Haven, CT: Yale University Press.

Riker, W. H., & Peter, C. O. (1968) A theory of the calculus of voting. *American Political Science Review*, 62(1), 25–42.

Roberts, T. (2015). 5 things you should know about Guinea's (peaceful!) election. In *The Monkey Cage* website. https://www.washingtonpost.com/news/monkey-cage/wp/2015/10/20/5-things-you-should-know-about-guineas-peaceful-election/?utm_term=.4d27279a736e

Robinson, A. (2016). Nationalism and ethnic-based trust: Evidence from an African border region. *Comparative Political Studies*, 49(14), 1819–1854.

Rogers, E. M., & F. Floyd. (1971). *Communication of Innovations*. New York: The Free Press.

Rood, L. (1976). Nationalisation and indigenisation in Africa. *Journal of Modern African Studies*, 14, 427–447.

Rosenstone, S. J., & Hansen, J. M. (1993). *Mobilization, Participation, and Democracy in America*. New York, NY: Macmillan.

Rosenzweig, S. (2015). Does electoral competition affect public goods provision in dominant-party regimes? Evidence from Tanzania. *Electoral Studies*, 39, 72–84.

Ross, M. L. (2001). Does oil hinder democracy? *World Politics*, 53(3), 325–361.

Rothchild, D. (1985). State-ethnic relations in middle Africa. In Gwendolyn Carter, & Patrick O'Meara, eds., *African Independence: The First 25 Years*. University of Indiana Press, 71–96.

Roubaud, F. (2003). La crise vue d'en bas à Abidjan: Ethnicité, gouvernance et démocratie. *Afrique Contemporaine*, 206, 57–86.

Sabatier, P. (1978). Elite' Education in French West Africa: The Era of Limits, 1903–1945. *International Journal of African Historical Studies*, 11(2), 247–266.

Sahn, D. E., & Stifel, D. C. (2003). Urban–rural inequality in living standards in Africa. *Journal of African Economies*, 12(4), 564–597.

Saine, A. S., N'Daiye, B., & Houngnikpo, M. C. (2011). *Elections and Democratization in West Africa, 1990–2009*. Trenton: Africa World Press.

Salih, M., ed. (2003). *African Political Parties: Evolution, Institutionalism and Governance*. Pluto Press.

ed. (2005). *African Parliaments: Between Governance and Government*. Berlin: Springer.

Samuels, D., & Snyder, R. (2001). The value of a vote: Malapportionment in comparative perspective. *British Journal of Political Science*, 31(4), 651–671.

Sartori, G. (1976). *Party and Party Systems. A Framework for Analysis*. Cambridge: Cambridge University Press.

Scacco, A. (2010). Who riots? Explaining individual participation in ethnic violence. New York: PhD Dissertation. Columbia University.

(2005). *Parties and Party Systems: A Framework for Analysis*. ECPR press.

Schaffer, F. C. (2000). *Democracy in Translation: Understanding Politics in an Unfamiliar Culture*. Cornell University Press.

ed. (2007). *Elections for Sale: The Causes and Consequences of Vote Buying*. Boulder, CO: Lynne Rienner Publishers.

Schatzberg, M. G. (2001). *Political Legitimacy in Middle Africa: Father, Family, Food*. Indiana University Press.

Schedler, A. (1998). What is democratic consolidation? *Journal of Democracy*, 9(2), 91–107.

(2002). The menu of manipulation. *Journal of Democracy*, 13(2), 36–50.

(2006). *Electoral Authoritarianism: The Dynamics of Unfree Competition*. Boulder, CO: Lynne Rienner.

(2013). *The Politics of Uncertainty: Sustaining and Subverting Electoral Authoritarianism*. Oxford: Oxford University Press.

Scheufele, D. A., & Matthew, C. N. (2002). Being a citizen online: New opportunities and dead ends. *Harvard International Journal of Press/Politics*, 7(3), 55–75.

Schmitter, P. C., & Karl, T. L. (1991). What democracy is … and is not. *Journal of democracy*, 2(3), 75–88.

Seely, J. C. (2005). The legacies of transition governments: Post-transition dynamics in Benin and Togo. *Democratization*, 12(3), 357–377.

Shefter, M. (1993). *Political Parties and the State: The American Historical Experience*. Princeton: Princeton University Press.

Sklar, R. L. (1963). *Nigerian Political Parties. Power in an Emergent African Nation*. Princeton, NJ: Princeton University Press.

(1965). Contradictions in the Nigerian political system. *The Journal of Modern African Studies*, 3(2), 201–213.

(1979). The nature of class domination in Africa. *The Journal of Modern African Studies*, 17(4), 531–552.

(1988). Beyond capitalism and socialism in Africa. *The Journal of Modern African Studies*, 26(1), 1–21.

Slater, D., & Simmons, E. (2013). Coping by colluding: Political uncertainty and promiscuous powersharing in Indonesia and Bolivia. *Comparative Political Studies*, 46(11), 1366–1393.

Slater, R. (2011). Cash transfers, social protection and poverty reduction. *International Journal of Social Welfare*, 20(3), 250–259.

Smith, L. (2013). *Making Citizens in Africa: Ethnicity, Gender, and National Identity in Ethiopia. No. 125.* Cambridge University Press.

Snyder Jr, J. M., & Strömberg, D. (2010). Press coverage and political accountability. *Journal of political Economy*, 118(2), 355–408.

Soares, B. F. (2009). The attempt to reform family law in Mali. *Die Welt des Islams*, 49(3–4), 398–428.

Souaré, I. K. (2017). Explaining the mixed fortunes of African opposition parties in their quest for state power: An institutional and strategic analysis. In Said Adejumobi. eds., *Voice and Power in Africa's Democracy*. New York: Routledge. 97–116.

Southall, R. (2006). Troubled visionary: Nyerere as a former president. In R. Southall and H. Melber eds., *Legacies of power. Leadership Change and Former Presidents in Africa Politics*. Uppsala, Sweden: The Nordic Africa Institute.

Stasavage, D. (2005). Democracy and education spending in Africa. *American Journal of Political Science*, 49(2), 343–358.

Stinchcombe, A. L. and J. G. March. (1965). Social structure and organizations. In and J. G. March, ed., Handbook of Organizations, 7, 142–193.

Stokes, D. E. (1963). Spatial models of party competition. *The American Political Science Review*. 57(2), 368–377.

Stokes, E. (1966). *Malawi Political Systems and the Introduction of Colonial Rule, 1891–1896. The Zambesian Past: Studies in Central African History*. Manchester.

Stokes, S. C., Dunning, T., Nazareno, M., & Brusco, V. (2013). *Brokers, Voters, and Clientelism: The Puzzle of Distributive Politics*. Cambridge University Press.

Stone, W. J., & Simas, E. N. (2010). Candidate valence and ideological positions in US House elections. *American Journal of Political Science*, 54(2), 371–388.

Straus, S. (2015). *Making and Unmaking Nations: War, Leadership, and Genocide in Modern Africa*. Cornell University Press.

Straus, S., & Taylor, C. (2012). Democratization and electoral Violence in sub-Saharan Africa, 1990–2008. In D. A. O. Bekoe, *Voting in fear: electoral violence in Sub-Saharan Africa*. Washington, DC: United states Institute of Peace. 15–38.

Stroh, A. (2010). The power of proximity: A concept of political party strategies applied to Burkina Faso. *Journal of Contemporary African Studies*, 28(1), 1–29.

Svasand, L. (2015). Political parties: Fragmentation and consolidation, Change and Stability. InN. Patel, M. Wahman eds., *The Malawi 2014 Tripartite Elections: Is Democracy Maturing*. Lilongwe: National Initiative for Civic Education, 86–103.

Svolik, M. W. (2012). The politics of authoritarian rule. Cambridge: Cambridge University Press.

Szeftel, M. (1998). Misunderstanding African politics: Corruption & the governance agenda. *Review of African Political Economy*, 25(76), 221–240.

Teorell, J., & Wahman, M. (2017). Institutional stepping stones for democracy: How and why multipartyism enhances democratic change. *Democratization*, 1–20.

Tendi, B. M. (2010). *Making History in Mugabe's Zimbabwe: Politics, Intellectuals and the Media*. New York, NY: Peter Lang.

Teorell, J., & Hadenius, A. (2009). Elections as levers of democracy: A global inquiry. *Democratization by Elections: A New Mode of Transition*, 77–100.

Themnér, A., ed. (2017). *Warlord Democrats in Africa: Ex-Military Leaders and Electoral Politics*. London: Zed Books.

(2004). "La consolidation des régimes post-transition en Afrique: le rôle des commissions électorales nationales." In Voter en Afrique: Comparaisons et differentiations, ed. P. Quantin. Paris: L'Harmattan, 129–47.

Thiriot, C. (1999). Sur Un Renouvellement Relatif des Elites au Mali. In J.-P. Daloz ed., *Le (Non-) Renouvellement Des Elites en Afrique Subsaharienne*. Bordeaux: Centre D'Etude d'Afrique Noire, 135–54.

Throup, D., & Hornsby, C. (1998). *Multi-Party Politics in Kenya: The Kenyatta & Moi States & the Triumph of the System in the 1992 Election*. Ohio University Press.

Tilly, C., & Tarrow, S. (2006). *Contentious Politics*. Boulder, CO: Paradigm.

Toulabor, C. M. (1986). *Le Togo sous Eyadéma*. Paris: Karthala Editions.

Tower, C. (2008). *Radio Ways: Society, Locality, and FM Technology in Koutiala, Mali*. PhD Dissertation. Northwestern University.

Trease, H. V. (2005). The operation of the single non-transferable vote system in Vanuatu. *Comparative and Commonwealth Studies*, 43(3), 296–332.

Tripp, A. M. (2015). *Women and Power in Post-Conflict Africa*. Cambridge University Press.

(2017). In pursuit of autonomy: Civil society and the state in Africa. In John Harberson, & Donald Rothchild, eds., Africa in World Politics: Constructing Political and Economic Order.

Tripp, A., & Kang, A. (2008). The global impact of electoral quotas: The fast track to increased legislative female representation. *Comparative Political Studies* 41(338).

Uppal, Y. (2009). The disadvantaged incumbents: Estimating incumbency effects in Indian state legislatures. *Public Choice*, 138(1), 9–27.

Van Cranenburgh, O. (2007). Big Men' Rule: Presidential power, regime type and democracy in 30 African countries. *Democratization*, 15(5), 952–973.

Van Eerd, J. (2017). *The Quality of Democracy in Africa: Opposition Competitiveness Rooted in Legacies of Cleavages*. Berlin: Springer.

Van Ham, C., & Lindberg, S. I. (2015). From sticks to carrots: Electoral manipulation in Africa, 1986–2012. *Government and Opposition*, 50(3), 521–548.

van Klinken, A. (2014). Homosexuality, politics and Pentecostal nationalism in Zambia. *Studies in World Christianity*, 20(3), 259–281.

van de Walle, N. (2001). *African Economies and the Politics of Permanent Crisis, 1979–1999*. Cambridge University Press.

(2003). Presidentialism and clientelism in Africa's emerging party systems. *Journal of Modern African Studies*, 41(2), 297–321.

(2006). Tipping games: When do opposition parties coalesce? In Andreas Schedler ed. *Electoral Authoritarianism: The Dynamics of Unfree Competition*, 77–94.

(2007). Meet the new boss, same as the old boss? The evolution of political clientelism in Africa. In Herbert Kitschelt, & Steve I. Wilkinson, eds., *Patrons, Clients, and Policies: Patterns of Democratic Accountability and Political Competition*. Cambridge: Cambridge University Press.

(2009). US policy towards Africa: The Bush legacy and the Obama administration. *African Affairs*, 109(434), 1–21.

(2016). Democracy fatigue and the ghost of modernization theory. In Filip Reyntjens, & Tobias Hagmann, eds., *Development without Democracy: Foreign Aid and Authoritarian Regimes in Africa*. London, Zed Books.

van de Walle, N., & Butler, K. (1999). Political parties and party systems in Africa's illiberal democracies. *Cambridge Review of International Affairs*, 12, 14–28.

Vicente, P. C. (2014). Is vote buying effective? Evidence from a field experiment in West Africa. *The Economic Journal*, 124(574), F356–F387.

Vicente, P. C., & Wantchekon, L. (2009). Clientelism and vote buying: Lessons from field experiments in African elections. *Oxford Review of Economic Policy*, 25(2), 292–305.

Verba, S., Scholzman, K., & Brady, H. (1995). *Voice and Equality: Civic Voluntarism in American Politics*. Cambridge: Harvard University Press.

Villalón, L. A. (1995). *Islamic Society and State Power in Senegal*. Cambridge: Cambridge University Press.

(2010). From argument to negotiation: Constructing democracy in African Muslim contexts. *Comparative Politics*, 42(4), 375–93.

Wahman, M. (2017). Nationalized incumbents and regional challengers: Opposition-and incumbent-party nationalization in Africa. *Party Politics*, 23(3), 309–322.

Wahman, M., & Boone, C. (2018). Captured countryside? Stability and change in sub-national support for African incumbent parties. Comparative Politics, 50(2), 189–216.

Wallsworth, G. (2015). Electoral violence: An empirical examination of existing theories.

Wanjohi, N. (2003). Sustainability of political parties in Kenya. In Mohamed Salih, ed., *African Political Parties: Evolution, Institutionalism and Governance*. Pluto Press, 239–258.

Wantchekon, L. (2003). Clientelism and voting behavior: Evidence from a field experiment in Benin. *World politics*, 55(3), 399–422.

Wantchekon, L., Novta, N., & Klašnja, M. (2013). Education and human capital externalities: Evidence from colonial Benin. Working Paper.

Weghorst, K. (2015). *Losing the Battle, Winning the War: Legislative Candidacy in Electoral Authoritarian Regimes*. PhD Dissertation, University of Florida, Department of Political Science.

(2017). *Activist Origins of Political Ambition: Opposition Candidacy in Electoral Authoritarian Regimes*. Unpublished manuscript, Vanderbilt University.

Weghorst, K. R., & Bernhard, M. (2014). From formlessness to structure? The institutionalization of competitive party systems in Africa. *Comparative Political Studies*, 47(12), 1707–1737.

Weghorst, K. R., & Lindberg, S. I. (2011). Effective opposition strategies: Collective goods or clientelism? *Democratization*, 18(5), 1193–1214.

(2013). What drives the swing voter in Africa? *American Journal of Political Science*, 57(3), 717–734.

Weylandt, M. (2015). The 2014 National Assembly and presidential elections in Namibia. *Electoral Studies*, 38, 82–136.

Whitaker, B. E. (2005). Citizens and foreigners: Democratization and the politics of exclusion in Africa. *African Studies Review*, 48(1), 109–126.

(2015). Playing the immigration card: The politics of exclusion in Côte d'Ivoire and Ghana, *Commonwealth & Comparative Politics*, 53(3), 274–293.

Whitaker, C. S. (1970). *The Politics of Tradition: Continuity and Change in Northern Nigeria, 1946–1966*. Princeton, NJ: Princeton University Press.

Whitehead, R. L. (2009). *Single-Party Rule in a Multiparty Age: Tanzania in Comparative Perspective*. Philadelphia: Temple University.

Whitfield, L. (2009). Change for a better Ghana: Party competition, institutionalization and alternation in Ghana's 2008 elections. *African Affairs*, 108(433), 621–641.

Widner, J. A. (1993). *The Rise of a Party-State in Kenya: From "Harambee!" to "Nyayo!"*. University of California Press.

Wilfahrt, M. (2015). *The Historic Origins of Public Goods: Local Distributional Politics in Rural West Africa, 1880–Present*. Working Paper. PhD Dissertation, Department of Government, Cornell University.

Willis, J., & al-Batthani, A. (2010). We changed the laws: Electoral practice and malpractice in Sudan since 1953. *African Affairs.*, 109(435), 191–212.

Wilson, E. J. (1990). Strategies of state control of the economy: Nationalization and indigenization in Africa. *Comparative Politics*, 22(4), 401–419.

Wing, S. (2012). Women's rights and family law reform in Francophone Africa. In Ellen M. Lust, & Stephen N. Ndegwa, eds., *Governing Africa's Changing Societies: Dynamics of Reform*. Boulder, CO: Lynne Rienner Publishers.

Wiseman, J. (1986). Urban riots in West Africa, 1977–85. *The Journal of Modern African Studies*, 24(3), 509–518.

Wiseman, J. A., ed. (1995). *Democracy and Political Change in Sub-Saharan Africa*. Psychology Press.

Wittmann, F., & Thiam, B. (2006). Deficient democracies, media pluralism and political advertising in West Africa. *The Sage Handbook of Political Advertising*, 417–428.

Yates, D. A. (1996). *The Rentier State in Africa: Oil Rent Dependency and Neocolonialism in the Republic of Gabon*. Africa World Press.

Youde, J. (2005). Economics and government popularity in Ghana. *Electoral Studies*, 24(1), 1–16.

Young, C. (2004). The end of the post-colonial state in Africa? Reflections on changing African political dynamics. *African Affairs*, 103, 23–49.

Young, L. (2015). Mobilization under threat: An experimental test of opposition party strategies in a repressive regime. Working Paper.

Young, T. (1993). Elections and electoral politics in Africa. *Journal of the International African Institute*, 63(3), 299–312.

Zimmerman, B. (2015). Voter response to scandal: Cashgate. In N. Patel and M. Wahman, eds., *The Malawi 2014: Tripartite Elections: Is Democracy Maturing?*. Lliongwe: The National Initiative for Civic Education (NICE).

Zolberg, A. R. (1966). *Creating Political Order: The Party-States of West Africa.* Chicago, IL: Rand McNally.

(1969). *One-Party Government in the Ivory Coast.* Princeton, NJ: Princeton University Press.

Other

Attiah, Karen. (2017). Rwanda loves to boast about women's empowerment, yet keeps arresting female presidential aspirants. *The Washington Post,* October, 25, 2017: https://www.washingtonpost.com/news/global-opinions/wp/2017/10/25/paul-kagames-senseless-war-against-one-woman/?noredirect=on&utm_term=.251c0c11b7df

An Arresting Event, (2016). *Africa Confidential* Vol 57 No 4, February 19, 2016: https://www.africa-confidential.com/article-preview/id/11512/An_arresting_event

How the next election will be won, (2016a). *Africa Confidential* 57 (3). February 5 2016: https://www.africa-confidential.com/article/id/11476/How_the_next_election_will_be_won

Protest grows over Museveni win (2016b). Volume 57 No 5, February 22, 2016: https://www.africa-confidential.com/articlepreview/id/11518/Protest_grows_over_Museveni_win

Democrats Under Fire. *Africa Confidential.* April 29, 2016.

Cendrowicz, Leo. (2013). Robert Mugabe's Zimbabwe election victory was a 'masterclass in electoral fraud' *The Independent* August 2, 2013: https://www.independent.co.uk/news/world/africa/robert-mugabes-zimbabwe-election-victory-was-a-masterclass-in-electoral-fraud-8744348.html

Outlook, Regional Economic. Sub-Saharan Africa. *IMF,* October (2015).

Nigeria: Presidential Election Marred by Fraud, Violence. (2007) *Human Rights Watch* April 25, 2007: https://www.hrw.org/news/2007/04/25/nigeria-presidential-election-marred-fraud-violence

UN Habitat Annual Report (2010). Eds Roman Rollnick andThierry Naudin. 2011. Nairobi: United Nations Human Settlements Programme.

Periodicals

Bongo's Incredible Win. *Africa Confidential.* September 9, 2016. Vol. 57, no. 18.

Immanuel, S. (2014). The land of the chosen few. The Namibian, 3 (Windhoek).

Tjihenuna, T., Kahiurika, N., Haidula, T., 2014, August 28. "Struggle kids" shot ... Police claim retaliation. Namibian Windhoek. Retrieved January 1, 2015, from www.namibian.com.na/indexx.php?archive_id1/4127312&page_type1/4archive_story_detail&page1/43

Muraranganda, E., 2014. Mbumba apologises for "peasants" remark. Sun November 24, Windhoek. Retrieved January 3, 2015, from www.sun.com.na/politics/mbumba-apologises-for-peasants-remark. 73812.

Policy Reports

Migration Policy Institute. The Ghanaian Diaspora in the United States, 2015, from www.migrationpolicy.org/sites/default/files/publications/RAD-Ghana.pdf

The World Bank. *Poverty in a Rising Africa*. The World Bank, Washington, DC, 2016.

The Economist (2016). Africa's Fragile Democracies: Political reform Stalls. pp. 10, 37–39.

The Economist. The Coup in Burkina Faso Follows the Usual script. September 18, 2015.

The Economist. Democracy in Africa: Stronger than you think. January 12, 2002, 15.

The Economist. The Democracy Bug is Fitfully Catching on. July 24, 2010, p. 45.

The Economist. China in Africa: One among many. January 17, 2015.

IMF, Regional Economic Outlook April 2016: SubSaharan Africa: Time for a Policy Reset. International Monetary Fund, Washington, DC, 2016.

Index